Marine Corps
Tank Battles in Korea

Also by Oscar E. Gilbert

Marine Tank Battles in the Pacific

Marine Corps
Tank Battles in Korea

Oscar E. Gilbert

CASEMATE

Havertown, PA

Published by
CASEMATE
2114 Darby Road, Havertown, PA
Phone: 610-853-9131

Typeset and design by
Savas Publishing & Consulting Group

ISBN 1-932033-13-0

First edition, first printing

Cataloging-in-Publication data is available
from the Library of Congress

Printed in the United States of America

For Oscar E Gilbert Sr., James D. Rittmann Sr., and all
the other soldiers, marines, sailors, airmen, and
"coasties" who did their duty
in anonymity.

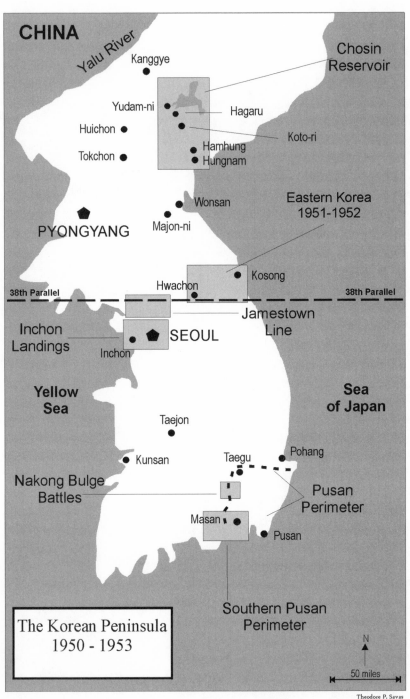

CHINA

Yalu River

Kanggye

Chosin
Reservoir

Yudam-ni   Hagaru

Huichon

Koto-ri

Tokchon

Hamhung
Hungnam

Wonsan

Eastern Korea
1951-1952

PYONGYANG   Majon-ni

Kosong

Hwachon

38th Parallel   38th Parallel

Jamestown
Line

Inchon
Landings   SEOUL

Inchon

Yellow
Sea

Sea
of Japan

Taejon

Kunsan   Taegu   Pohang

Nakong Bulge
Battles

Pusan
Perimeter

Masan

Pusan

The Korean Peninsula
1950 - 1953

Southern Pusan
Perimeter

N

50 miles

Theodore P. Savas

Contents

Maps and Illustrations

Photo inserts follow pages 122 and 218. Images of many of the Marines whose stories make up this book have been placed in the Epilogue.

Preface

I have worked as a scientist for over thirty years now, and one lesson I have learned from that career is that although you may start out with an idea you want to prove, the facts often lead down a very different path. So it was with the research for this book.

Lieutenant Colonel Ken Estes and I both began research into the real story of Able Company, 1st Tank Battalion in the defense of the Pusan Perimeter during the summer of 1950 (a project I hope we can one day complete). We both assumed that Able was a hand picked ("gold-plated" in the Marine Corps' vernacular) team. To our surprise, it turned out to have been cobbled together from whatever personnel were available—including a few transients who simply had the ill fortune to be passing through Camp Pendleton at the time. Like a real-life cliché from a Hollywood movie, this motley group went on to become one of the least known but most deadly armored units in American military history. Alas, the men of Able Company were not the super warriors of media myth. They were just typical Americans and Marines—good men well led. In their commonness they were representative of all the good men who struggled in the obscurity of the Korean War.

Korea has rightly been called "The Forgotten War," in part because it was fought at a time when the national attention was focused on the post-World War II economic boom. In a larger sense, the Korean conflict has been willfully forgotten, probably because it was the first war the United States lost. It was not "lost" in the traditional sense of a military defeat, but it was arguably the first struggle in which the nation was unable to impose its will, at least in the short term, by force of arms.

The forgetting began even as the war was being fought. Men and women served a tour in Korea and then, one by one, slipped quietly and gratefully back into society. No one wanted to hear their tales of mundane day-to-day terror with little in the way of tangible gain to show for it. In the end, there were no heroic accounts of final victory over a reviled enemy. And so the warriors of Korea slipped into the twilight of the national memory, overshadowed by the victors of World War II and eventually by the survivors of the even more frustrating struggle in Vietnam. It was a twilight ill-deserved.

Probably no one has been so forgotten as the tank and armored vehicle crewmen who served in Korea, not only those from the U. S. Marine Corps and U. S. Army, but also the contingents from the other United Nations forces. While the contributions of the tanks and tank crewmen were, at least in a relative sense, not so badly slighted as those of the men who fought World War II in the Pacific, published references are few. In large part this is because so little has been written about the war at all. What little has appeared deals largely with the "romance"—such as it was—of the first jet-powered war in the air, and the experiences of the infantry in their grisly day-to-day struggle for survival. The exceptions are some of the Fiftieth Anniversary Monographs published by the Marine Corps Historical Branch, Lee Ballenger's Korean War trilogy, and a few works by Jim Mesko and Simon Dunstan. The works of the latter two writers were designed for use by scale model builders rather than by the general reader, and as such are primarily pictorial rather than operational or experiential histories.

Marine Corps Tank Battles in Korea is a small effort to clarify some of the lesser-known aspects of the war, and to depict what the war was like for some of the doubly forgotten warriors. It is an effort that is, by its very nature, foredoomed to failure. Most of us, thank God, will live out our lives with no understanding of what the combat in Korea was like for these men.

Tanker Ben Busch summed it up well when he told me, "That's why I never talk to civilians. They ask, 'What was the war like?' How do you explain it? I don't even try."

Acknowledgments

Once again I must thank the cast of characters who played major roles in preserving a bit of history. Foremost, of course, are the men who were interviewed for this project, each of whom are listed separately in the section on interview sources.

Don Gagnon (Master Gunnery Sergeant USMC, Ret.), the editor of the *Marine Corps Tanker's Association Magazine,* not only suggested key people for interviews but also provided old copies of the Association's publications and invited me to annual meetings of the Association as his guest. Don also alerted me to a private reunion of the 3rd Platoon of Able Company, and interviews and discussions there allowed me to begin the task of pursuing the largely untold story of the tank company attached to the Provisional Marine Brigade in the defense of the Pusan Perimeter.

Colonel Ed Bale (USMC, Ret.), one of the legendary Marine tank officers, provided me with the means of contacting many officers who served in the latter part of the conflict. Gil Stauss was very helpful in my efforts to track down members of the 1st Marines Anti-Tank Company. Lee Ballenger freely shared materials, sources, and contacts from his own research that resulted in his two books (of a planned trilogy) on the war in Korea, and particularly the story of Operation Clambake.

Colonel John Williamson (USMC, Ret.) provided me with a copy of his privately published memoir of the war, and Colonel Vaughn Stuart (USMC, Ret.) supplied me with a copy of an unpublished manuscript detailing his experiences in the Chosin Reservoir Campaign. Both men have graciously allowed me to quote extensively from their works. Roger Chaput (Major, USMC, Ret.) provided a copy of the volume of memoirs, photographs, and general information he and his daughters compiled for the 3rd Platoon, A Company reunion.

Research Librarian Debbie Gummeiny and the staff of the Maude Marks Branch of the Harris County, Texas, Public Library helped track down and obtain copies of period references. Lena Kaljot of the Marine Corps Historical Center, and the staff of the National Archives at College Park, Maryland, helped locate the official photographs. Some of the quotations for chapter introductions are drawn from one of Lena's sidebars in *Fortitudine*, the bulletin of the Marine Corps Historical Program. Don Gagnon and Lt. Colonel Harry Milne (USMC, Ret.), Roger Chaput, and Jim Mesko helped me to locate and obtain additional official photographs unavailable through other sources. Harry Regan, Charles Batherson, Ben Beck, and Robert Schmitz provided personal photographs. Dieter Stenger and Ken Smith-Christmas of the Museums Branch helped me identify additional sources of information, and Col. Elliot Laine (USMC Ret.) helped clarify questions concerning the limited use of M4A3 (76mm.) tanks by the Marines.

Lieutenant Colonel Ken Estes (USMC, ret.) reviewed the manuscript with his usual keen eye for historical detail, and helped me to correct many sins of omission and commission. Ken also graciously provided a copy of the Operational Report for Able Company in the Pusan Perimeter, which he located in the National Archives.

I would also like to thank my publisher, David Farnsworth of Casemate, for agreeing to publish this book, and Theodore P. Savas, of El Dorado Hills, California, for his editorial expertise and maps.

As usual, my children Jordan, Bill, and Jillian, provided a wealth of technical support and services, and Jordan in particular provided her observations of local terrain and modern Korean society.

Above all, my wife Cathy has now spent thirty-two patient years in—to quote the words of the Marines' Hymn—"every clime and place," including being dragged through museums and archives, military bases, and across old battlefields in baking heat and bitter cold, snow and rain, mud and dust.

Ed Gilbert
Katy, Texas
October 2002

A Note on Language and Attitudes

Anyone who has been in the military knows that the language of fighting men is often obscene and cruel, both in the use of expletives and in racial or other epithets used in reference to enemy combatants.

In all of America's wars, men (and women) from every branch of the service made extensive use of familiar four letter expletives to express the gamut of emotions—frustration, disgust, horror—that war elicits. Paul Fussell, in his book *Wartime: Understanding and Behavior in the Second World War* (Oxford, 1990), ably describes this use of language. Because of casual and banal application, many of these expletives have lost the power to shock. Words never used in polite company are now a common staple in Hollywood movies, music, print, and even radio and television programs.

Readers of this book will note that the interviewees used little such language. Indeed, as one informed me before carefully sanitizing the content of a battlefield radio message, "I've got to watch my Marine Corps vernacular now!" These men are relics of a bygone age, when obscenities were used in moments of extreme stress or anger, and never in casual conversation with your grandmother.

Included inside this book are words like "gook," "chink," "goonie," or "Chinaman," all used to reference non-Caucasian enemy. The origin is unknown, but "gook" is probably a corruption of the derisive term "googoo," used to describe natives and *insurrectos* alike during the Philippines War of 1899-1902. By some strange twist of culture, such words have become the obscenities of our time. Many dictionaries do not even list the racial (or more properly, racist) definition of "gook," and one I examined prissily labeled it "a taboo word." (Ironically, the word "taboo" is Polynesian in origin, and was used to describe a thing too holy to be named; now it is used to describe something too obscene to mention. What must Pacific Islanders think of this bowdlerization of their language and culture?)

During wartime, such epithets pass into universal usage because they serve a very real purpose for individual soldiers. They help him distance himself from his victim while he accomplishes culturally sanctioned slaughter. In order for the front-line soldier to kill another human being in close physical proximity, he must first establish an emotional distance from his intended victim so as to reduce the enemy to something less than human—a process greatly facilitated by cultural or racial differences. This process—and its cynical manipulation by organizations and cultures—is described in Dave Grossman's *On Killing: The Psychological Cost of Learning to Kill in War and Society* (Little, Brown, & Co., 1996). Despite the tendency of we Americans to castigate ourselves for racism, the practice is global and has existed from the beginning of human history. John Dower's *War Without Mercy: Race & Power in the Pacific War* (Pantheon, 1987), ably described the overt racism and outright demonization of the foe from both sides of the conflict. Of course, one need look no further than the Balkans, central Africa, south Asia, or the Middle East for a plethora of contemporary examples.

Yet, even in the most brutal conflicts from World War II in the Pacific through Korea to Vietnam, American fighting men proved capable of acts of great compassion, even self-sacrifice, toward civilians in general, children in particular, and even defeated enemy soldiers—all while being utterly ruthless in their actions against armed combatants of the same race or nationality. You will also read about these acts of kindness within these pages.

Readers must keep in mind that these men were called upon to fight in, what was for them, an alien world. They were dumped into the middle of an ancient and strange land with many profound cultural differences. In addition, they fought against an inexplicable and unbelievably brutal North Korean soldiery who routinely tortured and murdered military prisoners and raped, brutalized, and starved South and North Korean civilians with equal gusto. This horrific situation was without precedent in the mental and emotional framework of most Americans. In this context the use of the word "gook" in particular reflects more than simple racism. It expressed another, now forgotten, definition of the word, a meaning that was better understood in the context of the war: a stranger.

In the end, the men who fought in Korea had, in some ways, more in common with their foes and the brutalized Korean civilians than with their own countrymen. While they were fighting a ruthless war under the most horrid conditions of climate and terrain, their fellow citizens were reveling in an economic boom and an unprecedented improvement in the standard of living. After a tour of duty in Korea, veterans returned home to a country of affluent strangers unmarked by the brutality and waste of war.

Perhaps Colonel John Williamson expressed this best in *Dearest Buckie: A Marine's Korean War Journal*, a collection of his wartime letters. Williamson wrote his wife that he would soon be coming home to the Yoosah— the USA—the place he defined as "the land of the white gooks."

After a year in Korea, we fat, dumb, and happy Americans must have seemed the strangest gooks of all.

"Duty is the sublimest word in our language. Do your duty in all things. You cannot do more. You should never wish to do less."

— General Robert Edward Lee

Prologue

When Duty Called

For weeks the seemingly invincible enemy tanks and masses of ruthless infantry swept everything before them. Every attempt to stop them had met with disaster. Hastily formed forces like the U. S. Army's Task Force Smith resisted valiantly, but the infantry was overrun in desperate rearguard battles. Artillery was smashed, and the American light tanks were contemptuously swept aside.

The enemy took prisoners. Then they tortured and murdered them.

Now the Eighth U.S. Army and the shredded remnants of the army of the Republic of Korea (ROK) had been pushed into a final corner in Pusan, their backs to the sea. Like wounded bears, they turned to fight to the death. And like bears, they would not go down easily.

The Provisional Marine Brigade, composed of a rifle regiment, a small artillery force, and a single company of tanks, was a scratch force assembled and trained in a matter of days before being thrown into the maw of this disaster. The tank crews spent all their time not training for combat, but cleaning unfamiliar equipment hurriedly removed from storage. Each tank crew had fired only four rounds from the main gun of their tank. Now they stood in the path of a powerful, confident, and battle-hardened enemy.

But these Marine tank crews were not novices at war. Many of the officers and sergeants were combat veterans, victors in a dozen brutal World War II campaigns where no quarter had been asked or given. The famous *esprit de corps* of Marines was high among the junior enlisted men. All were confident in the quality of their brand-new tanks—their M26s had been designed to duel with the legendary German Tiger tank.

When the North Korean enemy pushed a deep salient into the last-ditch defensive line around Pusan, the Marine Brigade was called upon to launch a desperate counterattack to salvage the situation. The Brigade marched through the night and on the morning of August 17, 1950, began to doggedly roll the enemy back at a place they came to call No-Name Ridge. Unfortunately, the battered and exhausted Army regiment fighting on the right flank of the Marines was unable to make any headway into the rugged hills, which left the Brigade's right flank dangling in the air.

In the stifling evening heat the Marine tankers received a coded radio signal: *FLASH PURPLE—Enemy tank attack.* The North Korean People's Army was once more on the attack, this time along a road that skirted the north end of No-Name Ridge. The Marine Brigade had already fought a terrible battle on the ridge, and its medical aid stations were choked with wounded. Its two rifle battalions were badly hurt, and still engaged in a savage battle far from the road.

If the combined enemy tank and infantry force broke through the thinly defended flank, the hospitals, support and headquarters units in the Brigade rear, and headquarters of the U S Army's 25th Division would be overrun. Worse still, the enemy would spill out onto the main road that carried communications and supplies for the entire northern flank of the defensive perimeter, and which led directly to the port of Pusan, the vulnerable throat of the entire Eighth Army.

Five tanks under Second Lieutenant Granville G. Sweet were in position to resist the onslaught. Sweet was a mustang. A former enlisted man commissioned from the ranks, he had been severely wounded at Pearl Harbor, but recovered to fight as a tank company First Sergeant on Guam and Iwo Jima. Sweet's men topped off their tanks with fuel and ammunition and raced westward to intercept the approaching enemy.

Some did not even pause long enough to close the caps on their fuel tanks. Sweet's Marines were supremely confident. They believed their M26 could defeat the enemy's feared T-34/85 tank in one-on-one combat. But under the circumstances, and with so much at risk, Sweet could not afford to take any chances.

A generation of Americans raised on video games and Hollywood's combat-fantasy films cannot grasp the choice Sweet faced. The goal was not simply to kill a compliant robotic enemy, to rack up a body count, to tally a score. Duty dictated that the enemy could not be allowed to pass—no matter who won the fight.

Fortunately, Sweet had fought over the same ground earlier that day, and he knew what had to be done. Without hesitation, he dispatched his tanks to the narrowest stretch of the road, where it passed through a narrow gap between hills too steep for tanks to climb. Once there, he positioned one M26 squarely in the middle of the narrow road, and one on either side in the ditch. He deployed his last two tanks (including his own) behind the other three, ready to plug any gap that might appear.

Sweet's prompt action satisfied the call of duty, guaranteeing that his battle was won before the first shot was fired. Even if his tanks were defeated, in death the forty-six ton hulks of the M26s would deny the use of the critical road to the enemy.

And so they waited, Marine tanks and their crews idling in a narrow pass in anticipation of the arrival of the enemy's *107th Tank Regiment*.

*   *   *

Exactly six weeks earlier, G. G. Sweet and his tankers had been sitting fat, dumb, and happy half a world away in southern California. Many had yet to meet. They were by no means fully prepared for war, but they were not alone.

America was not prepared for war in Korea or anywhere else in the summer of 1950. Indeed, America has never been fully prepared for war, which is perhaps one of our greatest strengths. To Americans, war is not a way of life but an odious task to be completed as quickly and efficiently as possible.

For Americans at the midpoint of the twentieth century, war was still a moral endeavor like the Civil War and the two World Wars. The only acceptable goal was to decisively crush the adversary. The two World Wars had been just such titanic crusades. Despite a few innovative new weapons like the tank and the airplane, they had been fought with huge numbers of conventional weapons that would have been generally familiar to soldiers of both Napoleon Bonaparte's and Ulysses S. Grant's armies. Scientific improvements to those weapons, however, had rendered them able to kill and destroy on a monstrous scale. The conflict in Korea would mark a major paradigm shift in the way America fought her wars.

By 1950, global alliances had shifted and some of America's former allies had become foes. Moreover, the introduction of nuclear weapons had resulted in a balance of terror that made all-out struggles of annihilation like World War II unthinkable. A struggle in which both sides rained nuclear destruction upon each other's cities could only be a war with two losers. The result was limited war.

Limited war was not a new concept to Europeans, with their long history of dynastic wars and struggles for limited territorial and colonial ambitions. For Americans, however, the idea of waging war for limited goals was an alien concept. This new and unpalatable struggle even had a new name. It was not a war, but a "police action."

Korea's agony would redefine the very nature of conflict between superpowers in the second half of the century. The prolonged struggle for supremacy between the West and communism would be waged on the soil and populations of proxy nations, from the jungles of Vietnam to the dry plains of Angola and the high deserts and mountains of Afghanistan. The Korean conflict spanned the transition between these two styles of war. Both sides sought decisive victory during the war's early months.

By 1951, however, the war had settled into a new pattern, with each side pursuing limited goals. Neither side was willing to escalate the war to the next highest logical level. The Communist forces of North Korea and the People's Republic of China still sought to drive the South Koreans and their United Nations protectors (mainly Americans) out of Korea. But the Chinese dared not risk an attack upon the tiny offshore islands along the Chinese coast, still held by Nationalist Chinese forces allied to the American and UN forces. For their part, U.N. forces fought to maintain the pre-war partition of unhappy Korea. They refused to advance to the Chinese border in the north, from which point they could directly threaten the Chinese industrial heartland.

In addition, a larger conflict threatened the direct intervention of Soviet Russia, with her huge conventional forces and nuclear arsenal—and global war. And so the "police action" wound down into a bloody stalemate, one of the most unpopular wars in American history.

Korea seemed an unlikely place for Marine Corps tanks to achieve battlefield distinction. Terrain that was not jagged mountain was rice paddy, sometimes dry and blowing dust but usually stinking black mud that could swallow a tank in minutes. But Marines are serious about the idea of the combined arms team, and so the tanks made the journey to the peninsula. And there they excelled, overcoming every obstacle of climate and terrain.

For the tanks and their crews, Korea was three different wars. In the first months of the war their role was to kill enemy tanks in the constant ebb and flow of a largely defensive campaign in and around the Pusan perimeter. For a few heady months they fought campaigns more befitting the offensive mind set of Marines, staging a bold amphibious landing, and then fixing and destroying the enemy through rapid fire and maneuver. Finally, when the war stagnated into a bloody exchange of minor hills, the Corps tankers became both mobile artillery and guardian angels of the infantry in modern-day trench warfare.

The ever-shifting nature of the war also provided a stern test of the adaptability of the individual Marine. In World War II the Corps had established a central school at Jacques Farm, California, to train tank crewmen. Under the direction of men like Lt. Col. William R. Collins, battle-experienced instructors trained the new men in both the basics and the niceties of their grim trade. This sophisticated school was one of the casualties of the post-World War II demobilization. Specialist training was once again conducted as it was in the days when Marines grabbed their muskets and climbed into the fighting tops of sailing ships—by individual tutelage within units in the field.

The stress of the rapid mobilization for the Korean conflict swamped this training system. It never recovered. From the very first days of the invasion at Inchon until the closing days of the war, all too many tank crewmen arrived in their units without ever having *seen* a tank. It was under these trying circumstances that individual Marines excelled. Their adaptability and initiative—the yardsticks by which elite troops are measured—served them and their nation in good stead.

Long-service professionals, Reservists called to the colors, and brand new Marines fresh from boot camp all met the challenges posed by the ever-shifting nature of the war. True to the traditions of their Corps, they all adapted to the new conditions and fulfilled their unpleasant, and usually thankless, duty as defined by the elected civilian leaders of the republic they protect.

Because duty is still the most sublime word to Marines.

Chapter 1

Repeating History
The Unexpected War

After the end of World War I, it took the world two decades to plunge
itself into another cycle of destruction. In the aftermath of World War II,
it took less than five years, and the chaos and destruction that flowed from
it is still felt today.

The collapse of the Japanese Empire in August 1945 virtually
assured the eventual collapse of European colonialism in Asia.
Debilitated European colonial armies faced not only pre-war nationalist
movements, but well-armed and organized Communist groups and
resistance movements that the Allies had sponsored in the fight against
Japan. The Japanese had been merciless colonial masters, but the peoples
of Asia had seen European armies humbled by fellow Asians. The
European powers launched protracted and ultimately futile struggles to
reestablish their dominance.

America tried to preserve the peace (and the ante-bellum Nationalist government) in northern China and to extricate itself from the remnant of its own empire in the Philippines. In China, the primary tasks of the Marine Corps were to disarm and repatriate the enormous Japanese army in northern China and provide minimal security for non-Chinese in the region. Unfortunately, both the Nationalist and Communist Chinese factions were determined to resume the civil war placed on hiatus while they fought the Japanese. As the power struggle escalated into full-scale warfare, the American presence in China withered. Most Marine Corps ground elements had left by 1947, and the last air units were withdrawn by 1949. The most forward-based Marine presence in the Asia-Pacific region, a single brigade based on Guam, was disbanded in 1947.

The legacy of Asian colonialism, as practiced by imperial Japan, also posed an intractable problem. The strategically located Korean peninsula had been fought over for centuries. Unbeknownst to most people, in 1882 the United States entered into a trade and protection treaty with the "Hermit Kingdom" (Korea), but later stood by as the armies of China, Russia, and finally, Japan, marched across the hapless country.

Japan annexed Korea as a "protectorate" after the Russo-Japanese War and ruled it as a colony from 1910 until 1945. Japan was a harsh ruler, and neither dissent nor nationalist sympathies were tolerated. In March 1919, a fledgling Korean nationalist movement promulgated a non-violent declaration of independence, and Japanese police slaughtered thousands in the months that followed.

Japanese dominance in Korea ended in August 1945 when the Soviet Union invaded the peninsula from Siberia. The Soviets leapfrogged along the northeastern coast in a series of amphibious assaults and overland marches against disorganized Japanese resistance. As had been previously agreed, the United States occupied the southern part of the peninsula up to an arbitrary line on a map—the 38th parallel. Both sides installed a local government, an aggressive Communist "democratic republic" in the north, and a squabbling and intractable "strong man democracy" in the south. The United States and the Soviets withdrew from Korea in 1948. The Soviets, however, left behind an entrenched dictatorship, arms sufficient to equip a powerful army, and a large cadre of combat-trained Koreans. Many North Koreans had been educated in the USSR or had fought either with the Communist forces in the Chinese civil wars, or in the Soviet Army in World War II.

The thankless presence in war-torn China was not the only problem faced by the Marine Corps from 1945 through 1949. The deadliest threat came from the halls of Congress, where a speedy movement was underway to disassemble America's massive wartime naval and military establishments. Each of the larger services fought to preserve its manpower and programs. Once again the small Marine Corps appeared the obvious target for massive budget cuts. Just as their predecessors had once argued that the machine gun and massed artillery made amphibious assaults impossible, a new generation of theorists argued that atomic bombs, targeted against shipping and the troops crowded into a beachhead, made amphibious assaults impossible. In other words, there was no longer a need for amphibious specialists, and the Marine Corps was deemed by many in Congress as an unnecessary luxury.

A War Department-Congressional alliance, with the sympathy of President Harry Truman's administration, wanted to streamline defense functions by absorbing land-based air assets into the newly independent Air Force, and by having the Army assume all significant ground combat functions.[1] The Marine Corps, if it still existed, would once more be a small naval security force, and would fill the old role of "colonial infantry."[2] Radical air power enthusiasts argued that the Air Force would become the nation's means of projecting its might around the world. Long-range bombers would be able to reach any spot on the globe and A-bomb any enemy into submission.

The potential dissolution of the Navy was never a serious threat, but the admirals still found themselves strategically disadvantaged. Just as in the 1920s, the Army's generals were preparing to replay its role in the last war, earnestly preparing for a conventional and nuclear struggle in central Europe. They were not interested in allocating resources to aid the Navy by capturing advanced bases.

Elements in the leadership of the Marine Corps were quick to perceive a threat to their existence and launched a massive publicity campaign in an effort to blunt Congressional tactics. The result was codified in the National Security Act of 1947, which not only assigned the Corps specific missions as amphibious specialists and the nation's "force in readiness," but also specified minimum force levels. Ironically, the Marine Corps found itself with more missions than it could reasonably carry out, including the capture of advanced bases intended for Air Force use. Another mission, in tacit acknowledgment of the new global strategic situation, was the protection of American interests in the Persian Gulf.[3]

Not content with simple survival, planners again sought to reinvent the Corps along more modern lines. One promising new technology was the helicopter, which would allow assault troops to be inserted into enemy territory from ships standing far out to sea, where they were less vulnerable to attack. Diffusion of the support ships over a larger area would also make them an uninviting target for nuclear attack. By 1948, a Marine Corps Special Board speculated on the potential role of the helicopter for air assaults in support of amphibious operations, although the Corps had only acquired its first helicopter in January of that year.[4]

If the Corps had a visionary in matters of armored doctrine, it was Lt. Col. Arthur J. ("Jeb") Stuart, the commanding officer of the 1st Tank Battalion in the bitter battles on Peleliu and Okinawa. Assessing war plans focusing on potential conflicts around the periphery of Europe and Asia, Stuart advocated the development of better anti-tank weapons and doctrine for the infantry to counter Soviet-style mechanized assaults, as well as more effective utilization of the tank in amphibious assaults. Stuart's vision also extended to the development of amphibian tractors capable of providing more protection against hostile fire, and specialized engineer vehicles for breaching minefields and defensive works.[5]

Unfortunately, neither the fresh ideas nor the new missions came with money attached. Despite the provisions of the National Security Act, by 1950 shrinking budgets had reduced the two surviving active duty divisions to skeletal proportions. The entire Corps consisted of eleven under-strength rifle battalions in two divisions, when each division should have fielded nine. Further plans were afoot to reduce the Fleet Marine Force to six rifle battalions.[6] There were also two active duty tank battalions, the 1st and 2nd, supported by two Reserve tank battalions, the 10th and 11th. The 1st Tank Battalion, which consisted of only a single company of obsolete M4A3 tanks, supported the 1st Marine Division.

Training suffered as school units were reduced or eliminated. The tank and amphibian tractor schools were merged into a single Tracked Vehicle School Company in 1947.[7] Tank crewmen were trained "on the job," within active field units.

The strong suit of the Corps was its Reserve system, an outstanding 127,000-man reservoir. Its members trained weekly while pursuing civilian careers. Of this number, 98% of the officers and 25% of the enlisted personnel were wartime veterans. Limited funds and facilities, however, handicapped effective training.[8] Unfortunately, the Reserve was ill-equipped. The Reserve 10th Tank Battalion, for example, had only four worn-out M4A3s tanks, and a single VTR.[9] Both active-duty and Reserve tank units used late-war versions of the M4A3 medium tank with improved suspension, armor protection, and armament. The improved POA-CWS-H5 flame tank version of the M4A3 replaced the older vehicles used in World War II. The H5 mounted the long-range flame gun alongside either a 75mm. gun or 105mm. howitzer. By 1950, the Marine Corps had standardized all their vehicles to the more powerful 105mm. howitzer. Not every tank, however, was actually fitted with the larger weapon, and most remained in storage.[10]

The newer M26 "General Pershing" tank[11] was not yet in common use. In 1945, the Corps Commandant authorized purchase of the M26, and by late 1949 the Corps had 102 of these tanks on hand. Most were in storage, and the two active-duty tank battalions had only five each, to be used for ". . . training purposes limited to special exercises, experiments, and demonstrations."[12] The most operating experience with this new tank was vested in the 2nd Tank Battalion at Camp Lejeune, North Carolina. The battalion eventually received ten of the new tanks, but requests for additional vehicles were refused. The 2nd Division routinely deployed a tank platoon to accompany the Battalion Landing Team aboard ship in the Mediterranean. In 1948, Lt. Col. Robert Denig requested a sufficient stock of vehicles to equip this platoon with five M26s, but the old M4A3s were used on all or most of these deployments.[13]

Although designed and constructed to counter the monstrous German Panther and Tiger tanks in World War II, the M26 only saw limited service in the waning days of the war in Europe. With thicker armor, improved mobility, and a powerful 90mm. main cannon, it was one of the most formidable tanks in the world. It was also one of the most expensive to operate, and was significantly heavier than the old M4A3s, which also made it harder to transport and land. There was another drawback: the explosive power of the 90mm. shell was not as effective as its 75mm. counterpart in the older tanks, which made the M26 less desirable as an infantry support tank—and infantry support was still the primary role of Marine Corps armor.

In addition to the main gun, the M26 carried two 30-caliber machine guns, one coaxial (mounted to fire parallel to the main cannon), the other low on the right side of the front of the hull. The latter gun was hard to aim without tracer bullets. According to Nik Frye, a talkative and naturally outgoing tank crewman, "The secret was to shoot at the ground, and then track it [onto the target]." Most of these vehicles were stored at the Barstow Depot in the California desert. Marine Corps doctrine also provided for an anti-tank platoon equipped with five tanks as part of each rifle regiment, but these units existed only on paper.[14]

Warrant Officer "Willie" Koontz and Sgt. A. J. Selinsky had a platoon of M26 tanks in Headquarters Company of the 1st Tank Battalion.[15] Basilo Chavarria, a quiet young man with a subtle sense of humor, was raised in Texas and served for three years before he was assigned to this platoon. "Before the Korean deal," he recalled, "they decided that they were going to Barstow and pick up a platoon of M26s in Headquarters and Service [Company]. Sort of a training [platoon]. Alternate guys went through. . . . June comes around, and here we are with one platoon of M26s, and all the others with them old tanks."

Many of the tankers never saw the M26s. Bill Robinson was a strong stocky man who had enlisted in 1946. By 1950, he was a technical sergeant and tank commander in the 2nd Platoon of A Company. His experience with the M26 tank before the war in Korea was all but nonexistent. "I think they ran one school through to train a few men on the new tanks," was about all he could say of that model.

The new and much smaller Marine Corps offered a chance for more realistic training, but the opportunity passed by unrealized. Captain Gearl M. "Max" English, a thin man with a strong east-Texas accent and cackling laugh, was a veteran of the tank fighting on Roi-Namur, Saipan, Tinian, and Iwo Jima with the 4th Tank Battalion. In 1950, Captain English was in Headquarters and Services Company of the stunted 1st Tank Battalion. "Things were happening," he said. "Somebody knew that something was going to take place. We had an awful lot of maneuvers. We only had the Fifth Marines. We were out night and day training with the Fifth."

Tankers always emphasized tank-infantry training. We broke our asses to do something for them. We would play-fight all day long. We would try to get them to stay in a foxhole and run a tank over them, and oh, no, they wouldn't do that. We would take a couple of crew members out of another tank, and put them in the same place and run over it to show the infantry that it wouldn't hurt them. Then we would tell the infantry to lay down like you're wounded, and let us come pick them up. Oh, no, no! We lay our own troops down there, and we would pick them up.

We trained to where they had confidence in us. That damn tank *can* come over you without killing you. They *can* pick you up and pull you in the escape hatch, and get you out.

A natural leader, English would put his experience to work in Korea, where his ability to make quick battlefield decisions would be repeatedly tested.

Another tanker, Joe Sleger, lamented that the new generation of infantrymen were not very well informed about the power of tanks: "They also took some of the tanks and went around to the infantry units for indoctrination. Koontz went out one day, and he was giving the lecture on the twenty-six [M26]. Some infantry guy there asked him if he threw a grenade in the track, if that would hurt it." Sleger paused a moment with a smile. "Old Willie said, 'I could stand here and I could piss on that track, and it would rust through before it [a grenade] would do any damage.'"

The tall and quiet C. J. 'Boogah'[16] Moss enlisted in 1940 and served as an infantryman in a Division Scout Company in World War II and in the 1st Tank Battalion in China.[17] According to Moss, the infantry had the same attitude toward tanks in 1950 held in World War II. "The infantry is always reluctant," he explained. "Their argument is that the tanks draw fire. Of course, my rebuttal is, 'So does a utility uniform.'"[18]

*   *   *

The leader of Communist North Korea, a Soviet-educated officer named Kim Il Sung, was determined to reunite the peninsula, by force if necessary. To that end, he organized and launched a series of incursions into South Korea. The last in a series of well publicized "peace proposals" was being floated by the Communists on June 10, 1950—even as their commandos were infiltrating into South Korea.

Washington, meanwhile, watched with growing concern but refused to directly intervene, wishing to avoid an Asian entanglement. Mixed signals were presented by Secretary of State Dean Acheson in a speech to the Washington press corps in January 1950 that seemed to imply Korea lay outside America's sphere of interests. The speech may have led the Communists to believe that the United States would not go to war to protect South Korea.[19] Matthew Ridgeway went so far as to state that Acheson was "merely voicing an already accepted United States policy."[20] Other historians have concluded that the assumption was groundless: Kim, now beyond the effective control of his Soviet patrons, would have invaded the southern peninsula regardless of the political situation in America.[21] Any uncertainty was resolved at 0400 hours local time in Korea on June 25, 1950, when 135,000 battle-hardened North Korean soldiers, including mechanized units supported by waves of tactical aircraft, swept across the border into the South.

The invasion should not have come as a complete surprise. Central Intelligence Agency reports had indicated the movement of North Korean troops into the border area, the evacuation of North Korean civilians, and the accumulation of extensive stockpiles of ammunition and other war supplies along the border.[22] The North Korean People's Army (NKPA) was the most lavishly equipped and heavily mechanized army in eastern Asia. Each of the seven NKPA Rifle Divisions in the initial assault included three rifle regiments, an artillery regiment, and supporting formations. Each rifle regiment included its own artillery battalion, an anti-tank formation, and an additional battalion of self-propelled artillery equipped with sixteen SU-76s, 76.2mm. field guns mounted on a light tank chassis.

Spearheading the assault on the South was the *105 Tank Division*, a powerful combined arms force. Although called a division, it was similar to an American regiment in strength. It included the *107, 109*, and *203 Medium Tank Regiments*, each with forty T-34/85 tanks organized into three battalions. Other organic units included the *206 Mechanized Infantry Regiment* (with its own artillery, heavy mortar, and anti-tank battalions), the *308 Armored Artillery Battalion* with sixteen SU-76 guns, and the *849 Anti-Tank Regiment* with 45mm. anti-tank guns. The *105 Tank Division* did not fight as a unit, but the three *Tank Regiments* were parceled out to support the infantry divisions.[23]

The T-34/85 Soviet-built tank was considered by many to have been the best all-around tank of World War II. When the original model of the T-34 made its debut during the opening weeks of Hitler's 1941 Operation Barbarossa, its combat worthiness shocked the German Army and served as the impetus for the development of the Panther and Tiger tanks. With a powerful diesel engine and wide tracks, the T-34/85 was fast, agile, and could cross soft ground where other tanks bogged down. The sloped armor increased the tendency of enemy rounds to bounce off without significant damage. The /85 portion of T-34/85 referred to a high-velocity 85mm. main gun derived from an anti-aircraft weapon.

To oppose this onslaught, the Army of the Republic of Korea fielded a variety of obsolete World War II-era equipment supplied by the United States. The 2.36-in. rocket launchers (bazookas), and the 37mm. and 57mm. anti-tank guns had proven ineffective against the late-war German tanks, and were by no means capable of countering the modern equipment of the NKPA. The heaviest weapons they possessed were a few 105mm. howitzers and light mortars that had not been fired for years. South Korea's armored vehicles, a few old six-wheeled M8 Armored Cars, mounted 37mm. guns that could barely damage the T-34. Twenty unarmed L-4 and L-5 liaison and spotter aircraft opposed hundreds of modern fighter aircraft and bombers of the North Korean Air Force.[24] The South Koreans, at least on paper, appeared to be doomed.

The NKPA easily drove the Republic of Korea (ROK) forces before them, meeting, attacking, and defeating each successive line of resistance. There were few exceptions to this repetitious scenario. The well-led ROK 6th Division stubbornly delayed the North Koreans for three days until the units on either flank were annihilated. The ROK 1st Division defended the capitol city of Seoul until it, too, was overrun. Some infantry units died to the last man.[25]

Despite fears that the attack was a diversion to distract attention in advance of a Soviet invasion of Western Europe, once the shooting began the United States unilaterally decided to defend South Korea. Taking advantage of a Soviet boycott of the United Nations Security Council,[26] a hasty coalition was organized under the auspices of the United Nations (although the bulk of forces would of necessity be American).

Exactly how the United States would defend the South Koreans was problematical. Four soft, under-strength, and ill-equipped divisions were maintained on occupation duty in Japan. Each was short of weapons and lacked the spare parts necessary to maintain what little equipment they possessed. The outfit best prepared for war was the 24th Division, which was rated at 65% combat readiness.[27] The only forces available to counter the NKPA's mechanized onslaught were the "tank battalions" of the infantry divisions. Each of the tank battalions was in reality a company equipped with M24 light scout tanks. These small vehicles were the heaviest the frail bridges and roads of Japan could accommodate.[28] Infantry and artillery components were at two-thirds of authorized strength, and there were no 90mm. anti-tank guns to be found.[29]

The first American unit committed to the maelstrom was Task Force Smith, two infantry companies from the 21st Infantry of the 24th Infantry Division, Battery A of the 52nd Field Artillery Battalion with six 105mm. howitzers,[30] two platoons of heavy mortars, with only one 75mm. recoilless rifle, and six 2.36-in. bazookas for anti-tank defense.[31]

On July 5, just ten days after the Communists invaded South Korea, Task Force Smith was attacked near Osan by a full NKPA division supported by thirty tanks.[32] The soldiers managed to delay the enemy through nine hours of desperate fighting, and the artillery destroyed or disabled five T-34s before the guns were overrun. By the end of the day, Task Force Smith was all but destroyed. The survivors managed to fall back on the positions of the 21st and 34th Infantry twelve miles to the south near Ch'onan, where they held out until July 9, when relentless armored attacks drove them rearward. The early fighting claimed the life of Col. Robert Martin, the commanding officer of the 34th Infantry, who was killed while attacking a T-34 with a bazooka.[33]

The outnumbered and outgunned 24th Infantry Division stubbornly traded space and lives for time until additional forces could be moved to Korea. Because the light tanks were ineffective against the T-34s, they adopted the simple expedient of retreating whenever enemy armor appeared. By July 12, the division had been pushed back to Taejon, a critical position on the road running south out of Seoul. When a major Communist attack was launched on July 19 and 20, 3.5-inch "Super Bazookas" airlifted from the United States proved somewhat more effective, but only at point-blank range. Even with their 76mm. guns, the old M4A3 tanks, hastily supplied from depot stocks in Japan, also provided unable to deal with the redoubtable T-34s. Major General

William Dean, the 24th Division commander, was captured attacking a T-34.[34] Three dilapidated M26s discovered in a Japanese depot were rushed to Korea but succumbed to mechanical failure before they encountered enemy tanks. All three fell into North Korean hands.

By August 1, 1950, the American and South Korean armies found themselves pressed into a perimeter around the port of Pusan, on the southeastern tip of the Korean peninsula. Four full U. S. Army and five surviving ROK divisions held a tenuous line. Resistance began to harden, however, as the NKPA supply lines grew longer and the UN lines shorter. The Communist commanders of the NKPA knew they had to crush the Pusan perimeter before the United States could bring to bear its full might—or face destruction themselves.

The deployment of the 7th, 24th, and 25th Infantry and 1st Cavalry (Dismounted) Divisions from Japan stripped U.S. resources to the bone. The four divisions represented fully one-third of Army and Marine Corps ground combat strength worldwide.[35] Meanwhile, concern still lingered that the Korean crisis was but a prelude to a Soviet onslaught in Europe.[36]

As early as June 28, Marine Commandant Gen. Clifton Cates urged the use of Fleet Marine Force units in Korea and offered a brigade of Marines. The Chief of Naval Operations, Adm. Forrest Sherman, waited two days before he advised Vice Adm. Turner Joy, commander of Far Eastern naval forces, that a Regimental Combat Team (RCT)[37] could be made available.[38] When Douglas MacArthur, the general of the Army, was advised of this offer he immediately requested a full Marine division, only to be told that a division was not immediately available. The offensive-minded MacArthur was already planning an amphibious counter stroke to behead the extended NKPA forces operating in South Korea. Before available Army units stationed in Japan were committed to the defense of the Pusan perimeter, MacArthur ordered small Marine Corps and Navy detachments to train the soldiers in the fine points of amphibious assault warfare.[39]

Lieutenant General Lemuel Shepherd, the commander of Fleet Marine Force, Pacific, flew to Japan to meet with MacArthur and the leaders of Eighth Army. Shepherd had served in the Marine Brigade in France in 1917-1918, and was painfully aware of the difficulties that could result from a Marine Brigade serving within an Army organization. Unable to communicate with Commandant Cates, he elected to push for the commitment of an entire Marine division. MacArthur explained his bold plan to Shepherd. When Shepherd assured him that an entire division could eventually be made available, MacArthur formally requested the full division from the Joint Chiefs of Staff.[40]

The commitment of a Marine division became inextricably entangled in the politics of MacArthur's proposed Inchon operation. When the Joint Chiefs questioned the feasibility of the operation, the implacable MacArthur dispatched a message saying his mind was made up on the issue. MacArthur was determined to put his bold plan into action even without a full Marine division. If it became necessary, he would land at Inchon with the Marine Brigade and the hastily trained 2nd Division of the U S Army.[41] Their bluff called, on July 25 the Joint Chiefs acceded to MacArthur's unyielding demands.

The personnel strength of the Corps was so depleted that only two RCTs, rather than the three of a full division, could be provided. The Marine Corps initially stripped the 2nd Division on the East Coast and other bases worldwide for trained personnel before mining the well of reserves. According to one scholarly treatment of Marine operations in Korea, by September 11 "the Organized Reserve (Ground) had in effect ceased to exist!"[42] No matter how great the effort, however, the third RCT—the 7th Marines—would not be ready for MacArthur's amphibious counter stroke.[43]

*   *   *

While MacArthur planned his offensive, the need for reinforcements to defend the last foothold in Korea grew more critical by the day. It was decided that the Marine Brigade was to be committed to the defensive effort. The "heavy" spearhead of the Brigade, however, consisted of a single company of tanks.

When the Brigade was formed, Able Company, 1st Tank Battalion, was the only active-duty line tank company on the west coast. It was equipped with old M4A3 tanks. When activated as part of the 1st Provisional Marine Brigade on July 7, Capt. Max English was transferred over to lead the company.[44] He could not have been happier when he received word that his company would be re-equipped with M26s. In a scenario all too familiar to the veteran tankers, however, his unit would be equipped with the new and unfamiliar tanks on the eve of their entry into combat. "We had the only M26s available in the entire western United States," remembered English. "As far as the rest of it, we weren't concerned about that. Hell, we were tankers. We could handle that."

Gunnery Sergeant Eugene Viveiros, a street-wise Massachussetts kid before joining the Corps, had been with the tanks since Guadalcanal. The aggressive Viveiros, who always wanted to be in the thick of the action, was the Company Gunny.[45] He, too, was not unimpressed by what he saw. "They wanted to know, when they picked up those M26s at Barstow, whether they wanted another one quipped with the [bull]dozer attachment. I knew nothing about the M26 at that time," he said, "and after I saw the underpowered rigs that came out of there, I was glad that I didn't try to hang a dozer on the end of this thing."

Instead of using an M26, a pair of M4A3s were assigned to the company, each equipped with a bulldozer blade. They were used "mainly for any blown-out areas that were impassable to other vehicles" and for "filling in [craters] until the engineers could reconstruct something on a narrow roadway. . . . The 105 was good," continued Viveiros, because its more powerful explosive shell made it more useful against some targets.

The M26 had thicker armor than the old M4 tanks, and it had slightly better mobility over soft ground. Veteran tanker Merl Bennett had trained on the old M4A3s, but had also attended a school on the M26. Unlike Viveiros, Bennett was more impressed with the tank. "That old M4 had that . . . stick shift, and the M26 had the Torquematic transmission. That helped out a little bit there, because that was the hardest part about driving that M4, shifting the gears. [The M26 required] less skill, and it was easier to train a guy."

The World War II veterans modified the tanks to help the hard-pressed infantry. Able Company tanks had racks welded over the fenders, which were then loaded with boxes of rifle and light machine gun ammunition.[46] According to North Hampshire Yankee Roger Chaput, "Any of the grunts were running low and needed some, they just run up and take one out of the rack."

There was also a scramble to reorganize the company and integrate new personnel from all points of the national compass. C. J. Moss was assigned as the light section leader for the 2nd Platoon.[47] "It was confusing," he recalled. "We had to drop people and pick up new ones, and that went on for about two weeks." The unit was dropping "Short-timers. Those who had less than a year to do, that didn't volunteer to . . . extend their enlistment. We had to drop 'em from the rolls."

Bill Robinson was in Kansas when he received "a telegram to report back to the base. I went down to Lowrey Air Force Base [Denver, CO], and showed them my telegram. . . . They put me on a fighter plane, gave me a parachute, and flew me to March Air Force Base."

Merl Bennett had a similar experience in Indiana. "I was on leave, having my birthday party two days early, and I got a telegram to come back to the base. I showed my telegram over at Wright-Patterson [Air Force Base] and got a hop out of there to Ogden, Utah. Then I went down to Denver," Bennett continued. "I couldn't get anything going to San Diego or El Toro, so I went up to Travis Air Force Base and got a bus out of San Francisco down to Camp Pendleton."

Some personnel gaps were filled with experienced men like Robert B. Miller, a thin and craggy-faced Marine whose primary concern was always the welfare of his men. A veteran of the tank platoon in the defense of Midway, and of the fighting on Guam and Okinawa in World War II, Miller was assigned to the 1st Platoon under 1st Lt. William D. Pomeroy.[48] G. G. Sweet was another mustang like Max English, and the leader of 2nd Platoon. Handsome and square-jawed, the Chicago Irishman had served with English in the Tank School at Jacques Farm, California in 1942, and was a veteran of the fighting on Guam and Iwo Jima. "That was the only trained platoon," said Sweet, "all right out of boot camp, trained tankers." The experienced Sweet was switched over to lead 3rd Platoon, cobbled-up from personnel drawn from various sources. J. A. Merlino was a typical personnel acquisition. He returned from a posting to Guam and arrived at Camp Pendleton just in time to be plugged into Sweet's newly constituted 3rd Platoon.[49]

The skeleton tank battalion[50] had only the handful of M26s in the Headquarters and Services Company.[51] "When they started putting crews together in A Company," Everett Dial recalled, "we had all the experience with M26s. We were trying to rotate people through them, when the balloon went up. There really wasn't a lot of hand picking to 'em. In fact, our platoon was kind of the tail end of the crop."

"Chester Churchill was going to be the Platoon Sergeant, and he was on leave when the war started," remembered Joe Sleger. "I was a section leader, and G. G. [Sweet] told me to go ahead and start getting the platoon ready with him. We worked our butts off getting the platoon ready. The morning we were scheduled to leave, I came in from my home over in . . . housing, and I was walking up the side of the barracks, and this guy yelled out the top window—he was leaning out the window—and it was Churchill! I just sank down, and thought, 'Aw, man! After all my work there goes my platoon.'" Sleger's outlook changed, however, when Sweet clarified the situation by telling him, "You're gonna be the Platoon Sergeant." The handsome big man with the wavy hair could not have been happier. As he later remembered, "I was in seventh heaven."

Churchill had not yet fully recovered from wounds received in World War II, and was kept stateside to train new tank crewmen.[52] "B [Company] was just a skeleton. It was not a full company, and H&S was pretty much a full company," added Sleger. "We drew as much from battalion level, and formed a full A Company."

Sweet had only two weeks to organize a functional platoon. As for the M26, Sweet noted that virtually none of his men had "[seen] the damn things before, never fired 'em. But I had one man who was trained in the M26, and that was Chavarria. That's why I got him over into the platoon. I had just finished going through a school, training a whole platoon, and it was all on the M4."

Sergeant Don Gagnon confirmed Sweet's recollection. "I never got on a damn M26 until they said, 'Okay, here's your tank.' We're down at the Reserve Center in San Diego, with a steam jenny[53] that we couldn't get any heat out of, and [used] gasoline because we didn't have any more cleaning solvent. We're scrounging around for rags. . . . We worked on those tanks seven days a damn week. We worked sixteen hours a day."

On July 7, 1950, the company took two of the tanks to the firing range. The gunner and loader from each crew received a short orientation on the new weapon, and fired a grand total of two rounds.[54] Advance instruction was inadequate, as Joe Sleger quickly discovered. "I remember going to the range because we had the old leather tank helmets that looked like the football helmets," said Sleger. "The first time we fired the ninety I had this helmet on. On the M4s we would stand up in the turret hatch and spot the rounds. I called 'Fire!' and I thought the skin was gonna peel off my face. I thought, 'What the hell! Something must be wrong with the gun.' Stupidly, I stayed standing up and I called for

another round. This time I felt like screaming, a spontaneous screaming."
The second blast from the discharge had twisted Sleger's helmet around
until "the [ear] flap was in front of my face!"[55]

Sleger was one of the lucky ones. Many did not receive any advance
instruction at all.[56] "First time I drove one was backing it aboard ship,"
remembered John Haynie, a tall, thin, and slow-talking Marine. Able
Company would not fire its guns again until it arrived in the combat zone
in Korea.[57]

There was little advance warning before orders arrived to ship out for
Korea. "The families were abandoned," said Sleger, who had two sons,
one a toddler and the other an infant. "I left home in the morning, and that
was the last time I saw the family. We knew we were going, but there
wasn't enough time to pack them up."

Sleger continued:

> They railed [transported] in the twenty-sixes [M26s]. There was a
> beach area outside of San Diego where the LCUs could beach. We
> got the tanks off [the] flatcars, and the OEM gear[58] was still boxed
> up. . . . We opened all the boxes and loaded everything, put it in its
> proper place. Then we went aboard the LCUs, and they took us out
> to the LSD, which was offshore, and we deck-loaded[59] the
> company. Then we started to work, cleaning all the guns. Before we
> went aboard ship we got a load of ammunition. We test-fired the
> machine guns off the fantail, got all the equipment stowed. All the
> tank commanders in our platoon had their manuals. . . .

The company sailed out of San Diego aboard the LSDs *Fort Marion* and
Gunston Hall on July 12.

It took less than twenty-four hours for a major crisis to strike. "I'm
the seasick guy," said Don Gagnon. "Everybody's in the galley, and I've
gotta go throw up again, so I run down. As I go by that passageway, I look
down and I see this water bubbling up in the well deck. I forgot that I was
sick, and I run down and go to the galley. [Walter E.] Sandy [Platoon
Sergeant, 1st Platoon] was there, and I holler, 'The well deck is flooded!'
They're looking at me like 'April Fool—You're gonna get your ass in a
jam coming in here talkin' like that!'" It was clear that no one believed
him. "'Come and look!'" retorted Gagnon, whose short stature contained
a large well of assertiveness that would eventually earn him the nickname

"Mighty Mouse." "By the time they got people to shut the damn valves off, there was [water] up into the slip ring.[60] I wasn't sick after that."

Captain English remembered the same event. "We were out of San Diego about eight hours, and security came up to the wardroom and he told me, 'Skipper, the well deck's under water!' I said, 'Oh, my God,' so we dash out there, and the well deck was under water! We had tank turrets just showing above salt water. Everything was stowed down there," continued English. "Ammunition, jeeps, six-by-sixes,[61] everything was in there. . . . They closed the sea cocks real fast, and pumped all that water out. We sent a message to the commanding general, Camp Pendleton, that the well deck was flooded, the tanks had all been flooded, and sent a copy to Marine Corps Headquarters."

The five feet of salt water damaged fourteen of the precious tanks, 300 rounds of 90mm. ammunition, and 5,000 rounds of .30-caliber machine gun ammunition. The damaged ammunition included all 250 rounds of High-Velocity Armor-Piercing (HVAP) ammunition in Marine Corps stocks.[62]

"We jettisoned that stuff, the rounds that were in the very bottom of the ammo racks, underneath the turret," explained Sergeant Robinson. "We had ready racks on the side, and racks underneath the turret, one or two layers. They said that if there was any water at all [that touched the HVAP rounds] to jettison, because it would have a chemical reaction on that ammo." The concern was apparently specific to the HVAP rounds.[63]

Unfortunately, no new stocks of HVAP, or hyper-shot, were immediately available. Brigadier General Craig, the brigade's commanding general, authorized English to dump the ammunition over the side and return to San Diego. New tanks would have to be rushed to San Diego as quickly as possible.[64]

The authorization to return to southern California did not sit well with Max English. "We had a problem. We were being told to turn the ship around and come back to the United States because the tanks would be no good. We said, 'Wait, let's look at this. . . .' English turned for advice to his communications officer, Prentiss Baughman.

"'Bo, what are we supposed to do?' asked the captain.

His answer, as recalled by English, was: "'[W]e're gonna . . . take all the radios out. We'll take them up to the ship's ovens, and we'll bake the salt water out!"

The solution seemed reasonable to English, and a message was sent to the Commandant of the Marine Corps "that we could repair these vehicles between here and Japan."[65]

Prentiss Baughman was another old breed Marine who had enlisted in 1937. He had served in the infantry and as a communications specialist before transferring to tanks in 1948. His new responsibility was as English's Communication Officer and the Platoon Leader of the Headquarters Platoon.

The shipboard problem was but the first crisis in which the unusual composition of Baughman's platoon would prove critical to ultimate success. "In our company, we were self-contained," boasted English. "We did our own maintenance and everything. . . . I had an OCM man,[66] which ordinarily wasn't given to anybody [at company level]."

"Myself, and Warrant Officer [Robert] Plumley, my assistant, cleared all the boards out, the ignitions and all, washed them all with fresh water, and put them in the baking machine to dry out," explained Baughman. All those tank radios had been fabricated for [temporary submersion] underwater, in case we got hung up going ashore. I figured if we got the salt water off so it wouldn't corrode 'em, and dry 'em out, they'd work. Probably. We were quite successful."

"Plumley was an old salt Marine," recalled English with no little pride. "He told me, 'Don't you worry. All we're gonna do is flush the engines with new oil, and the instrument panels will be taken out and baked.' The ordnance officer said we had a problem with ammunition. We looked at it real good. We had to throw a lot of ammunition over the side."

The effort was both resourceful and successful "We got everything going but one tank," said English. "One tank had to be wired around the instrument panel, but the Army had a replacement for us when we got there. They put one on a fast ship from Hawaii, and it beat us to Korea. When we offloaded, we traded with them."

Eventually is was determined that two tanks needed additional work, and replacement parts were flown to Japan,[67] and additional 90mm. ammunition was loaded aboard a fast convoy from California.[68]

The crewmen also made modifications to some of the tanks during the overseas journey, including moving the roof-mounted heavy .50 caliber machine gun from its position on the rear roof of the turret to a position in front of the commander's cupola, in order to make it more useful against ground targets.[69]

After some three weeks at sea the Brigade finally arrived in Korea late on August 2. "We got to Pusan, and we were unloaded by crane," Sleger recalled. "They drove around down the line . . . and there were flatcars alongside a warehouse. We went right up on the flatcars." It did not take long for word from "an Army source" to reach the American tankers that the men at the front "were having difficulty penetrating the T-34. We revised our [ammunition] load, and we got an additional supply of HVAP,"[70] explained Sleger.

Tank commander Cecil Fullerton, a thin baby-faced staff sergeant, would often find himself riding in the lead tank in Korea. He had joined the Marines in November 1945 at the young age of sixteen, and served as a truck driver in the Headquarters and Service Company, 2nd Tank Battalion. When he was in northern China with 1st Tank Battalion after World War II, Fullerton thought driving a tank "looked like a lot more fun than driving a truck." Still, the thought of facing the heavily armed North Koreans gave everyone pause. "All the way over to Korea, we had heard nothing but how invincible that T-34 was. It couldn't be stopped. We were a little concerned, naturally."

The next morning at 0600 the Brigade began its movement to the front aboard trains and fifty borrowed Army trucks. By 1600 that afternoon, every element of the Brigade, except one tank platoon, had arrived in Changwon, west of Pusan.[71]

"We loaded on flatcars and went out of Pusan about twenty-five miles," said Max English. "[We] sat in a railway station, looked up on the side of a mountain, and saw a big old gash on the side of [it]." Using the landslide scar as a target, the tank crews zeroed-in the big guns without ever unloading from the train cars. It was time for target practice.

The big tanks were so wide that the track hung over each side of the little flatcars.[72] According to Don Gagnon, the M26's were perched precariously on the little flatcars. "Instead of turning the guns at a ninety degree angle, we took it off at maybe thirty degrees. Wasn't enough to actually throw the weight off and a little bit back."

As Prentiss Baughman remembered it, "The muzzle blast from those things may have knocked every window out of that railroad station. The army colonel came out, and he was really raising hell with us."

"We were ready to go shooting," recalled English with a smile.

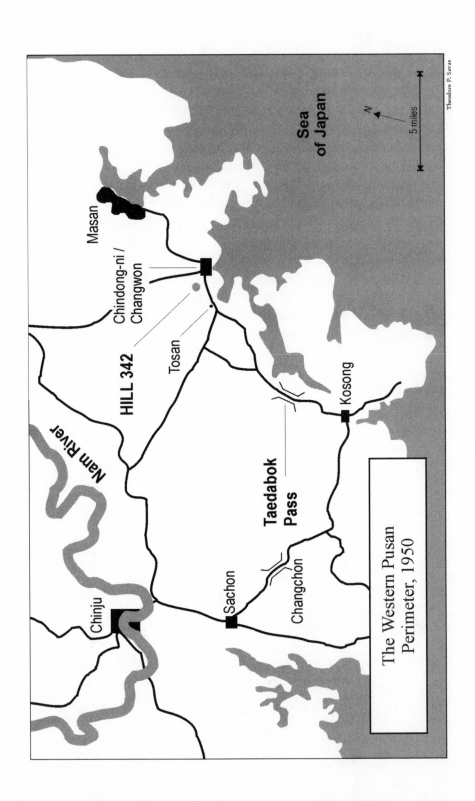

The Western Pusan
Perimeter, 1950

Theodore P. Savas

"The most vital quality a soldier can possess is
self-confidence, utter, complete, and bumptious."
— Lieutenant General George S. Patton

Chapter 2

One Company's War

The Defense of the Pusan Perimeter

By early August 1950, the mauled remnants of the U. S. Army and
ROK (Republic of Korea) divisions had fought the NKPA to a near
standstill, a feat for which they were, and still are, given little credit. The
NKPA continued to batter the Pusan perimeter in a final effort to crush
the UN forces. The entire UN front was overextended, and sizeable
NKPA forces infiltrated the thin defensive line.

There were two critical points in the defensive perimeter: the town of
Taegu in the northern sector, and on the western side of the perimeter
where the NKPA was exerting powerful pressure. Taegu's fall would
open up three possible roads along which the NKPA could launch a drive
against the port of Pusan, severing the UN's supply lines. A breakthrough
in the west, where there was a relatively dense net of coastal roads, would
more directly threaten Pusan. The loss of either point would spell the
doom of the Pusan defenders.

The American plan to disrupt the enemy's offensives involved an
attack westward parallel to the southern coast, where intelligence

suggested that the NKPA was not deployed in strength. The Army's 25th Division and 5th Regimental Combat Team, together with the fresh Marine Brigade, was ordered to pre-empt the enemy offensive by striking west from the village of Chindong-ni. On August 6, the Marine Brigade was attached to the 25th Division and moved forward to relieve a battered Army regiment and screen the Main Supply Route (MSR).

The Brigade advanced swiftly from the railhead at Changwon and quickly discovered NKPA units wandering far to the rear of the front lines. The marines assembled in stifling heat and clouds of dust, and during the following night were called upon to rush a rifle platoon onto Hill 342 northwest of the town to aid an Army platoon in danger of annihilation. The movement did not work out as planned when the relieving force quickly found itself under siege. The Brigade had stumbled into the path of the NKPA *6th Division's* offensive.

"That night we got our baptism of fire," remembered Joe Sleger. "That was the 6th of August. Artillery [fire]. It was like rain. We didn't have time to get into the tanks. We were working on the outside of the tanks, and we went underneath. I think that's where Dial got hit with the rocks."

"Next thing we know," said Everett Dial, continuing Sleger's story, "in comes these 122mm. mortars. I dove underneath the tank [and] was holding my head . . . One of them landed right beside the tracks, and blew all these rocks and some shrapnel inside. I got hurt worse by the rocks than I did the shrapnel." Although the rocks and debris had shredded Dial's clothes, his perpetual smile remained plastered to his face. He later joked that the damage was far worse when Basilo Chavarria cut his jacket off and "operated"on him with his Kabar fighting knife.[1]

According to Sleger, "Max English came up the next morning. I was walking away from the tank, going to check on one of the other tanks. He got out of the jeep, and he said 'Sleger. How'd things go last night?' I told him about the artillery, that we got quite a bit of artillery, and . . . it was about one o'clock [when] it let up a little. But we got harassing fire on the hour."

According to Sleger, English looked at his watch and asked, "Seven o'clock round come in yet?"

"No, sir!"

Sleger had just uttered his answer when an artillery round was lobbed in their direction. "That was the last we saw of each other," he joked. "He went one way and I went the other!"

In the confused fighting that followed, the enemy attacked across the rough terrain and broke through the American lines, blocking the MSR. The entire area was infested with NKPA, and the tanks were a prime target of their ambushes.

The Marines had to drive the NKPA out of the valleys and hills, but even some of the gentle slopes presented an unanticipated problem for the American tanks. The M26 was a powerful vehicle, but as the tank crews soon discovered, if it stopped on a steep gradient the transmission would slip, and it was difficult or impossible to get it moving again. Help was needed and Eugene Viveiros, who, with one of the Headquarters Platoon blade tanks, attached himself to the 3rd Platoon, was ready to supply it. He was called upon "to pat them on the butt end with the blade of the 'dozer tank to shove 'em up and get 'em going again. Once they got traction, then they were all right," Viveiros explained.

Three days of bitter fighting in the steep hills followed. The situation did not look good to Eighth Army command, which considered the units in and around Chindong-ni to be cut off. No one really knew whether the Army's 5th RCT or the NKPA controlled the critical road junction at Tosan, west of Chindong-ni.[2] The situation cleared somewhat when the NKPA finally broke off its offensive and withdrew on August 9, its strength spent.

The retreating North Koreans found themselves in a perilous position. The two roads that led west converged fifteen miles to the northwest near Chinju, a strategic crossing of the Nam River. The Communist forces had to defend both roads, lest the more mobile Americans advance rapidly along either and cut their line of withdrawal. The Marine Brigade was assigned the longer southern route, while the 5th RCT advanced along the northern axis.

The weary Marines began their advance at 0115 hours on August 10, Lt. William D. Pomeroy's 1st Platoon tanks in support. At 0500 the lead tank broke through one of the fragile bridges and jammed itself amid the rubble.[3] "That was Joe Welsch's tank [A-13]," remembered Bob Miller. "The road was so narrow, and we were going over this hill. [T]hey would use brush and everything else for a fill, because these little roads were designed for an oxen with a cart behind it. When the tanks went through, of course they crushed these things. You [also] had to be real careful on braking, so you didn't dig up the road too much. When that tank ... broke through, it caused the firing pin on the thirty caliber to strike a shell, which hit the poor guy in the foot who was guiding the tank."

Welsch's tank suffered a damaged main gun and could not be recovered from the rubble of the bridge, so it was destroyed.[4] His mishap also triggered other problems. Pomeroy's tank (A-11) threw a track while trying to bypass the collapsed bridge, blocking the advance until engineers could construct a bypass.

Other than these minor accidents, however, the Marines met little in the way of resistance. They pushed forward by mounting parts of a rifle company and the Reconnaissance Company in jeeps and trucks. This force advanced as far as Taedabok Pass, where at 1500 hours it was ambushed and pinned down for an hour and a half until the tanks came forward to drive the NKPA off the high ground. This pattern of ambush and extraction was repeated the rest of the day while the enemy bought time to execute their fighting retreat.

Nightfall found the Marines still short of the next small town, Kosong, which was located at the head of a small bay. A pre-dawn spoiling attack by the Communist forces failed in its objective, and by 0800 hours 3rd Battalion, 5th Marine Regiment (3/5)[5] was attacking southward along the road. The Marines reached the outskirts of the town two hours later, impeded only by small delaying actions along the way.

Bill Robinson's tank, part of Lieutenant Winters's 2nd Platoon, was leading the column toward Kosong. "All of a sudden I looked down, and this captain leaned out of his jeep and waved me off the road. [He] wanted to get by," recalled Robinson, who told his driver to move the tank onto the shoulder. The jeep accelerated past the tank. "He got about fifty yards in front of me, and the whole jeep exploded." Directly in front of the column, "about a hundred and fifty yards [away] was one of these Jap forty-seven [millimeter] AT guns.[6] They threw another round in, and they didn't depress enough. The round went over the top of the turret. My gunner saw the [muzzle] flash."

Robinson knew exactly what to do. "Henry," he shouted, "you see that?"

"Yeah!"

"Let 'em have it!"

One well-placed round destroyed the anti-tank weapon. When Robinson looked down, he saw a Marine rifleman sprawled on the ground, knocked down by the muzzle blast of his cannon. "This poor guy was spread-eagled on the side of the road, his dungaree jacket was all unbuttoned, and he was just laying there. I didn't know if the poor guy was dead, or what. We just kept on going."[7]

With the gun destroyed, Robinson drove his tank forward. "The AT gun crew was knocked out. We mounted a fire team on the tank and took on off.[8] We went down the road a ways, and they had left someone with a burp gun, and [he] sprayed the tank. The fire wounded several of the men riding on the tank, so consequently I radioed back saying, 'Receiving small arms fire, some casualties.'" The order, however, was to hold up. A disappointed Robinson added, "we never did get to catch 'em."

The tanks and infantry cleared the northern part of the town, but the enemy was still very active, with anti-tank gun emplacements and machine guns sited to cover their withdrawal. It was here that the an event known as the Kosong Turkey Shoot occurred when Marine aircraft caught the NKPA *83rd Motorcycle Regiment* fleeing south from the town into an apparent cul-de-sac on a peninsula. The planes virtually annihilated the unit. The slaughter, reported Robinson, "[left] a lot of goodies. Motorcycles, jeeps, all kinds of equipment."[9]

That afternoon, the Marines advanced several miles west of Kosong. The tanks led the column and provided "reconnaissance by fire"—blasting away at suspicious locations to disrupt potential ambushes. Driver John Haynie explained what transpired at one ambush. "There was a road that went up this way, and it turned. There was a big hillside over here. [Technical Sergeant Cecil] Fullerton's tank was just ahead of us. We were second, and the lieutenant [Sweet] was on my tank that particular day. Fullerton ran over a land mine in the road, just before he got to the turn."

Earlier that day, a spare crewman named Walter Oberle had replaced Fullerton's usual assistant driver. He had spent much of his time detonating exposed anti-tank mines in the road with machine gun fire. One passed unseen. "[They] fooled us. They had it hidden real well," conceded Fullerton. "When we hit it, up went a big cloud of smoke, and of course it rattled us, shook us up for about five seconds. There was no sound."

Fullerton yelled out, "Is everybody all right?"

According to Fullerton, Oberle came on the intercom, and said, "'You know, it's days like this a guy really misses his mother.' That broke it then. That's when I told Ski [the gunner, Stanley Tarnowski] to keep his gun on the trees up ahead."

At the time, no one was sure exactly what had caused the explosion. "I didn't know whether we had been hit by an AT gun, or what," explained Fullerton. "I told my driver, 'Back her down, Andy.' We tried to back down behind a building there. I looked out, and our track [was] unwinding out behind us. I said, 'Never mind. We aren't going anywhere.'"

Sweet radioed Fullerton and told him he thought his tank had hit a mine. "[Sweet] said, 'I know darn well you hit a mine.' The fender had torn off my tank, and . . . almost took his head off back there." Justifiably cautious, Sweet was reluctant to send another tank around what was essentially a blind curve.

"The lieutenant called for the tank behind us, the bulldozer tank, to go up on the hill and see what's over there," Haynie remembered.

As Sweet tells it, "I told [Master Sergeant Charles J.] 'Tiny' Rhoades to go up on the high ground above me and see if there was anything around this curve before we go around it. I've got to watch my Marine Corps vernacular now," he explained, "because I'm gonna quote something. This guy (Rhoades) gets on the mike. 'Mister Sweet,' he says, 'there's a tank over here.' I said, 'What the frig are you whispering about?' He acted like the enemy could hear him, you know. I said, 'I'm comin' up.'

"[Rhoades] had a one hundred five millimeter gun, but it was nothing like we had," continued Sweet, "and we had HVAP armor-piercing ammo. I said, 'When I come up to the top of the ridge, you hit him with a white phosphorus, and we'll take care of him.'" Sweet's plan worked brilliantly. "We loaded HV and started up the hill. Tiny let a white phosphorus go on the tank, so that would allow us to pull up and get the bottom of our tank the hell out of sight of them.[10] We could get pointing downhill to get our front slope plate at 'em, where we had four inches of homogeneous armor plate."

Sweet drove his tank over the crest and opened fire. "We just loaded shells into that goddamn thing. It was just a bonfire. That tank was burning from one end to the other in no time at all."

"It shot right through that tank," confirmed Haynie. "The HV rounds went right through that T-34."

Fullerton, meanwhile, was finally able to dismount and check the damage to his tank. The mine had taken "off the track and the first two sets of road wheels. They were blown completely off." Rainy weather only added to the misery, but did nothing to dampen the abilities of the maintenance crew which was "magnificent that day." The VTR pulled the damaged tank into the village immediately to their rear.[11] In addition to a constant flow of ambulances through the village, "there was artillery coming in every once in a while. . . . I rolled away at midnight that night," explained a pleasantly surprised Fullerton, "completely mended."

As in so many Marine Corps campaigns where the tanks were operating far from major support organizations, the rapid and efficient work of the maintenance support team was critical to success. "Robert Plumley was our Maintenance Officer for the tanks," explained Prentiss Baughman. "He had a group of tank mechanics with him. He had the Service Platoon. . . . We carried the Exec's tank, the CO's tank, and [three] spare tanks in the Headquarters Platoon. We had a specially equipped jeep we sent out on liaison duty. Two or three men would go out on that . . . and scout the territory."

Another of Baughman's many jobs was to facilitate coordination with the infantry. "Each platoon was assigned to a battalion of the Fifth Marines, for their support. As they needed them, they asked for them. It was up us to get the frequency they operated on, and see that the tank radios were in operating condition on their frequency," said Baughman.

The following morning, August 12, the Brigade moved out toward Sachon, the next otherwise unimportant village about ten miles to the northwest. Two tanks led the column, followed by B/1/5, and the other three tanks of Pomeroy's platoon. About noon the column entered a broad valley southeast of the road junction at Changchon. When the tanks and infantry opened fire on what appeared to be a group of stragglers, a torrent of return fire poured down upon them from the hills on either side. The unsuspecting Marines had prematurely triggered a massive ambush.

The tanks, trapped on the road by the soft ground in the valley and unable to climb the steep ridges, did their best to support the riflemen with long-range fire while providing cover for the evacuation of wounded from the valley floor. The firefight continued through the day and into that night.

At midnight, the Marines received orders for one rifle battalion and a battery of artillery to break contact with the enemy southeast of Changchon and move twenty-five miles back along the route they had just traversed. While they had been fighting the enemy that day, a large Communist force had attacked out of the range of hills separating the Brigade and the 5th RCT, overrunning three Army artillery batteries west of Tosan. The sudden thrust had again severed the 25th Division's MSR.

The next morning found the Brigade launching two separate attacks in opposite directions. By 1000 hours, the Marines, aided by light Army tanks, were driving the NKPA off the ridges and reopening the roads west of Tosan. On August 14, the entire Brigade was ordered to break contact and fall back from Changchon. Frustrated, the Marines began a hasty retrograde movement eastward in the direction of Kosong, with engineers and tanks acting as the rearguard.

After the fight below Changchon, the Marine Brigade was shifted north when one of Eighth Army's nightmares came true. On August 6, the NKPA breached the Naktong River line, the last natural defensive barrier protecting the highway between Taegu and Pusan. Utilizing a Soviet technique, the NKPA had stealthily constructed submerged bridges of rocks and logs so that they could quickly move heavy equipment across the river. The Army's 24th Division was unable to dislodge the enemy from the jagged ridges, and by August 10 the entire NKPA *4th Division* (the *5th, 16th,* and *18th Rifle Regiments* and the attached *107 Tank Regiment*) was entrenched on the eastern bank. Desperate American counterattacks on August 11 and again on August 14 and 15 failed to dent the NKPA positions.

Long distance movements, like the one the Marine Brigade undertook on August 15, were a nightmare. The tanks were transported by rail as far as possible, and Sweet was sent on a reconnaissance to determine which bridges could accommodate the tanks.[12] "I remember one time when I immediately knew what kind of people I had," said Sweet. "We had such a short time for the infantry kickoff, and we gotta get into position. We're charging up this road, and we come to a bridge that had cement pedestals on it, about four feet apart. No way to get around, and a mud hole on either side. I called Sleger, and I said, 'Send a man up with a sledgehammer off all the tanks.' I was out there trying to sledgehammer one of the pillars off. He just got those sledgehammers and knocked those pillars down and then we went over the coarse stuff and made it to our [departure line]." After the tanks crossed the bridge, Sweet thought to himself, "Geez, these guys are as eager as I am!"

On August 15, the Marine Brigade became part of Task Force Hill. Colonel John G. Hill of the 9th Infantry (2nd Division) commanded a powerful force including the 9th RCT, the 19th and 34th Infantry of the 24th Division, and the Marine Brigade. The Marine Brigade was given a troublesome dual responsibility: attack the Obong-ni Ridge while simultaneously protecting Cloverleaf Hill, a height three miles west of Obong-ni that screened the 24th Division Headquarters and the Miryong Road, which provided a direct route to the Pusan-Taegu highway.

The Marines called the Obong-ni Ridge "No-Name Ridge," and most still use this name today. The ridge was a formidable position—high, steep, and stony, with several peaks aligned northwest to southeast. Numerous spurs ran down to the lower ground and overlooked the village and Observation Hill, which was occupied by the Marines. Overextended and operating with limited resources, the Marines planned to assault the ridge by capturing the high northwestern end, and then move along the crest and clear it of enemy forces.

On August 17, the Brigade's artillery began shelling the high rocky ground, and at 0800 hours D and E Companies of 2/5 moved out across the low divide connecting Observation Hill to the main ridge line. The men absorbed a terrific enemy fire on the open ground, and D Company was also exposed to a deadly flanking fire from the village of Tugok, to the north in the 9th Regiment's zone. Sweet's 3rd Platoon tanks fired over the heads of the advancing Marines and were credited with the destruction of twelve anti-tank guns and numerous machine guns. Their heavy armor withstood numerous hits from enemy mortars and twenty-three hits from enemy anti-tank guns.[13] Unfortunately, the best efforts of this handful of tanks were not enough. The riflemen slowly fought their way onto the peak at the northern end of the ridge, but were forced to withdraw at noon. There were simply no reserves to hold the ground they had taken.

The retiring Marines passed through A and B Companies of the First Battalion, which were moving in for their own attack. One section of Sweet's tanks moved forward along the road that skirted the northern end of the ridge, between it and Tugok, to help suppress the fire coming from the village. "That was the day I sent Sleger down the hill," remembered Sweet. "I said, 'Don't go down too deep, but reconnoiter the area and see if there's something down there.' He went down and turned around, and took his position. The NKPA must have seen him come down and back up."

The area was littered with abandoned American and NKPA equipment, which impeded Sleger's reconnaissance. "I remember driving over a jeep," said driver Haynie. "It was about this tall when we got through," he said, holding his hands about a foot apart, "but it was in our way, and no one would move it."[14]

"We went down and to the other side of that slope to see if we would draw fire," explained Sleger. "The old pucker factor was riding pretty high. We didn't draw any fire, but there were some abandoned vehicles there. We destroyed them, and came back." The patrol returned at about 1600 hours.

The tanks repeatedly ran short of fuel and ammunition, and several times retired to a supply point and Forward Command Post behind Observation Hill. Stretcher parties flooded back down from the ridge, filling the medical aid stations with casualties.[15] In the early evening, the tanks retired to refuel and replenish ammunition for the fifth time at the Forward CP, about 1,000 yards to the rear.[16]

At 2000 hours observers reported a force of NKPA infantry, led by four T-34 tanks, moving along the road toward Tugok. With one of its rifle battalions mauled, another entangled with the NKPA forward on the ridge crest, and the Army's 9th Infantry unable to advance into the high ground to the north, the right flank of the Brigade was desperately vulnerable to the looming counterattack.

Max English relayed the information that the enemy attack was underway. Sweet recalled that English had spent most of the Pusan Campaign on General E. A. Craig's staff, as the tank expert.[17] "Most everything that we did, we did without orders."

"G. G. [Sweet] was my Rock of Gibraltar," said English. "If something was going on, I'd say, 'G. G., let's get going.' So he'd come in, rearm and refuel, and I'd say, 'You got to get your ass back out again.'" English recalled clearly the circumstances that sent Sweet into one of the most desperate situations he would face in Korea: "G. G. was down there getting some ammunition and gas that had been sent up there close to his area. The word was passed that tanks were coming, and he moved his platoon up there and made a roadblock."

"It wasn't a matter of who was leading who," said Sweet, "but whoever had their tank ready. These guys were handling fifty-five gallon drums of gas, and loading ammunition off a truck. We had been shootin' all day long and had just pulled back from the ridge that we knew like the back of our hand."

As Sweet implied, the refueling process was backbreaking labor. "We never had a deal like the Army, where big fuel trucks come and refuel the tanks," lamented tanker Chavarria. "We had fifty-five gallon drums. We used to manhandle those drums. . . . It [the bung] was threaded. Put [in] a nozzle, and then two guys used to get that fifty-five gallon drum and tip it over."

Nik Frye was on radio watch inside Sweet's tank. "I heard 'FLASH PURPLE!' That was the infantry sign for a tank attack." Sweet also remembered the moment. "All of a sudden we get the message, and man these guys were just taking off. Really charging. I, the leader, I think I was about the fourth tank, and Sleger was behind me. I laugh like hell when I think of it," he continued, "but we never even had the gas caps on the tanks. Everyone was so eager get in it that we charged up that hill!"

Fullerton's crew had completed refueling and were dining on C-rations when the order came to move out.[18] "Sweet told me, 'You go ahead, Fullerton, and we'll catch up soon as we get refueled here, and finish loading with ammo.' So I took off up the road. On the way, down the road came this Army jeep. [The men in the jeep were] waving their arms. I told my driver, 'Hold up, Andy. Let's see what they want.'"

The men in the jeep stopped close to Fullerton's tank and one of its occupants yelled out, "Don't go up there! There's tanks up there!"

"What do you think this thing is?" yelled back Fullerton. "Get out of the way!"

Fullerton drove his tank forward. "On the way up we ran into a couple of abandoned jeeps that we just pushed off the road." Ahead he spotted a large truck filled with ammunition. "I told the driver to hold it up," said Fullerton, who jumped out, ran up to the truck, jumped inside and drove it into a cut in the left side of the road where mortars had been set up.

The move did not please one of the mortar crew, who screamed at Fullerton, "Get that truck out of here!"

"You drive it out of here or I'll run over you and it, too!" came his terse reply. "When I saw his Major's [oak] leaves on his collar," said Fullerton, "and I ran and got in the tank and we took off."

Fullerton's tank sped past wounded soldiers littering the sides of the road. When he was about fifty yards from the curve, he instructed his gunner to "Sight in on the curve."

The 1st Recoilless Gun Platoon was entrenched on the northern slope of Observation Hill, overlooking the road, and 3.5-inch rocket launcher teams were waiting on the slopes of Hill 125. Both these weapons had already proven less than effective against the enemy T-34s. The 75mm. recoilless guns often failed to penetrate the T-34's armor. The rocket launcher could be deadly, but only in the hands of experienced gunners who were cool enough to take on the big tanks at close range. The Marine tankers were confident that the M26 was a match for the T-34, but the stakes were too high to take a chance. The T-34s had to be stopped—even if they could not be destroyed.

The defile where the road passed through the ridge was very narrow, and when Sweet arrived on the scene, it was there he chose to make his stand. "We came up, and there was a cut, and we heard the enemy tanks were coming. I told them where to go, and get hub to hub, and close that thing off."

Joe Sleger explained Sweet's thinking. "He blocked that pass, because down behind and to the rear of that hill mass was the battalion medevac station. He put two tanks[19] down in the road, so that even if they got knocked out you couldn't get anything past them." Max English agreed. "There was no way they could get through him even [if] they knocked him out."

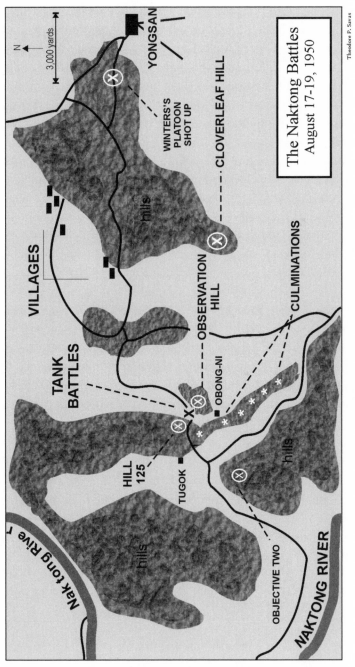

The Naktong Battles
August 17-19, 1950

Theodore P. Savas

"I can remember that kid, Fullerton [tank A-34] . . . was on the left, [Gerald] Swinicke [tank A-33] was in the middle, and Chavarria [tank A-32] was on the right," continued Sweet. "I was sitting right behind them." Swinicke's tank was staggered slightly back from Fullerton's, with his gun muzzle beside the rear of Fullerton's turret.[20] The three tanks in the cut, however, blocked Sweet's own field of fire. "We couldn't fire anything. In fact, I made the loader take the shell out of the chamber because all I had was three turrets in front of me. I was looking between the first and second tank."

A mechanical failure had already knocked one of the Marine tanks out of the fight. "My elevation and traversing mechanism wouldn't allow the gun to go down," grumbled Nik Frye. "The enemy tanks were below us, coming up the road. I couldn't depress the gun enough to shoot at 'em."

While Sweet's tankers waited, an attack by Marine aircraft reportedly damaged one of the advancing enemy tanks and dispersed the infantry, but the balance of the NKPA tankers rolled confidently forward, approaching the narrow gap where the road passed between Observation Hill on the south and Hill 125 on the north. The North Koreans had every reason to be confident. For months they had brushed aside American tanks, and although they had suffered losses, most had been the result of air attacks or suffered in battle when overwhelmed by American infantry. As they understood the situation, an opportunity existed to drive into the American flank and rear and get in among the vulnerable support units—a tanker's dream.

When the enemy tanks came into range, Sweet called Fullerton and said, "'try one of those hyper-velocity shells on those tanks.' At that range the muzzle velocity was 3,350 feet per second." Before Fullerton could react, American rocket gunners on Hill 125 struck first, pounding one of the advancing enemy vehicles. The tank kept coming even though its track was damaged and external fuel tanks aflame. When it moved into the sights of Fullerton's tank at a range of only 100 yards, he ordered his gunner, Sgt. Stanley Tarnowski, to let him have it. Three 90mm. rounds were sent flying.

"Tarnowski hardly ever missed," recalled Fullerton. This time, however, he was convinced his shot went wide of the target because there was no explosion or other indication of a hit.

"You missed, Ski," Fullerton yelled.

As Fullerton recalled it, his gunner turned around with big tears in his eyes. "I don't miss, Sergeant Fullerton."

"And he was right. When the men checked the dead tank later that day, they discovered he hadn't missed. I had just forgotten there were no explosions [with armor-piercing ammunition]," explained Fullerton.

Tarnowski's shots had passed right through the tank and hit Obong-ni Ridge, over 1,000 yards away. When the shells struck around them, the American infantry on the ridge were convinced they were taking friendly fire, and called the tankers to tell them as much.

Tarnowski's first round had struck "the first tank in the bow gun mount," remembered Fullerton. "The projectile was just a tungsten carbide core. It didn't explode. It just punched its way through armor. It went through the bow gun, through the turret [base] . . . tore half the engine of that T-34 out, went on through, and hit on that hill over there, on Obong-ni Ridge. We [had] just tried that out, to see what it would do to a tank."[21]

Lieutenant Sweet, of course, was satisfied with the result. "We blew them right off the face of the earth! There was only one guy [who] moved in this first group of tanks we hit. He must have been the tank commander. He was trying to get out [of] the top, and he just got splattered. No one got out."

At the refueling point, a considerable amount of fuel had been spilled onto the decks of the American tanks. "When they took the drum off they spilled a lot of gas in the turret ring," remembered Frye. "When Swinicke would fire, he would light Fullerton off, and he'd fire and put Fullerton out. So we're all saying, 'Fullerton! Fullerton! You're on fire!' and then Bang! He'd be out."

Sweet confirmed Frye's recollection. "Every time the one on the right would fire, he would set off the gasoline . . . I didn't know whether they had their gas caps on or not, but they spilled a lot. . . . Then the other tank would fire, and blow it out. We had fires going on all three tanks."

In the fast and confused action north of Observation Hill, some of the infantry claimed they knocked out the enemy tanks. Not so, claimed Fullerton, who added, "In action like this, everyone says they got the tanks. The infantry says they hit 'em with bazookas and blew their tracks off and everything. All I know is the first one came around that curve under full power, and we hit him. He went off the road, and started burning."

The second T-34 did not fare any better than the first. Even though it was smothered with anti-tank rockets and recoilless gun rounds, it kept rolling toward Sweet's tankers.[22] "Before we could get a second round in,"[23] remembered Fullerton, "[it] came around with his gun pointed right at us. For some reason, and to this day I don't know why, he didn't fire. Just as we hit his turret, it spun to the left, and he fired into the bank beside the road. That's how close it was." Fullerton had a theory why the enemy tank had withheld fire. "They were so used to . . . coming up against Army M4 Sherman tanks [that] he was temporarily stunned to look and see that big ol' ninety millimeter, that M26, sitting there."

The shot had knocked the second tank off the road as well, "and then the third one came around." A fourth T-34 lurched to a stop in defilade behind the flaming leader and continued to fire across the narrow gap at the Marines on Observation Hill. One of Sweet's M26s squeezed past the burning tank and into the road. The Marine tankers put six rounds into the T-34, setting it ablaze. "The Korean crewmen started coming out of the hatches when they first got hit, and Cecil and the other tank opened up with the machine guns," recalled Sweet. "They closed the hatch and went back in. . . . They never came out of the tank. It was real fast."

The third tough Russian-made tank took another seven 90mm. rounds before it, too, exploded. The turret hatch flew open and someone finally tried to climb out, but a 3.5-in. rocket with a white phosphorus warhead hit the open hatch cover, ricocheted inside, and exploded. No survivors emerged.

Sweet's tankers were consumed with the fire of battle. "I had one hell of a time . . . getting them to quit shooting," explained Sweet. "They were beatin' them tanks up like tomato cans. And they kept pourin' that ninety into 'em, and I'm yelling 'Cease fire! Cease fire!' They must have fired twenty more rounds after I told 'em to quit. They all knew enough to hit the turret ring first [to jam the turret], and then they were hittin' everything." The result was a bloody mess. ""It was a scene that nobody would want to see. You could see when they got hit, see them trying to bail out of their tanks, and it was really a pretty sad sight."

The 2nd Platoon tanks, with Viveiros in the 105mm. M4A3 in support, were positioned about fifty yards apart on a ridge to the north.[24]

While Sweet's 3rd Platoon tankers were wiping out advancing Communist armor, 2nd Platoon had its own unique experience, although against attacking enemy infantry.

Don Gagnon watched in horror as hundreds of foot soldiers he initially took as American infantry advanced toward his position. "I'm looking out through my periscope, and I'm yelling 'Cease fire! Cease fire! We're shootin' at our own people!'"

Boogah Moss heard him and shouted back, "Those are not our people. Those are people dressed in our uniforms. Take a closer look!"

Gagnon did and agreed. "Okay, you're right!"

As he later explained it, "They were North Koreans, coming down off that hill, just like a parade had just broken up and they're all coming down. . . . We're shootin' high explosives into those people with delayed fuses, to bounce them off the ground. They were just slaughtered.

"They [3rd Platoon] had just finished with those tanks around the corner," continued Gagnon, "and these people were coming down the hill. That was really a massacre on our part." Moss believes the enemy infantry were trying to escape following the bloody failure of their tank attack.[25]

In retrospect, Sweet concluded that the NKPA tankers just "did not have the training. That eighty-eight [sic] could have put holes in us. . . . I figured they should have gotten three or four rounds off, but [they] never got anything off."

The enemy tankers had not impressed Fullerton, who was amazed with "how dumb North Korean tank tactics were. If we're in a column and go around a curve, and the first tank is hit, we're not just gonna go busting right around one after the other."

The fight at the gap raised the morale of the Marine tankers and wiped away the mystique of the once-dreaded T-34. "We were looking for 'em from then on, hoping to run into some," recalled Fullerton. "It was no problem with 'em at all. It was like a Cadillac up against a Model T Ford as far as we were concerned. Most of the time when you hit them the top of the turret would blow completely off. I guess it was just welded on up there."

By comparison, the M26 was much safer. "We had a couple of tanks hit . . . and if you don't hit the fuel tank, nothing really bad happened."

When the late summer darkness finally fell, the Marine riflemen held defensible positions atop the two northernmost knobs of Obong-ni Ridge, and in the words of the official history, the tanks had "shattered the myth of the T-34 in five flaming minutes."[26]

Obong-ni Ridge was a critical position for the Communists in what had become known as the Naktong Bulge. If they could not hold it, the whole NKPA position east of the Naktong River was in peril. At 0230 hours on August 18, Communist forces began a series of desperate counterattacks against the Marine positions, launched from the high hills to the west of the ridge, and along the ridge crest from Hill 117, an enemy-held position. Although some American positions were overrun, by dawn the enemy's strength was spent and the Marines were still firmly in control of the northern third of the ridge.

The remainder of the day was spent in a costly yard-by-yard struggle south along the ridge crest, a bloody fight for each inch of rocky terrain. Other Marines pushed westward onto Objective Two, a higher and even more rugged hill mass. The tankers provided support for both operations, firing over the heads of the advancing riflemen.

The NKPA knew that once the Americans controlled the Objective Two hill mass, their tanks and vehicles could sweep down the road from Tugok and into the open valley that led down to the river. Although the random tangle of high hills closer to the river was a strong position, it would also turn into a trap if the Americans controlled the river crossings. Unable to halt the American advance, the North Koreans began falling back, first in an orderly fashion, and eventually in mass retreat. American artillery and mortars opened fire on the fleeing infantry, turning the river crossings into slaughterhouses. Large stocks of ammunition and equipment were left behind. Early the following morning, August 19, 1st Platoon moved down to the banks of the river, where it found nine abandoned field guns and howitzers.[27]

"We had probably a battalion or two battalions of people breaking off and trying to get across the river. We fired so much we burned up our machine guns," recalled Bill Robinson. "We were only about seven hundred yards [from the river]. We were lucky, though. Earlier that day we had run across all these Army tanks that they had just left, abandoned. We stopped by and I had my loader go in there, and he pulled out all the machine guns. It worked out real good."

The stunning string of successes left the Marines "salty," a bit of Marine slang for "cocky." Many grew beards because water was too precious for shaving. When Colonel Murray of the 5th Marines "read the riot act" to Max English about his beard, English passed down the word that the beards had to go.[28] "We all left mustaches to keep it in line," laughed Sweet. "That was kind of legal."

"We were using artillery grease [on the mustaches], but that didn't taste very good," remembered Frye. "Somebody wrote to Colgate Palmolive Pete or something, and the girl sent us a whole case of mustache wax. Everybody had a toothbrush and a tube of mustache wax."

Sweet sported an enormous red handlebar mustache, curled at the tips.[29] "I remember the time I woke up. . . . I was just laying there unconscious, and I was lying on the side. This side of the mustache was pushed right down on my mouth, and the other was still waxed up there. I went over to a six-by sitting there. I looked in the mirror and said, 'Holy Christ!'"

*   *   *

Following the elimination of the Naktong Bulge, the Marine Brigade went into reserve, patrolling rear areas while it integrated replacements and prepared for its next assignment. The troops, of course, were not informed that they were being rested before they joined the rest of the 1st Marine Division for the planned Inchon landing.

Certain units were assigned secondary duties. A stint as security troops for the Brigade command post resulted in a very odd gift—a large aluminum pot presented to C. J. Moss by General Craig.[30] "That was my reward," said Moss. "I used it to make coffee, heat C-rations. We'd pool five C-rations, put 'em in one pot, and—hot meal! He gave me a bazooka and an M-1 rifle as well. I said, 'What in the world am I gonna do with all this?'"

Most other crews had similar communal cooking arrangements. Merl Bennett had no idea how he "wound up being the cook most of the time. We'd mix some good goulash out of [C-rations]. Get the five-in-one rations [and we thought] we'd died and gone to heaven."[31]

Still determined to crush the Pusan position, the NKPA attacked again on September 1, pushing the U S Army's 2nd and 25th Divisions back and again occupying the Naktong Bulge. By September 2 the Communists had put their *9th* and *4th Infantry Divisions* and supporting units—a total of thirteen infantry and three security regiments, and tanks—across the river. This time, however, the American defense was not as effective, and the North Koreans penetrated past Cloverleaf Hill and threatened the town of Yongsan, on the Pusan–Taegu road.

The deep thrust precipitated a crisis in UN high command circles. Eighth Army saw an immediate and critical need to use the Marines as a "fire brigade" to push the Communists back, and proposed that the 32nd Infantry, a unit not adequately trained in amphibious assault, be substituted for the Marine Brigade in the Inchon operation. The suggestion was completely unacceptable to the Marine Corps and the Navy. In a hasty compromise, it was agreed that the 32nd Infantry would be rushed to the Naktong area as quickly as possible. Until then, the Marine Brigade could be used to contain the Naktong Bulge. One non-negotiable condition was that the Brigade would be released no later than September 5.[32] The situation along the Naktong River and in the bulge, meanwhile, grew steadily worse for UN forces. On the night of September 2-3, the NKPA attacked 9th RCT, and NKPA forces filtered into Yongsan itself.

The Marine Brigade began to move north during the night. "All of the tank commanders had to get out and walk in front of the tanks," remembered Sleger. "We were in total blackout conditions. We walked the entire night, leading the tanks down the road to where we were supposed to jump off."

The sudden movements baffled most of the Marines. Chavarria said, "I didn't understand. We would go across, and then we'd come back, and go across and come back. It was real dumb, I'll tell you."

The heat and living conditions, as well as the constant fighting and marches, began to wear the men down. "I only remember about two hot meals," continued Chavarria. "We would fill our canteens and stuff from the rice paddies, and use the [Halazone] pellets. [And it was] hot. When we'd go back to fuel and rearm, we'd take our jackets off and wring them out and put them on the engine doors to dry out. . . . After about two or three days of that, it really got smelly in the turret."

John Haynie remembered how miserable it was inside the cramped hull. "I got out of my driver's hatch one time, and I didn't have a dry stitch on me. . . . I looked down in that seat for some reason, and there was a little puddle. I did not wet my pants. It was just moisture coming off my body."

The Marine infantry arrived by truck in the pre-dawn darkness and were deployed to attack the hills west of Yongsan. Before they could do so, however, they found themselves embroiled in a bitter fight with the NKPA inside the city. By 0630 they had fought their way west of the town, where they discovered the broken remnants of the Army's 9th Infantry falling back amid the burning hulks of American and North Korean tanks.

At 0645 the Marines hastily positioned themselves to meet the main body of the oncoming NKPA forces. The developing engagement promised to be a brisk one. Second Lieutenant Robert Winters led his platoon of tanks into hull-down positions on a small hill west of the town, where they began engaging the advancing enemy infantry. He was soon joined by a group of surviving Army tanks, and the combined firepower drove the enemy back.

The tank commanders were standing exposed in their hatches, hammering away at the North Korean troops with the big .50 caliber machine guns. In World War II, the tank crews seldom used this weapon, but on the more open terrain of Korea, it was deadly against exposed infantry. "It was very good," confirmed Bill Robinson. "I could pick guys off at eighteen hundred yards. It was unbelievable. . . . They thought they were safe."

"I never used my tank commander's seat," explained Sleger, "because I felt that I wouldn't be alert enough if I sat. I always stood on the tread deck." That habit exposed the tankers to enemy fire, and the first to suffer its effects was Lieutenant Winters.

"Winters," recalled C. J. Moss, "was standing on top of the tank. I recommended that he get the hell off the tank. They were shooting at him, the bullets hitting the turret. He ignored that, and he was hit eventually."

Gagnon was "sitting right behind Winters when he got hit, parked right next to him. There were six tanks up there. Winters got hit, and [General] Craig was standing behind the tank."[33] Two men who attempted to assist Winters's were also wounded. Others who had dismounted or exposed themselves atop their vehicles were also hit in the exchange of fire.

The casualty list continued to grow. According to Gagnon, Platoon Sergeant John Cottrell "had a whole bunch of brass in front of his tank commander's hatch because we moved the fifty [machine gun] from back here [the turret roof behind the hatch] up to the front. A round came in—I don't know what caliber it was—and busted up a whole bunch of those fifty caliber empty casings, and threw shrapnel into his stomach."

"There was a lot of us hit up on that hill," remembered Robinson. "Winters was hit in the neck, then Cottrell was hit, my loader was hit, and I was hit. I went out to get a machine gun. We'd burned up the bow gun and the other one [the coaxial], so I went out to get one of those [spare] guns out of the sponson box." Luckily for Robinson, he suffered only a minor shrapnel wound.

Merl Bennett had also climbed out of the tank. "I bent over to hand some thirty caliber ammo to the infantry, a machine gunner. . . . Di Noto [the loader] got hit. They took him back to Taegu, to an aid station back there. He never did come back up. He was too young to be in combat."[34]

The same series of rounds that struck Di Noto also hit Bennett. "I got part of the bullet spray in the butt. It was kind of hard to sit down for a while, but not bad enough to be evacuated. I had a nice soft cushion down there anyway, a pillow I think I got aboard the LSD-22, *Fort Marion*, on the way over there. When Sweet's platoon pulled through," continued Bennett, "we all went down there. They had Winters laying on a stretcher, and Cottrell was on one, and the rest of us were waiting for the corpsman to get around to us."

Moss took over for the wounded Cottrell, and 2nd Lt. John S. Carson replaced Winters. "He was Recon, and when Winters was hit, he took over the platoon," said Moss.

The night was rainy and miserable. Sleger's section of tanks were moved up to an over-watch position during the pre-dawn darkness. At 0855 the next morning, the infantry of A and B Companies attacked the high hills west of the town and south of the main east-west road. They were supported by long-range fire from an Army tank destroyer that had worked its way up onto high ground to their rear. The exhausted tankers fought off one last enemy surge west of the town, destroying in the process three T-34s with long-range fire.

Sometime during the morning, Sweet and the rest of 3rd Platoon joined the band of tanks on the small hill, which were still firing at targets in the valley. With his attention riveted on an exchange of fire, Sleger was not aware that Sweet had joined him. "We had a good hull-defilade position," said Sleger. "We were getting rounds in front of the tank. Sizeable rounds. We could hear rounds going over the turret. Apparently, when they would depress, they would hit in front of us, when they would elevate they would go right over us."

"We thought we were fighting AT guns," continued Sleger. "We were using HE [high explosive]. Then I saw a flash, a soft flash. It was in a dried out stream bed, and there were some poplar trees right on the edge of the stream bed. In between the poplar trees, I saw the flash." Sweet, who was on another ridge, saw it as well.

"Sleger, put a round of AP in there and see what happens," he suggested.

Sleger, who had not thought of that, launched the round "and the flash didn't come back. Just as the smoke was clearing . . . and waited around, a thin trail of smoke came up from behind the poplar trees. Then we got the word to jump off in the continuation of the attack." Sleger's tankers passed the poplar-lined stream bed. "We were exchanging rounds at 800 yards, and [there] was a T-34 sitting there . . . knocked out."

By noon, the Marines had occupied the hill mass south of the road, and the 3rd Battalion was attacking the hill mass to the north of the road. The 2nd Platoon tanks moved down the valley, shelling likely centers of resistance. The 45mm. anti-tank guns were not very effective, but Lieutenant Carson was directing the tanks from a standing position in his hatch. "He took several rounds of fifty-one caliber in his guts," said Moss. "He was killed instantly."[35]

Several other tank commanders were wounded by small arms fire. "The others that were wounded were exposed where they shouldn't have been at that time, because they were manning the fifty caliber machine gun which was mounted on the outside of the turret," explained Moss. "That's a no-no. In fact, the company commander [English] after that action ordered all the fifty caliber machine guns removed and stored. He couldn't afford to lose any more people on that basis."

Moss assumed temporary command of the platoon until Viveiros was sent down to take over.[36] Sweet suggested that this was a welcome opportunity for Viveiros. "Every time I'd go out, old Viveiros used to volunteer to go with me. He said, 'I hate this fuckin' CP.'"

Some tank commanders were far more circumspect than Winters and Carson. "Swinicke was overly cautious," Dial remembered. "I guess he figured somebody had his number. We'd all be out looking around, or stickin' up out of the turret, and here'd be Swinicke with his turret cracked with his steel helmet on his head—which none of us ever wore—with his eyes rotating around the cupola."[37]

"I guess that was more my fault than anybody's," explained Sweet, "because I was always on people's ass for cracking their hatch." Both Sweet and English were veterans of World War II, and in that war the first casualty in English's own company was killed when he needlessly exposed himself.[38]

The poor visibility from inside the tank, which prompted many commanders to expose themselves, was a common complaint. Even the driver seldom knew what was going on during combat. "You're driving along looking out a periscope, and your vision is like this," said Haynie, gesturing was though looking out through a narrow tube. "You're looking around for anything in your way, land mines, anything. You're just not seeing everything that someone else might."

The loader, however, had it the worst of all. He worked completely cut off from the outside world, and he had other problems beyond visibility. As Roger Chaput described it, "We didn't have bore evacuators. You fired, it would counter-recoil and go back into battery, and then a big blue flame would come out of the breech. We all had mustaches, so you said, 'Fire! Bang!' You'd cover up your mustache so you didn't get it singed off."

Each time the big gun fired and recoiled, the breechblock automatically flew open and ejected the empty, blistering-hot brass shell casing. The turret quickly filled with choking, acidic fumes. One of the loader's tasks was to pick up the expended casing and shove it out the pistol port, a small hatch on the left side of the turret. "You had to bend down and pick up a round—a spent round," explained Chaput. "You always had those flames [unburned propellant] shooting out of the breechblock. I didn't have any eyelashes or eyebrows left." There was only so much a loader could stand. "We fired twenty or twenty-five rounds, and that was almost my limit. . . . Once in a while I would slip open a [pistol] port, and stick my nose and mouth out that way, and get some fresh air."

*   *   *

On the afternoon of September 4, the Marines continued their attack along both sides of the road, advancing about 3,000 yards before darkness and rain ended operations for the day. By dawn on September 5, the Marines were back in a familiar spot, with 3/5 preparing to attack Obong-ni Ridge from Observation Hill. Another miserable night was spent under intermittent rain and shell fire.

The events of the following day, September 6, were eerily parallel to those of August 17, but with grimly different results. As the same rifle battalion moved out to attack the north end of the ridge, the 1st Platoon tanks under Lieutenant Pomeroy waited in the road cut between Observation Hill and Hill 125 to the north. The infantrymen of B/1/5 on Hill 125 saw a pair of T-34s, followed by an armored personnel carrier,[39] advancing east along the road toward the gap. They tried to alert Pomeroy, but the infantry radio, unreliable at the best of times, malfunctioned at that moment.

Pomeroy sent his tanks single file through the narrow gap to support the infantry attack on the ridge. The turrets were slewed ninety degrees to the left, so that when they rounded the right-hand bend on the far side, the big guns would be pointed at the ridge and ready to fire. The tanks had loaded their ready ammunition racks with High Explosive rounds in preparation to engage enemy positions on No-Name Ridge.[40]

The leading M26 emerged directly into the path of the first T-34. This time the enemy crew did not hesitate and hold their fire. Several rounds slammed into the side of the American turret. The crew of the stricken M26 scrambled out through the escape hatch in the belly of the tank and spilled onto the road. The second M26 tried to squeeze past its stricken brother, but the T-34 put several rounds into it at close range. The crew of the second tank also escaped, but the narrow defile was nearly plugged by the hulks of the big tanks. According to the official history, neither tank crew suffered any casualties, but Joe Sleger disagrees, claiming that the crews fell back through their position, and that one had been killed and another wounded.[41]

Bob Miller's tank was still behind the ridge when the first two were knocked out of action.[42] "One of the guys, Steve Duro, got up there and pulled one of the drivers out that had tried to get out the escape hatch," said Miller. "Seems to me he had his foot shot off, or partially shot off . . . with a round.[43] Duro hauled him off in his arms. Brought him back off of there."

Assault squads from B/1/5 rushed down the hill and, according to the official version of events, killed all three of the NKPA vehicles with rocket launcher fire delivered at close range. The tankers say that a third M26 commanded by Joe Welsch squeezed by the two wrecked tanks and had also engaged the T-34s. With no armor-piercing rounds in the loader's ready rack, Welsch was forced to scramble to recover rounds from the "honeycomb," the storage racks below the turret, while the main gun recoiled above his head.[44]

One of the wounded tankers was Pomeroy's platoon sergeant, but there were two other staff sergeants in the platoon available to take his place. As Miller recalled, "Pomeroy said, 'Whichever one of you guys is senior is the Platoon Sergeant.'" And that was it.

Joe Sleger's section from 3rd Platoon moved into the same position. "I told them to close the hatches. Sweet's [order] was that . . . as soon as we crossed the line of departure, we had to button up. [Bud] Cornelius[45] had his hatch open. . . . As he closed the hatch, on the assistant driver's seat . . . we took a round right at the junction of the hatch and the hull. One second earlier, and he would have had his head blown off."

The round that struck the tank had been fired from an anti-tank shoulder rifle.[46] "And then they really worked us over with those things," said Sleger. "Shot all our sponsons up, tore everything up on the side of the tank. The rounds—especially on the slope plate—would go in and gouge, and ricochet out. That was the first encounter that we had with the anti-tank shoulder rifle."

Max English brought a contingent from Brigade headquarters, including civilian correspondents, to see the damage. Sleger recalled the humorous event: "Max was showing them around our tank. He said Sleger didn't mind this round, and he didn't mind this one. But when they shot up the coffee can, that really pissed him off!'"

The old anti-tank rifles were more effective against the M4A3s than the M26 model. Frye remembered that this weapon "penetrated the M4 in certain places, so Tiny Rhoades put about fifty-six tons of extra track and railroad iron on his tank. Of course, when he got in a mud hole, he couldn't get out."

The battles for the hills north and south of the road continued under a steady rain that began with the falling darkness. The 23rd Infantry Regiment arrived that night, and at midnight the Marines, true to their orders, began to move back down off the ridges to board trucks for the trip to Pusan and the Inchon expedition.

The two tanks of Pomeroy's platoon disabled in the ambush could not be recovered before the Marines were pulled from the front. Moss said that "bazookas [were] fired at 'em and missed. They sent some private up there with a five-gallon can of gasoline, poured it on 'em, and set 'em on fire. That's how they were destroyed."

These two tanks could likely have been recovered and repaired had the Brigade not been under orders to depart immediately. In the final analysis, they were the only two Marine Corps tanks that would be lost by fire in tank vs. tank combat; by contrast, the enemy lost fourteen T-34s.[47]

To Frye, the most memorable part of the withdrawal was what awaited the tired Marines in the rear. "We got one of our first hot meals, and clean clothes. We got great big hunks of breaded Spam. That was a real treat."

"I know that this operation will be sort of helter-skelter. But the 1st Marine Division is going to win the war by landing at Inchon."

— General of the Army Douglas MacArthur

Chapter 3

The Masterstroke

The Inchon and Seoul Operations

Like the Marine Brigade, the balance of the 1st Marine Division was one of the most experienced units America has ever sent to war. The tank battalion was comprised of veterans from top to bottom.

Battalion Commander Lt. Col. Harry Milne, commissioned through the University of Oregon, had been a member of a ship's Marine Detachment at Pearl Harbor, transferred to tanks in 1944, landed as an observer at Peleliu, and was the Executive Officer of the 6th Tank Battalion on Okinawa in 1945.[1] Already a square-faced and middle-aged grandfatherly type, Milne had just finished Senior School at Quantico and had orders to go to the 1st Tank Battalion at Camp Pendleton. Before his leave ended early that summer in 1950, the Korean War had begun. "By the time I checked in at Camp Pendleton, A Company had just left with the 1st Marine Brigade for Korea," remembered Milne. "I never had one day of training with the battalion, one day of training with any of the tank companies. We were trying to form the other three companies into a battalion. All my training was trying to get the thing together. We only

had Baker Company at Camp Pendleton at the time. My Charlie
Company came from Camp Lejeune [North Carolina]. Dog Company
came in later, mostly from Reserves." Milne did not even see Dog
Company "until after the landing at Inchon."[2]

The senior Reservist called for the front was Captain Phil Morell, a
precise, detail-oriented officer who could be unfailingly relied upon to
make things run smoothly in whatever capacity he was assigned. Morell
had served as a tank company commander on Guam and Okinawa. He
was summoned to active duty while serving as the Executive Officer of
the 11th Tank Battalion, Marine Corps Reserve. According to Morell,
"They had their line company commanders all set, so Lieutenant Colonel
Milne, whom I knew from the 6th Tank Battalion in World War II, gave
me Service Company, which was a huge company. We had truck repair,
truck platoons—we had eighteen or twenty trucks—and machine shops."

Many of the junior officers like Vaughn Stuart were also veterans.
Vaughn, who stood three inches taller than six feet (particularly tall for a
tanker), had served as an enlisted man in World War II, and had been in
Korea as part of the contingent that accepted the surrender of Japanese
forces there in 1945. Commissioned a lieutenant, he had served on other
duties before being transferred back to the 1st Tank Battalion just as A
Company embarked for Korea. When no tank platoon positions were
available, Vaughn was assigned as maintenance officer in Service
Company, then Radiological Officer in Headquarters Company. Clean
and neat under even the worst of circumstances, the handsome Stuart
was, to some, analogous to a walking recruiting poster.[3]

Meaningful preparation for war on the Korean peninsula was
hampered by limited communications and intelligence, together with the
confusion of integrating new personnel from active duty and reserve
units and absorbing new and unfamiliar equipment. "Headquarters and
Service Company was at Camp Pendleton, plus Baker Company. Charlie
Company was on the east coast," said Phil Morell, explaining the
confused state of affairs. "The reserves came in from San Diego. They
were called up on the 24th of August, and fitted into the other companies.
[We were] trying to get a semblance of battalion integrity without really
having the whole battalion together."

Both Morell and Milne agreed that there was little or no information
on the combat experiences of A Company. "We got their little action

reports that were submitted once in a while, but we had no communication with them," said Morell. "That's why when we landed at Inchon, the battalion officers didn't know Max English's officers, or G. G. Sweet, or any of those guys, or how they functioned, or anything."

Truck driver Len Maffioli was another World War II veteran who had stayed on with the 11th Tank Battalion. "I was in the unit for two years, and had just been discharged from the Reserves in 1950," recalled Maffioli. "In a couple of months the Korean War broke out, and I ran down and reenlisted with that unit. Within two weeks we were activated and on our way to Korea." Maffioli's 11th Tank Battalion was absorbed into the 1st Tank Battalion, and Maffioli was back in the "Motor T" section of Service Company.

Reservists were hastily integrated into unusual positions. Darrell Snideman had served in the Navy in World War II, and a co-worker convinced him to obtain a discharge from the Naval Reserve and join a Marine Reserve Signal Company with the rank of sergeant.[4] Explained Snideman, "When we got to Pendleton, they interviewed everybody, and this gunner asked me what I had done in the service before. I said I was a Seabee, a heavy equipment operator. So he said, 'You're a tank operator now.'" As the surprised Snideman remembered, "I never saw a tank until we got to [Japan]."

Ben Busch, a short and stocky Reservist, was a amphibious tractor operator. "They probably read that wrong or something and figured tractors are close to tanks, so we'll stick him in tanks!" laughed Busch.

In World War II, Jim Edwards served in a Navy unit that salvaged damaged landing craft from invasion beaches. During this time he worked closely with three Marine divisions. After the war, Edwards transferred to the Marines, who "didn't know what to do with me," so they made him a supply sergeant. When the Korean conflict began, Edwards thought he was being assigned to a weapons repair unit. "When I got in the truck and transferred over from Pendleton," he remembered, "there was a great big sign across the road that said 'First Tank Battalion.' I thought 'Uh-oh.' That's how I got into the tanks."

"When I reported in, I had a couple of hash-marks," continued Edwards.[5] "The lieutenant took a look at me and stood up. He shook hands with me and said he was sure glad to have 'experienced tankers.' I told him, 'I hate to burst your bubble, lieutenant, but I've never seen the

inside of a tank.' He got on the telephone and raised all sorts of hell."
Edwards was given the usual military tasks, like "[S]tenciling tank
[battalion] logos on a lot of stuff."

Paul Sanders's entire platoon joined the battalion by a most
roundabout route. Sanders had enlisted in the Marines in December 1941,
and had fought on Guadalcanal. In 1949, he was a first lieutenant and the
Executive Officer of an infantry company. Sanders had just returned
from a deployment to the Mediterranean with the Sixth Fleet when the
Commandant of the Marine Corps issued an order encouraging cross
training. He took the encouragement to heart and volunteered to go to the
2nd Tank Battalion. "They gave me good men, and they taught me the
fundamentals," Sanders explained. "I studied and by the time I felt I was
okay, I knew every damn nut and screw in [the tank]. Then we went out
and ran maneuvers and so forth."

One afternoon, the colonel called him into his office and told him,
"Sandy, I understand you've been over in the Med not too long ago for six
months."

"Yes, sir, that's right."

"We got a problem. We have to choose a tank platoon [to go to the
Mediterranean] on an LST. All the other boys don't want to go, and since
you're junior in this outfit, you're it, boy."

It worked out pretty well, Sanders said, because "they provided me
with my pick of the men in the tank battalion. I picked up the guys I knew
were pretty damn good."

Sanders's time in the Mediterranean proved limited. Two months
after their arrival there, he and his tankers were ordered to join the 1st
Tank Battalion in Japan. "They took us off the LST, and the LST took the
tanks back to the United States. We went aboard a troopship that went
through the Suez [Canal] and on around to [Japan]."[6]

The men who had it the worst were those who staffed each rifle
regiment's Anti-Tank Platoon. Not only did they receive little or no
training, but they also belonged to tiny "orphan" units. Mike Wiggins, a
soft-spoken Regular from North Carolina stationed at Fort Mifflin,
Pennsylvania, had some experience with tanks in the closing days of
World War II. "All the Marines who were at guard duty stations and other
separate units were shipped to Camp Pendleton," he remembered. "It was
segregated at that time. Tanks didn't become part of the Marine Corps as

far as blacks were concerned until 1950. When I got to Camp Pendleton, with my background and previous heavy equipment and tractor operations, stuff like that, I was assigned to the 7th Marines. I was assigned to the Anti-Tank Company." These units, organic to each of the rifle regiments, had two platoons of 75mm. recoilless anti-tank guns, and a platoon of five M26 tanks. "The regimental commander could use them as his defense."

Sergeant Donald R. Bennett lied about his age to join the Marine Reserve at age fifteen. He served three years while still in high school. He was assigned to Baker Company tanks, where he found that the other companies received even less preparation than A Company. "When we got to the dock in San Diego [at the Naval Station], none of us had ever been on [an M26] tank," explained Bennett, who estimates that his company consisted of perhaps 60% Regulars, many from the east coast, 20% World War II veterans from the Reserve, and the balance green reservists like himself.[7] "We had one man in the company, a maintenance man, who had been to an Army school on the M26 tank. He told us how to hook up the batteries. After we checked the oil and other things, he started each vehicle and drove it off the flatcar, and parked it there at Thirty-Second Street [San Diego Naval Station]. We were told at the time that we were going to Japan for three months training. That was the standard line that was being passed out. We were also told not to clean any Cosmoline[8] off any of the weapons. They said, 'Store the [O. V. M] items where the manual says they're stored, and we'll clean the Cosmoline out of 'em when we get to Japan."

The next day civilian workers showed up and began welding fording gear onto the tanks. "I knew then we weren't going on any three months of training in Japan," recalled Bennett. "Those vehicles were driven by that same guy down [to the docks] and they were loaded, one at a time, on board a tramp steamer. Lieutenant Gover selected six or seven people, including himself, and they went with the ship, with the tanks, for the purpose of keeping them dogged down and watching 'em."

Harry Bruce was a Reservist assigned to the First Replacement Draft, destined to replace the casualties suffered by the First Brigade. "I got as far as San Francisco. They shipped me from Frisco down to Pendleton." When the men fell us out one morning, the officers "called my name out, and they said, 'We got a work detail down at North Island.' I believe there was a longshoreman's strike going on at that time, so they didn't have anybody to load and unload ammo. We went down there and worked for a week, twelve hours a day, unloading ammo and stacking it up."

When Bruce and his comrades finished, they went back to Pendleton. "One morning, " he continued, "they called my name out, and said, 'You're in Tank Battalion. Report to Camp Del Mar by noon.' I got there by noon. They said, 'Ship your stuff home. You're going aboard ship at six o'clock.'" Like so many other tankers destined for the new war, Bruce "did not see a tank" until he got to Korea.[9]

The bulk of these men were embarked on the *U.S.S. General Meigs*. Don Bennett turned nineteen the day they boarded the troopship, August 15, 1950.[10] Conditions on the old troopship, hastily pulled out of mothballs and manned by a civilian crew, were less than ideal. Once aboard, the Navy held the ship for another three days because, as Bennett explained it, "they kept finding people and things to put on there."

The Battalion Maintenance Officer, Chief Warrant Officer William F. "Mac" McMillian, was a veteran tanker from the 1930s whose considerable luck in Korea would keep him alive long after it had abandoned so many others less fortunate. McMillian had fought in the Solomon Islands, on Tarawa and Saipan, and was wounded on Tinian. Mac and Bruce Williams (who later took over as CO of B Company) managed to secure a dozen extra power packs—tank engines and transmissions combined—and some additional trucks. "I politicked into letting me have 'em, and got the extra power packs," explained McMillian.

Bruce witnessed McMillian's efforts and asked, "How you gonna get 'em aboard ship?"

"You wait and see," came the reply.

The smooth-talking McMillian, who would later become a Louisiana politician, smuggled the extra power packs aboard the transport ships.

The men also obtained other non-issue items that would later prove useful. "I went by the armory, and he gave us each one of those old issue shotguns, twelve gauge," McMillian remembered.[11]

Training efforts were unfortunately laughable. The tank commanders were told to take the manuals for the new tanks aboard the troopships and train their men as best they could. According to Don Bennett, "All the way over on the *General Meigs* we had classes. We sat there in circles, and listened to: 'Here's how you turn on the master switch,' and 'Here's the booster, here's how you start it, here's how you check the oil.'"

Things were little better at higher levels. "On the way to Japan, the battalion staff and some of the company officers were on one of the Liberty ships.[12] We had some classes and that sort of thing; tried to pull things together," said Phil Morell.

Problems continued to plague the battalion. "Somewhere right outside Kobe, Japan, there was a fire started on that ship," Don Bennett said. "In trying to put that fire out, they really covered those tanks with salt water, which didn't do 'em any good." The Cosmoline still on critical components probably helped save them from serious damage.

When the troopship arrived at Kobe, the teenaged Sergeant Bennett was so excited that he stayed on deck watching the other ships in the exotic port—and missed evening chow. "Next morning when I got up, people were talking about the terrible storm they had last night. A typhoon had hit and broken the ship from its moorings, and we were wedged between two piers. And I had slept through it," he remembered.

When the crews disembarked, they were sent to a baseball field where the tanks were waiting for them.[13]

The old M4A3s that would serve as dozer and flame tanks had been stripped down for storage. According to Darrell Snideman, "They had all these tanks that they had brought over. Nothing was in them except the heavy weapons. We had to put everything in them, and I learned quickly how a tank works, inside and out." Snideman was assigned to B Company's VTR. "If you have a tank that's broken down—throws a track or whatever, and is sidelined off on the road, could be under fire . . . could be daylight, could be dark—you have to go out and either repair the tank at the time, or hook it up and bring it back in. Just like a tow truck." The company VTR was responsible for recovery and light repairs; extensive repairs were the responsibility of the repair section in Service Company.[14]

As many of the neophyte tankers soon discovered, one of the touchiest problems was the hydraulic fluid in the recoil system for the main gun. "They had a tape that went in this cylinder-like affair," explained Bennett. The tape, like the dipstick in an automobile engine or transmission, measured the proper fill level, which was critical to the proper function of the recoil system. "[T]hey had to get another tank and push up against the [gun] tube to exercise that system. . ."

The tankers experimented with their new machines. "I bore sighted[15] the ninety and the sights on a building there in Kobe," said Bennett. "Everybody was running around taking care of their own vehicle. The lieutenant would show up every once in a while to see what we were doing, give us a little guidance, and be gone. I figure they were going to briefings, doing all the logistical things that had to be done."

For the officers, the situation really was a nightmare. Phil Morell recalled that it was almost impossible to "have an officer's meeting or anything. It was just get in and get ready to go. Milne had a hell of a job to do."

To make matters worse, the tanks and guns had never been safety tested. "These guns had never been fired!" exclaimed Morell. "In the Marine Corps, when you got a tank with a new gun on it, you're supposed to tie a [line] on the cocking lever up there. Everybody gets out of the tank. You put a round in there, and fire it [from] outside the tank by pulling this string. The first time these tanks [guns] were fired, it was in combat!"

Tank gunnery was hardly a precise science in that era, and the fact that there was little or no training for the gunners only compounded the problem. Aiming was done by estimation and ranging shots, and a procedure known as "burst on target." As Ben Busch explained, "The tank commander would give you the yardage and you'd crank that on the gun, and then lay your gun on the target. You'd watch where your round burst. Usually you never hit it the first time." Busch continued: "Soon as you fired, that tank would kick back. Soon as it kicked forward again, came back to where it was, you immediately picked up that burst, re-laid your crosshair on the target. Then when the burst happened, you'd move that burst onto the target, and fire a second round. Do it right, and you're gonna get a second-round kill."

As Busch and many others learned, estimating ranges was a tough job, but "after a while you just get a thing for it, like anything else. It takes a while. If you're looking up, things look closer, and if you're looking down things look further [away] than they really are. If you're looking across something flat things look further [away], and if you're looking across a river things look closer. All those things come into play."

Shooting the tank's main gun was not the only first for these tankers. "Inside that ballpark was the first time the men who were going to be drivers got to drive their tanks. We made a mess out of that damn ballpark," reminisced Don Bennett. After peeling around for a time, the novice drivers moved the tanks aboard LCUs, then loaded them aboard the LSD *Gunston Hall*.[16]

Paul Sanders's platoon assigned to D Company arrived in Japan after most of the battalion had already sailed for Inchon. "The Quartermaster got me and says, 'Paul, get your platoon together and I'll run you out to where your tanks are.' I said, 'What tanks are they?' and he says, 'the M26.' I'd never seen one. They had put them out at Barstow . . . we still used the old M Three [sic] with the howitzer on it. The Quartermaster says to me, 'You got two days [to learn the new tanks].'"

Paul and his comrades boarded a train and road a few miles to "an area about three times the size of a football field," where five tanks sat waiting for their arrival. "They still had the stuff in the boxes," remembered Sanders. "We all gathered around one tank. I had a Gunnery Sergeant who was sharp on everything. I said 'Okay, you're in charge. Let's learn about this tank.'"

Over the course of the next two days the men taught themselves to drive the tanks and learned the rudiments of the unfamiliar vehicles. They even test-fired the machine guns. Sanders remembered that two days into the process, "they came and got us, and said, 'You're gonna be in Dog Company Tanks.' I said, 'Where are they?' and he said, 'They're comin' over on a ship.' The ship pulled in the next day. Our tanks went aboard and I got to meet my new Commanding Officer, who was Reserve called up, and the Exec, who was a Reserve called up."

Captain Lester Chase decided to split Sanders's platoon up into three parts and spread his handpicked men through the other platoons as a cadre.[17]

*   *   *

While the tankers trained as best they could, General Douglas MacArthur continued planning his masterstroke. He had begun doing so even before Eighth Army was driven into the Pusan perimeter. The military geography of Korea both controlled the axis of the Communist onslaught and provided the foundation for its eventual defeat. The mountainous terrain east of Seoul channeled all major north-south road and railway communications, with the exception of a single highway along the east coast, through the narrow coastal strip between Seoul and the sea. From Seoul, the roads and rail lines fanned out to the north and south, but Seoul was the choke point.

MacArthur's genius was to recognize that if a single bold amphibious stroke quickly recaptured Seoul, it would sever the communications and supply lines of the North Korean forces and leave them vulnerable to a counterattack by Eighth Army. Other American commanders argued for a more conservative operation. MacArthur's formidable reputation overawed these men, and the Inchon operation was set for mid-September.

The major objection voiced by the Navy and Marine Corps leadership was the difficulty of landing at Inchon, the port city that served the Seoul area. Inchon presented virtually every possible obstacle to an amphibious assault. Instead of onto open beaches, the landings would have to be made directly into an urban area. Complicating matters was the 32-foot tidal range, one of the most extreme in the world. At high tide ships can navigate up the lengthy Flying Fish Channel. At low tide, however, the entire area west and southwest of the city becomes a vast plain of stinking deep black mud capable of swallowing men and vehicles alike. Any invading force landed at high tide would be completely isolated and vulnerable to counterattack until the next high tide. The Korean tidal cycle limited possible invasion dates to only three or four days out of each month.[18]

Complicating MacArthur's planned operation were the harbor's prominent geographic features. Two islands on the western side of the harbor, Wolmi-do (Moon Tip Island) and Sowolmi-do (South Moon Tip Island), were connected to the mainland by a causeway carrying a heavy-duty road. The hills on these islands overlooked the approaches to the best landing beaches. Their towering positions meant that both islands would have to be taken on one high tide and held without reinforcement until the next tidal cycle. The enemy, therefore, would have twelve hours to cross the causeway, overwhelm the initial landing force on the islands, and prepare for the main assault.

An undaunted MacArthur moved forward with his plans, essentially operating autonomously and unrestrained by his nominal superiors. At a meeting on August 23, the Joint Chiefs made another attempt to forestall the Inchon operation. Impressed by MacArthur's oratory, the representatives accepted the plan, but the next day calmer heads elected to make one last effort to convince the general to consider other options. MacArthur's Chief of Staff, Lt. Gen. Ned Almond, intercepted Marine Lt. Gen. Lemuel Shepherd and in a heated argument informed him that the decision was already made, and thus not subject to change.[19]

X Corps, an essentially autonomous formation, was created by MacArthur to execute the dangerous landing. Lieutenant General Shepherd had "some expectation" of commanding X Corps because of his amphibious expertise, but MacArthur had promised the command to Ned Almond who, against both logic and normal practice, continued to function as Eighth Army Chief of Staff. X Corps included the Army's 1st Cavalry Division (Dismounted) and the 1st Marine Division, minus the 7th Marine Regiment and D Company of the 1st Tank Battalion. Due to logistical difficulties, however, the 7th Marines and their accompanying tanks would not be able to reach the area in time to participate in the landings.

Harry Milne and his battalion staff faced the monumental task of organizing an assault landing utilizing officers and units, like Max English's A Company, who were strangers to each other. "We just followed the division orders," explained Milne many years later. "Max English said that he would have his Third Platoon land on Wolmi-do as the first tanks ashore."

The bulk of the 1st Tank Battalion was embarked in two LSDs with three LCUs each to carry the tanks, and six LSTs (Landing Ship, Tank) to transport additional tanks and other vehicles. Many of the LSTs used in the Inchon operation were vessels that had been transferred to the Japanese, and had been used as civilian coastal transports under control of a US agency until their requisition for the Inchon operation.[20] Thirty of these vessels would go into action with civilian Japanese crews.[21]

The commander of the 1st Marine Division was Maj. Gen. Oliver P. Smith, a calm, deliberate, professorial officer—but a stubborn man when convinced he was right. These attributes came in handy when Ned Almond's subordinates began to pressure Smith to provide troops for a number of "special missions." One of the more hare-brained ideas was to land an Army infantry battalion and have them "barrel" down the main Seoul highway and capture Kimpo Airfield ahead of the main Marine Corps force.[22] Smith wisely managed to thwart this and similarly risky schemes.

Equally ambitious plans were being prepared for the Marines, who were still not completely organized. Jim Edwards recalls that he did not see the tank he was assigned "until I was on the LST out of Japan, heading for Korea. I still didn't have the vaguest idea what the inside of the tank looked like. They had made me radio operator and loader. So I couldn't get too many things wrong. You're the low man on the totem pole. As it turned out, I got assigned to a Sherman, an old M4 with a dozer blade."

The preliminary air attacks on Wolmi-do island, which began on September 10, included napalm to burn off small trees and dense underbrush. On the following day, tank crews were informed of the date and objective off the operation. D-Day was scheduled for September 15. Able Company was still attached to the 5th Marines, and thus under its tactical control.[23]

Two days before the scheduled landing, naval vessels began shelling Wolmi-do. The pace of the bombardment quickened on the morning of D-Day when air attacks and barrages from LSM(R)s, heavy landing ships equipped with rocket batteries, opened on the island. Reconnaissance indicated that wreckage and rocks made much of the shore line of Wolmi-do unusable by the wooden-hulled LCVPs (Landing Craft, Vehicle and Personnel) that would carry most of the infantry. As it turned out, useful beach front was only fifty yards wide.

At 0633 on September 15, the first wave of seven LCVPs ground their way ashore carrying a platoon from G Company and three platoons of H Company, 3/5. A second wave carried the balance of the two companies. At 0646 the tanks arrived aboard three LCUs launched from *Fort Marion*. The small force consisted of Lieutenant G. G. Sweet's 3rd Platoon, A Company, reinforced with a single M4A3 POA-CWS-H5 flame tank, two M4A3 105mm. howitzer tanks equipped with dozer blades, and a VTR.

It was an unnerving experience for the first men ashore. As Joe Sleger remembered it, the shoreline was obscured by smoke and dust. "We waited and circled while the bombardment completely blacked out

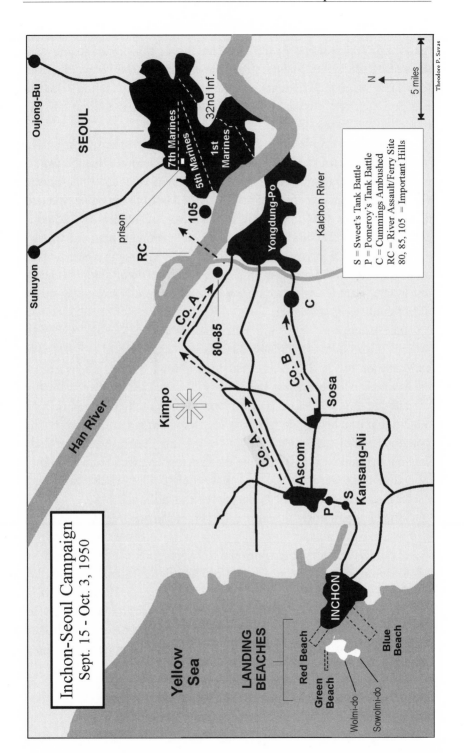

Inchon-Seoul Campaign
Sept. 15 - Oct. 3, 1950

Theodore P. Savas

N

5 miles

S = Sweet's Tank Battle
P = Pomeroy's Tank Battle
C = Cummings Ambushed
RC = River Assault/Ferry Site
80, 85, 105 = Important Hills

Oujong-Bu

SEOUL

7th Marines

32nd Inf.

5th Marines

1st Marines

prison

105

RC

Suhuyon

Yongdung-Po

Kalchon River

Han River

Co. A

80-85

Co. B

C

Kimpo

Co. A

Sosa

Ascom

Kansang-Ni

Co. A

P   S

Yellow
Sea

LANDING
BEACHES

Red Beach

Green
Beach

Blue
Beach

INCHON

Wolmi-do

Sowolmi-do

the island. You couldn't see the island at all. Last thing they did, they had three of the old rocket boats. . . . They came in, and as they were all in line, they let loose. . . . We went through the smoke. You couldn't see the island. . . . It was absolutely devastating." For Sleger and his tankers, limited visibility was but the first of many problems.

As the tankers quickly learned, maneuvering a tracked vehicle off a landing boat is a tricky task. "I was the last tank coming off, and the boat would go in," remembered Sleger's driver John Haynie.[24] "It went in almost up against the bank, so I had to give a hard right. I just lost a track! I sat right there while they fought the battle of Wolmi-do." Platoon Sergeant Sleger climbed out of the disabled tank and sought out another vehicle.[25] An ordnance crew arrived to help the tankers put the tread back on the tank. "They got put in for a Bronze Star, for working on the tank under fire," said Haynie. "Our crew was out there helping too, but they didn't think about us getting a medal."

Item Company—the rifle battalion reserve—followed the tanks ashore. To the surprise of many, the seaward side of the island proved to be lightly defended. The crest of the high ground, dubbed Radio Hill by the Marines, was secured by 0655.

Haynie took over as tank commander, and got the repaired tank up the hill that dominated the island. "We were sitting there firing into the city, and I couldn't tell where my blast was hitting, because all those ships way out behind us were firing into the city too," he recalled. "I couldn't tell where mine were going." Haynie went on to relate an exchange with the tank's gunner that aptly demonstrated this difficulty.

After the gunner shot, he turned to Haynie and asked, "Where'd that go?"

"I dunno," answered Haynie truthfully.

"You don't know where I'm hittin?" asked the frustrated gunner.

"No, I can't tell."

In an effort to rectify the situation, Haynie grabbed a pair of binoculars and focused on a distant point. The gunner launched another round. Haynie hesitated, still not sure where the shell landed. "I think it's over there," he answered, pointing with his hand.

"You *think* it's over there?"

"Fire again."

Throughout the exchange enemy fire was dropping close by. "Three or four big explosions" landed around Haynie's tank.

While Haynie and his gunner were trying to figure out where their shells were landing, Item Company, 3/5, moved around to attack the harbor side of Wolmi-do. They ran into a hornet's nest of NKPA troops in caves and buildings. A three-tank section rolled forward to blast the positions with their 90mm. guns. Tanker Basilo Chavarria fired his main gun at one of the caves while Sergeant Rhoades helped him with the flamethrower. The deadly weapon shot forth a long stream of flame. "Some guys start coming [out]. They were on fire," remembered Chavarria.

Another group of about thirty stunned North Koreans surrendered, but most of those who hid out in the caves and rocky ground fought to the bitter end. The intentions of at least one of their officers was not as clear. During the action Lieutenant Sweet had dismounted from his tank to confer with Sergeant Moore from the Headquarters Platoon. As they were speaking, Moore spotted a Korean soldier approaching from behind. As Sweet recalled it, the sergeant "started screaming 'Look out, Lieutenant! Look out!'" Without hesitating, Sweet swung around and shot. The man might have been trying to surrender. "He was a North Korean officer with [white] rags or something," continued Sweet. "He had it in his hand, but he didn't let the white rags out. I felt real bad about that. I crawled up on the back of the tank . . . and I said [to Chavarria], 'Hey, I really screwed up. This time the chaplain will really be after me.'"

The NKPA officer shot by Sweet suffered a kinder fate than many of his comrades. When the remaining pockets of defenders refused to surrender, dozer tanks advanced and heaped rock and dirt over the cave openings, entombing the stubborn enemy inside.

Joe Sleger, meanwhile, with other tanks and support from G Company riflemen, attacked across the causeway toward Sowolmi-do.[26] By 1115 the smaller island was secured. Engineers had already scurried out onto the broad causeway connecting Wolmi-do to the mainland, planting mines and erecting obstacles to hold back the expected Communist counterattack. Sweet's tanks took up defensive positions overlooking the roadway. They would have to hold for a good twelve hours without additional support.

By noon, the receding tide had left the Marines on the two islands isolated, beyond any aid except air strikes and long-range naval gunfire. Fortunately for the American spearhead, the NKPA was too disorganized by the surprise attack to respond effectively. Most of their efforts consisted of alerting units near Seoul to move toward Inchon. When the expected counterattack did not materialize, the battalion commander on Wolmi-do, Lieutenant Colonel Taplett, requested permission to advance across the causeway. His bold request was denied.

The main landing at the next high tide was as risky as any operation ever undertaken by the Marine Corps. The operation took place late in the day, and the small force of assault troops had just two hours to seize a defensible beachhead before they, too, would be isolated by the next fall of the tide. In order to interdict critical road junctions, four rifle battalions were expected to take and hold an immense perimeter. Without the 7th Marines, there was no reserve available except two partially trained battalions of the new Korean Marine Corps.[27]

At 1730 hours, two battalions of the 5th Marines landed north of the causeway on RED Beach. The beach was very narrow, forcing the riflemen to come ashore in twenty-five separate waves of boats. The men were equipped with scaling ladders to climb from the boats directly over the seawall, and the Marines fought a short but desperate battle for control of the top of the wall. Compared to some of the assault landings of World War II, casualties were few—despite misgivings about launching an assault directly into the heart of the town.

Max English went along as liaison with the infantry landing on RED Beach. "I was scared as hell," he remembered decades later. "You know why? I had to get in one of these little landing craft with Colonel [Ray] Murray and make a landing on a beach. I had always landed in a tank. Before we got to the beach, we had small arms fire hitting that damn small boat like nothing." Four civilians—a photographer and three correspondents (including Marguerite 'Maggie' Higgins of the *New York Herald-Tribune*) landed with the Marines.

Harry Bruce was now serving as a loader in one of the nine flame tanks of Headquarters Company. His tank was one of those that went ashore in the RED Beach assault. "They took all the ammunition racks out of the bottom of the tank and they put four seventy-five gallon tanks of napalm down there," said Bruce. "They used three CO-two bottles to pressurize it. They took the coaxial machine gun out of the turret and put a tube there. That's where the flame spout was."

Traditional ammunition was not plentiful. "I think we had seven rounds of regular one-oh-five ammo, because we had a regular rack on the turret floor," continued Bruce. "That was all the ammo we had other than the machine guns. We had a fifty up on top, and a thirty down in front at the assistant [driver's] place."

Lieutenant Sweet's tanks on Wolmi-do supported the amphibious assault with their fire. Sleger remembered the landing well: "When the main landings came that afternoon, we pulled out of our positions and crossed the causeway as they were landing. So we made two landings in one day." After Sleger and his comrades of 3rd Platoon crossed into the city, they sought out their commander. "Max English had a piece of corrugated roofing propped up and he was under there with the CP set up," said Sleger. "We reported in. We got the word that we were going to continue the attack in the morning."

Things were far more confused on the south side of town, where the 1st Marines were landing at BLUE Beach, led ashore by eighteen lightly-armored LVT(A)-5 amphibian tanks.[28] Rain and smoke obscured the beaches, and the LVT-3 troop-carrying tractors began to go off course. Some units landed two miles from their assigned positions.[29] Unable to find the expected gaps through the seawall and under fire, the LVT crews used their own hands to dismantle part of the wall in a desperate effort to get their vehicles ashore. Once on terra firma, they found their advance blocked by a deep drainage ditch that aerial reconnaissance had misinterpreted as a road.[30]

Although the fighting in the town was confused and expected to be desperate, the Marines ended up not needing all of the firepower they had brought ashore for the task. Harry Bruce, for example, remembers that he and his fellow tankers arrived ashore at night and "sat on the beach, up on a hill, all night long."

Problems arose when it came time to land the artillery and the rest of the tanks, particularly those designated as support for the 1st Marines. The soft ground behind BLUE Beach would limit their usefulness in that area, but if the bulk of the tank battalion landed at GREEN Beach on Wolmi-do, it might be trapped if the enemy had planted demolitions to destroy the causeway. The operational planners decided to delay their landing, which meant that B Company and the battalion command post came ashore at GREEN Beach on September 16.[31]

"I was supposed to be in the assault group, but the LCU didn't make it to the beach," remembered Don Bennett, who was now in the 2nd Platoon of B Company. "We were about two to three hundred yards off the beach when the tide went out sufficiently that we hung up. So I got to watch the assault and the operation there on Wolmi-do Island on the morning of the fifteenth." The delay ultimately proved unimportant. "The Navy just didn't get us in there soon enough to get us ashore. There [were] three tanks that were on this LCU. By the time we got ashore they had secured the island, and were getting ready to go across the causeway."[32] As Bennett quickly discovered, the ubiquitous mud flats stretched for miles at low tide. "There was no getting out. They had kind of gullies in it." As it turned out C Company was not able to land until the next day, September 17.

The resourceful Mac McMillian landed his maintenance units on GREEN Beach. He easily recalled the moment. "The minute we touched the beach, we came under Army [X Corps] ordnance. There was a lieutenant colonel, and he was the ordnance officer. He got the Medal of Merit for having the foresight to bring extra power packs for the M26 tank to Korea. . . . Every minute this was going on, I was liable to be court-martialed [for purloining the unauthorized power packs!]"

B Company tanks established a bivouac area on the far side of the city, and tank crewmen were sent out with machine guns to establish listening posts.[33] "Every bush moved out there in front of us," Bennett vividly remembered decades later. "Your imagination goes wild. But we of course didn't fire, or have anything happen to us that evening."

Like most of the city, the bivouac area was filled with enemy stragglers. "After we got all set up we found five or six North Korean soldiers hiding there," Bennett continued. "They didn't try anything at all. They had been overwhelmed, and here they're in the midst of a bunch of tanks and Marines. When they were discovered they gave up, but that made us feel pretty unsure of ourselves. . . . We didn't find them for an hour or so after we set up. They were made prisoners, and it was an uneventful evening, to the best of my memory."

"During the night [a] Republic of Korea Army platoon pulled in alongside of us," related Darrell Snideman while recalling his first experience with Korean Army methods. "I guess they thought they were safe with us. Next morning soon as it got daylight, their sergeant went around, and doesn't tell 'em it's reveille. He just goes over and kicks each one. As they were getting up, one had a BAR [Browning Automatic Rifle]. As he got up, the BAR went off and shot another one through the leg. The sergeant ran over there, and picked up a steel helmet, and beat that guy right down to the ground, [hitting him] on the head with that steel helmet."

The 2nd Platoon of Able Company was placed in support of the Korean Marine Corps Battalion. The tankers found the Korean marines extremely proficient, and the discipline similarly harsh. Bill Robinson remembered the Spartan aspects of their officers' conduct. "We didn't even have to put any guards out at night. . . . It was like a vacation. Tell them guys to be three feet apart, and if they were four feet apart, their Gunnery Sergeant [would] walk up and put a carbine stock in back of their head or their shoulder. They were all squared away."

When the Marines pushed their way through the city, the tanks supported the infantry by reducing several stubborn obstacles. The armor operated in direct support of the rifle regiments.[34] "This is something that's important. We did not attach tank companies to regiments, per se. We direct-supported. That was the division orders," explained Harry Milne. "We had found out that attaching to regiments was not the best way to go, because they wanted tanks to do a lot of things it was impossible [for us] to do." Milne provided one such example: "They would say, 'Well, you got mines on the road. Just go over 'em and get 'em off the road.' I'm not trying to be facetious, but they expected tanks to do a lot of things that tanks couldn't do."

Phil Morell agreed with the lieutenant colonel: "If the tanks are in direct support, that means that the battalion [headquarters] is still in control. If they're attached, then we're not in control. We all had good working relationships. You'd send a company up and say, 'You're going to work with Chesty Puller's regiment today,' or 'You're going to work with the Second Battalion, First Marines,' or whatever. The company commander would just go up and report in, listen to what their infantry CO wanted to do that day." The liaison was between the infantry unit and the tank unit. "We had a battalion command channel, but we didn't control any of the action," said Morell. "We might at the end of the day say, 'Okay, B Company you come on back here, you're going up to Seventh Marines tomorrow,' or whatever."

For Lieutenant Colonel Milne, even more so than with many other officers, good communications were essential—especially if you wore two hats. Milne, for example, was both Battalion Commander and Division Tank Officer.[35] Prentiss Baughman explained it: as division tank officer, Milne monitored all tank communications, and the tank company commanders often monitored operations from the battalion CP.[36]

Milne acknowledged the same thing: "My task was to see that all the companies had what ammunition and supplies they needed. I would follow them along to the front, and see that they were working all right, and assigned various companies to support each regiment." In order to build better coordination, whenever possible the tank battalion tried arrange it so that the same tank company worked with the same infantry unit.[37]

Even though not in immediate tactical command of his tanks, Milne did not view his duties as primarily administrative. Far from it. Phil Morell related a story about the brave officer. "[Milne] had guts," he began. "I was up with him a couple of times. We took two tanks up to check a bridge. We got out of the tanks because we couldn't get down this little road. . . . We're ahead of the front lines. Suddenly these big guns start to shoot at us. We ran back to get in our tanks. He jumps in his tank and pulled the hatch down. It came down on his wrist and broke his arm. So I was writing love letters to his wife, while he was trying to get his arm healed."

As it turned out, Milne had less combat experience in tanks than some of his officers. "He [Milne] was sharp enough to listen to us," Morell said with admiration. "I was in tanks since forty-two, and I figured I was a real vet. He listened to me. I would recommend things. The way I usually functioned was to go up each company in a jeep, and come back and report to him. I'd say I would recommend maybe take a platoon and send it over here, or whatever, and he would do that. But he would go up, too."

As Morell well knew from experience, with the tanks so widely scattered logistical support had to remain flexible. "If they were too far out, we would truck up the gas and ammunition," recalled Morell.

"Somewhere between the front lines and the tank park we would refuel them in the field and give them the ammo. Or, if they were close enough, we would try to bring them back to the tank park, where we would load them up and try to give them some hot coffee, maybe some hot chow. . . . Service Company was in charge of that."

Many aspects of the early fighting in Korea were the result of hasty organizational efforts to get fighting men on the peninsula as soon as possible. One of the consequences of swiftly organizing the tank battalion, for example, was that it ended up with extra personnel. Some were inexperienced men like Ben Busch, who recalled simply, "I went ashore on foot."[38]

When another human spare in the form of Radiological Officer Vaughn Stuart finally got ashore and reported to Lieutenant Colonel Milne, he was assigned yet another task.[39] "I was sort of the reconnaissance officer. There wasn't really a billet for me, but they had me in another billet that had to do with radiological defense, but we didn't have anything to defend against. I really was the assistant [battalion S-Three Operations Officer], but I really did the reconnaissance work, and other kinds of liaison." It was, as Stuart remembered, "Me, a recon NCO, and a driver." There were very few roads and bridges able to support the tanks, so Stuart often reconnoitered the roads to and from the two assault regiments. "I did a lot of work just delivering messages," he continued. "If we got a Division Order, I'd go up to Division and pick it up. That was real late at night. Generally I went with Colonel Milne wherever he went. Even in the tank I rode with him. I was the gunner on the tank; I was a lieutenant, but I was the gunner for his tank. Milne was always forward," he said, echoing Morell's recollection of the battalion leader's method of operating in the field.

The lull that night ended at about 0700, when American airplanes spotted a column composed of six of the dreaded T-34s headed down the highway from Seoul. The less experienced tankers in B Company listened to the radio traffic with some trepidation. Don Bennett remembers how the day's fighting opened: "The airplanes were diving, and the artillery fired. . . . What we were hearing was that there were a bunch of T-34s coming down the road. We were expecting that we were going to have to fight these monsters that we had heard about. There was that lull, and then we heard the infantry firing and the rockets firing."

The planes, however, drove home an air attack that exploded one of the tanks, while another lost its track in the road. A third, for reasons not readily apparent, appeared to be immobilized. The airmen claimed three T-34s destroyed. A second group of airplanes streaked across the sky, delivered their ordnance, and pulled away believing all six enemy tanks had been knocked out.[40]

The NKPA dispatched reinforcements in piecemeal fashion against the advancing Marines, and in desperation even tried some Hollywood expedients. Following Sweet's instructions not to leave the roadway, Joe Sleger was parked with his tank in the road when he beheld a baffling sight he did not readily appreciate as a threat. The NKPA had set fire to an ammunition cart hauled by an ox, and it was moving in the direction of the Marines.

Sleger radioed Sweet, who was "up on the high ground," and told him what was going on. "I could actually see it," remembered Sweet. "I could see the fire burning on the ammunition boxes in the back."

"What should I do?" asked Sleger.

"Shoot the friggin' cow!" yelled back Sweet.

Later that morning, the Marine task force approached the hills where the aircraft had reportedly destroyed the T-34s. Wary of an ambush, Sweet sent Sleger's section to the top of a hill so they could provide covering fire while the riflemen moved around a blind curve. "Sweet sent myself and Cecil [Fullerton's tank] up this road to this high ground," explained Sleger. "We looked down, and just beyond the bend, there's three tanks—T-34s."

Visibility was partially blocked by the buildings on the hill. "I could see two of them, and Cecil could see two of them, but between the two of us we could see all three," continued Sleger. "We positioned ourselves abreast of each other, and pumped rounds into the broadside of these three tanks. I think we put about twenty rounds of ammunition into them. They were still there, intact, waiting for [our] infantry to come around the bend."[41]

As the Marine column resumed its advance, Sleger experienced a personal moment he would never forget:

> We came out of our positions, and we took the lead again. As we came around the bend, just beyond where these three tanks were, there was a dead [body] in the road. He was crossways in the road.

For some reason I felt humane. I didn't want to run over him, so I stopped and I jumped out of the tank. I grabbed him by the uniform—he was still in uniform, face down—and I threw him in the ditch. Where I had picked him up, he had a burp gun under him.[42] He had been hit in the stomach area. The burp gun and the jacket were all filled with his guts. I took the burp gun and threw it up on the tank, and we took off."

As Sleger and his fellow tankers soon discovered, NKPA resistance was disorganized, consisting of numerous small-scale ambushes. "We were in column with the tanks, and there was a ditch on either side of the road. We had our pistol port open. We never used to keep our pistol port open, but that day we had our pistol port open. We were so intent on observing to our front [that we never noticed there were some NKPA in the ditch]. One stood up and tried to pitch a grenade through the pistol port." Sleger paused a few seconds, recalling the tense moment. "He missed, and it fell down by the gas cap and blew up. It didn't do any damage to the tank." A few inches in another direction, and Sleger and his comrades would have been killed.

Threats to the tanks came in many forms, as Don Gagnon of the 2nd Platoon, A Company, found out on the Inchon-Seoul highway. Gagnon had been firing all day, and was in the process of withdrawing to replenish his supply of HE [High Explosive] ammunition when he had a memorable run-in with a railway track. "We backed up a little ways, and we get the track caught in the rail in such a manner that it ripped the track just a little bit, but it raised that rail," he remembered. "I looked up, and there's about twenty feet [of rail]. I see that damn thing coming up in the air, and I tell the driver to hold it up, otherwise we're gonna tear our fender off. We sort of maneuvered around a little bit . . . and were able to get off the railroad bed." The torn track damaged the fender and put the tank out of action for a full day.

That same afternoon, Sweet's tanks and 2/5 approached the village of Kansong-ni, where the road to Seoul curved to the north around a series of hills and approached the old American logistical center called Ascom City, near Kimpo Airfield. The 3rd Platoon had expended much of its ammunition, recalled Sleger. "Somebody passed through us; we were off to the right of the road, refueling and rearming." It was Lieutenant Pomeroy's 1st Platoon. To Sleger's amazement, "[General] MacArthur came up with his entourage. He had about four or five jeeps, with his MPs leading and trailing."

The little convoy passed by the Marine tank column. "He [MacArthur] came up to where we were at," remembered an equally stunned Bob Miller. "My tank was over far enough so that I wasn't close enough to him. He gave a couple of the guys medals who were close by him. Of course, that's what MacArthur could do, you know. He just hands you a medal, and you're a hero, I guess."

The day was winding down and everyone was exhausted. Few knew exactly where they were, including the high ranking officers. The general's entourage drove beyond the lines before someone yelled out, "Hey, you guys are out ahead of the lines here!" The jeeps quickly turned around and drove back to safety. "They had no idea where the lines were," recalled John Haynie with some amusement.

The Marines took up night defensive positions on the hills overlooking the road, ready to resume their advance into the built-up area of Ascom City the next morning. The NKPA, however, continued throwing units piecemeal down the road without knowing exactly where the advancing Americans were located. Just before midnight, a fast-moving North Korean truck drove right through the blocking position established by the infantry and suddenly found itself in the middle of Lieutenant Pomeroy's 1st Platoon tanks. The truck and all its occupants were quickly taken prisoner.[43]

The truck incident served to remind everyone just how quickly disaster could strike. The Marines were more alert when at 0615 hours, just before dawn on September 17, another NKPA column consisting of six T-34s of the *42nd Mechanized Regiment*, together with about 200 to 300 infantry of the NKPA *18th Division*, blundered down the same road. Some of the infantrymen were riding on the engine decks of the tanks, while others jogged along behind them. The North Koreans advanced blissfully unaware of the American positions, their infantry talking and shouting loud enough to be heard over the noise of their tanks. Some were eating on the march. None of them were ready for sudden combat.

The 2nd Platoon of D/2/5 opened against the tank-infantry column at close range. The initial blast of machine gun and rifle fire swept the lounging infantry from the decks of the tanks, spilling their broken bodies onto the roadway. Many of those who had been marching alongside, talking and eating just seconds before, fell dead or wounded. Rockets from the Marine platoon's 2.36-inch and 3.5-inch rocket launchers mortally wounded one of the tanks and disabled a second. Taken unawares, the remaining four tanks veered about on the road before swerving into adjacent fields, crushing their own infantrymen between the steel treads and the road's hard surface. The Marines, meanwhile, continued to mercilessly rake the enemy infantry with everything they could throw at them.

Pomeroy's tanks opened fire at 600 yards range with deadly effect. There was a strategy as to which vehicle to go after first, as Phil Morell explained: "We used to tell our gunners, 'Don't hit the lead tank. Take on the last tank, and then work your way up so you get 'em all.'" This practice says a great deal about the aggressive mentality of the Marine tankers. Official doctrine—and the logic of self-preservation—is to attack the closest, and thus most dangerous, threat. The tactic described by Morell, however, was designed to make sure none of the enemy escape.

Pomeroy's gunners made the same error as Sweet's platoon at the First Battle of the Naktong when they loaded HVAP ammunition into the barrels. "We loaded anticipating the tanks," said Bob Miller. "My God, I fired two rounds and it looked like I missed the damn thing! I decided what I was doing was going in one side and out the other. We loaded HEs, and that blew the darn turrets off. That busted 'em up." Miller speculated that the quality of the Soviet armor was not as good as the American-made material.[44]

Within minutes the Marines had slaughtered the rest of the enemy infantry. Between the tank guns and infantry anti-tank weapons, they also destroyed all six enemy tanks. Miller believed most of the enemy infantry got off the tanks, but added, "Oh, God, it was terrible. It was just a bloodbath for them. It was a bad news deal. We had a terrible time getting through it all, and had to leave the road . . . so we wouldn't be driving over the bodies. My God, it makes you sick to think about it."

The tactics used by the Communist infantry amazed Miller: "The whole thing is ridiculous when you think about it, just ridiculous. They just marched like they were in platoon formation, close order drill, coming up the road. When they were strafed by the infantry, and by the air and tanks and everything like that, we're talking about just piles of

[dead] people. It was ridiculous." Phil Morell's last recollection of the engagement has remained with him to this day: charred corpses perched on the engine decks of the destroyed tanks for weeks after the battle.

Lieutenant Pomeroy's platoon helped clear the margins of Ascom City, a warren of buildings north of the highway, and then moved northeast toward the big Kimpo Airfield. The problems caused by the nightmarish maze of roads, trails, and small villages were complicated by the absence of adequate maps. The few that existed were mainly old Japanese renderings from the occupation era. Locating positions, and particularly calling for artillery and air strikes, was a major problem. "Maps were very poor. Rather than have coordinates transmitted to headquarters, I had our staff of the battalion pick out a bridge or a crossroads and letter them," explained Harry Milne. "The tank company commander could say, 'I'm a hundred yards, or a thousand yards, from A or B or Double A,' or whatever it was. They all had those on the maps. We passed those out to the companies. It was convenient." This clever technique also provided some degree of security against enemy interception of radio messages.[45]

While A Company was engaged south of Kimpo, the tanks of Captain Bruce Williams's B Company led an attack eastward along the Seoul Highway in support of 3/1. As far as Don Bennett was concerned, Williams was "a Southern gentleman. [He] had been an enlisted man prior to World War Two. When he went to meet Colonel Puller, the regimental commander that we were in support of, Colonel Puller said, 'I know you, son.' Captain Williams responded, 'Yes, sir. I served with you on the *Augusta*.'[46] Puller replied, 'Oh, let me shake your hand again, son.' That was a bond," explained Bennett. "It seemed that we were always in support of the First Regiment after that."

The tanks of Lieutenant Robert Gover's 1st Platoon and G/3/1 led the assault column, followed by the balance of 3/1 mounted in LVT-3s. Near Mahang-ri the tanks spotted a T-34 emplaced inside a building, with the gun tube protruding out a window. This was a common practice for both sides, especially in barren terrain. "One of our tricks was to put a tank into a native hut, mud huts with thatched roofs," recalled Phil Morell. "Just drive a tank into it and poke your tube out the window at the enemy. You had perfect camouflage." The Marine tanks destroyed the enemy tank before it could spring its ambush and secured the village at about 1600 hours.[47]

Williams's B Company tankers were new to both their tanks and combat. Bennett and his crew had never fired their main gun, and were not certain it would function properly. "That was the first day I fired the ninety," he explained. "I told the gunner the distance, gave him the range—might have been a thousand yards—at an enemy hut with infantry in and around it, with HE. What a surprise it was when that ninety millimeter went off. I actually had closed my eyes!"

Bennett continued:

> I had read the manual. We had no training at all—none—in this tank. There were a lot of warnings about the hydraulic fluid in the recoil [system] of the gun, to have it just right. When that gun fired, I expected to see it go all the way back into the radios, and wipe out the radios. To his great surpirse, after the gun fired he opened his eyes "and the brass was coming out and hitting the deck, and the ninety was going back into battery. . . . I knew that I had gotten the hydraulic system oil all set up right. I was real happy!

The crews in the tank platoons of the regimental Anti-Tank Companies had received even less training than Bennett and his comrades, but according to Mike Wiggins of the 7th Marines, "It didn't take long to really get familiar with it. Practical application. You had a lot of things you could shoot at, zero in and learn the small mechanicals of how to operate. There's nothing like learning quickly when your life is on the line."

The Baker Company column continued down the road toward Sosa, the next village, with the 2nd Platoon of B Company tanks, under Lt. Bryan Cummings, in the van. Some of the G Company infantry was riding on the decks of the tanks, with others following on foot. For the North Koreans, the best defensive terrain lay halfway to Sosa, where the road passed through a narrow cut in a north-south ridge. When the tank column, with Cummings in the lead, entered the narrowest part of the passage, all hell broke loose. Small arms fire swept the decks of the tanks, and enemy anti-tank guns and a hidden T-34 opened fire on the lead vehicle. Cummings's driver tried to back up, but the tank stalled. The lieutenant barely had time to grab one of the riflemen by the collar and drag him through the hatch and into the tank before enemy infantry swarmed down the embankments and onto the vehicle.

The tank's crew, meanwhile, returned fire with machine guns and cannon. Before long a well-placed enemy round broke the track, immobilizing the tank. Acrid fumes from the machine guns and the gas that rushed out whenever the loader opened the breech of the main gun filled the vehicle. The harried Cummings discovered what many World War II tankers had learned the hard way: otherwise hardened infantrymen grew extremely claustrophobic when locked inside cramped tanks with enemy fire hammering on the hull. When the rifleman he had just saved from death or capture went berserk inside the besieged vehicle, Cummings knocked him unconscious.

Gasping for breath, Cummings opened the pistol port on the side of the turret to let some of the choking gas escape. Almost immediately a North Korean grenade flew through the opening and exploded inside the turret. The shrapnel wounded Cummings, his gunner, and the incapacitated rifleman. With no time to spare, Sergeant Marion Altaire moved his own M26 into the road cut and "scratched the back" of Cummings's immobilized tank with machine gun fire, knocking the NKPA attackers to the ground. More help was on the way. Sergeant Arthur R. "Slope Plate" MacDonald led his section into the cut to assist the trapped Americans. He slammed round after round at the anti-tank guns at close range. Although at the time no one could see the effect of the fire, after the chaotic fight ended the Marines counted six anti-tank guns and a T-34 destroyed.

Bennett remembered the action vividly many years later: "An AT [anti-tank] shell hit the slope [plate] of the lieutenant's tank, and didn't do any harm to any of the crew. If it penetrated, it wasn't much. I was the youngest of the sergeants, and I was a tank commander. He came back and took over my tank. Then I got to mother this tank that had been damaged, and that crew. It was kind of scary, when I had to go back to where his tank was. No password, no nothing, running into the infantry. I wouldn't forget that for a while."

Darrell Snideman's B Company VTR was waiting at a road junction in the rear of the action. "This little girl toddler came down the road. All by herself. We thought, 'Gee, that's kind of strange.'" The soldiers swept up the child and carried her to their tank, where she would be better protected should fighting break out in their area. "We opened up the goodie package in the C-rations, and gave her the candy," said Snideman. Before long, an officer with a photographer in tow came along and snapped a picture, which ended up in Snideman's hometown newspaper. The incident was highly unusual, because the terrified Korean civilians were "awful shy. They stayed away from you. The real, real old timers used to try to wander through your compound. You never saw the young girls. They were afraid for their safety, I think. They hid them out."

Before nightfall on September 17, the 5th Marines moved out onto the runways of Kimpo Airfield, assisted by two tank platoons from A Company. "We were the first unit onto Kimpo Airfield," said Joe Sleger proudly. "We drove into the hangar with the tank, and there was this intact Yak-Nine fighter. We got pulled back to the infantry, who had been mustering at the edge of one of the major runways. We set up positions on line."

The Marines dug in along a line far too long to be held by such a small force. The new line extended from south of the main Inchon-Seoul road north and across the open ground of the huge airfield. The northern portion of the line consisted of widely separated company perimeters that were subjected to sporadic counterattacks and artillery fire all night long. Fortunately, the disorganized and demoralized NKPA forces were busy packing themselves into the small pocket of remaining ground south of the Han River. The NKPA *1st Air Force Division*, however, launched several ill-coordinated counterattacks in the hours after midnight.

"About two o'clock in the morning we got a lot of small-arms fire coming from right abreast of us," remembered Sleger. "There was a lot of noise, a lot of yelling. These guys were yelling banzai or some damn thing. Screaming and walking and shooting, in the upright position, approaching the tanks. And then everything went dead. Completely silent. We were told to hold our fire. I don't know if they went back, and then came in again, or if it was another wave, but here it came again." The enemy attacked three times. "That third time was their mistake. It was just getting light, and we got the word to jump off in the attack. We caught these guys in between the two runways, in this tall grass."

The NKPA survivors went to ground among the scattered Marine perimeters, and at daylight on September 18 had to be rooted out of the airfield. It was dangerous and bloody work. "Not one would stand up and surrender," said Sleger. "Not one. We did the whole bunch in. When we jumped off I had to tell Haynie to stop so we could get the gun low enough to fire the coaxial. These guys were crawling, on their hands and knees, and they wouldn't stand up. There you saw the true shock action of the tank. We were firing everything. We had our hatches open. It was the only time I ever fired my pistol in combat. We saw one big clump of them. They were huddled together . . . about four of them. They were holding each other, and they were laying down in this tall grass."

Sleger's assistant driver, J. A. Merlino, was shooting the bow machine gun but the grass blocked his view. "Most of the time the enemy was hiding in there [in the tall grass]," he explained. "They hear all this noise, and they jump up, and you see them." It was not always easy to distinguish combatants from civilians, however, because the NKPA often masqueraded in civilian clothing. It was something "you always had .. in your mind," remembered Merlino. "Is this a civilian, or is this the enemy? But then you had to get that out of your mind, because the ones you thought were civilians were attacking you at night. You had to be careful."

Driver Haynie employed a unique—and controversial—method to kill the enemy soldiers: "The infantry was up ahead of us," he said. "Our tank and another tank were ordered to go clean that out. I realized they were all in this ditch. I just put one track in that ditch, and started running down that ditch." Some other tankers later criticized Haynie for his action. "Why people do that I don't know," he replied. "I got heavily criticized for that. If that's the enemy, he's a mortal enemy. If I run over him, they're dead. I made sure he was dead." Sleger seemed to agree with Haynie. "We ran over them. That's when I used my pistol, because I looked down, and the ground was soft, and they were just, like, pressed, from the track."

That same day, September 18, when the last of the battalion's tanks were landing at Inchon,[48] the Marines continued encircling the enemy pocket south of the river around the industrial suburb of Yongdung-po. B Company tanks led a mounted column into the hills south of the river. The company's dozer tank, B-43, supported whatever platoon was in the lead at any particular time. Jim Edwards, a radioman and loader in a dozer tank, remembered their role during these operations: "You either used the dozer as the lead tank or the end tank. I can understand the end part, because if you had problems you could shove other tanks off the road, or clear debris, or something like that. As we went toward Seoul the road was mined, so they put us up on a railroad track that ran directly into downtown Seoul. I was lead tank all of that time."

The B Company column churned up a hornet's nest of activity. "We ran into a pretty heavy firefight," remembered Edwards. "We had three engineers that were sweeping ahead of my tank. All of a sudden one of 'em just keeled over, and I [thought], 'What the hell happened here?' Then I started hearing the ping-ping-ping on the side of the tank, and we had a full infantry company hit us."

The only gun Edwards could bring to bear was the 30-caliber in the turret, because the bow machine gun "was pointing directly down the railroad tracks, and we couldn't swing around." The two surviving engineers had disappeared from view. Edward had no idea where the engineers were. "I was assuming they were huddled up against the front of that dozer blade." Even with the single gun, Edwards managed to exact a bloody enemy toll. "I never saw actual figures. I heard that with that one thirty caliber we had killed roughly a hundred and twenty-three infantry, and there were quite a few prisoners. . . . I never saw this in print. It was just talk through the company."

When one of the B Company tanks was disabled, Snideman's VTR was sent to recover it. By the time they had the tank hooked to the big Y-shaped tow bar, recalled Snideman, "The infantry guys came over with a prisoner they had captured. We sat him up on the fender of the tank we were towing, and we had to guard him 'til we got down to the prison camp and kicked him off. I guess he was scared to death," he added. "If he had fell off that tank, I'd have shot him. But I didn't have to, so that was alright."

The trip to the rear, however, did not turn out as Snideman anticipated it might. The crew towed the disabled tank down the main highway from Seoul toward Inchon. "As we were coming back, we were going down a hill, and there was a long, sweeping turn," he explained. "An Army convoy came by, with a bunch of nurses in a bus; they just happened to be going from one place to another. As they passed us, my tank driver pulled a left turn lever, and it locked. We were on the outside lane, pulling this heavy tank behind us, and it wouldn't release!" The heavy tow jackknifed the lighter VTR, and both veered into the oncoming traffic. "As we started to turn toward the cut, an Army truck was going by, and it had a bunch of guys sitting up on top of all the stuff on it. It threw this one guy off. He landed right in front of the retriever, and the retriever rolled right up on his leg. I was sitting up there on the front, and so I jumped off and I signaled to back up." The weight "broke his leg, popped the calf of his leg open, from the pressure. He thought he was killed." Snideman added. "This busload of nurses came along and picked him up, and he was really living! That guy was in heaven! "

The next major task facing the Marines was to force a crossing of the broad Han River. The engineer assets of X Corps, however, were inadequate to the task. Although infantry and most supplies could be moved across in LVTs, the enemy had destroyed the only bridges capable of carrying tanks. The original plan was for the division Reconnaissance Company to establish a perimeter by stealth on the north shore. The attempt failed when the noise of the tractors transporting them revealed the movement, and they were driven back with significant losses. Colonel Ray Murray of the 5th Marines had anticipated potential problems and launched a two-pronged attack strategy. A full-scale assault by Item/3/5 drove ahead and established a beachhead at 0650 on September 19 and then the infantrymen attacked Hill 125 overlooking the crossing sites. With the enemy's attention riveted on Item Company, a second assault crossing by H/3/5 met less resistance and the men quickly seized Hill 51.[49]

On the south bank of the river, C/1/5 captured Hill 118 at 1100 hours and pushed onward with the support of the 3rd Platoon of A Company tanks. By 1650, they had secured Hills 85 and 80 overlooking Yongdung-po. That night NKPA troops trapped on the south shore launched local counterattacks against the Marines. Bob Miller was there and remembered the action: "We had set up for the night. We had infantry all around us, of course, and we had gone out and got the azimuth, as far as we could traverse so you wouldn't shoot the infantry sitting out there."

In the darkness the tanks would fire along azimuth-bearings relative to the fore and aft axis of the tank, indicated by the traverse indicator inside the turret.[50] "We looked right down the tank barrel, and aimed right at 'em, and then took that azimuth," Miller explained. "We got that attack that night, and the next morning we went over there. One of the guys showed me the ammo can that had a couple of holes in it that we put in it. We were right close, right to the edge of our area. God almighty! But we didn't shoot any infantrymen."

The darkness only compounded the tanker's problem. "It's dark at night, you can't see nothing. When you fire you have to duck your head back inside, but you can't close up [the hatches]. You have to be able to see, and you couldn't see at all if you tried to do it in the dark. The tank commander had to be out where you could see."[51]

The situation was as confused for the Marines as for the NKPA, and there were no secure communications with the 5th Marines on the north bank of the Han River. Milne dispatched Vaughn Stuart with a written message. Stuart, his driver, and Corporal Reinche, the Recon NCO, quickly became disoriented in the maze of roads around Kimpo Airfield.[52] Stuart still has a clear recollection of his experience:

The meager road led to Kimpo Airfield and then on to the ferry crossing. At least, that is what the map indicated. But we could not find the road out the other side of the field, and after two or three passes around the place, I stopped to ask directions. I cannot remember the organization where I inquired, but the unit commander offered his interpreter, an American who had lived in the area several years, to lead us to the ferry crossing.

By then it was pitch black, but off we went toward the river, his jeep leading mine, a war-party of four Marines and an unarmed civilian. We had gone several miles without seeing any Marines, all the while getting closer to "Chesty" Puller's burning city and the trapped North Korean Regiment, when the interpreter stopped his jeep in the middle of a totally darkened village, explaining that he was not about to go any farther in this direction. Turns out that the ferry crossing he had in mind crossed the river between the burning city and Seoul. He had taken us almost into a penned-up North Korean Regiment that was still filled with fight, and we were miles past our own front lines.

We got the hell out of there and back within our lines in record time, and I found the proper ferry crossing with no more outside assistance.[53]

Nightfall brought no rest for the exhasted tankers. They rode into battle, but in other respects their lives were little different from those of the riflemen. "I didn't know what it was like to see a bed," said Lieutenant Sweet. "Maybe if we could get out of the tank, we usually ended up in streambeds someplace, and sleeping on rocks. They had a little warmth from the day."

Streambeds were chosen for pragmatic reasons, as Sweet explained: "We had all this work to do. After shooting all day we would pull back to re-ammo, clean guns, and everything—a tanker's duties. He might fight all day, but then he's got to go to work. Clean all the barrels on all the machine guns. Do all the maintenance on all the air cleaners and stuff, and it's dustier than hell. A streambed was a nice clean spot to work. You couldn't do it in a brush pile. We always ended up in a streambed because you didn't have to do any preparation for the tank park we were making. Spent a lot of nights in streambeds." As much as Sweet liked parking at night in a stream bed, he thoroughly detested nighttime movement orders. "I only had one thing I didn't like—I always hated it when they would give me a radio message about nine o'clock at night say to come to the Colonel's CP. That's the only time I didn't want to walk around at night, with all these trigger-happy goddamn people around."

To the south, the 1st Marines attacked eastward from Sosa toward Yongdung-po proper. Captain Rice Taylor's C Company tanks lead the way. One of the young tankers was Michael O'Sullivan, who had volunteered for service at age at seventeen because he did not get along with his new stepfather. O'Sullivan transferred from Service Company, of the 2nd Marine Division, and ended up in the Headquarters Platoon of C Company tanks.[54] As his company advanced, O'Sullivan heard, of all things, exotic music. On the Yongdung-po Road, he later remembered, is "where our company met—believe it or not—a kid who played the bagpipes! He was on the road, playing a bagpipe, and we don't know where in the hell he was from. I guess every time his company went anywhere, he played the damn bagpipes."

The Scottish serenade did not last long. Some 500 yards out of Sosa the lead M26 tank hit a box mine. The huge explosion lifted the tank into the air, ripped off the right track and two road wheels, and the tank settled back into the crater. The other C Company tanks tried with little success to detonate visible mines with machine gun fire. With the road effectively blocked to armor, the infantry moved on without tank support. As they moved forward, engineers arrived and breached the minefield by 1300 hours. The tanks rolled slowly forward for another mile when the dozer tank hit another mine, blocking the road a second time. The Marines were held up well short of Yongdung-po. Despite their meager gains, however, their right flank was exposed to to the enemy because the Army's 7th Division, tasked to support it, had delayed their attack until the next day.

By that afternoon the perimeter on the north bank of the Han had grown quite large, and the engineers had rigged an M4A2 raft capable of carrying tanks. It was a tedious process. "We crossed the Han in a couple of different ways," said Phil Morell. "We got some huge rubber rafts from the Navy, and put planks on them. It would take one tank. They had outboard motors, which were kind of slow, but they would get across that way. They finally made a rubber boat bridge with planking on it. One tank at a time would cross the river that way."

The 2nd Platoon, A Company tanks, were the first across at 1410 hours, followed by the 1st Platoon at 1600. Bill Robinson was driving his tank onto the precarious raft when "This guy on this barge told me to bring the tank a little bit farther ahead. I did, and looked down and here's this jeep coming aboard, with this blonde gal, this Marguerite Higgins." (Higgins, it will be remembered, was the reporter for the *New York Herald-Tribune*.)

G. G. Sweet's 3rd Platoon was still embroiled in the fight for the hills around Yongdung-po, and did not cross the Han until late that night. "Everything got all screwed up," complained Gene Viveiros, and it was late in the evening before they crossed on the pontoons. "The previous day an anti-tank rifle punched a hole through one of the tank's cupola blocks. . . . Didn't come through the glass, it came through the metal. I got sprayed with something in the face, nothing serious. I went to look out through the block, and I seen where this thing had punched a hole through it."

The stress of daily non-stop combat was making everyone ill-tempered, as Viveiros related in a story to the author:

> The next thing I know, they tell us, "Well, gonna have to go with what you've got. Can't get anything else across. We can't get you no fuel, can't get you no reload of ammunition." I looked around and I think there was about three C-ration cans left. Had some coffee grounds, a day old, [in a] gallon can. I told the guys, "Okay, get out the Coleman [stove], get some coffee going." Wilkie, he went to sleep. He's tired out. So I said, "Well, save a little coffee for when Wilkie wakes up, and we'll leave one can of meat and beans

or something." The next thing, old Wilkie he comes awake, and oh, he's in a bad mood, like a bear out of hibernation.

"Where's the chow?"

I said, "They can't get anything across to us. We gotta make do with what we got 'til tomorrow, daylight again. We saved you one can of meat and beans and . . ."

Next thing I know . . . he went walking by the Coleman where the bucket was up, and he knocked it over and that was the end of his coffee. Then he went into a rage again.

Prentiss Baughman's supporting units were also experiencing difficulty crossing the Han. "There was no way to get across the river. I waited with three tanks for about four days to get across."

The North Koreans were unwilling to give up the last positions on the south bank without a fight, and that night they reoccupied Hills 80 and 85. Just before dawn on September 20, another strong enemy force attacked down the Seoul-Inchon highway, but as usual seemed to have no idea where the Americans were deployed. A truck loaded with ammunition led the column. Perhaps it was a suicide bomb, intended to attack any American roadblock or tank it encountered. No one knows for sure. Five T-34s rumbled behind it, with more trucks and marching infantry in trail.

At 0430 the column moved into an L-shaped ambush set up by all three companies of 2/1, supported by C Company tanks. The ammunition truck blew up in a titanic explosion, showering the tanks and infantry with fire and debris. When the melee was over, two T-34s sat burning in the roadway, and a third had been abandoned intact. About 300 enemy soldiers lay dead and wounded.

The 2nd and 3rd Platoons of C Company moved up to the riverbank to support an assault crossing of the small Kalchon River on September 21. The Kalchon is a small tributary that flows north into the Han, and was the last terrain barrier protecting Yongdung-po. The tanks covered the crossing by B/1/1 with overhead fire. The main obstacle on the far bank was a series of flood dikes that sheltered the enemy. The tanks fired high explosive rounds into the thick earthen embankments, with little effect.

While this fight was taking place, to the south A/1/1 penetrated far into Yongdung-po, blowing up the NKPA's main ammunition dump, and positioning themselves atop one of the flood control dikes on the opposite side of the city. That night the Marine unit was attacked by five T-34s.

The enemy army flailed away at the dikes with cannon and machine gun fire that inflicted little damage, but in turn suffered one tank destroyed and two damaged by 3.5-inch rocket fire.[55] Five separate assaults by enemy infantry also failed to dislodge the 1st Marines.

The next day, the 5th Marines and the Korean Marine Corps Battalion, supported by A Company tanks, assaulted the hill complex north of the river, destroying three 76.2mm. anti-tank guns[56] and initiating a devastating three-day struggle.

South of the river, meanwhile, the 1st Marines struggled to clear Yongdung-po and captured four T-34s that could not be withdrawn across the river. The Marine tanks dueled other T-34s on the far bank of the broad waterway. O'Sullivan remembered the action: "Across the river there were some T-34s that were in a railroad tunnel. It was a little on the comical side, because it was like one of those shooting gallery games. They would race back and forth in and out through this [railway] tunnel. We were sitting on the banks of the Han River, shooting at 'em. It was kinda crazy. Like, 'Hey, here comes another one.' Boom! Fire off a ninety and when the dust cleared you see what the hell happened. It was strange really. They'd race out, spin their turret around, fire a shot across the river at us, and then back up like crazy right back into the tunnel again."

Although the encounter appeared comical with the passage of many years, it was anything but funny during the event. "The first time we fired, we were a bunch of nervous kids, and we put HVAP— which was High Velocity Armor Piercing," explained O'Sullivan. "We put a round right on through the T-34 and we didn't think we hit it. Our tank commander was Lieutenant Paul Curtis. Gene Flannery was our gunner, and the lieutenant was yelling at Gene, 'You missed 'em! You missed 'em!' 'No, I hit 'im, sir, I hit 'im!' says Gene. We wound up shooting HE at him—high explosive—and it blew the turret off it. But the first shot hit him. It went right on through." According to O'Sullivan, when the tankers returned to their command posts, "all the HVAP came out of the tank, and everything was HE and WP [white phosphorus]." C Company destroyed three T-34s and six more anti-tank guns in this long-range shooting match.[57]

Leon Mullins was in boot camp when World War II ended, and he decided to stay in the inactive Reserve. He had just transferred into the active Reserve when the Korean War began, and was immediately called to active duty. Like so many others, Mullins had no training in his assignment and was made the company supply sergeant of the 1st Marine Regiment Anti-Tank Company. "My MOS [Military Occupational Specialty] was line company, from my first tour of duty," he said. "The captain said that because I had a couple of years of college, I was the best educated of the enlisted men, and he wanted good records kept. So that's how I got stuck on that."

The commander of the Tank Platoon was former fighter pilot Lt. Chester Tucker, a leader Mullins and his comrades grew to respect. "They needed tank commanders," continued Mullins. "[Tucker] probably weighed a hundred and thirty-five pounds. Had one of these long mustaches, waxed on the ends, and he operated those five tanks like combat planes. They would do so much firing—they would joke about it—that the guys in the tank would pass out from the fumes in the tank. Another tank would come up and hook on behind it, and pull it back. They'd open the hatch. I don't know how much of that was true, but they'd joke about it. He was really a super person. The tankers loved him."

Mullins also recalled the strange way the Americans found beer in Yongdung-po. The tankers "crashed through the walls, into [a] brewery. I can still visualize where they had those kegs of beer when they came back. They sent a keg of it over to [Colonel] Puller, but I have no idea whether he drank any of it. We tried it. It didn't taste very good as well as I remember, but it was just something different."

Korean beer was not the only thing those tankers found distasteful. "When we were back in reserve in Seoul, everyone was cleaning weapons," continued Mullins:

> One of the tankers, a kid from El Paso, was working on the [tank] tread. They had decapitated a North Korean. Not intentionally, but the guy was dead and the tank ran over him, and his head was wedged in the track. This Army general,[58] who was one of [President] Truman's personal representatives, came up in his jeep along the side. We had seen him before. He'd go around with a fifty caliber machine gun mounted on his jeep, and a little South Korean soldier sitting down with his hands raised up to hold onto the handles. He wouldn't have been much help.

The general walked up beside the tank and the track, and he said, 'Son, are you having any problem?'

I've forgotten the kid's name. He looked up and said, 'Aw, general, I'm tryin' to get this God damn gook's head out of here.'

He peered around, and the head was all disfigured, from being scrunched into the track. He turned around, and kind of grabbed his stomach. He walked back to his jeep, never said a word, and got in it [and drove off]. We all burst out laughing.

"It really wasn't funny," concluded Mullins, "but you have to get immune to some of that, or you'll crack up."

The next day, A Company tanks and a platoon from B Company supported attacks against the hills north of the river by 2/5, 3/5, and the Korean Marine Corps. The tanks quickly bogged down in the soft ground and could only support the infantry with long-range fire. This battle remained primarily an infantry struggle through September 24.

The tankers soon discovered that even enemy small arms could be effective against armored vehicles in the close-range fighting. "Cecil was to our left, and then there was a tank to our right, and then Chavarria's tank," recalled Joe Sleger. "We were in a staggered line, off the road. There was a sniper somewhere, a damned sniper, and we couldn't find him. He shot off every one of our periscopes. . . . Put the periscope up and Pow! He'd shoot the thing out."

The tanks were also exposed to anti-tank gun and artillery fire from the hills above. Gene Viveiros had fought from Guadalcanal to Inchon. Unfortunately, much of his legendary luck ran out on September 24. "[Lieutenant] Sweet sent a couple of tanks down to a road down there," remembered Viveiros, who was in one of them. Enemy anti-tank guns ranged in on Viveiros's tank, and "Next damn thing I know, 'Blam!' And then the next one, 'Blam!.' He's really got the range on this thing, and I'm yellin' at Jim—he's drivin' me at this time—he got all shook up there with these hits from the artillery. I'm tellin' him, 'Move this son-of-a-bitch! Find a defilade and drop into it!'"

To Viveiros's dismay, the tank did not move. "All I could hear was him tryin' to shift that thing, put it in gear. 'Hrrrrr. Hrrrr. Hrrr.'"

Desperate to avoid a potentially fatal shot, Viveiros reached through the opening at the base of the turret and "whopped [Jim] in the back of the head. . . . That's all it took." All the while, enemy rounds continued to pour down upon the tank.

Joe Sleger also remembers the engagement well: "It was one of these situations where we couldn't tell where the rounds were coming from. All of a sudden I spotted the flash from the gun, up in a saddle, on the MLR. I called over to Vi [Viveiros] on the radio, and I told him I saw the flash of the gun. I was gonna put some white phosphorus on it, and then we'd concentrate our fire. He never called me back." A round had scored a direct hit on Viveiros's already-damaged cupola.

"The whole goddamned cupola got torn away on it," grumbled Viveiros, who was lucky to have gotten out of the tank alive. "The fifty caliber that was mounted up there, it was all screwed up.[59] This corpsman came up and he talked to me a while. . . . He stabbed me with his morphine syringe, and then I remember I dropped back. [To] Corporal Sweet, I said I had to drop out. I said, 'I got a pretty good hit here.'"[60]

After he was carried a short distance to the rear, Viveiros remembers seeing Colonel Murray and a chaplain, who was holding services for all fallen infantrymen gathered there. Murray asked what happened. Viveiros described the action "usin' all my favorite adjectives . . . and he looked white. [Colonel Murray told me], 'Gunny, the chaplain's over there tryin' to hold services!'"

Sleger and his comrades were determined to knock out the gun that had destroyed Viveiros's tank, but before they could do so, their own tank suffered an electrical failure. In an exposed position and with the machine gun bullets sounding like "BBs on a rain barrel," Sleger and his crew continued to fire until their main gun ammunition was exhausted. With no operable ventilator fans, the tank filled with propellant fumes, and possibly also with toxic gasses from the batteries. No one remembers if they opened the pistol port to try and vent some of the gasses.[61]

"I felt myself passing out, and I started punching myself in the face to try to keep myself awake," recalled Sleger. "We fired our last round, and Merlino [the loader] reached down and picked up the hot brass with his bare hands, and threw it [back] into the chamber. Wham! He hit the deck, and he went into shock."

Merlino remembered the painful moment well. "Actually, I thought we were hit," he explained. "When the fumes got me, I fell over and hit my head on the tank, on the turret. Meantime that's when I grabbed a shell, and I grabbed a hot one. Pretty hot. . . . Messed up my hand a little bit, that I couldn't use it right away." In the miasma of the fumes, Merlino did not feel the pain of his burned hands.[62]

Driver John Haynie recalls, "[R. W.] Hoffman trying to get out of the escape hatch, and I told him no, we were told to stay in there, and we were going to stay in there. We did have a message that Lieutenant Sweet said he was going to get us out of there. We had one channel on one radio. . . . We heard one channel from Sweet, and he said, 'We're gonna come get you. We're gonna pull you off!'"

"Nobody leaves this damn tank. We're all staying in it!" was Sleger's last conscious order. "The next thing I know, Haynie called me and said Hoffman had passed out. I was starting to feel woozy, and that's when I started punching myself. Next thing I know I woke up and I was on my back, wedged between the collector ring and the gunner's seat. I could see, and I could hear, and I could talk. But I couldn't move. When I woke up, I looked up and [the gunner, H. L.] Roth had put my tank commander's seat down and he was on it like a monkey, and he was talking into a dead mike."

At that moment Nik Frye's tank pulled up behind the Sleger's disabled vehicle. "[Frye] came up behind our tank and . . . butted it, and dropped the [escape] hatch. Frye came out and hooked the cables up," said Sleger.

While Frye was dragging Sleger's crippled tank out of harm's way, a semi-conscious Haynie tried to follow the confusing messages pouring through the radio. "When they started pulling us off of there, I was trying to guide, and seeing where the road was," he explained. "They were pulling us backwards, off the line. I heard [Sweet in the radio] say, 'left brake!' and I gave left brake. I heard Sweet yell, 'No, no! Not you, Haynie! I'll tell you if I want you to give left brake or right brake!'" By this time it was too late, and Haynie's tank had moved off the road and into a ditch filled with infantry.

Sleger and his fellow tankers were just happy to be alive. "They got us out of the tank and they put me on a stretcher and pushed me into a culvert under the road," he said.[63] "I stayed there for two days. They gave me some hot soup, and by that time we got a new tank and we took off."

Merlino's experience was different: "I think when I woke up, I was in a MASH tent. Then I was off and on [between bouts of consciousness] there. All you do is lay there and sleep, and wait to be transferred."

According to Haynie, the crewmen who had managed to remain conscious received somewhat better treatment. "Lieutenant Sweet put us in a tent, and said, 'You guys sleep in here tonight.' He gave us a shot of whiskey. Where he got that, I don't know." Haynie was still not aware enough to realize that Sleger was not with them. "Never did get our [old] tank fixed," he lamented, "and I have no idea what the electrical problem was."

One other bizarre episode occurred during the struggle for Hill 296. A tall, fair-skinned enemy officer on a nearby hill appeared immune to fire from the Marines. Small arms, mortars and even artillery failed to deter him as he continually walked about in full sight of the Americans. Finally, the frustrated commander of 3/5 called a tank forward, but even long-range sniping with the 90mm. gun failed to scare the officer the Marines nicknamed "Fireproof Phil."[64]

MacArthur's brilliant landing at Inchon essentially severed the North Korean supply line, but like a reptile that does not know when it is dead, the NKPA continued to strike at the Pusan perimeter. Time, however, was now on the side of the Allies. Eighth Army's Lt. Gen. Walton Walker was constantly bedeviled by General MacArthur's demands that he break out of the perimeter, but Walker's battered command simply did not have the strength to do so. On September 23, however, the NKPA attacks slacken perceptibly, and the enemy began to flee northward.[65]

The next day, the 1st Marines crossed the Han River against minimal resistance, and B and C Company tanks were sent back to the ferry crossing. The 1st Platoon of B Company was detached from A Company and committed to the fight on the north end of the hill complex, and immediately suffered one tank destroyed by a mine, and another lost to heavy mortar fire.[66]

Harry Smith had joined the 3rd Division in World War II after Iwo Jima, and had served in China after the war as a truck driver and quartermaster. He was in college at San Diego State when the 11th Tank Battalion was activated, and he served through the first part of the Inchon campaign in H&S Company as an untrained tank mechanic. As he remembered it, "The section leader came down and said, 'Smith, you're going up to a line company.' So I went. The CP was in a railroad embankment, like a stone bridge, with laterals on it." Smith was called up to join Joe Sleger's crew as the replacement for Merlino.

The A Company tanks had at last fought their way through the hills and into position overlooking Seoul, a rambling city of over one million citizens. "We moved up into position and set up for the night," explained Sleger. "We had the dozer tank up to dig us some revetments. We didn't know it until we dug in, we were in a graveyard! These graveyards are ancient, and the ground was just permeated with sticky clay. The stench of the dead bodies! We spent the whole night in the damn graveyard, a dug-up graveyard."

Taking the cue from his boss MacArthur, Ned Almond continually pressed the deliberate General Oliver Smith to attack more aggressively. When he did not get the results he wanted, Almond even went so far as to skip over Smith and give orders directly to the Marine regimental commanders.[67]

At 0700 hours on September 25, the attack into Seoul commenced. It was a complex plan, with five regiments attacking along convergent axes. The 32nd Infantry of the Army's 7th Division and the 17th ROK Regiment attacked northward from the river through the hills east of the city. The 1st Marines attacked north through the heart of the city, while the 7th Marines attacked from the hills bordering the west side of Seoul. Between them, the 1st and 7th regiments would pinch out the battered 5th Marines in the center of the city at the Capitol Building.

The depleted 5th Marines were overextended, so a small task force consisting of the 2nd and 3rd Platoons of B Company tanks, together with a platoon each of engineers and infantry, was hastily organized to cover a gap between the 1st and 5th Marines. One of the objectives assigned to this task force was Hill 105-S, supposedly already secured. Unbeknownst to the Marines, however, the NKPA had reoccupied the hill and raked the engineers and infantry with heavy fire.

Captain Bruce Williams dispatched a flame tank and a single M26 around the left flank of the hill. The flame tank hosed the enemy trenches with flames and drove the survivors out into the massed fire spewing from from Lieutenant Cummings's tanks. About 150 enemy soldiers were flushed out and killed in this manner. An even larger number sought refuge in the caves and huts dotting the hill until ferreted out by the engineers and tanks. One section of tanks was assigned the unusual duty of escorting 121 prisoners to the rear.[68]

At noon, Cummings's platoon crossed the unit boundary to support the 1st Marines in their advance through the city. The struggle for Seoul became known as "The Battle of the Barricades." Harry Bruce explained why: "We ran into roadblocks. Just about every intersection was barricaded." Walls of rubble, rice bags filled with dirt or broken rock, and anything else available jammed the roads. Mines and anti-tank guns protected the approaches to these barriers. The reduction of each street-corner fortress required a slow, systematic and bloody effort. The infantry hunted out snipers, engineers rushed in to lift mines, and the tanks methodically crashed the barricades one by one. It required about an hour to reduce each such street-corner fortress,[69] so progress was exasperatingly slow and deadly. NKPA snipers infested the rooftops and windows, picking off advancing Marines. Others hurled improvised gasoline bombs from the rooftops. This entire nightmare scenario unfolded amidst drifting smoke, flaming buildings, battered corpses, and a milling throng of terrified Korean civilians.

The old M4A3 tanks came into their own in the narrow streets of Seoul. "Surprisingly enough," said Jim Edwards, "the one-oh-five was a better gun in the city, because you got into these little narrow streets, the Pershings with the nineties couldn't traverse. They'd hit the sides of the buildings. With the little short-barreled one-oh-five, we could turn three hundred sixty five degrees. It became the asked-for tank when the infantry was looking for some backup."

Harry Bruce agreed, adding, "The dozers were there too, and they had the one-oh-five on them too, but they also could take that blade and push stuff out of the way. We used the one-oh-fives. We didn't burn any buildings down in there. We didn't run into any caves, and that was where they came in the best."

Although snipers offered sudden death, mines posed the greatest overall threat to the advance. Many of the other NKPA weapons, like the anti-tank rifles, were less efficacious. "We got shot up pretty bad in there with what they called anti-tank guns, little ol' 14mm. things," remembered Sweet. "They wouldn't penetrate the tank, but they would knock big holes in that armor. They would shoot a hole about an inch in diameter, and penetrate about a half inch to an inch." The M26 had three inches of armor on the turret, four and a half inches on the turret face.

"They knocked some periscopes out. If they hit that glass periscope, it knocked them out. That's about the worst damage I remember receiving." Others recalled a different risk that quickly became familiar to the tank crews. For O'Sullivan, "the biggest thing we ran into all the time was the telephone lines. They'd wind up around your tracks, and you'd have to stop and get out, to clear the tracks. [We] used wire cutters. We weren't very friendly with the communications people. We'd snag 'em on the turrets, and pull the telephone poles down." Exiting the tanks to clear the wire, however, exposed the tankers to sniper fire, which only added to their frustration and misery.

Nightfall found the 1st Marines still entangled in the streets and alleyways of the old city, while the enemy stubbornly resisted the advance of the 5th Marines in the hills west of the city center. The impatient Ned Almond ordered the attack to continue through the night. General Smith, commander of the 1st Marine Division, requested clarification of this unusual order. Even the aggressive Chesty Puller, commanding officer of the 1st Marines, balked at advancing into the warren of narrow passages in the darkness. He delayed his attack until 0200 hours.

The NKPA resolved the dilemma by launching a series of their own attacks that night. The first came just before midnight and just west of the city against 3/5 on Hill 105-North. The main attack came at 0158, when at least 500 infantry of the NKPA *25th Brigade*, supported by seven T-34s and a pair of SU-76 self-propelled guns, rushed Marine positions on Ma Po Boulevard. With the aid of massive artillery fire, the Marines smashed the attack by 0230, although one stubborn SU-76 continued to blast away at the Marine positions until dawn.[70]

At daylight on September 26, the 1st Marines and B Company tanks advanced slowly along the main streetcar line, wending their way deeper into the wrecked city. Although the infantry proved remarkably adept at protecting the vulnerable tanks in the narrow streets, losses were unavoidable. Cummings's tank hit a mine that had been laid by Marine engineers during the night for defense, but had been forgotten in the confused aftermath of the enemy attack. The blast crippled the vehicle. A flame tank was disabled when a suicidal attacker rushed in and threw a satchel charge onto the engine deck, wrecking the engine and immolating himself in the process.

The infantry had to remain close to defend the tanks against such attacks, but staying too close to the big cannon could be hazardous. "Many a time we were shooting and infantrymen were hiding around our tank," recalled Sweet. "I always felt sorry for them, cause there was a guy with no eardrums for the rest of his life." Haynie agreed, adding, "A lieutenant or somebody was standing right there in front of the tank. We fired, and boy, it burned his face, singed his beard. He probably didn't hear for a while."

Since coming ashore four days earlier, the 7th Marines and the supporting Dog Company tanks had screened the broad left flank of the division between the coast and Seoul, then hooked in northwest of the city. Although this flanking movement did not meet the powerful resistance encountered in front of the city, Paul Sanders's platoon still lost one tank to a mine.[71]

Captain Chase of Dog Company did not have a command tank. "He [Chase] needed one to go up and look around, so I would act as his loader," said Sanders. "We drove up, and damned if we didn't run into a mortar barrage that set us on fire.[72] I finally got the thing backed up around a curve, and we finally got the [engine] fire out. All the stuff that was on the outside was all stripped off. All the equipment, the aerials, and stuff like that. A radio man came up and gave us a new aerial."

Meanwhile, on the northwest side of the city 2/7 advanced down a valley between two tall and rugged hill masses until blocked by the stubborn defense in the massive walls of the old Sodaewon Prison. More enemy troops rushed down out of the hills to either side, and before long D/2/7 was trapped in the narrow valley. Even a tank column failed to drive the enemy out of this strong position. It was not until the following morning that Dog Company tanks and the other rifle companies were able extricate the trapped (and grateful) unit.

Once the 5th Marines finally breached the hill defenses on the morning of September 27, three rifle regiments began converging on the heart of the city. After a night of work to repair the damage inflicted by the Marine mine, Lieutenant Cummings's tank took the van and led his armor platoon in the attack. Tanks of A Company's 2nd Platoon, supporting 3/5, handily destroyed a pair of SU-76s in a short battle at a major intersection. Cummings's hard-luck tank, however, hit yet another mine and was again disabled.

In the confused street fighting that followed, the NKPA experienced trouble coordinating units and understanding where the Marines were actually deployed. Sleger: "We went down the big boulevard toward the palace. To the west of the palace, up that road, that's where we ran into a platoon [of NKPA] in formation. They marched right into the face of our tanks." The enemy force was coming down the street, bordered on one side by a brick wall. "We were right here, the lead tank. I said we'll wait 'til they're on this wall, and we'll open up with the ninety. I yelled, 'Fire!' and Roth pressed the machine gun stud, and they scattered. I thought we were gonna have the shot of the war."

The 2nd Platoon of A Company supported the Korean Marine Corps, which was supposed to recapture the City Hall.[73] "Here we are in a concrete jungle, and they've got these little square holes dug in the concrete," reminisced Don Gagnon. "I'm straddling them or going around them, and for some reason [Bill Robinson] hit one, and it was a land mine!"

Robinson recalled the moment: "I had the point, but I hit a land mine. Blew one of my bogey wheels off, so we just laid up. We just stopped there right beside the Post Office. The rest of the platoon continued on. We were there for about four hours until we got the maintenance and retriever up, and replaced the bogey wheel and so forth."

As they had in World War II, the company maintenance crews performed miraculous repairs. "They had to pull that [torsion bar] all out. They lifted up the tank with the retriever, the boom," explained Robinson. These major repairs were usually done in rear area shops, but "lift that up and there's no pressure. All you have to do is pull that torsion bar out, and put a new one in. They put the bogey wheel back on, put some new [track] block on, and we were ready to go," continued Robinson. "My loader and I, we took on off and walked around in the buildings and everything. One person said they had a bunch of arms or something up in this garage. All it was was a bunch of junk, really."

Don Gagnon remembered several close calls inside the city. "An infantryman came up to me, and said, 'We can't open [a pedestrian] gate. Would you open the gates for us?' I said sure, I'll open the gates for you. Get away from the gate.'" Gagnon backed his tank into the opening. "I knocked the gate down, and of course the gate exploded because it was booby-trapped. All my oil cans and water cans that were on the back were perforated, and there was water and oil running down off the fenders. That infantryman was too damn close, and he got some shrapnel in his leg."

Some time later, Gagnon continued, "some engineers raised up their hands and wanted us to stop. I opened up my hatch and leaned out, talking to these two guys standing on the ground. One of them spun around like a top. We knew he got hit right away, so I jumped back in and pulled the hatch shut, because that round was meant for me. It missed me, and hit the engineer." Gagnon continued: "We were going into an alleyway, and I look up and I see this clock tower. I say to myself, 'That's where that sniper is.' I told the gunner to lay an HE round into that clock tower, and we never had any more trouble after that."

At 1630 hours organized enemy resistance inexplicably collapsed, and the NKPA abandoned the city in a rush. X Corps spent the next day consolidating its position and clearing the urban area of enemy stragglers, although trapped bands of NKPA made local attacks for two more days. Gagnon: "The CP was in a schoolyard. We never used the buildings for quarters. We stayed on our tanks. First of all, you're too far from your tank if you have to fight, and number two, if they bombard the building with artillery, you're gonna get caught in that. So we stayed out on the tanks all the time."

The following days were relatively quiet ones for the tankers, who enjoyed their respite while the infantry eliminated the enemy's scattered rearguards and stragglers. Losses, however, accumulated as the result of enemy mines and erratic small arms fire, which crippled two tanks and inflicted five casualties.[74]

At 0630 on October 1, the Marines pushed north along the two main roads out of Seoul. The more powerful of the two advances—the 7th Marines, reinforced by a battalion of artillery, a company each of engineers, the Korean Marine Corps, and Captain Lester Chase's D Company tanks—fought their way along the broad valley toward Ouijong-bu, sixteen miles to the north. Their mission was a difficult one. The NKPA was entrenched along high ridges on either side of the road. In a narrow defile known as Nuwon-pi Pass, powerful hilltop positions protected a dense minefield.

The Marines relied heavily upon air and artillery support, which worked well in clearing the enemy off the hillsides. This operation marked the first use of the Porcupine communications tank to coordinate and control supporting arms.[75] The Porcupine was an old M4A3 from Headquarters Company with its interior and armament stripped away. It was equipped with a dummy cannon barrel, and its interior fitted with additional radios and map tables, which allowed its occupants to simultaneously communicate with the infantry, artillery, and air controllers on multiple radio nets. The nickname "Porcupine" was derived from the array of radio antennae that poked out and waved wildly in all directions.

For the tankers, perhaps the most memorable incident of the operation north of Seoul took place on October 2, when an enemy rifle round went down the gun tube of an M4A3 blade tank and ricocheted inside the turret, wounding two of the crewmen inside.[76]

Once the Nuwon-pi Pass position was broken, the NKPA had few resources left with which to contest the advance. By 1700 hours on October 3, the head of the Allied column entered the town of Ouijong-bu.

The second advance or wing of the October 1 movement consisted of a much smaller force—3/5, supported by the 3rd Platoon of A Company tanks and engineers. It attacked northwest toward the town of Suyuhyon. "[There were] no flank guards. We just went up as fast as we could," said Sleger. "We went as far as we could that day. The tanks pulled off to the left side of the road, and we set up in a kind of a three-quarter perimeter. The road was here," he said, gesturing with his hand. "This was a big rice paddy field, dried up but the embankments were still there. Our tank was looking right out in this area as part of our sector." The infantry set up on higher ground, on the other side of the road.[77]

Sleger recounted what followed:

> About one-twenty, one-thirty I came off watch, out of the turret, and lay down on the engine doors. I covered myself with a poncho and a blanket. The engine doors were nice and warm. I was just dozing off . . . and holy chee, out in front of the tank a guy screamed like I've never heard a man scream in my life. I thought the outpost got knifed. When he screamed flares went up over our perimeter, and all hell broke loose."[78]
> I jumped up and threw my poncho and blanket down. . . . I yelled for everybody to get in the tank. We got in there and loaded up, and

it was a pretty good show. The dozer had dozed out revetments for us and Cecil [Fullerton] was on this revetment on the outside of the tank with his Thompson, and shooting. I was yelling to him, 'Get in the tank!' Everybody was screaming, telling everybody to get in the tanks.

Sleger continued:

> [In front of our position] some guy stood up and he ran across the rice paddy ridge. He must have had a flare in his back pocket, because the machine gun was firing as he was running across that rice paddy ridge with that flare going off in his pocket. I don't remember him being cut down, but I'm sure somebody got him. The next morning we went out and checked the area, and there were somewhere between forty or sixty bodies."

E. D. Dial, speaking about the same evening action, added: "The next morning one of the infantry officers came down and wanted to know what the hell was going on. They took him out into the rice paddies and showed him these bodies laying around all over the place, and said, 'That's what's going on.'"

Despite the NKPA counterattack, the task force mananged to secure the town on October 2. Late in the day, Sleger's section saw some unidentified vehicles on another road, and thought they looked like Russian-made NKPA vehicles. "I told the tanks to hold their fire for positive identification," he explained. "I called back to G. G. [Sweet], and asked if there were any friendlies in that area. The call came back, 'No friendlies in your area.' As they got in position for us to shoot, we identified them. They were Army jeeps. Where the hell they came from, I don't know. There was an Army major in command."

The officer got out of his jeep and approached Sleger. "Were you tracking us?"

"We sure as hell were," replied Sleger, who remembered that the major "went to every tank and thanked them for not shooting."

Sleger also remembered another, rather disturbing event. "We captured the chief of police [a North Korean appointee] from one of the villages, and were about to put him on the fender of the tank. But before he got [there] . . . the villagers came out, and they just stomped this guy. I mean they just stomped him! We put him up on the fender, and there was a correspondent, and a photographer. . . . I told him what had happened, and he said, 'Gee, I'd sure like to get a picture of that.' And the villagers came out and they pulled him off the tank, and they stomped him again."

After securing the two towns screening Seoul, the Marines settled in to defend the city. During lulls like these, the dozer tanks worked harder than ever. Jim Edwards remembered digging "latrines with the thing. We scraped off areas to flatten them out to put tents on. Cleared roads. Just general duty stuff."

Phil Morell was promoted under a new Marine Corps policy in which Marine Reserve officers, who were on a slower promotion schedule, were advanced to the rank of their peers in Regular service.[79] "I was promoted to major," Morell said. "I didn't know this, but suddenly I'm the senior major in the battalion, so Milne made me the XO."

The battalion was "suddenly [sent] back to Inchon," and made the trip from October 5 through 7, remembered Morrell. "Down on the beach . . . we had every welder in the division, working around the clock, welding fording kits on." This respite provided an opportunity for the men to "get together. There was a unity that developed within the battalion at that time. It was a little grim."

The battalion would need all the unit cohesion it could muster. The situation for the Marines was not going to get better any time soon. In fact, it was about to get substantially worse, for a new and vastly more difficult mission awaited them in northeastern Korea.

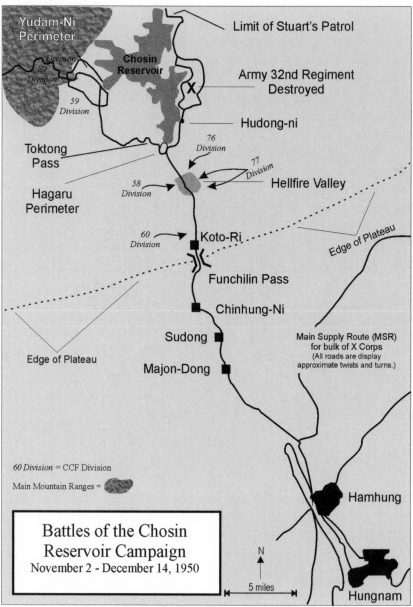

Yudam-Ni
Perimeter

Chosin
Reservoir

*79
Division*

*89
Division*

*59
Division*

Limit of Stuart's Patrol

X

Army 32nd Regiment
Destroyed

Hudong-ni

Toktong
Pass

*76
Division*

*77
Division*

Hagaru
Perimeter

*58
Division*

Hellfire Valley

*60
Division*

Koto-Ri

Edge of Plateau

Funchilin Pass

Chinhung-Ni

Edge of Plateau

Sudong

Main Supply Route (MSR)
for bulk of X Corps
(All roads are display
approximate twists and turns.)

Majon-Dong

Hamhung

60 Division = CCF Division

Main Mountain Ranges =

**Battles of the Chosin
Reservoir Campaign**
November 2 - December 14, 1950

N

5 miles

Hungnam

Theodore P. Savas

"Into the eternal darkness, into fire and into ice."

— Dante Alighieri

Chapter 4

The Lowest Circle of Hell

The Chosin Reservoir Campaign: Encirclement

In Dante's *Divine Comedy*, the worst of sinners are perpetually frozen in a lake of ice. X Corps was about to be thrown into just such a frozen hell.

As the result of General MacArthur's masterstroke at Inchon, the NKPA experienced one of the most complete collapses of any army in modern times. The goal of the UN operation had been to drive back the invaders and restore the ante-bellum division of Korea. The collapse of the NKPA, however, offered up the tempting possibility that Korea could be reunited as a pro-Western entity. In Washington, political leaders were still troubled by the possibility that Korea was a diversion, and they worried that an advance into North Korea would lead to the active involvement of the Soviet Union.[1]

Presenting their allies with a *fait accompli*, the ROK Army crossed the old frontier on October 1, 1950, and soon thereafter the US Joint Chiefs of Staff authorized American troops to advance north after their South Korean comrades.

* * *

The obvious mission for X Corps was the seizure of the port, industrial complex, and airfields at Wonsan, in North Korea. The harbor was one of the best on the entire peninsula, and control of the port would ease logistical limitations on UN forces. Redeployment of X Corps, however, was hamstrung by congestion in Inchon and Pusan, and D-Day for the planned assault landing at Wonsan began to slip. X Corps did not sail from Inchon until the day of the planned landing, and I ROK Corps captured Wonsan while X Corps was still afloat.[2]

Over 2,000 naval mines seeded by the North Koreans blocked the approaches to the harbor.[3] While the Navy's handful of minesweepers struggled to open the port, the ships carrying the Marines sailed to and fro, their human cargo plagued with seasickness and intestinal ailments.

"We just floated around out there, and watched old movies that the Navy had aboard," said Phil Morell. "We finally landed [on October 26], and God, what an embarrassing thing! There's an old airstrip there that's all abandoned. There's a big old hangar there, and by God, Bob Hope and some beautiful blonde are putting on a USO show in this hangar!" The initial landing was indeed anti-climactic. "We hung around there, sort of defending that thing, because we had bypassed a lot of the North Koreans," Morell continued. "We were told to set our tanks out and try to intercept them, because some were coming up the beach on rafts and that sort of stuff."

Two days earlier on October 24, MacArthur had authorized a general advance all the way to the Yalu River—the border with China and the USSR. The ramifications of the planned offensive were readily obvious and greatly disturbed the Joint Chiefs. Nonetheless, no one took any steps to rein in the general.

Once ashore, the reorganization of the tank battalion already underway continued. Able Company had been sent overseas with a disproportionately high percentage of the senior NCOs (the 1st Platoon alone had four Staff Sergeants rather than one), so Bob Miller was transferred to D Company.[4] "I think there were two of us who went from A Company to D Company," he remembered.

The Marines were soon scattered over a vast expanse of eastern Korea. The 1st Marines were assigned to patrol a large area around Wonsan, while the 5th and 7th Marines advanced northward. This dispersal scattered the division across 15,000 square miles of hostile terrain. The 1st Marines could do little more than hold strategic road junctions and patrol the narrow winding roads. The region was infested with NKPA stragglers and guerilla bands up to battalion strength, and these groups regularly ambushed patrols and besieged the scattered garrisons. Some of these enemy forces were not "guerillas" in the regular military understanding of that term. For example, one of the attacks was launched by some 1,000 men of the NKPA *10th Regiment*. Their objective was the base at Kojo, forty miles south of Wonsan, which they attacked on the night of October 27-28. The Kojo garrison—the 1/1 reinforced by a battery of artillery and supporting units—was badly outnumbered. Still, the besieged troops managed to hold out through the night and the next morning the regimental commander, newly promoted Brig. Gen. "Chesty" Puller, dispatched an additional battalion by train, and ten tanks of C Company were loaded aboard *LST883* to help relieve the embattled garrison. The ship ran aground twice in the poorly charted waters, and did not arrive until after the enemy had been driven off with heavy loss.

The remaining battalion, 3/1, was ordered to shift north toward the important road junction at Majon-ni, west of Wonsan, which left only service units to defend the Wonsan. Majon-ni was isolated in a bowl-shaped valley in the mountains, and the main service road (MSR) was nothing more than a single lane dirt road the Marines called Ambush Alley.

The time for hard and bloody action was rapidly approaching. The Marines were ordered to prepare to launch themselves into the mountains of northern Korea by November 16. The 1st Division began its displacement, with the 5th Marines and A Company tanks screening the inland flanking operation by establishing a series of blocking positions.

Lieutenant Sweet's 3rd Platoon of A Company was still given a wide variety of difficult tasks. Its commander recalled why: "The reason that we got so many things to do, Captain English would hold a meeting every night. . . . All the platoon leaders would come in, and he'd say, 'Well, okay, who's got five tanks ready to go in the morning?' He would say, 'Second Platoon always had some kind of problem, but Third Platoon was always ready to go.' I knew that if there was one down or two down,

English would let me borrow Forty-One or Forty-Two [tanks from the Headquarters Platoon]."

Over the years, a myth has arisen that the Chinese intervention in Korea came as a sudden shock in late November. In reality, the Marines and ROK troops had been locked in battle with the Communist Chinese Forces (CCF) for weeks. At the end of October, the 7th Marines relieved an ROK regiment at the hamlet of Oro-ri, in the hills ten miles north of the city of Hamhung. The South Koreans had captured 16 Chinese prisoners who readily revealed that they had crossed the Yalu River on October 16 with the Chinese *124 Division*. The Marines were struck by small CCF probes beginning at 0600 hours on November 2, and skirmished with small bands throughout the day. The regiment established a night perimeter below the town of Sudong, a few miles north of Majon-Dong. At 2300 hours, the CCF began probing the eastern side of its periphery. Within two hours the regiment was under full-scale attack by the *124 Division*, which was supported by five T-34s of the NKPA *344 Tank Regiment.*[5] The road to the north, which led toward the Chosin Reservoir, was too narrow to allow the passage of NKPA tanks, leaving them trapped below the mountains.[6]

The Chinese infantry pressed into the low ground, attacking support units in the valley. One T-34 broke through the lines of A/1/7 on the north side of the perimeter below Sudong, prowling through the company's rear areas until a round from a 3.5-inch rocket launcher set fire to the sandbags stacked around the base of the turret. The blazing tank drove around for some time, lighting up the area before turning around and breaking out through the American lines.

Dawn on November 3 found the Marines in a peculiar deployment. The rifle companies occupied the hills, while the valley was filled with small, mixed perimeters of Marine headquarters and support units—and Chinese soldiers. It took most the day (until 1800 hours) and difficult bloody work to secure the low ground within the Marine perimeter.

The next day, the Marines resumed their advance toward the Chosin Reservoir. They moved several miles north, meeting only slight resistance as far as the village of Chinhung-ni. The Recon Company, augmented by a section of 75mm. recoilless guns, was engaged in a firefight with a small band of Chinese when they noticed a T-34 on the opposite side of the road and behind them buried under a pile of tree limbs. Three men jumped onto the tank, smashed a periscope glass, and dropped a grenade inside the turret. The tank began to move, but a second grenade caused it to lurch to a halt and begin to spew smoke. The Forward Air Controller called for help, summoning Corsair fighter-bombers. Just then, another T-34 emerged from a crumbling hut up the road and began to traverse its 85mm. gun toward the Marines on the open ground. A hail of 75mm. and 3.5-inch rounds had little effect on the Russian-built tank, but one of the Corsairs scored direct hits with a pair of rockets and the vehicle exploded with a deafening roar of flame and smoke. As the Marines passed the burning hulk, they spotted yet third T-34 behind the recently killed vehicle, and yet another tank farther to the rear, both of which they had previously overlooked. Quick action disabled one and captured the other.

Throughout the remainder of the day and both days on November 5 and 6, the 7th Marines fought a series of bitter battles for control of the hills overlooking the lower end of Funchilin Pass. On the morning of November 7, the Marines found that the CCF had disappeared during the night. The Chinese had deliberately withdrawn from contact. The CCF referred to this engagement and related spoiling actions as their Phase One Offensive.

Between November 5 through 9, the 5th Marines reconnoitered the vast area between Huksu-ri and the Fusin Reservoir. The sweep captured another garrulous Chinese prisoner. What he had to say shocked those who heard him: the CCF had committed twenty-four divisions to Korea. On November 7, patrols from 1/7 reported over 2,000 NKPA troops moving east from Huksu-ri and into the flank of the division. A major enemy movement was underway.

The critical rail line from Wonsan, still guarded by patrols from the 1st Marines and D Company tanks, was under constant attack by guerillas and closed to nighttime traffic.[7] During the days, "We went out on foot patrols, but we didn't run into nothing," said Ben Busch. "You're a rifleman first. They'd send a few guys out every day, make up a patrol. We'd go out and snoop and poop around, see if we could find anything." Paul Sanders also recalled the foot patrols, saying, "We'd stay out from dawn 'til dusk, and then they picked us up. Next day a platoon might go out in another area. It was awful hilly."

Don Bennett, a junior sergeant with a bottomless well of patience for enlisted men and subordinates, had been reassigned to the 1st Platoon of B Company tanks. "I remember the day—it was November 10th—we started a two-day road march from Wonsan to Hamhung. They were starting to have quite a bit of trouble [with guerillas]. We spent a night about halfway up." The tank company spent the night in a separate perimeter not far from a Puerto Rican National Guard unit. "They were really jumpy. They did a lot of shooting during the night," said Bennett.

Despite signs of Chinese activity, on November 11 Lt. Gen. Ned Almond promulgated X Corps Operations Order Number Six, authorizing an advance to the banks of the Yalu River. As envisioned, the plan would scatter X Corps over a huge area in the nearly roadless mountains. The 1st Marine Division was expected to defend nearly forty miles of front.[8]

When they were about ten miles inland from the coast along a thin dirt road, remembered Phil Morell, "We set up in a schoolyard, and sent different companies out. This was a little narrow ribbon of road that ran all the way up to Yongdongpo-ri, which was at the base of the little narrow road that went up about 9.4 miles to Koto-ri, which is up on the level with the [Chosin] Reservoir. Chesty Puller took his regiment, with one of our companies of tanks [B Company], and set up his perimeter there [at Koto-ri]."

By this time the weather had turned bitterly cold, as John Haynie discovered one morning when he tried to eat breakfast: "We had hot cakes one morning. Boy, it was nice to walk into the cook tent. . . . I was kind of looking down at my hot cakes with the syrup and the butter they had just put on there. I walked past the end of that tent flap and the syrup—whew!—it just clouded over, just like that. You had to break the syrup!" The extreme cold brought with it unexpected problems for the tanks. During the slightly warmer days, snow would melt and if the crews were not careful, the next night ice would form around the turret ring, jamming the turret.[9]

On November 15, the port at Hungnam was finally opened, relieving some of the logistical pressures on the men ashore. On the same day, MacArthur instructed X Corps to push westward, deep into the mountains to assist ROK forces and support the advance of Eighth Army. The Army's 3rd Division was ordered to relieve the Marines in the fighting still going on around Wonsan. Oliver Smith's 1st Marine Division would be responsible for a broad front facing the mountains, extending east to the Fusin Reservoir. General Smith questioned the wisdom of pushing his troops into the rugged mountains in winter because this would string his division out along 120 miles of a single, vulnerable road. He dispatched a letter to the Commandant of the Marine Corps stating as much, and that he had reason to "doubt the feasibility of supplying troops in this area during the winter or providing for the evacuation of sick and wounded."[10] A careful and cautious commander, Smith sought to concentrate his division, but the task was slow since the road into the mountains had to be widened to support the division's tanks and heavy vehicles.

Following a personal reconnaissance on November 17, Lt. Col. Harry Milne concluded that only the old M4A3s could negotiate the narrow road in its existing condition. The next day, Milne organized a Provisional Tank platoon under Capt. R. M. Krippner. This platoon consisted of two M4A3 dozer tanks from B Company, three dozer tanks and a radio jeep, with a radio operator and medical corpsman from D Company, and a two and one-half ton truck with a driver and two maintenance men from the Service Company.[11] After the battle for Seoul, Vaughn Stuart had been reassigned as a liaison officer to Division headquarters, and he was to play a key role in the fate of this platoon. Stuart recorded that the newly formed Provisional Tank Platoon included dozer tanks D-43, D-44, D-45, and B-43.[12]

Jim Edwards experienced engine trouble with his M4A3 dozer tank and wasted several days at a battalion machine shop trying to fix the problem. As a result, he was separated from B Company.[13] "Because [the roads] were so narrow we finally had to dump the dozer blade," he said. "You couldn't use the thing because the edges of it sticking out there were constantly running into the side of the mountain. If you were on frozen ice, it didn't take too much of a push to shove you right over the side."[14]

Vaughn Stuart experienced the same thing: "I had four of the gun tanks. We left the dozer blade on one, and dropped the other three dozer blades. I had another vehicle there they called "The Porcupine." It was loaded with communications gear. From inside there, you could talk to anybody in the Division area, or [aircraft] above it." As Stuart described it, "They took out the guts of it, put on a telephone pole for the gun so it would look like all the rest of 'em, and just loaded it down on the inside with all sorts of communications." As noted earlier, the nickname came from the array of radio antennae that adorned the old tank.[15] The Provisional Tank Platoon advanced as far as Hagaru-ri on November 19, but the movement of the tanks required the closure of the road to critical truck traffic from 0700 until 1300 hours.[16]

Meanwhile, the heavier M26 tanks provided security around Hamhung and Hungnam. The tanks of the regimental anti-tank platoons were under the control of the tank battalion, and were used to establish roadblocks along the MSR.[17] Don Bennett remembered "checking a lot of people at roadblocks, looking for pack marks, looking at their hands.[18] If there was somebody that looked of a soldier age, we looked 'em over real close. . . . We checked 'em. We weren't experts by any chance. The main thing is they didn't go by us with any weapons, ammunition, etc. That's what we were checkin' for." Their job was not an easy one. "We didn't have anybody that spoke Korean, so it was a case of just lookin' at 'em. If we thought there was a suspicious one, we hauled 'em back." Questionable cases were handed over to South Korean troops for questioning.

General Smith was unable to concentrate his force until November 20-21, when the 3rd Division replaced the 1st Marines in the Huksu-ri area, and the battalion-sized 41 Royal Marine Commando was attached to the division.

When the Marine Division continued its shift northward, A Company was at last given a break, assigned a variety of duties in the rear. "We had over ninety-three tanks in that battalion, and it was way too many," said Harry Milne, explaining why this company was tasked away from the front. "The TOE called for that. It was way too many for that type of operation and that type of terrain. We had to limit the number of tanks that could go up north. The engineers had to widen the road for the M26s."

Although he remembers guarding a bridge during this period, Cpl. Roger Chaput could never figure out why. "We were in a circle of wagons [near Sudong]. There was a bridge down there. I just assumed that we were there to watch that bridge. I thought there was a dry creek, so what

The Chosin Reservoir Campaign   109

the hell, anybody could just go around it!" The tank company was supporting a Puerto Rican National Guard unit.

Driver J. A. Merlino, who had spent a month in a hospital in Japan to recover from the bad burns on his hands, rejoined the unit at this time.[19] Prentiss Baughman was transferred to Service Company, which remained at the lower end of the Funchilin Pass. "They had a tank they couldn't fix up there, we'd send good tanks up, to bring theirs back and work on them in the rear area," said Baughman. "We had about three spare tanks in our company."

For the two tank companies ordered to advance into the mountains, the narrow icy roads proved to be a nightmare. "We didn't have the rubber pads on the tracks," said Michael O'Sullivan. "Ours were steel tracks all the way, so it was like a pair of ice skates. You'd get on a downward slope, and you could put on all the brakes you wanted to, and you just kept sliding 'til the damn thing decided to stop."

Other than the Provisional Platoon, the most advanced tank position was miles to the rear at Majon-dong, where D Company was garrisoned with 1/5. As of November 23, the tank battalion was assigned to "protect the MSR from positions in the vicinity of Majon-dong and Soyong-ni."[20] Pending the widening of the road north of Majon-dong, Dog Company was told to stand by to move one platoon north up the narrow mountain road to Hagaru, where it would consolidate with the Provisional Platoon.[21]

The M4A3s spent time patrolling the constricted secondary roads. Harry Bruce: "We were making quite a few runs off the side of the main MSR. We'd turn and go up into a valley. We'd hear one shot, and we'd go up in there and there wouldn't be anybody. They were playing hide and seek with us at that time." These patrols Bruce and others were participating in were a screen—and the only security—for the west flank of the division as it advanced into the mountains "mostly to the west of us, which was back farther into the mountains," said Bruce. "I don't remember ever going east off the MSR." The weather only got worse as they advanced. "It snowed, and . . . they came and picked up all the tents and everything that the tank battalion had, and took them north. We were left out in the open, because they needed those tents farther north."

By November 24, patrols from the 5th Marines were combing the desolate terrain east of the Chosin Reservoir. "We were at Hagaru," said

Vaughn Stuart. "We really didn't have too much activity when I first arrived, but I got a call from the S-Three of the 5th Marines one afternoon kind of late." Stuart received orders to support Lt. Col. Taplett's 3/5 on the east side of the huge reservoir. "He gave me an order to go up there. I had to go several miles up the east side of the reservoir. Taplett's battalion held that area that the Army RCT [Regimental Combat Team] later came into. I had a mission, with two tanks, to join one of the rifle platoons and go all the way [north] to the dam of the Chosin Reservoir.[22] I can't remember how many miles it was up there, but we traveled all day."

Stuart and his comrades "ran into what looked like a couple of squads, but that might have been a Chinese platoon. They were in a little valley, in some houses. I guess they chased the Koreans out of it. We came up over the hill, and they just bolted out every door and window and charged up the other side of the hill, with all of us shooting at them. I don't know how many casualties we got, if any. We didn't take any, but I don't think we inflicted any, either."

The same problem that had bedeviled Max English was encountered by Stuart: in the heat of the moment, the infantry tended to forget proper procedures. "Second Lt. Danny Cashion, who was running the platoon, was a close friend of mine.[23] He motioned me forward. They were taking the advance, and he really frenetically motioned me to come forward. I roared up there. He was trying to tell me, from the outside of the tank, what he wanted me to do. We had that tank-infantry phone on the back of the tank. It was encased in a steel box. He could have gotten behind the tank and told me. I heard the bullets coming by, they were so close. I ducked back down in the tank, and he just looked kind of frustrated. I don't know why he didn't get on that tank-infantry phone. I don't know why he didn't communicate by radio. He just wanted me so bad to shoot all those Chinese."

Stuart eventually managed to get Cashion to communicate by radio. The infantry had smaller man-portable radios, but the signal from the powerful tank radios carried farther through the rugged mountains. Stuart recalled the conversation:

> . . . my radio conversation with Danny carried back to the battalion headquarters. The one-sided communications likely sounded strange to Colonel Taplett and his staff, particularly on his battalion tactical net, not knowing who I was, and not having heard from

Danny since we got out of sight that morning. Instead of using the formal call signs for our respective units, we were using "Stu" for Stuart and "Cash" for Cashion just to keep the radio procedure brief. My radio must have provided the stronger signal, being powered by the tank batteries, and over the radio came, "Stu, this is Tapp."

I knew who he was and he wanted to know who I was and what I was doing in his network. I guardedly gave him enough information to satisfy him as to our bona fides, and for the remainder of the patrol, I relayed information to him and his instructions to Danny.[24]

Although the advance had gone fairly well thus far, the strategic situation was growing ominous. "We went on around there and up toward the dam, and the Platoon Leader of the infantry left me on the road with a squad," said Stuart. "He took two squads up to observe the dam or anything around the dam. Ran into five Chinese soldiers, and they just assaulted and killed all the Chinese. We went farther north than anybody else did, that one patrol. The Army went further up, over on the eastern flank [of the Corps, in far northeastern Korea], but I don't think they ever really ran into any Chinese over there, *and we had no contact with them*," Stuart concluded. This simple, chilling, statement summarizes the precarious tactical situation of X Corps. The individual divisions were trying to cover impossibly large areas, and were separated by huge swaths of unknown and unpatrolled territory. It was a recipe for disaster.

At noon the next day, November 25, the Army's 1/32 of the 7th Infantry Division formally relieved the 5th Marines of responsibility for the area east of the huge lake, freeing up Oliver's 1st Marine Division for the advance to the west. Foreboding news was received that strong CCF forces had savaged I ROK Corps at Tokchon, a key road junction 70 miles southwest of Yudam-ni.

By dawn the next day the division was at last reunited, though still strung out over seventy miles of road. Two rifle regiments and much of the artillery were entrenched in advanced positions. The most advanced tank units were the Provisional Platoon at Hagaru-ri, and the 2nd Platoon of D Company at Chinhung-ni, far back down the road. The 7th Marines were still embroiled in continuous fights with small bands of Chinese. Enemy prisoners, many of whom spoke freely, boasted that the CCF's *58, 59* and *60 Divisions* were already in position and poised to cut the MSR south of Yudam-ni.[25]

The CCF divisions committed in Korea, each with 7,000 to 8,500 men, were light infantry formations. Each consisted of three rifle regiments, an artillery battalion equipped with Soviet-made 76.2mm. field guns, and other supporting units. The individual rifle regiments included three 700-man rifle battalions, a battery of four to six 76.2mm. guns, and several supporting companies, including a mortar company. This latter formation included the enemy's most formidable firepower, Soviet-made 122mm. mortars. These weapons would play a particularly significant role, because many of the field guns were left behind because of transportation difficulties. Each rifle battalion consisted of three rifle companies and a heavy weapons company with heavy machine guns and 82mm. infantry mortars.[26]

Despite overwhelming evidence of a looming enemy attack, MacArthur's command in Tokyo steadfastly held to the plan for a victorious advance to the Yalu River. That evening, 7th Marines rifle company commanders were issued orders to continue advancing into the rugged mountains. The division as a whole was directed to cut behind the enemy facing Eighth Army, a move designed to facilitate the advance of that far larger force.[27]

At 0300 hours on November 27, four M4A3 gun tanks of the Provisional Tank Platoon attempted to cross the pass to Yudam-ni west of Chosin Reservoir. Vaughn Stuart: "They didn't want us on the road in daylight hours, because they needed to have the trucks to transport troops, materiel, or food, whatever, up that road. Our tanks would just block it." The move was undertaken during the freezing and dark early hours of the morning. "The ice was just hard as steel. We didn't get very far out of Hagaru 'til all four tanks were off the side of the road. Just slid off. We just could not control it." Stuart was quick to point out that the problem was not due to poor driving. "I had good drivers. We had steel tracks, and the tracks simply would not hold into that ice. We got three of them out of the ditches and back on the road. Another one threw a track in the ditch."

Without a VTR, the men of the platoon were hard-pressed to recover the stuck tanks. "We just had a heck of a time. It wasn't really a deep ditch. I had attached one tank by a cable, and we were trying to pull it out, and we just had the devil of a time. The ice was so hard. It was really cold." Eventually, when vehicles began rolling again along the road,

Stuart explained that he "got the other three tanks back to Hagaru. Took the guns and breechblock out of the M4 that had thrown the track. We were gonna come back the next day and repair that and drag it out."[28]

Later that morning, a single M26 from the 2nd Platoon of D Company tanks, now at Hagaru-ri, made another attempt to get over the icy pass. Lieutenant Richard Primrose rode and walked ahead of tank D-23, driven by Sergeant Clyde Kidd. The difficulty of the effort was noted by Michael O'Sullivan, who observed that "The road was only thirteen feet wide, and the tank is a little over eleven feet wide, so you didn't have much to play with."[29]

Vaughn Stuart followed part of the way, watching the M26 move along the road that had thwarted his own tanks. "This tank had rubber treads on it. I don't know if they mashed down and gave a little better traction on that ice, or if it was just the fact that this driver was just outstanding. I followed along with that, and at times the rear end of that tank would swing way out over a drop on the side of the road. It was amazing to me, but just outstanding driving." Sergeant Kidd rode the brakes in a controlled slide down from the crest of the pass, deliberately colliding with roadside embankments to slow the tank.

Soon after Lieutenant Primrose and Kidd arrived in Yudam-ni late that afternoon, they were flown back to Hagaru-ri.[30] The plan was that they would lead the rest of the 2nd Platoon across the pass the following day. The two men never returned for their tank.

Shortly after the 7th Marines began their cold weather advance, sudden and heavy resistance brought the movement to a sudden standstill. No one knows why the CCF did not wait and strike the Marines after they had advanced deep into the rugged mountains, where they could have been hacked to pieces in detail. This strategic misstep was one cause of their ultimate undoing.

One the fighting began, the 5th and 7th Marines, together with the bulk of the 11th Marines' artillery, pulled back into the more defensible valley east of the reservoir and town to ride out the enemy onslaught. By 2100 hours on November 27, the large perimeter at Yudam-ni was under full-scale attack, with the greatest threat directed against the Northwest Ridge and the 7th Marines, which was strung out along the road to the west. The CCF *79* and *89 Divisions* assaulted the perimeter from the north and northwest, respectively, while the *59 Division* slipped around to the west to close the Toktong Pass behind and below Yudam-ni near the southern tip of the reservoir.

The immediate effect of the sudden enemy movement became clear to Vaughn Stuart at daybreak when he went back in an attempt to recover his abandoned tank left behind with the thrown track: "The next morning the Chinese had set a roadblock up almost right on top of the tank. We lost that one. Never recovered."

Stuart was disappointed, but General Smith's worst fear had materialized: his strung-out division had marched into a major and well organized enemy attack in inhospitable terrain. He quickly concluded that the only place he could assemble his scattered forces was fourteen miles southeast at Hagaru-ri, which sat in a topographic bowl at the southern end of the Chosin Reservoir just east of the Toktong Pass. The main road diverged at Hagaru-ri, with one leg leading northwest to Yudam-ni carrying the bulk of Smith's Marine division, and the other heading north and hugging the eastern flank of the reservoir, where the Army's 31st RCT was operating. The critical position was the crest above Toktong Pass, about midway between Hagaru-ri and Yudam-ni. It had to be held at all costs. F/2/7 occupied a hill there that overlooked the important road.

It did not take long for the CCF *59 Division* to strike Hagaru, which was garrisoned by two rifle companies, half of an infantry heavy weapons company, two batteries of artillery, and a handful of tanks. Chinese heavy mortars and field guns dueled with Marines howitzers along the four-mile perimeter, which was far too long to be defended by such a small force. The fighting was intense, prolonged, and memorable. One officer of 1st Engineer Battalion, fighting in the hills north of Hagaru, remembered that the artillery and mortar fire "fused into a great ring of living flame, and the thousands of explosions blended into one steady, low-pitched roar."[31]

That night, while the Marines were fighting at Yudam-ni and clinging to Hagaru-ri, the destruction of the Army Regimental Combat Team east of the reservoir began. Vaughn Stuart had watched earlier in the day as much of the army outfit and its accompanying vehicles passed by his unit's warming tents. "About ten o'clock that night, we were alerted by incessant artillery fire from the vicinity of the Army regiment," he remembered. "We were shivering in our sleeping bags, but we were laughing because we thought the Army had merely become spooked and had started shooting at their imaginations." Within a short time, no one would be laughing.[32]

On the other side of the reservoir, the importance of holding the Hagaru-ri position was obvious from the outset of the fighting. The 1st Marines were ordered to send a column of reinforcements north from Koto-ri "at all costs." The distance to Hagaru was about eleven miles, but the column only managed to make about one mile before it, too, came under attack by elements of the CCF *60 Division*. Unable to contest the advance, the reinforcements turned back at 1730 hours. More firepower was needed before the contested road to Hagaru-ri could be safely opened.

Don Bennett remembered the aborted attempt to reinforce Hagaru. The B Company tanks were bivouacked at an abandoned power plant, sleeping in the buildings.[33] "We were wakened in the middle of the night, and told to break down what we had there. . . . We were gonna move to the Yalu, as far as we knew. [B]efore sunrise, we started a road march to go up the mountain. Dog Company, I don't know how many of them, had went ahead of us."

Meanwhile, matters continued to deteriorate around Hagaru. While the opposing artillery and mortars dueled, and the infantry traded small arms fire, the Provisional Tank Platoon, the main armored force at Hagaru, moved forward to reinforce weak spots along the four-mile long perimeter. The strongest Chinese attacks were directed against the southern margin of the Hagaru enclave on the night of November 28. The Marine perimeter in that region ran across the broad flat valley floor in order to encompass enough ground to enclose an airstrip.

Vaughn Stuart said that he and his comrades "knew they [the enemy] were there, but it took them several days before they decided to attack. That was after they had hit that Army Regimental Combat Team." Stuart took three tanks and moved out to support the infantry struggling to defend the flat open terrain in front of a hospital. Behind the medical facility, recalled Stuart, were "a bunch of floodlights [where] they were constructing the airfield. The [rifle company] executive officer, who had been commissioned with me, came out and told me where they wanted the tanks set in. He said, 'There are no alternate positions. This is it. We're gonna have to stay here, because the hospital is right there!'"

The tanks were set up in the front line of infantry, with a second line of infantry positions behind them.[34] Waiting in the tanks was a miserable experience. The crews had to sleep sitting up, and contact with the cold steel sapped body heat even faster than lying in the snow. "It must have been about ten o'clock at night, the listening post alerted the front lines, and pulled back in to the MLR. The Chinese were coming in," said Stuart. "We fought all night long. We fired about everything that we could fire. If a Chinaman got through—a couple of times they got up on the tanks—the infantry behind us would shoot 'em off."

There were thatch-roof houses in that area, several of which were set on fire by the tracers. Stuart watched with some interest as Chinese soldiers moved up to take advantage of the heat. "They would come up there and bunch up," he recalled. "We waited until they got bunched up, and then we'd put a round of one-oh-five in the middle of 'em. We did that all night long. Plus machine gun fire. We were really active with machine gun fire."

The extremely cold weather played hell with the weapons, which began to malfunction. "After I'd fired maybe half a dozen rounds from my tank gun, it got to where the round wouldn't fully seat," Stuart remembered. "It would go almost all the way into the chamber, but not completely." Cold or no cold, the tankers had little choice but to find a way to keep firing their weapons—or be overrun and killed or forced back. "My driver—probably the most dangerous thing we did all that night—took a mallet, I guess it was made of some kind of hide. We would hammer the round into the chamber. You know if you hit the primer on that thing, it would just destroy the tank. . . . We worked that way."

Many Marines reported that the Chinese soldiers often appeared bewildered, and seemed to have no clear tactical goal in mind. "I don't understand the logic behind them, because they didn't stop," said Jim Edwards. "They kept right on going. They'd run by the tank. Shoot at it. Throw grenades at it. Keep right on going."

At 0630 the following morning, the beleaguered Marines still held their positions, though they had been pushed off East Hill, a key piece of high ground northeast of Hagaru-ri.

Vaughn Stuart vividly remembered the carnage exposed by the spreading sunlight: "The next morning, in the first fifty yards, we counted over five hundred dead Chinese." The enemy had been both physically and emotionally brutalized by the night battle. Cultural barriers kept the Marine infantry with Stuart from understanding the puzzling intentions of individual enemy soldiers. "One lone Chinese soldier, obviously disoriented, came wandering toward our lines, and suddenly discovering us less than a hundred feet away, he looked nervously around, turned, and took a couple of steps away from us. The first rifle shot missed, and the soldier waved his open palms to us in what appeared to be an appeal, then dropped on all fours to commence crawling. The next shot hit him in the side of the head, and his upper body flattened onto the snow, but his rear-end remained raised thigh-high in the air.[35]

While the widespread fighting continued largely unabated, new Allied units poured into Koto-ri. On the night of November 28, the 41 Commando, Royal Marines, arrived. On November 29, a scratch force consisting of the 41 Commando, G/3/1, and B/1/31,[36] all under the command of Lt. Col. Douglas Drysdale, Royal Marines, was assembled for an attack north to relieve Hagaru-ri. The Motor Transport Section of Service Company, 1st Tank Battalion and Motor Transport Battalion, 7th Marines, provided most of the trucks for the effort. Two days earlier the tank battalion had furnished fourteen trucks and crews on "indefinite" loan to the Royal Marines.[37]

"There were a lot more units that wanted to get up north, and they knew the Chinese were lining that little narrow ten mile valley we had to go through," remembered Len Maffioli. "There was a kind of safety in numbers thing. . . . The next morning we've got over a hundred and forty vehicles and about seven hundred men, waiting to go that ten miles."

The column left the perimeter at 0930 hours on November 29, but quickly became embroiled in a battle with the CCF. The enemy was strong enough to convince Lieutenant Colonel Drysdale to wait until tanks were brought up to add their firepower to the head of the procession. When D Company tanks arrived and refueled, Paul Sanders's 1st Platoon moved up to help Drysdale's Royal Marines and G/3/1 attack the Chinese positions that had stalled the column and forced B/1/31 to deploy along the road. "We started out and got about a mile out. There was a long ridge up there, and there were quite a few gooks up there shooting. The road went right by it," Sanders said. "I was in the lead. I got up there and found we had a bridge—or where a bridge used to be. I told the rest of my platoon, and called the company commander.

'Why don't you just go ahead with the 2nd Platoon, and I'll fall in behind them.'

'Well,' answered the company commander, "they're finding out whether they want to go back or not.'"

While he waited for the decision to be made, Sanders received one of the most chilling messages to ever come across his radio. "I was fooling around on the radio, and bang! Clear as a bell came a message from somebody asking, 'Can you hear me? Can you hear me!' It was some guy up in Hagaru," explained Sanders. "He said, 'Boy, whoever you are . . . tell your people we can't hold without you!' That's all he could say, 'We're in a hell of a lot of trouble.'"

Word soon arrived that the column was going to head back for Koto-ri. Sanders was mortified. The men up ahead were counting on their arrival to survive. "I got word we were gonna turn back, so I told Captain [Bruce Clark] about this, what I had just heard. He radioed back to Drysdale, and decided to continue on." As Sanders remembered it, Drysdale wanted to intersperse the tanks within the column, "but our company commander says, 'Hell no! We'll lead you up there, but I don't want to get my tanks separated.' We got separated anyhow," Sanders said "but that was the flap right there. I think there were a lot of hurt feelings on that, but that was not my business. I just followed orders." Sanders's platoon was already under strength, because one tank had been left at the foot of the pass with engine problems, and another had run out of fuel.[38]

Since he was in the lead, Sanders moved out as the van tank of Drysdale's column. Before long, he noticed that the tail of the line was falling behind. Drysdale was determined to push ahead, however, and the column moved as swiftly as it could through where Baker Company, 31st Infantry, was assembling on the road.[39]

"I fell in behind the second or third tank of my platoon," Sanders said. "We started up again. In the meantime, a lot of the trucks and other vehicles got ahead of us. There was a little action, shooting here or there. You couldn't see a hell of a lot, but you could shoot where you think it's coming from."

The improvised march order helped determine the fate of what was known as Task Force Drysdale. The 1st Platoon of D Company tanks under Paul Sanders was at the head of the task force to punch through any roadblocks. Seven more tanks from D Company and another five from the Anti-Tank Company, 5th Marines, followed. Behind the armor was a long column of trucks and jeeps carrying G/3/1 (22 vehicles), the 41 Commando (31 vehicles), followed at some distance by B/1/31 (22 vehicles) and detachments of the Division Headquarters Battalion and 1st Signal Battalion (66 vehicles). This arrangement left the lengthy string of vulnerable vehicles without the protection of the tanks.[40]

A short distance behind Sanders and his fellow tankers an enemy round struck a truck, which caught on fire and blocked the narrow road. American and British Marines worked feverishly to clear the blockage out of the way, but B/1/31 and everything that followed behind it was brought to a dead stop by a single disabled truck.[41] Sheer bad luck had sliced Task Force Drysdale into two pieces in a place the men would come to call Hellfire Valley. Its fate was now sealed.

South of the Drysdale column, B Company tanks and their supporting trucks fought their way into Koto-ri, the last intact unit to arrive at that now embattled enclave. "Things were happening pretty fast," remembered Phil Morell. "I had gone up to reconnoiter a place for the tanks at Hagaru-ri. Everything was kind of screwed up. Chesty Puller is partially responsible for this, because he had that perimeter [Koto-ri]." Puller detached the 2nd Platoon from B Company for local defense. "He shouldn't have done that, because they were in direct support, not attached. Of course, Chesty Puller did a lot of things on his own, you know," said Morell knowingly. Colonel Milne knew nothing of Puller's action.[42]

Meanwhile, miles south of Task Force Drysdale at Koto-Ri, another column, including the B Company tanks, was scraped together to reach the stranded soldiers. Don Bennett: "We were gassed up. We got a couple of fifty-five gallon drums and we poured the gas in the vehicles because we had used up a good percentage of it climbing up that long pass. Chesty Puller, the regimental commander, requested that one platoon be left behind, so that left the First Platoon and the Third Platoon, and the CO's and XO's tank[s]." B Company started north to try and overtake the Drysdale column.

Ben Busch's tank, which was supposed to be with Drysdale's original column, had gotten separated from the rest of D Company. "We had thrown a bunch of fan belts climbing up that hill," he explained. Loose engine belts were a chronic problem on the M26 tanks.[43] "Shift it wrong, or accelerate wrong, and you'd snap a belt. Anyway, we snapped some belts." Left behind in Koto-ri, Busch and his crew fixed the problem as fast as possible, and "around four-thirty or five o'clock in the afternoon were told we'd lead the cooks, bakers and candlestick makers up." Busch's orphaned tank was tucked into the B Company relief column.

Unfortunately, the powerful tank radios proved unreliable in the mountainous terrain. As a result, Phil Morell explained, Capt. Bruce Williams and B Company, trying to catch up with the Drysdale column, were completely unaware of the problems plaguing Captain Bruce Clark and D Company at the head of the column.

The gaggle of B Company tanks and a variety of soft-skinned vehicles set off in pursuit of the Drysdale column. "Now it's getting dark," said Bennett. "I don't know what, five o'clock or four-thirty, but it's getting dark when we left, and ended up trying to find that convoy."

The progress of the main Drysdale column was fitful as local fights developed along the line of march, and the inch-worm progress inevitably resulted in the vehicles becoming spread out along the road. At 1615, the head of the column ground to a stop only four miles north of Koto-ri. When the column halted, the trucks pulled off the road and became mixed together. Unit integrity dissolved.

"My part of the convoy got just about halfway, about five miles," said Len Maffioli. "The Chinese were smart enough to let [D Company] tanks through. They did not disperse the tanks throughout the convoy as some people had suggested. In fact, Drysdale requested it. The tank company commander [Bruce Clark] said no, he can't spread his vehicles out like that without infantry protection. The [enemy] let the tanks get through, and about a third of the wheeled vehicles." When the Chinese hit the convoy, "about a third of us were trapped," continued Maffioli. "The road was narrow, very narrow, barely enough for two vehicles to pass if one wasn't a tank."

The Army infantry company, B/1/31, came under heavy attack. Chinese infiltrated right onto the road, tossing grenades and setting fire to trucks. The column was slowly chopped into pieces. Within a short time the convoy was reduced to four separate perimeters spread over 1,200 yards of road.[44]

Bob Miller had been ordered to join Vaughn Stuart as the Platoon Sergeant of the Provisional Tank Platoon at Hagaru. Riding in the cab of one of the trucks, Miller had reached Koto-ri just in time to be included in Drysdale's convoy. Miller was holding the driver's rifle, just to keep it from bouncing around on the rough road.[45] "The minute we got stopped, he left!" said an amazed Miller. "The driver grabbed that rifle, and was gone so quick you couldn't believe it! Left me with my pistol!" The enemy, as Miller easily recalled, "broke up the convoy right there. At that point we had one tank still in with that group of trucks. It was still not midnight, but in the evening hours. When they attacked it was with bugles, and racket, and shooting, all of that type of thing." To Miller's surprise, "one of the weapons they had that we retrieved from them were the Thompson submachine guns that we gave 'em after the Second World War. Naturally. In the tanks we had what we called the 'grease gun,' a terrible looking weapon.[46] We just threw those things in the ditch and grabbed the Chinese Thompsons."

The situation was grim indeed, and virtually every part of the stalled Drysdale column was under attack. Both Bruce Clark and Paul Sanders advised Drysdale that they thought the tanks could fight through the enemy fire tearing up the road and reach Hagaru-ri, but that the trucks would not make it. Drysdale, however, decided to try and forge ahead anyway. The lead group of tanks, G/3/1, and most of the Royal Marines lumbered on, unsure of the fate of the besieged units trapped behind them.

Far to the rear, Bennett and the rest of the B Company tanks were racing out of Koto-ri to catch up with Drysdale's severed column before darkness fell. The company's own soft-skinned vehicles—twenty-three trucks, jeeps, and Weasels[47]—were sandwiched between two groups of six tanks each. The 3rd Platoon was in the lead, with orders to bull through any opposition. When the head of the tank column rounded a bend near Hills 1236 and 1182, it nearly collided with wreckage from rear elements of Drysdale's column.

Don Bennett estimated that the head of the column had traveled "four or five miles, and it was dark when the lead tank ran into an area where trucks and jeeps had been abandoned. It was just darker than all get-out. There was some shooting going on." The lead tank commander started receiving fire from a hill," Bennett continued. "He didn't know exactly whether there were any Americans there, or [if] they were all Chinese. I'm not certain how much firing back they did, because I was back a few tanks." Ben Busch was even farther back in the same column. "I was sitting in the assistant driver's seat, the hatch open, and all of a sudden some mortar rounds hit right in front of the tank, right on the road!" he said. "The Chinese clobbered the wheeled vehicles."

With his column raked by fire, Captain Bruce Williams realized that there was no way to fight through the wreckage clotting the road. He ordered his command to turn around, but enemy fire was already shredding his unarmored vehicles, and the narrow road made the effort doubly difficult. Still, somehow the men managed to pull off the nearly impossible feat. "Captain Williams made the decision in the middle of the night that it was not a healthy situation for us to go any farther," said Don Bennett. "[So] we turned around."

The trailing tanks of 3rd Platoon, together with a handful of trucks, suddenly found themselves in the lead and heading south. No one was aware of what was happening to the rest of the company, because their radio antennae had been shot away. Somehow this small group managed to fight its way back to Koto-ri.

One platoon of tanks, Captain Williams's command group, and Ben Busch, the orphan from D Company, found themselves trapped, the road blocked by their own wrecked trucks. "After we turned around, I found myself the next to the last tank," Bennett said. "We headed back toward Koto-ri. We had not traveled very far, when all at once there was a lot of shooting up in front of me. I could see tracers going over my head. We were fighting with the hatches open. I got down. I ordered the loader to close the hatch. His name was [PFC John C.] 'Frenchy' Lirette." As soon as Lirette's hatch was shut, Bennett jumped up and grabbed the tank commander's hatch. He "wiggled it real hard. It was stuck, and it felt like it took forever to get that hatch closed. I knew if I didn't, that very soon there would be a grenade coming through there." The driver and assistant driver quickly closed their hatches."[48]

Bennett's fight on the road back toward Koto-ri was harrowing and nearly fatal. We were receiving quite a bit of fire from the east," he began:

The Battles of Naktong and Pusan

This 1st Marine Division review was held in early summer of 1950. These tanks are a mixture of M4A3s armed with 105mm. howitzers and 75mm. guns, although the 75mm. gun tanks were supposed to have been phased out of service by this time. (Marine Corps)

Above: Tank A-23, commanded by Don Gagnon of 2nd Platoon, A Company and infantry of 2nd Battalion, 5th Marines at the Changwon railway station, August 3, 1950. At this stage of the war, the company did not include the company letter in the tactical marking. Note how the rail car sags under the weight of the tank. *Below*: "Reconnoiter the area and see if there's something down there," ordered G. G. Sweet. The view west from Hill 125 toward Tugok on August 17, 1950. The lower slopes of No-Name Ridge on the left. Tanks from Joe Sleger's section are moving past the village. NKPA tanks later attacked down this road from the west. *NA*

Above: Eugene Viveiros's blade tank pushes the burned hulks of T-34s off the road after the First Battle of the Naktong. The markings are USMC 103247. The number 43 indicates Headquarters Platoon, third tank. Damage to the T-34s is visible as penetrations in the turret side of the far tank, and the blown out machine gun mount on the near tank. *NA*

Left: A close-up of damage to one of the T-34s, perhaps one destroyed by Cecil Fullerton's crew. Two rounds penetrated the slope plate, one caving in the hull machine gunner's position at left. These rounds went completely through the tank, from front to rear. *Marine Corps*

An assortment of NKPA weapons captured by the Marines near the Naktong. The larger gun in the background is a Soviet 45mm. anti-tank gun, the standard weapon of the NKPA anti-tank units. The smaller weapon is a Soviet Maxim 1910 heavy machine gun, an old but effective weapon. (National Archives)

The tankers from Joe Sleger's A-35 brief infantry during the rest and retraining interval between the First and Second Battles of the Naktong. This photo is dated August 23, 1950. The uniforms are clean but old, as indicated by the peculiar "butt pouch" of the limited-issue HBT P1944 (mod) utility trousers visible on the nearest man. (National Archives)

Above: A tank commander confers with other Marines during the Second Battle of the Naktong, while the exhausted loader naps. Note the discarded packing tubes for 90mm. rounds. Both G. G. Sweet and Max English sought to discourage such congregations, as they provided targets of opportunity for the enemy. (National Archives)

Below: The crew of tank A-25 hammers away at the enemy with the heavy turret machine gun at the Second Battle of the Naktong. Moments after this photo was taken, John Cottrell (firing the machine gun), DiNoto (kneeling), and Merl Bennett (standing) were wounded by enemy machine gun fire. (National Archives)

Tank A-34, commanded by Staff Sergeant Cecil Fullerton, enters the village of Katkol, west of Yongsan, during the Second Battle of the Naktong, September 3, 1950. Tanks were at their most vulnerable in populated areas because their freedom of maneuver was severely restricted. (National Archives)

Below: The crewmen of the Able Company VTR, from Prentiss Baughman's Headquarters Platoon, scramble for cover when they come under enemy fire while trying to recover a damaged blade tank. Note that the VTR seems to carry the same number as one of the blade tanks—A43! (National Archives)

The Inchon-Seoul Campaigns

Tank crews from Headquarters Platoon, A Company, unpack and stow ammunition aboard an LCT en route to Inchon. The smaller vehicles are jeeps, trailers, and an M29 Weasel utility vehicle. The middle tank, A-41, would have been Max English's, but was usually used as a spare. *NA*

Above: M4 dozer and flame tanks move off an LCT and onto the beach at Wolmi-do. The M26 in the background is Gerald Swinicke's tank, with Eugene Viveiros's tank in the foreground. Note how the .50 caliber machine gun mounts have been moved forward of the tank commander's hatches. *NA*

Below: Gerald Swinicke's Tank A-33 moves cautiously along the crest of the ridge that formed the spine of Wolmi-do. *NA*

Above: The Inchon-Seoul Road led through a series of small villages. Note the Marines in the ditch along the right side of the road, providing covering fire as other Marines and Lt. William D. Pomeroy's tank A-11 advance along the highway. *NA*

Below: The cuts where roads passed through steep ridges south of Seoul were natural sites for ambushes of the type that disabled Lt. Bryan Cummings's tank. Here, Marines have dispatched a squad to the crest to check out the other side before proceeding. *NA*

Above: Tiny Rhoades's blade tank struggles up the steep northern bank of the Han River. The practice of welding extra track blocks to the side of the hull as extra armor was first used by the 6th Tank Battalion in World War II, but was rare in Korea. *NA*

Below: Eugene Viveiros's dozer tank, disabled by a mine. At some time after the company rejoined the battalion at Inchon the white stars and turret bustle marking were obliterated with dark paint, and the letter "A" was added in front of the "43." Note where the track blocks added for the Inchon landings have been knocked off. *NA*

Above: Several tanks from the 1st Platoon of Company B advance past a breached barricade on the main boulevard through central Seoul. The tank in the front center is B11. Note that the Marines have used the remains of the enemy barricades to establish a protected command post. *Marine Corps*

Left: Lt. Col. Harry Milne in his command tank. The standard stencil on the sand shield— Radio Installed Harnes for SCR-504 AV/TAC 3 OVM Complete—indicates the type of radio and communications capabilities of the tank, and that all Outer Vehicle Maintenance equipment was in place at time of issue. *Marine Corps*

The Chosin Reservoir

The tank-infantry phone allowed infantrymen on the ground to direct tanks from a position of relative safety for both the infantryman and the tank commander. As Vaughn Stuart would learn to his dismay, many infantry officers forgot about it in moments of stress—as they would on several occasions during the terrible Chosin Reservoir fighting. This photo is dated March 7, 1951. (National Archives)

Above: Tanks of the 2nd Platoon, Company B, near the electrical power generating plant at Wonsan in November 1950. North Korea controlled most of the divided nation's heavy industry at that time, and Wonsan was a major port and industrial center. (National Archives)

Below: An M26 of the 2nd Platoon, Company D, with its wading gear still attached waits beside the airfield at Wonsan. The pistol port, which is the small door forward of the tactical numbers, is open for ventilation. Note that the number "22" was carefully applied in white, with the yellow "D" added later. (National Archives)

Above: The roads through the mountains of northeastern Korea were too narrow for heavy vehicles, and the NKPA abandoned many in working order. This T-34/85 and several SU-76 self-propelled guns were found loaded on heavy railway cars. (National Archives)

Below: Men of the Provisional Tank Platoon labor to extricate B-43 from a ditch on the road west of Hagaru, November 27, 1950. The truck waiting for the tanks to clear the road is a Dodge 1-1/2 ton 6x6, leading the last convoy bound for Yudam-ni. *USMC via Jim Mesko*

Above: Tanks of the Army's 31st Regiment Tank Company wait in a blizzard at Hagaru after their parent formation was destroyed east of the Chosin Reservoir. These M4A3 tanks with long-barreled 76mm. guns are frequently misidentified as Marine tanks, but Marine tank units used this model only for training. (See Chapter 7). (National Archives)

Below: A gaggle of tanks waits south of Koto-ri for the signal to move down into the Funchilin Pass. The tank to the left of B-25 is the "Porcupine" communications vehicle, and the vehicles to the right are Army M4A3s with 76mm. guns. (National Archives)

Above: Tanks and infantry of Chesty Puller's 1st Marines wait to move out as the rear guard for the retreat down the Funchilin Pass. The snow thwarted both air support and concealed Chinese infiltrators. (Marine Corps via Milne)

Below: The blown bridge at the valve house in Funchilin Pass, before emplacement of the Treadway bridge. On the left, the mountain drops some 2,000 feet. (National Archives)

and there was a large number of people behind a railroad track, [and] between the railroad track and the road. They were shooting at us, and there was plenty going on up in front of us. I had the gunner, which was [Cpl.] Eugene E. McGuire, lower the tank gun, and fired the first HE. When it's that dark, the sights are no good at all, and we went over the railroad track and hit the hill behind it. The next round I had him come down . . . and the next round hit right on top of the railroad track. We were receiving a lot of fire from the ditch also, so I had him bring the cannon down and we fired two or three more rounds of HE into the ditch.

In the middle of this fierce fighting the unthinkable happened: the gun stopped working. "All at once the loader . . .

was throwing a round into the tube, and it wouldn't go in any further. It wouldn't go all the way in. It just stopped. I tried to get it out, [but] it wasn't pulling back. I even got in behind the breech and tried to kick it in with my boot. A dumb thing to do, but I wanted to get that tank's ninety back in operation. I wasn't gonna get that ninety shell in or out. I happened to look behind, through the prism that went around the cupola, and I could see that the tank behind me—which happened to be B Fifteen, I had B Thirteen—was on fire."

The trailing tank had been hit in the thinly armored rear plate; the pillar of fire he saw was rising from the engine deck.[49] Matters were about to get considerably more tense. The always observant Bennett, with his trademark stub of a cigar clenched between his teeth,

decided that what I should do was to get back there and help them. I had my driver back down the road. I don't know how far they were from me, fifty yards at the most, maybe thirty-five. . . . When we hit the tank, the gunner—he's over there peeking out of the loader's hatch—had the tommy gun in his hand. With the intercom, I was directing the driver back. When we touched the other tank, McGuire jumped up . . . to give some cover to the people (crew of B-15), and he came tumbling back down. He didn't get even waist high. He . . . had taken a round in the arm. The tommy gun fell back inside with him. . . . I asked him, 'Did you see any of them [the stranded tankers]?' He said, 'Yeah, I seen 'em gettin' out of the hatches. . . . They all fell, and they have to be dead.'

For Bennett, every decision was a life and death choice. "I'm setting there and I can see the fire. I call the lieutenant, Gover, and I told the lieutenant I was back with B Fifteen and it was on fire, and I was going to wait two minutes to see if I got any response from them. If not, I would go ahead and pull away." The tanker eyed his watch. "Why I said two minutes, I don't have the vaguest idea. I was sorry I said it. I was sitting there watching my watch, [waiting] for that two minutes to go by."

Just when Bennett started telling his driver to move out, "a voice comes over the intercom and says, 'Bennett, don't move the tank. This is Swearinger.' [Swearinger was tank commander of tank B-15.] My driver heard that too. . . . Swearinger had gotten the tank-infantry phone out of the box and pulled it down underneath the tank. They had gone out of the escape hatch in that tank of theirs, and got under our tank."

Bennett was now faced with an entirely new and vexing situation. "I was concerned that his tank was gonna blow up, gasoline plus ammunition. I asked him how the room was down below. I told my assistant driver to drop the escape hatch. . . . He couldn't make it drop. It was frozen."

While Bennett's trial of nerves continued, the rest of the 1st Platoon, the two Headquarters tanks, and Busch's orphan had continued moving down the road in the direction of Koto-Ri.[50] This larger force was also in trouble. Trapped between the wreckage of Task Force Drysdale and that of his own trucks, Captain Williams drew his tanks up into a tight group. He deployed his surviving men from the trucks, together with such wounded as he could gather, around the tanks and prepared to fight it out through the night.[51]

Bennett, who could see the trucks and four tanks stopped about 300 yards down the road, recalled that "Captain Williams was there, and Lieutenant [William T.] Unger, who was the Executive Officer, the First Sergeant, the Gunny Sergeant. All the Headquarters personnel were in those trucks."

Ben Busch was one of the tankers with Williams's embattled group. "We set up a perimeter there, all that night," he remembered. "The Chinese kept shooting at us and getting in among us. We used the main gun, but it got to the point we couldn't use it any more. . . . I think it was because the blast was screwing up the ground troops. We could have used some canister that night, but we didn't have any. Ninety millimeter didn't have canister in that day and age."

The situation did not take long to deteriorate. "My tank commander, John Murphy, got hit in the stomach," continued Busch. "We evacuated him out of the tank. . . . They set up a medical place under one of the six-by's, and we wrapped all the wounded in blankets and stored them under there. There was a corpsman who was taking care of them." The men set up a thirty-caliber machine gun in the ditch, "something I could never understand," continued Busch. "We were ordered to do that. . . . Some lieutenant jumped up on the tank after Murphy got hit, and told us to do that."

Back up the road, meanwhile, the cool-headed Bennett had made a decision. His own nearly crippled tank, with Swearinger's crew trapped beneath it, was inching its way down the frozen road toward Williams's armored laager. The men below the tank would crawl forward between the tracks until they reached the front of the vehicle. At that point, the driver would slowly pull forward until they were beneath the rear of the tank, and the entire tedious process would be repeated—over and over and all the while under fire.[52]

Bennett knew the effort was at best a stopgap measure, and that eventually he would have to find a way to get the trapped tankers inside his vehicle. The wearisome procedure eventually carried the tank to a spot in the road where the fire was less intense. Sensing the time was right, Bennett ordered the assistant driver to disassemble his seat, and the space was used to repeatedly hurl a full box of machine gun ammunition at the frozen hatch. It took several times, but "finally the escape hatch broke out. Then we took in that crew. . . . It was like sardines in there. I had one man wounded on the floor . . . I had people all over us."

Bennett radioed Gover for permission to enter Williams's main perimeter. To his dismay, his request was denied.[53] "The Chinese were trying to get to the people who had been in the other trucks. I was out there, and every once in a while I would see a Chinese [soldier] standing next to my tank. They hit me with rifle grenades, anti-tank grenades. They'd hit me with something that would rattle the hell out of that tank." The constant onslaught shredded the vehicle's exterior fittings. "I didn't have any cans left the next day. The fifty-caliber was gone. . . . I had procured some cots for us. . . . There were just threads left of them the next day. Every time I could see they were getting up close to the tank, I would call the other tanks and have them fire on me. They would dust me down with thirty caliber fire, and the Chinese would pull back and leave me alone for a while."

Unfortunately, the harrowing ordeal was only just beginning for Bennett and his beleaguered comrades. While doing his best to fend off the determined enemy, he received a radio call from Gover asking if he had rescued all of the crew from B-15. According to Gover, a man outside the perimeter was calling out that he was a Marine tanker. Bennett took a quick headcount inside the crammed and darkened tank and found, to his alarm, that he had only nine men instead of the ten he thought he had picked up. The tenth tanker had given up hope that Bennett would ever get the escape hatch to open, so he "took off running down that road. How he made that two or three hundred yards, I don't know," said Bennett.

One bold Chinese soldier climbed onto the tank, and Bennett spotted him through the vision blocks of the cupola. The man was actually standing on the engine deck, directly in front of the coaxial machine gun. Bennett yelled out instructions for someone to fire the gun, but with seven men jammed inside the turret, no one could reach the controls. The enemy soldier made the best of his own difficult situation. Bennett continued the story:

> He crawled up on top. . . . The first thing he did, he shot out the periscope for the loader. If you've ever seen the periscope, it's just a tin deal with some mirrors . . . nothing that would have stopped a bullet. Then he went over and shot off my two antenna bases. I could no longer get any more help. . . . Radios were piss-poor in those days, but without an antenna, that was the end. Then he saw me watching him through the prisms . . . and I could see that he was gonna get down and shoot out that periscope. I moved that thing [spinning the rotating cupola] on those ball bearings as hard as I could go, and lo and behold he stopped it. I don't know what with, but it about broke my wrist! We had the red lights on inside the tank, and he could see me looking up at him through the prisms. He just held this pistol there at the prism—eight or ten layers of glass on an angle. I watched that pistol go off, the yellow flash, and I thought to myself, 'Oh! I'm dead!'"

In desperation, Bennett instructed the driver to move the tank forward, accelerating and braking in an attempt to dislodge their tormentor. "Mack said to me, 'If I do I'll throw all my fan belts!' I hollered back, 'I don't give a blankety-blank how many fan belts you throw, get this Chinaman off the top of the tank!' He revved her up and shot down the road a ways, and threw the brakes on. That Chinaman went off the top of that turret and landed out there somewhere. We didn't have anyone else crawl up on the tank that night."

The crowded and wounded tank crawled down the road to a position about 150 yards from the main perimeter.[54] The tankers were afraid the Chinese might find the open escape hatch. "Sergeant Swearinger spent the night with his forty-five out, right above that open escape hatch. We really expected that someone would come crawling underneath there. They didn't throw any grenades under there . . . so I guess they didn't know there was a hole there," explained Bennett. "It was hard to judge the time, but "that ambush must have went on until eleven or twelve o'clock."

As Captain Williams's small perimeter battled the attacking Chinese, a radioman contacted Koto-ri and requested spotter rounds from the artillery.[55] "Once he got that spotter round out there, he called in the directions and put some artillery in on where he thought the main body of Chinese were," said tanker Ben Busch. "That helped tremendously, once he got that artillery concentration. They knew then that these people were willing to fight. Luckily we only had one man killed. He was the First Sergeant," Busch continued. "He got it right between the eyes."

All through the night the Chinese continued to launch infantry assaults on the tank unit perimeter. Although the light carbines and grenades proved unreliable in the cold, the tankers managed to fight back with the more reliable M-1 Garand rifles, Thompson submachine guns, and Captain Williams's twelve-gauge shotgun that Chief Warrant Officer William McMillan had procured for him back in California.[56]

Just to the north of Williams's surrounded group, the trapped survivors of Drysdale's column had taken to the meager shelter offered by the ditch and railroad embankment along the right side of the road. Their heaviest weapons were rifles. When the column stopped moving, explained Bob Miller, "the truck I was in didn't get hit or anything—the driver jumped out on one side, I jumped out on another. We got down in the ditches alongside the road.[57] The fighting is right up to the edge of the railway track. The Chinese are jibbering and jabbering and raising Caine."

Len Maffioli, too, was trapped in Hellfire Valley not far from Miller and his other unfortunate comrades, Marines and Army men alike. "There was an Army weapons carrier right behind my truck a little ways that had a 75mm. recoilless rifle mounted on it," he recalled. "There was a mortar right off in the frozen river bottom that was really peppering us, and killing or wounding people all over again right in the ditch. We were dragging our wounded and dead into the ditch."

As all hell was breaking loose, Maffioli remembers that "somebody yelled, 'Hey, on that recoilless rifle! If there's a crew around, my God, get it going!' They had to get up into the truck, as it was mounted on a bipod at the rear of the cab. Several of them got hit right away, but they did get a couple of rounds off, and that particular mortar did not fire again that night. Just about all that Army crew were killed or wounded."

Unfortunately for the trapped men, there were few medical personnel and even fewer supplies to deal with the flood of casualties. "We had only two corpsmen, a navy medical corpsman and a medic that belonged to Baker Company, Thirty-first Regiment," lamented Maffioli. "They used up every bit of medical supplies they had, and they started calling for that little first aid kit that we carried on our cartridge belt. We turned them all in, and they ran out of them pretty quickly, too."

The Dog Company tanks that had broken out ahead of Drysdale's trapped column were also caught in a fire sack. Paul Sanders: "It started getting dark, and God-dang all hell broke loose. My tanks got separated, with trucks trying to go around them and sliding off the side of the road. It was a mess. I tried telling my men, 'Make sure you stay right in the center of that road. Don't go too fast!' In spite of all that, including me, we just slipped off the side of the road. . . . My tank slipped off, and by God I couldn't get it out."

It was about midnight before Sanders was finally able to get out of his tank, make his way to the tank behind him, attach the towing cable, and have the other vehicle pull him out and up on the road. "I put the stuff back, got in, and went down about half a mile and dang! In spite of what the driver was trying to do, [we] went off the side of the road again!" he groused. "I finally got the tank at ninety-degree angles to the road, and that allowed us to get back on. I didn't know where anybody was. I didn't have a map, but it didn't make much difference."

Sanders's tanks struggled northward unaware of the carnage behind them in Hellfire Valley. Sanders eventually received a radio message from 1st Lt. Herbert Barrow Turner, the Reservist Executive Officer of Dog Company tanks. According to Sanders, Turner yelled, "'We're catchin' hell back here, Paul! What's the holdup!' I said, 'I can't tell you, but they're sure catchin' hell up here, too!' That's the last I heard of him before he was captured."

Only 2,200 yards short of the Hagaru-ri perimeter, the head of the column was halted at a blown bridge. A Chinese soldier rushed in and tossed a satchel charge onto the engine gratings of one tank, disabling it. Sanders, too, had a close call. "I had the hatch open, and damned if two gooks didn't walk up behind the tank," he recalled. "They couldn't see me because the engine was throwing out flame and stuff. They were just standing there clear as a bell. I was about ten or fifteen feet away, so I shot 'em both with my pistol. They went down. We finally got [the tanks] back on the road and we headed out for Hagaru. If the gunner saw any green tracers,[58] he'd shoot at 'em. We just got to the roadblocks," he concluded, "and the damn tank ran out of gas!"

At some point in the growing confusion, Drysdale fell wounded. Captain Carl Sitter assumed command of the column and formed the survivors into a hasty perimeter that managed to beat back the worst of the attacks. When the CCF assaults finally slackened, Sitter brought the severed head of his portion of the column into Hagaru-ri at 1915 hours.

Precise casualties in the Drysdale debacle will never be known because no one knows how many men were in the convoy. The shattered column had consisted of about 850 men, Of these, 162 were eventually listed as killed or missing and more than 450 captured; 159 of the wounded were exchanged by the Chinese. The destruction of the column was a disaster not only in terms of losses, but in the realization that Hagaru-ri could not reinforced.

Maffioli and his comrades, meanwhile, remained trapped in Hellfire Valley. "We were surrounded by this noise all night, bugles, whistles, and they said some sort of instrument that sounded almost like a cymbal from an orchestra," he recalled. "They would do this in four directions, to let you know you were surrounded. They just kept coming across the field, and we kept mowing them down. Some of them hardly would take cover. We just kept popping ammo. We had, fortunately, a lot of carbine ammo and rifle ammo with us." Maffioli took note of the weather and surreal surroundings in which he found himself: "It was almost pitch dark. It was snowing, then it quit snowing, but there was not much light except for one of the trucks had caught on fire, and was burning real slow. It never did explode. It just burned all night. That threw an eerie glow out over the frozen river bottom on the west side and that flat land up to the foothills on the east side."

Bob Miller and his other unknown companions fared little better in their ditch. "We used to wear our dungaree hats underneath our helmet. I don't remember now why I had both of them on, but that was the way to work it. It was colder than the dickens, of course." The men, to their intense discomfort, were not in a defensive perimeter, but instead "stretched out along this silly road." The Chinese continued to attack the position all night, and many of the units in the trap did not have the unit integrity to survive. "Bugles blasting all night, harassing, and I'm without a unit. I'm kind of like all by myself all night. I've got people around me, of course, but I don't have a tank platoon with me, you know! It was kind of a nutty position to be in with a forty-five [pistol]. . . . Of course, I wouldn't shoot that unless the guy was standing right in front of me. I wasn't about to be out of ammo, because you don't carry ammo for a forty-five, just a couple of clips. So you don't shoot it just to be shooting."

As if to prove Miller's point, a Chinese soldier threw a concussion grenade into the ditch, and it exploded near Miller's head. "It does make your ears ring. It's just a big, terrible blast." Only his hat saved him from blindness—or worse. "The bill of my cap hit me, because the blast was against the bill of my cap . . . and flattened it against my face. That's what gave me the black eyes, was that thing coming down on my face. Without that, it would have blown both my eyes out, I'm sure."

Following one of the ubiquitous Chinese bugle calls at about 0200, the shooting suddenly stopped. Chinese troops popped up from behind cover, some only a few yards from the ditch full of marines and soldiers. "When this cease-fire was called on their account, they started popping up," remembered a surprised Maffioli. "I remember three of them not fifty yards in front of me, and I could see them in the glow of the fire. . . . I guess it was happening all over. I just threw my carbine on automatic, and started on the left and got all of them with one little burst. They were screaming and moaning out there like 'No fair, cease-fire.' But nobody told us there was a cease-fire, and of course we didn't understand Chinese bugle calls."

The cease-fire ended almost before it began, but in the lull two soldiers and an Associated Press photographer named Frank Noll tried to go for help. They were caught, but thankfully sent back by their captors to explain the cease-fire and arrange a meeting. The formalities were out of a bygone age. Maffioli: "They knew it was getting toward dawn, and they knew our air [support] would come in. They said there would be no quarter. If you don't surrender, then it's all over when we do come in. The senior man by this time was a Marine major[59] who was actually the liaison officer between the First Marine Division and the Army's X Corps. He just happened to be in the convoy, trying to get up to the Division headquarters like everybody else." Maffioli and his comrades made it crystal clear that capitulation was out of the question. "We told the major we're not surrendering. We didn't give a thought—most of us—about Chinese. We thought we were still battling North Koreans. I'm a corporal, and what do I know about who we're fighting? There were rumors of Chinese, but we didn't know they had come in force."

Still, regardless of who he was fighting, Maffioli was convinced the game was over. "We went around shaking hands like, 'Well, this is it, buddy. Goodbye. We'll take as many of them as we can, but it looks like this is it.' We were not surrendering, because the North Koreans—the horror stories of how they treated prisoners—had been well publicized. They did not have a good track record with POWs, particularly Americans."

The Chinese offered to let the wounded return to Marine lines if the others surrendered. It was a terrible choice for the survivors to make. "The thought of surrender is horrible, particularly to a Marine," explained Maffioli, "but we looked at those poor bastards in the ditch. We had by that time a count that showed forty dead and one hundred sixty wounded laying in the ditches. A little over a hundred of us could still stand. Nobody bled to death, unless it was a big wound, because blood froze as soon as it hit the surface. It was that cold. We looked at those poor bastards and said, 'Jeez, if they could get back to our own lines, we'll take a chance.'" The major negotiated surrender terms. The unthinkable had taken place.

"The next thing I know," continued Maffioli, "I'm standing in the middle of the road breaking my carbine, swinging it by the barrel, breaking the stock and bolt, trying to smash it against the bumper of my truck. Somebody taps me on the middle of the back, and I turn around, and there's this old Chinese soldier. The guy must have been in his mid-forties or more. He's about five foot two or three. He had a Thompson sub-machine gun slung over his left shoulder. He sticks his hand out, and I thought he wanted my carbine. I handed it to him and he threw it away. He grabs my hand and shakes it, congratulating me for surrendering. That was their bit."[60]

The captives were herded up onto the rugged, pine-clad slopes where the Chinese had constructed log cabins that had gone completely undetected by the Americans. For Maffioli and so many others, the next six months were marked by night treks over the frozen mountains, little food, and relentless political indoctrination.

After the main group of Task Force Drysdale survivors capitulated, the smaller perimeters around them fell silent one by one as the infantry squads exhausted their ammunition against continuous enemy attacks in the bitter cold. "The Chinese finally broke off maybe around three or four o'clock in the morning," said Ben Busch. "They send up some red, green flares, I can't remember. . . . All of a sudden . . . they were gone."

Of the large groups, only Captain Williams's B Company tank perimeter survived largely intact. Bob Miller was also lucky, and made it back to Koto-ri the next morning.[61] Just as daylight came, B Company's Don Bennett grabbed the tommy gun and crawled out onto the top of the tank. "I didn't realize it 'til after daylight that there was also a hole in the barrel there of that [tommy] gun. . . . I might have killed myself if I'd had to fire it."

With the Chinese gone, they made their way back up the road to the abandoned tank. An anti-tank grenade had damaged the electrical system, so its crew could not turn the engine off when it was abandoned. The Chinese had thrown incendiary charges onto the exhausts. "What I was seeing was the exhausts, the satchel charges, burning. . . . It might have also been some transmission oil being thrown up there also burned. That tank did not burn."

While Bennett was preparing to tow the damaged armor vehicle away, "some British Marines come straggling in, about six of them, maybe seven," he said. "They had a wounded fellow with them. They asked me if I would take their wounded buddy. I said certainly I would, because one of our wounded was put on the back of the tank. . . . We only had two colored Marines in the unit, and it was one of them, Private Wells. . . . I put the British Marine up there by him."

The Royal Marines then asked for ammunition. "They only had one round between the six or seven of them." Bennett gave them a load of grenades and forty-five caliber ammunition for their tommy guns. "They told me they were going back a ways there. They had some wounded buddies, and they were gonna be back in less than an hour." It took Bennett and his crew another two hours to get under way, but "I never saw those British Marines again. Never heard a shot fired, or an explosion, so I don't know what happened to them."

Williams withdrew his battered company into Koto-ri, towing some of his damaged trucks on the rims, while Bennett dragged the disabled tank.[62] After Bennett dropped off his load of wounded, he decided to try and shove free the round that had jammed in his main tank gun during the early stages of the fight in Hellfire Valley. "We started out with just about four men on the rammer staff. I was inside to catch it when they knocked it loose." Eventually twenty Marines were trying to push the round out of the chamber.[63] When it popped out . . . I got the round. After we got it out of there, we looked at it, and one if not two rounds of [small arms] ammo had gone into the HE fuse. At least two, maybe three more rounds had lodged in that projectile, in the tube, and kept us from putting it in any farther." The impact of what he was witnessing was not lost on Bennett. "If my loader hadn't been real fast, we'd have had a half a dozen slugs running around inside [inside the turret]."

Bennett gingerly carried the damaged cannon shell away and dumped it into a stream. He later heard that the Chinese had been taught to fire down the gun tube of a tank immediately after it fired, in an effort to get rounds inside the turret while the breech was open.[64] If that was the case, "He wasn't fast enough, and I was lucky," he concluded. He was right on both counts.

Among those caught in the destruction of Task Force Drysdale were several senior officers of the tank battalion, as well as tank crewmen being sent up to Hagaru as replacements. Captain Lester Chase, now the Battalion Operations Officer, and 1st Lieutenant Herbert Barrow Turner, the Executive Officer of D Company, were both missing. "[Chase] was riding in a jeep along with them, and they just ran into all sorts of stuff," remembered Vaughn Stuart. "It was after my patrols. They knew that there were people there. . . ." Ben Busch's best friend, Ted Overshaw, was killed in the Hellfire ambush.[65]

Paul Sanders reached the relative safety of Hagaru, and "the next day they put my tanks on the road that led [northwest] to Yudam-ni. It was in support of the First Battalion, First Marines, I think. I had a buddy in there who was the battalion S-One, Danny Evans. His tent used to be about seventy-five yards from where our tanks were, so I could go over and get some hot coffee. . . ."

General Oliver Smith was still eager to reinforce the critical position at the crest of the Toktong Pass, the high ground separating Hagaru and Yudam-ni. "They asked me if I thought I could get up the road to get to Fox Company," continued Sanders. "I tried, and hell, there's no way I could get up there. . . . Just bump the side of the hill and hope you don't slide over [a cliff]. Trying to do that in the dark—it would have been undoable."

Sanders thought that they might have gotten up the pass had they been able to ground-guide the tank, as had been done with D-23.[66] With the Chinese holding the road, however, the attempt would have been suicidal.

"We've been looking for the enemy for several days now. We've finally found them. We're surrounded. That simplifies our problem of getting to these people and killing them."

— Brigadier General Lewis B. Puller

Chapter Five

Deliverance
The Chosin Reservoir Campaign—Breakout

The defeat and destruction of Task Force Drysdale effectively ended the Allied effort to seriously reinforce the trapped forces fighting around Hagaru. The inability to break through and open a route of retreat left the bulk of the 1st Marine Division isolated on the far side of the Toktong Pass on the west side of the Chosin Reservoir. There was only one viable option left: the units trapped there to fight their way out.

Unless one has been in combat or perhaps struggled to survive outdoors in an arctic environment, it is impossible to fully comprehend the daunting task that faced the embattled division. Under the best of conditions, moving a single-file column of thousands of vehicles and marching men along a narrow mountain road required prodigious feats of organization. The tail units of such a column, for example, would have to wait nearly two days and nights before its time to march would arrive. Worse still was that once it started to move the column could not stop, for fear it would become snarled in the stop-and-go pattern that helped lead to the destruction of Task Force Drysdale. Moving such a column down an icy mountain road in sub-zero windy and snowy conditions, all the while under constant enemy attack and often in pitch darkness, therefore, was nearly impossible. And yet, that is exactly what the division had to accomplish in order to survive. Such a feets would require an heroic effort from every man, from Oliver Smith to the lowest private.

While the Marines prepared to fight their way out of the trap at Yudam-ni, and while Task Force Drysdale fought its final desperate battle, a handful of Marines were inserted deeper into the trap set by the Communist forces. At the request of Colonel Litzenburg of the 7th Marines, Staff Sergeant Russell A. Munsell and a pickup crew belonging to the Executive Officer's tank from Captain "Roughhouse" Taylor's C Company, were flown into Yudam-ni to take over the tank that had required so much effort to bring in just days before.[1]

"Our tank was Charlie Forty-two," remembered Michael O'Sullivan, who was one of those men tasked with the job. "Paul Curtis, I guess, offered us. He said, 'You can take my crew.' There were Rusty [Dexter R.] Ayers, Russ Munsell was the tank commander, Gene Flannery, myself, and a Reservist, Bob Figaroa. They flew us in at night because the gooks were taking shots at everything in that area, up at Yudam-ni."

Helicopters were relatively new to the battlefield, and O'Sullivan recalls that the ride was "kinda scary. . . . It vibrates like a crazy man—shake, rattle and roll. You look out and you see there's no wings out there and you think, 'Hey, wait a minute. This ain't right.' They were shooting at the helicopters. That's why the pilots weren't too happy about that kind of flight."

The last thing O'Sullivan remembers of the flight was the pilot's order just before the helicopter touched down: "'Get the hell out!'"

Once the men were on the ground, they located Colonel Litzenburg and were told where to find the abandoned tank. It was sitting "in the middle of the compound," said O'Sullivan, "and the batteries were dead! We tried jumping it off from a six-by, but the battery of a six-by is only twelve volts, and you need at least twenty-four to get these monsters going."

Russ Munsell later told Marine Corps combat correspondents that "within 45 minutes after we radioed for parts for the tank (new batteries and fan belts, mainly), they arrived by helicopter from Hagaru."[2]

The men were not out of the woods by a long shot. O'Sullivan: "We changed batteries under fire, and once we got the tank started, we were pulling roadblock duty up at the north end of the town of Yudam-ni with some elements of the 7th Marines. I guess maybe they thought we still were gonna go north. I don't know. I was just a little ol' PFC, doing what I was told to do."

The decision to extricate tank D-23 was a tiny part of a much bigger and far more controversial decision. At a command meeting on November 30 at the division CP in Hagaru-ri, Lieutenant General Almond urged Oliver Smith to destroy all his heavy equipment. Smith refused, arguing that his primary responsibility was to bring out his wounded and to preserve his division as a fighting force. The record of an interview with one of the participants, Col. Alpha Bowser, the Operations Officer of the 1st Marine Division, indicates the meeting was acrimonious.[3] The decision to bring out the heavy equipment ignited a controversy that still simmers today. Some partisans claim the Marines scavenged Army equipment and brought it out at the cost of Marine lives, but Smith's decision to preserve the division's cohesion proved critical to its survival.[4]

Harry Milne appreciated the problem his division commander faced: "[Smith] had to [bring out the equipment] to make it work. . . . You've got to have a cohesive unit. It was well planned. The execution wasn't perfect, but it was sure well-planned, and that's how we made out as good as we did."

By 0100 hours on December 1, most of the service troops inside the embattled perimeter had been committed to the lines. Strong enemy attacks throughout the night consumed most of the CCF's *58* and *59 Divisions*. Dawn counterattacks by the Marines negated most of the gains made by the Chinese.

As bad as it was at Hagaru, the most heartbreaking problem for the Americans was the drama playing out east of the Chosin Reservoir, where three Army battalions and supporting units were trapped and fighting for their existence. A massive pre-dawn artillery barrage triggered the beginning of their Calvary. Vaughn Stuart and others on November 28 heard the distant thunder, knowing it rained down upon their comrades. The Army regiment was soon immobilized, burdened with more than 500 wounded. Steady enemy pressure snapped the regiment into two large perimeters, though both managed to hold out against two days of brutal attacks. During an attempt to consolidate his position, the regiment's commander, Col. Allan D. (Mac) MacLean was shot and killed on November 29. The remnants were reorganized as Task Force Faith under the command of Lt. Col. Don C. Faith. The three companies of Marines, themselves staked in place by the incessant CCF attacks against the key road junction at Hagaru-ri, were unable to offer any help.

Faith extricated his men early on December 1 by uniting the battalions and conducting a fighting withdrawal along the road leading south toward Hudong-Ni. Low on ammunition and bombed by their own planes, the soldiers continued their bloody trek, with trucks carrying those too badly wounded to walk. Faith demonstrated extraordinary leadership during the retreat and was himself struck down by a grenade. He died in great pain lying in the back of a freezing truck. (Faith was posthumously awarded the Medal of Honor.) Major Robert E. Jones assumed command, but it was too late to accomplish much of anything. The column largely disintegrated into a holocaust of death. The wounded were killed inside the trucks by gleeful Chinese, who trotted along the stranded vehicles and tossed grenades inside. Equipment was scattered and abandoned, and pockets of men ran, walked, and crawled toward the Marine perimeter at Hagaru. The first batch of survivors reached the lines there about 2200 on December 1, spreading word of the annihilation of the army regiment. The next day, Marine patrols made their way up the eastern road and onto the ice of the frozen reservoir in order to bring in the wounded and frostbitten.

Paul Sanders's tanks provided cover for rescue operations. He reported to the officer in charge, Lt. Col. Olin Beall of the 1st Motor Transport Battalion: "I walked up to him and saluted, and I said, 'Do you remember me?' He looked at me and said, 'You used to mow my yard.'" Sanders had returned to the United States from Guadalcanal eight years earlier suffering from chronic malaria. Captain Beall had watched over the young sick enlisted man and kept the cash from his accumulated combat pay in his personal safe.[5]

"I got my tanks out as far as I dared to go, and covered [Beall and his men] with guns and machine guns," explained Sanders. "I don't think we did much shooting, 'cause for some reason the Chinese weren't shooting, except for every once in a while they made up their mind to shoot at 'em."

Vaughn Stuart reported that an Army tank company arrived and set up positions alongside his own tanks.[6] To Stuart, the soldiers appeared completely demoralized and did little to help rescue their comrades.[7]

Of the 2,500 soldiers caught in the debacle east of the reservoir, only 385 survivors were fit to take up arms in the defense of Hagaru. Paul Sanders: "They took all the able bodied soldiers, and if they could walk and carry a rifle, they were put in the front lines." Another 665 were later evacuated.

Unfortunately, the battering absorbed by the survivors of the fighting east of the reservoir rendered most of the men unfit for practical duty. A few nights after their arrival, Sanders was sitting with his friend Danny Evans. "It was about midnight or one in the morning when some old Gunnery Sergeant came in . . . and he was crying. He was a great big guy, bearded, dirty. . .."

"Sergeant, how come you're crying?" asked Evans.

"You remember them soldiers you gave me to put in line?" asked the Sergeant. "Well, I took 'em up in the area and put 'em on line. There was a sergeant there, so I put him in charge, and I told him who was on his left, and took him over there, and who was on his right and took him over there. Told him his area of fire and so forth.

"I said, 'Got any questions?' and he said, 'Yeah. Where's the bug out route?'

"What did you tell him," Evans asked.

"I told him, 'We got no bug out route! This is where it is.' His response was, 'What'll we do if they attack?' I told him, 'You'll fight, you son-of-a-bitch! That's what you're paid for!'"

At that, remembered Sanders, "Danny and I fell off our chairs laughing, because here's this old grungy, scroungy Gunnery Sergeant crying, and you could see what it was for. He was frustrated. . . ."

Some of the frustration was smoothed over with hot food, a rare commodity in Korea during the winter months. The Marine infantry, recalled Sanders, would sometimes take advantage of the nearby tanks to improve their living conditions: "There's a little deflector behind the exhaust, just wide enough to hold several cans of food. A guy would come up and say, 'Hey tanker! Start her up.' We'd start her up, and throw their food in there. In about three minutes it was red-hot. We were quite popular."

Frustration and cold food notwithstanding, the Marines were still trapped west (at Yudam-ni) and south (at Hagaru) of the reservoir, and finding a way to safety was on everyone's mind. Vaughn Stuart remembers reconnoitering the road south out of Hagaru. His orders were simple, but the experience would remain with him forever: "They told me to take three tanks and go down the road until you come in contact with the enemy." After leaving the relative safety of the Hagaru perimeter, Stuart, who "had a habit of standing about waist high out of the tank commander's hatch," carefully scanned the embankments running along the road. "The Chinese had carved in under the sod at the top of the bank, a place they could individually hide in," he explained. "The first one I saw, I got on the phone and was gonna alert my tank crews that the Chinese were all around, and to watch what they were doing. About that time something hit on the front of my tank and burst. It just filled my face—it felt like a handful of gravel had been slammed into my face. There was so much blood I couldn't see anything. Everybody got their hatches closed but me." The road at that point was bounded by a deep ditch on one side and a steep bank on the other, and was thus too narrow for the tanks to turn around.[8] "I remembered that there was a place just down the road that was open, where we could get into. I had my tanks move toward that. I still couldn't see anything."

Stuart and his men had motored just a short distance when "it felt like the tank had been knocked about halfway around. It was really confusing me. We got it straightened out, and got on down the road. I still couldn't get my tank hatch closed, because you could hear the bullets hitting up on top of it. We sort of got the wagons circled, so to speak, and I got the blood kind of cleared out of my eyes. There were Chinese all over the place. You could have shot anything, a pistol even, and hit a Chinese. They were just all over."

Stuart later wrote that:

> About that time I got a heavy blow in my left shoulder. An anti-tank rifle grenade had come in through my open hatch, hit me in the shoulder, and dropped onto the tank deck and didn't explode. You can imagine what that would have done if it had exploded. My driver just looked at me quizzically, and threw it out.

The Chinese didn't seem to be too much afraid of the tanks. They simply did not exhibit any fear of tanks, but we were firing everything we had, eventually thinning them out enough to have made the foray worthwhile in the first place. They followed us closely, keeping up a steady fire until we reentered the perimeter defensive positions.[9]

Once in a safer environment, Stuart asked the commander of the tank behind him why the tank was jarred sideways during the time he was blinded with blood in his eyes. The answer, he remembers, was unsettling: "He said that before he could get his gun around and get ready, a Chinese soldier got out if the ditch with a satchel charge. It's like a broom-handle with a big ball of stuff on the end of it.[10] He threw it. The idea is to swing and knock the wheels out from under the tank. He missed, and got the sponson up over the wheels. He said it knocked that tank a quarter of a turn around. I tell people I'd be down there pushing the daisies up, or whatever flowers there are now, if he had hit those tracks."

Still bleeding badly, Stuart walked to the Navy field hospital, set up in the village school building. It was a disturbing sight:

> The place was so filled with wounded that I had to step over prone bodies just to get inside, and the doctors were slipping around on the bloody floors. I talked to a few of the wounded, and most of these were from Captain Barber's rifle company defending a mountain pass between us and Yudam-ni. Even though I was still dripping blood from my chin, when I saw such severely wounded Marines, I got a little ashamed to be there, but as I was leaving, a corpsman pulled me into a side room, cleaned up my face, and dug out the larger pieces of metal. He assured me that my eyes were not seriously damaged.[11]

On December 1, Harry Milne paid a surprise visit to Hagaru to assess the situation and determine whether tanks could be sent over the Toktong Pass north to Yudam-ni.[12] He joined his forward units at Hagaru, where the Provisional Tank Platoon was deployed east of the village. "I had been up there a while, so we had warming tents and stuff," explained Stuart. "The Chinese weren't active during the daytime. All of a sudden one day Colonel Milne walked in. One of the other platoon leaders—I was still a second lieutenant, I wasn't too pushy with colonels—said, 'What in the hell are you doing here?'"

"Well," answered the colonel, "I just thought I'd come up here and go down the hill with you guys."

"I had two tank companies up there," explained Milne, "and I wanted somebody to take command. That's me. So I talked the division into flying me up, and they said 'If you come up, you're not gonna fly back.' They had a little OY.[13] It took me up and landed at the airstrip at Hagaru. Looking down, it looked as peaceful as a walk in the park. Couldn't see anybody. I had been up there two or three days before, and tried to get the M4s up to Yudam-ni."

The colonel's actions impressed Stuart. "Milne wasn't sure whether we were gonna get out of there, but he sure came up to be with us."

The Provisional Tank Platoon, assigned to defend the critical artillery positions at Hagaru,[14] was ordered to conduct yet another reconnaissance of the road south of the perimeter. Vaughn Stuart, complete with an aching chin and scarred face, joined the effort: "We went out on a short patrol one day, out of Hagaru. We knew the Chinese were there. They had already blocked the road, and nobody could get through that road, at least by jeep or anything. They sent me to support a rifle platoon . . . to go as far toward Koto-ri as we could.

The column made it about three miles down the road and then "ran into all kind of Chinese." During the "severe firefight," Stuart observed that the Chinese seemed to pay little attention to his tanks, even when he fired at them.[15] "An observation plane, one of those little OEs [sic], dropped us a message, and said there are three hundred Chinese trying to get around behind us and cut us off from getting back into Hagaru. The infantry had already taken some casualties, and it was pretty obvious we weren't going to be able to go any further. I just put the tanks in between the infantry and the Chinese, and we broke contact and went on back to the perimeter."

On December 1, the same day Colonel Milne flew into Hagaru, and the Army survivors from Task Force Faith stumbled into the Hagaru perimeter, General Smith's effort to break out was launched. Like some great deadly inch-worm, the two rifle regiments at Yudam-ni contracted themselves into a tighter perimeter and struck out south under a heavy fire for the Toktong Pass. After the last stocks of ammunition was fired from the big 155mm. howitzers of 4/11, their personnel formed into provisional rifle platoons and joined the retreat. The howitzers and tractors brought up the rear to avoid blocking the road if they were wrecked. Captain William Barber's F/2/7 was ordered to hold the crest, the most critical position along the evacuation route. His isolated company, however was bleeding away under relentless Chinese attacks launched through a howling blizzard. A stripped-down rifle battalion, 1/7, was sent on a harrowing cross-country march to aid Barber's Fox Company.

Tank D-23 led the attack/breakout, supporting a platoon from H/3/5 and a platoon of engineers. "They moved us to the head of the column, and they had a D-Eight, a big engineering company tractor, right behind us," remembered O'Sullivan. "In the event anything happened to the tank, this thing was supposed to shove us off the road and keep the road open. That was the way it went."

While CCF forces pressed relentlessly against the rearguard, individual enemy soldiers eased their way into the road from along its sides and infiltrated the Marine column. By this time the temperature had fallen to minus 25 degrees Fahrenheit (-31 degrees Celsius), and falling snow limited visibility. Coupled with howling winds, these appalling conditions sucked the life from men on both sides. It was easier to just lie down and die than to go on living, and the officers and NCOs had to drive the men relentlessly to keep them on their feet and alive.

The Chinese were not about to let such a large prize slip through their fingers without a fight. They contested every yard of road up to the crest of the pass. American infantry marked targets by climbing onto tanks and firing roof-mounted machine guns. O'Sullivan: "We fired sixty-eight rounds of ninety, thirty thousand rounds of and fifty and thirty caliber, mixed."

In an effort to stop the American withdrawal, the Chinese had constructed fifty-three separate roadblocks along the grade leading up to the crest of Toktong Pass. "We'd fire a ninety at it, and then go over and mutilate whatever the hell was left," was how O'Sullivan explained their efforts to breach the roadblocks. "Sandbags, trees, rocks. . . . I don't think the little Chinamen initially realized the power of a tank. . . . They thought if they put a couple of big rocks on the road the tank would stop, and somebody would have to get out and move 'em. They'd set up periphery fire all around it."

Breaking through was much more difficult than O'Sullivan described it. At one point he was overcome by the fumes from the 90mm. gun, so Russell Munsell put him outside and shanghaied another loader from the infantry. When O'Sullivan recovered his senses, he ran alongside the tank until he was able to get aboard, open a hatch, and summarily evict his replacement.[16]

The merciless cold spared neither man nor machine. O'Sullivan continued: "The heater didn't work. The Little Joe, the auxiliary engine that you used to keep the batteries charged up, that gas line was so small that it froze. We had to keep the tank running. Twenty-four hours a day for three solid days, coming eighteen miles . . . from Yudam-ni to Hagaru."

The routine maintenance required to keep the tank running was a nightmare. "Everything you touched was cold as all hell. . . . If you went to tighten the end connectors on the tracks, you had to be really careful . . . because you'd snap them right off. . . . The guys in the jeeps were breaking their springs, and stuff like that, because everything was frozen so hard. It was really crazy." Even firing the main gun required special care and patience. "Every time we fired a ninety round, we had to wait for [the gun] to go back into battery, because the hydraulic oil and everything in the recoil mechanism had turned like molasses. The only thing that fired consistently was the thirty caliber and the fifty caliber machine guns, because they were gas operated."

Logistical orphans, the tankers had to scrounge for fuel. "Bob Figaroa and I got out, and we'd go back up into the infantry areas, and if a jeep had a five-gallon can of gas on the back end of it, it was ours," mused O'Sullivan. "We was robbing gas like bandits." Food was even more scarce than gas. "We didn't have any food. Tootsie Rolls and Charms [candy]. The greatest thing was the Tootsie Rolls, because you could put them in your mouth and let them slowly melt. We used to get the five-pack of C-rations, and everybody would look for the jellies and jams, stuff like that. The cans of meat and vegetables were frozen. . . . It was like concrete. We lived for nearly a week and a half on Tootsie Rolls and Charms."

Although the distance was short, the fight was long and bitter, and it was not until December 3 that the column was able to link up with 1/7 coming down from the crest of the pass. The forces guarding the pass fell in behind the lone tank for the downhill run to Hagaru-ri.

O'Sullivan remembers the difficulties he and his comrades faced during their drive for Hagaru: "Our driver originally was Rusty Ayers, and our co-driver was Bob Figaroa. I was the loader. . . . When we came into the Toktong Pass area, Rusty picks up some shrapnel off the slope plate, into his face, and he couldn't drive any more. We were getting peppered a lot with small arms fire, constantly, and Rusty had the hatch open so he could see the road better. Evidently some flakes came off the front slope plate and hit him in the head." Because Figaroa, as a Reservist, had never driven a tank, O'Sullivan suddenly found himself acting as the driver. The wounded Ayers took over as the co-driver, and Figaroa assumed the task of loader.

The crew of D-23 was bloodied, freezing, starving, and faced sudden death with each passing moment. O'Sullivan remarked on the sheer exhaustion that engulfed everyone involved: "We couldn't sleep because you couldn't shut the tank off. You didn't want to race the engine. . . . I slid off the road twice. We got it out on its own power. Very carefully, because on one side of the road there was like a three thousand foot drop. Very gingerly."

Although Munsell confirmed O'Sullvan's recollection, he noted that the situation was somewhat more precarious than his buddy let on:

> At one point the Chinese were rolling grenades down a hillside into the road, and we backed the tank to take them under fire.
> That was when we ended up with one track hanging off the road, in thin air over a cliff—firing up the hillside at the Chinks and hoping the tank wouldn't slip and plunge into the valley below. We tried several times afterwards to pull her back on the road, but it was a no-go. We were about to abandon the tank, but we gave it one more try—and she pulled back onto the road.[17]

Royal Marines and a platoon of tanks assisted the breakout by attacking north from Hagaru to help clear the way, and at 1900 hours on December 3, the head of the column reached the relative safety of the Hagaru perimeter. "Just before we reached Hagaru, there was a tank burning on the side of the road,"[18] remembered O'Sullivan. "That got our attention real quick. It was sitting up on the side of a hill, in flames. We thought, 'Oh, Jesus. Now we're really in for it. They've got something big enough that it's gonna take us out.' That brought us all back to life real quick."

The small but important victory of just reaching Hagaru was an emotional event for everyone involved. Paul Sanders stated forthrightly that he "sat there and cried" while watching the head of the column enter Hagaru. "Some of the first ones came in were guys I knew. As they came down off the hill and got on level ground, suddenly they all started marching in rhythm. The damnedest thing. You could see 'em throwing their shoulders back. No one was counting cadence, but that's one of the grandest marches I ever saw. It was something that will stick in memory. It was just what the Marines were all about."

A long thin column still stretched back up across the mountains, however, and the convoy inevitably fell victim to a stop-and-go pattern, a slow, lurching, and fatiguing movement. The CCF took advantage of this inch-worm style motion and pressed in for the kill. The artillerymen at the tail of the column proved particularly vulnerable. Many of those able to enter Hagaru the next day did so without several of the big howitzers, which had to be abandoned when their tow tractors ran out of fuel or were lost to enemy fire.

O'Sullivan was greeted in Hagaru by the original crew of D-23, who demanded that the tank be returned to them. "We said, 'Up yours, Benny. We got it this far, we're goin' all the way with it.'" The exhausted crew was given Lt. Colonel Milne's tent for the night, and O'Sullivan got the colonel's own sleeping bag. Milne had a staff officer prepare a hot meal for the men.[19]

As wonderful as it was for the men to reach Hagaru, the battle to escape was only half won. While O'Sullivan and his comrades were fighting their way south, the men trapped in the Hagaru perimeter were enduring a bitter siege, and the entire MSR (Main Supply Route) was under assault by the Chinese. A few miles south at Koto-ri, one platoon of B Company was ordered to move south down the road toward Hamhung and engage enemy forces firing upon traffic below the town.[20] While General Smith was planning and then launching his breakout from Yudam-ni, other units were moving north along the MSR—deeper into the enemy trap.

On December 2, Max English was reassigned as the battalion Operations Officer.[21] "The S-Three [Captain Chase] had gotten killed, and the Old Man, Colonel Milne, decided that he needed another [Three]. I told him he didn't need me," said English. After a brief argument, which Milne of course won, English headed north.[22] Traffic clogged the few sections of the icy MSR still open to traffic. "My jeep couldn't move, and I would walk through a valley," recalled English. "I know that laying and waiting out there and looking at me were hundreds of Chinese. It just amazes me, the fact that I was able to walk through there, and climb up that hill again, why somebody didn't reach out and trip me, or knock me in the head or something. They were waiting until a certain time. They hit us right after that, the next day. They came out of all those valleys."

Although the reports emanating from Korea had darkened the mood in America, optimism prevailed in Hagaru.[23] The Marine division was nearly whole again and on the attack. Aircraft evacuated 4,312 casualties from Hagaru, and replacements and ammunition were flown in.[24] With the units from Yudam-ni now safe within the fold, Smith was confident he could salvage his division. He decided to rest and reorganize his command before striking out for the final push to the sea, and simultaneously stabilize the Hagaru position as a base—despite the time this would give the CCF for further preparation. In addition to the three enemy divisions mauled at Yudam-ni, intelligence had now identified the CCF *58, 60, 76*, and *80 Divisions*, and possibly the *77* and *78 Divisions*, all of which were surrounding the Marines.

The most critical point along Smith's route of escape would be just south of Koto-ri, below the valve house in Funchilin Pass, where the road crossed over a concrete bridge. The valve house was perched on a narrow shelf cut into a cliff. The road passed over a concrete shelf hanging out over huge pipes, called penstocks, which dropped off 2,000 feet to the generator houses on the Chagjin River. The Chinese had captured the concrete span on two occasions, only to be driven off by Allied counterattacks. On December 4, General Smith received the disturbing news that the Chinese had again attacked the bridge, but this time had blown a sixteen-foot gap in the span.

Despite the bad news, Don Bennett remained confident that he and his buddies would make good their escape. "Seems like we never had any doubts that we were gonna get out somehow. I don't know why we were so confident as young kids." Jim Edwards recalls thinking, "'I'm not gonna worry about getting shot. What I'm gonna worry about is freezing to death.' In looking back at it," he added, "we really didn't have it half as bad . . . as those poor infantry guys outside there."

Of the several key points of attack, explained Ben Busch, the CCF made its major effort against Hagaru: "Soon as the sun went down, seems like they started harassing us. But they really didn't carry out a big-scale attack at Koto-ri, like they did on Hagaru."

Other units helped hold open the MSR. Mike Wiggins was one of those tasked with guarding the primary road. "We guarded the main route, going and coming. Roadblocks and what have you, from Hamhung and Hungnam on up," he explained. "We were on roadblocks, and you'd send out patrols from your position. You'd send out a section of tanks with a couple of squads of infantry." When they were attacked by groups of the enemy, Wiggins added, the Allies were "blessed to have artillery fire. If you couldn't reach 'em by direct fire, you could always call in artillery."

Able Company was assigned to support Army units defending the MSR on the low ground below the plateau. Despite the efforts of the Marines and Army troops, the persistent Chinese achieved minor tactical victories all along the MSR—including the destruction of a bridge near A Company's position at Majon-dong on December 3.[25] Harry Smith remembers when "word came that the Chinese were gonna blow up the bridges at midnight. They brought in a battalion of Army anti-aircraft. . . . Captain English went down and wanted to coordinate with them. He volunteered to put a couple of tanks up there with some infantry. They said, 'No, we're gonna cover the bridge by fire. That's what we did in Europe.' Right at midnight, Poom! The bridge went up. You could have walked on the tracers and what have you that were going on down below us."

The Chinese directed one attack after another against the Hagaru perimeter. Through December 5 a critical sector lay along the eastern side, where the Chinese had captured the dominating East Hill mass. Repeated American efforts to recapture the heights were thrown back. Vaughn Stuart remembers one enemy effort: "We had some tents set up across the road from that hill mass. The Chinese tried one night to come in through there, but it was kind of a halfhearted attempt, and they didn't get through. We had at least three tanks on the road that night, plus a lot of logistics folks who came out into the lines at night with rifles and machine guns. . . ."

While the Allies were throwing back the Chinese attacks, General Smith and his subordinate officers were planning their breakout. On December 4, the D Company tanks at Hagaru destroyed the eight howitzers that had been abandoned outside the perimeter.[26] D-45, a damaged M26 tank, was destroyed because it could not be repaired in time.[27] Just maintaining undamaged tanks was nightmare. When damaged radiators leaked irreplaceable anti-freeze, maintenance crews were forced to substitute a mixture of diesel fuel and gasoline. Ice clogged the cloth diaphragms in the fuel pumps, which were replaced with new ones cut from rubberized poncho cloth.[28] The problems seemed endless.

The escape effort was formally launched about 0900 on December 6, when a mixed force of Army and Marine units attacked CCF positions on East Hill. The Chinese defense collapsed and within two hours Americans controlled the hill mass overlooking the withdrawal route. Moving almost an entire division out of an embattled perimeter and down a single lane road while under attack, however, was a difficult proposition. The plan was for the Marines to hold the door of the escape route open while miles of slow-moving vehicles and marching men flowed down the narrow road. General Smith armed the column with a small armored spearhead, but most of its length consisted of two Division Trains of trucks and non-combat vehicles.

Because of his experience with moving heavy vehicles and in his capacity as Division Tank Officer, Lieutenant Colonel Milne was placed in charge of Division Train Two. This amalgam, he explained, included, "[An] Army engineer company, whatever other service people [who weren't] in Train One. They just filled it up with a mishmash of everything. The main body was the Army engineer company that had gotten as far as Hagaru. . . . I guess I didn't thank 'em, but I was there, anyway."

Gus Banks, the commanding officer of the Division Service Battalion, was in charge of Train One.[29] "He started out with the 7th Marines," recalled Milne. "Train Two was behind that, [and] behind us was the 5th Marine Regiment. What tanks we had at Hagaru were in support of the 7th Marines."

The difficulties of coordinating the movement of some 20,000 men and thousands of vehicles down a single-lane road in the Siberian-cold winter cannot be overestimated. Milne recalls talking "with them all. I called all the senior officers of each unit that were supposed to be in it. Of course some of them were just partial platoons, cooks and bakers, and you know. We had a plan, and said, 'This is where you're gonna be in the column,' and so forth." There were no Military Police or other coordinating units. "They were just happy to be together, to get the hell out of there."

At 0630 on December 6, the head of the column, led by the 2nd Platoon of D Company tanks and 2/7, moved out onto the road. The infantry's losses had been filled with jobless artillerymen from the 11th Marines. Progress was slow and deliberate, the pace controlled by the men moving on foot in the bitter cold, and by constant CCF roadblocks. The Chinese allowed the leading companies to pass unmolested, then opened fire on the units that followed. At the first roadblock, three rounds from a captured 3.5-inch rocket launcher disabled a tank. The glacial pace slowed even further. The second roadblock, only about 4,000 yards south of Hagaru, was not cleared until nearly 1500 hours. Under constant enemy attack, the column crept slowly onward through the night.

The infantry, supported by tank fire from the roadway, struggled to push the Chinese off the ridges to the left of the road. At each roadblock enemy fire drove men into the ditches for cover, which resulted in numerous halts that backed the column up for miles. Long-range machine gun fire raked the column, striking men in the trucks as well as those riding on the rear decks of the tanks. Many of wounded who had been placed on the engine decks for warmth received additional wounds or were killed by this fire.[30]

It was at one of these road blocks that Paul Sanders found it impossible to traverse his main gun. When he inquired what was causing it, someone on the tank-infantry phone informed him that a corpse had jammed the turret.[31]

The beleaguered column wended its way through Hellfire Valley and the wreckage of Task Force Drysdale until, at 2200 hours, an expertly sited enemy machine gun on a hillside raked the road with a deadly fire that completely halted the column for two precious hours. It was not until midnight that an Army tank finally managed to lay a round directly on the enemy position, and the division resumed its halting progress. The lead elements of 2/7 entered Koto-ri after midnight.

By this time it had become painfully obvious to the Chinese that if they did not cut off and capture or destroy the column soon, the entire prize might slip through their grasp. At 0200 on December 7, the most ferocious attacks of the entire campaign were launched against Hagaru in an attempt to overwhelm the position. The primary attack was concentrated against the north flank of the perimeter. Wave after wave of Chinese rushed the defenses, only to fall in heaps before the guns of the defenders.

Rounds flew thick and fast in every direction. One vehicle of the Provisional Tank Platoon was hit in the engine by an armor-piercing projectile that badly damaged the radiators. A pair of Army tanks from the 31st Regiment Tank Company were assigned to this small formation,[32] which made up the rear guard.[33] Vaughn Stuart wrote vividly of the horrendous action that took place that night:

> During the intense part of the fighting, one of the Army tanks suddenly started up, and with considerable haste, made for the area where my maintenance section with my hospital corpsman was ensconced. When the tank left the lines, I ran right behind it, ready to shoot the Tank Commander when I caught up with him, but the Chinese had already done that, so I had my corpsman get him to the battalion aid station while I found a Marine Corporal to put in command of the Army tank. This [guy], Corporal Einar A. Anderson, took the tank back into position and fired mostly white phosphorus rounds the rest of the night, literally frying the Chinese that came at the tank. To get to the tank the next morning, I was compelled to walk on their charred and frozen bodies.
>
> After daylight, I walked the perimeter and talked to each of my tank crews. There were dead bodies all over the place. I thought this was normal to all skirmishes, but later it became manifest to me that it took considerable effort to kill men, and from that point on, I had an even more profound respect for the tenacity of Marines.[34]

At about 0200 hours, the Chinese rushed the road in Hellfire Valley and broke into Division Train One. Item Company of 3/7 and a platoon of tanks were dispatched back north, into Hellfire Valley, and at 1100 hours 1/7 was sent back to secure the MSR through that critical defile. This unit searched the valley and rescued twenty-two Royal Marines who had been hiding there since the destruction of Task Force Drysdale.

By 1700 on December 7, all of the 7th Marines survivors had reached Koto-ri. As it turned out, the support troops suffered more than the combat formations, largely because burning trucks had blocked the column and exposed them to enemy fire for longer periods of time. Headquarters troops and artillerymen and fought off Chinese assaults at point-blank ranges, and the gunners unlimbered their pieces to fire for two hours over open sights.

Harry Milne's Division Train Two left Hagaru-ri after nightfall, but because of the blockage on the road, were barely past the perimeter by midnight. The delay proved a blessing in disguise, because they were able to pass through Hellfire Valley in daylight. "Train One got hit up pretty good, but we didn't get hit at all as far as I know," remembered Milne. "We didn't have any casualties. Not because we were smart. By the time we got there it was over. I'm not trying to brag that we were the best. That's just the way it happened." Milne remembers that supporting aircraft helped their cause by bombing the now-visible enemy positions. "I could watch them dropping napalm right alongside the road. We had daylight." Vaughn Stuart recalls that when the column passed through the wreckage of Task Force Drysdale, the men picked up all the wounded and whatever equipment was still salvageable. "They found Chase's body at that time. I think they suspected he was dead. That's really all I know about it." By midnight the rearguard, 2/5, was also safely inside the perimeter at Koto-ri.

The only Americans still inside defending Hagaru in the pre-dawn hours of December 7 were elements of 2/5 and the Provisional Tank Platoon, who were charged with protecting the engineers and ordnance men who would burn or blow up the supplies that could not be removed. Despite everyone's best efforts, three disabled tanks, D-41, D-42, and B-15,[35] could not be towed down the treacherous road. Don Bennett "had the privilege of putting a few rounds into a couple of disabled tanks we left behind. We pulled out of there with no real resistance."

In the milling combat confusion, two D Company tank crewmen on guard duty near the road past East Hill were almost left behind for the enemy. George Duncan and another Marine named "Hart" had constructed a comfy fighting hole complete with a roof and heater, and were overlooked during the evacuation. They watched the tanks and trucks move past, but "gave it no thought," Duncan explained. Fortunately, an infantry officer spotted the pair and sent them slogging through the snow with his own men. Duncan described the ensuing three days of fighting his way south with the infantry, armed with a Chinese submachine gun, as "pure hell."[36]

The Provisional Tank Platoon covered the withdrawal, and in the confusion Stuart lost track of the engineers he was supposed to help escort. He sent his tanks down the road at fifty-yard intervals, and believes that he may have been the last Marine to see the burning village from the ground.[37]

A short distance down the road the M4A3 dozer tank with the damaged radiators overheated and the engine caught fire. Stuart vetoed the crew's requests to try and save it, and all night they could see the glow and explosions as ammunition cooked off inside the burning hulk.[38]

The frozen and exhausted remnants of the Provisional Tank Platoon entered Koto-ri just before dawn on December 8. During the previous thirty-eight hours of constant fighting, the division had removed 10,000 men and over 1,000 vehicles from a seemingly inescapable trap. The division paused again to rest and reorganize for the main phase of the breakout.

George Duncan, one of the two Marines almost left behind in the evacuation of Hagaru, was still searching for D Company when he was scooped up by yet another infantry company, given a rifle and a new sleeping bag, and put to work defending the Koto-ri perimeter. Duncan fought all night from his shelter beneath an ammunition trailer. When the fighting finally slackened at dawn, he discovered he had been shot through the arm, and the sleeve of his parka was filled with frozen blood.[39]

The next leg of the attack toward the sea required Smith's Marine Division to force its way through Funchilin Pass, a narrow defile where the road dropped down a narrow gorge from the high mountainous plateau. As stated earlier, this was the most constricted and treacherous stretch of the road, and the site where the CCF had blown the critical bridge at the valve house. Unfortunately for the Marines, there was no time to build a trestle bridge. Although it had never been done, Air Force commanders believed they could successfully drop prefabricated

Treadway Bridge sections. Smith's decision to withdraw and save his heavy equipment paid off. Caught with the Marines at Koto-ri was the Army's 185th Engineer Battalion, with four of the big Brockway trucks used to transport and launch the bridge sections.

On December 7, Air Force planes dropped eight bridge sections and the special decking that would allow the bridge to carry narrow vehicles like jeeps. Although one section was damaged beyond use and another was lost to the Chinese, only four sections were required to span the gap. The next day, the Marines attacked from above and below the Funchilin Pass in an effort to open it and allow the column to advance. At 0200 hours, 1/1 started north from Chinghung-ni, a few miles below the pass, supported by M16 "Quad 50s" and 40mm M19s of the Army's B Company, 50th Anti-Aircraft Artillery (Automatic Weapons) Battalion.[40] At 0800, the 7th Marines attacked south from Koto-ri, supported by tanks of the Anti-Tank Platoon, 5th Marines.

The tanks left Koto-ri ahead of the main column. Some were put on outpost duty to screen the procession against attack from the nearby hills, but most were held in a large open area south of the town until all of the other vehicles had safely passed. Although the armored firepower of the tanks would be desperately needed at the front of the column, the role of rearguard was forced upon the tanks by necessity. "In some places about half of a tank tread would be hanging over the edge of this road, going down the cliff," explained Phil Morell. "You had to be very careful." One or more of the forty-six ton goliaths disabled in the road could spell the end of the entire division.

Ben Busch's tank watched and waited for two days while the other vehicles passed by his exposed position. The bitter cold showed no mercy to either side. One morning Busch woke up and looked at the surrounding infantry.

"Hey," he told one infantryman, "you better get your buddy up. Gettin' late."

"That's our company commander. He froze to death during the night," was the man's reply.

Like many others, Paul Sanders believes that the Chinese suffered far more from the intense cold. "Those poor bastards didn't have anything. They only had about a week's supply of food. They were supposed to march right in, knock us off, and take our food." During the withdrawal

Sanders remembers seeing something moving in the bushes, so he asked one of his comrade, "'What the hell's that in there?' Damned if it wasn't a Chinaman. He came out. We had a fire going, cooking something or other. We motioned him over, to get to the fire. He stuck his feet right in the fire. They were frozen. He undoubtedly lost them. They took him prisoner, and took him down the hill." The recollection has never left Sanders. "It was kind of strange. Here's a guy who's part of the opposing forces, and suddenly he's a guy who is just about ready to hand in his chips from the weather."

The Provisional Tank Platoon was dissolved when it reached Koto-ri, where Vaughn Stuart found himself "relegated to the walking unemployed in the column, hoofing it down the mountain to the railhead." There was no time to gather up the scattered remnants of units, and men like Stuart and Bob Miller were simply swept along in the southward flow.[41]

The push into the pass lasted all through the next day and long into the following night. Beginning on the morning of December 9, A/1/1 fought a bitter battle for control of Hill 1081, securing the critical south end of the defile by 1500 hours. Baker Company pushed on through along a nearby cable car track to secure other nearby hills overlooking the road. Attacking from the north, C/1/7 secured the bridge and valve house just after noon, and the engineers began the painstaking task of assembling the bridge.

When the first units began to cross the bridge, a bulldozer towing a scraping pan used to repair the road ahead of the column crashed through the decking. The engineers managed to extricate the heavy tractor and make jury-rigged repairs by changing the spacing of the bridge members, but this left vehicle drivers with little margin for error. Small vehicles like jeeps had only one-half inch of space to maneuver from side to side—any more than that and the vehicle and its occupants would slip between the stringers and into the chasm below.

All night long a chain of vehicles crept across the bridge in the darkness. The bitter cold and wind howling down the gorge offered a respite from CCF attacks. At 0245 on December 10, the leading elements of 1/7 arrived in Chinhung-ni. Throughout the next day, the single file line of trucks crawled down the road, all the while under Chinese attack. The enemy cut the road at Sudong, south of Chinhung-ni, on two occasions, but were beaten back each time after heavy fighting. It was not until 1700 that afternoon that the rear guard of the 1st Marines, covered by tanks, left Koto-ri.

The rearguard consisted of the Headquarters and Service Company, 1st Marines, followed by the heavy vehicles of the 185th Engineer Battalion. Next in line was 2/31 and 2/1. The last group was comprised of forty tanks of B and D Companies of the 1st Tank Battalion, the M4A3s of the Army's Medium Tank Company, and Anti-Tank Platoon 5th Marines, all screened by the division Reconnaissance Company.

The huge gaggle of tanks was assembled on open terrain near the summit of the pass south of Koto-ri, engines idling, ready to move out at a moments notice. The idling engines, however, consumed precious fuel, which in turn prompted Captain Bruce Clarke to move back to try and locate fuel trucks in Division Train Two. "[Clarke] went up to find fuel and never came back," said Paul Sanders. Unbeknownst to his men at the time, somewhere in the confusion Clarke was shot in the heel. Dosed with morphine, he was bundled into an ambulance and driven unseen down the road past his waiting tanks.[42]

The fuel trucks also passed unnoticed before Harry Milne appeared with the last few cargo trucks. With Captain Clarke wounded and the Executive Officer missing, Milne passed the command of D Company to Sanders.[43] "We got a little gas somewhere, but it wasn't much," said Sanders. "We took what we could get. Going down the hill, one of my tanks ran out of gas, and we had to push it over the side." The tanks finally started down the pass at midnight on December 10.[44]

Vaughn Stuart would eventually took over Sanders's platoon,[45] but that night he walked down the mountain. By 0300 hours he was so exhausted he ignored orders and climbed into a truck beside the driver and went to sleep. Some time later he awoke in panic when he could not feel his left leg. Walking up and down the column restored some circulation, although he suffered minor frostbite. Stuart considered himself lucky. That night he saw a young Chinese soldier near the power station bridge. "His hands were frozen so solid that they clinked like glass when he hit them together. He was laughing at the time."[46]

Leon Mullins of the 1st Marines' Anti-Tank Company remembers well the long withdrawal, the negotiation of the last pass, and a haunting conversation with a fellow soldier. The march, he explained, was . . .

one firefight after another. Cold. Ambushed a lot. I remember one Army major—some of the Army units had disintegrated, and their fellows had just integrated with the Marines. This Army major was walking beside me. We were just south of Koto-ri, starting out. He'd been in Europe in World War II.

He says, "As soon as I get back, I'm resigning my commission, getting out of this G D Army." A firefight erupted, and I dropped to the ground. I remembered watching him—he was on my left, and he was a tall fellow. I remember he dropped to the ground. I dropped to the ground and started rolling, and found a depressed area. After the firefight was over, I went back and was checking on casualties. He had dropped and taken a round right through the side of the head. The round had gone right over my head, and because he was the tallest, he was out of the Army—bless his heart—the next second after he said that.

The road itself was a nightmare, as Don Bennett explained: "It was very, very dark and the road was extremely icy, from all of the people packing down the snow. . . . We didn't know there was any [enemy] infantry anywhere around. We turned on our lights, and were driving down that mountain. . . . Most of the personnel were outside the tanks because the terrain was so slippery. Some rode on the left fender so they could jump off quickly if the tank went over the side."[47] The tankers had their lights on because of Sanders, who on his own initiative had given them permission. Even so, Sanders said, "It took a hell of a lot of courage for the driver to stay in the tank and drive it."

Captain Bruce Williams's B Company followed at the extreme end of the column. Williams had worked out an arrangement with the leader of a platoon from the Recon Company, about twenty-seven men under 1st Lt. Ernie Hargett, to screen the tail of the tank column.[48] The men in Sanders's platoon trained their guns to the rear, but could not support the tanks behind them because of the steep cliffs and winding road.[49]

The climactic moment came on December 11, near the damaged bridge. The tank column was moving forward, constantly harried by CCF attacks, when a horde of wretched Korean refugees pressed against the rear of the column. Chinese soldiers had infiltrated the throng. Lieutenant Hargett's men protected the last group of ten tanks as best they could, struggling to keep the refugees from intermingling with the tanks.

About 0100 hours, disaster befell the tail of the B Company column, 1st Lt. Philip Ronzone's 2nd Platoon. According to Don Bennett, "[A vehicle] two tanks ahead of me could not negotiate the turn."[50] Phil Morell picked up the sad tale: "About halfway down, the fifth tank from the end [of the column], the left track . . . seized on the inboard side, going into the mountain."[51] The tank slid sideways, embedding a track and fender in the bank on the uphill side of the road. "He couldn't go any place except forward or backing up a little bit. He couldn't steer. They tried to figure out a way to just throw the tank off [the cliff], but they couldn't."

Don Bennett believes that the steel tracks on the icy road were the real problem:

> The tracks on the M-26 had steel chevrons and not rubber as on later tanks. All the trucks and vehicles had been down this road for the last two days, packing the snow beneath them so that it became very slick ice. I believe B-11 slid off the road into the ditch when it tried to turn the corner. We could not get it out of the ditch, though many attempts were made.[52]

The hairpin turns bordered by rocky cliffs apparently blocked even the powerful tank radio,[53] so Lieutenant Ronzone dismounted from tank B-21 (the fifth from the tail of the column) and walked forward to confer with the men trying to resolve the traffic jam.

Accounts of what happened next differ. Don Bennett, who was closest to the action, remembered that "It was a sheer drop on the right on that corner, and there was just barely enough room. . . . The Chinese had evidently decided to attack the rear."

Unbeknownst to the men on the highway, the infantry assigned to hold the high ground above the road had left their positions and moved down the road toward the bridge.[54]

Lieutenant Gover was the senior of the two officers present, and Ronzone was urging him to make a decision, because the trapped tanks were now far behind the main column. Don Bennett picked up the story: "The two lieutenants there were conversing . . . and a decision was made to abandon the tanks. . . . The rest of the column was forty-five minutes to an hour down the road. They had actually went across the bridge."

The tanks ahead of the jam inched slowly across the structure, starting at about 2300 hours. The tanks, nearly blind even when the driver had his head out of the hatch, had but two inches to spare on the slippery bridge. Fortunately it was dark, said O'Sullivan. "I couldn't see how far down it was." O'Sullivan was rapidly becoming an expert driver the hard way. "It was a scary sucker, because they were afraid that if you slid one way or another—it's like going up on the thing to get your car greased—you're gonna block that whole bridge. . . . A foot man out front of you, holding one hand up, the other hand up, showing you which brake to pull. . . . We're doing it in the dark."

Don Bennett was still with the trapped tanks: "I guess the lieutenants knew that they had instructions that as soon as the last tank went over the bridge, there was no more chance. It would be blown. The decision was made to save the men, so we all took off [on foot].[55] We go down the road quite a ways. A mish-mash of weapons—pistols, tommy guns, carbines, whatever you had with you." Up the road, meanwhile, the men of the Recon platoon were still fighting a valiant but confused action to screen the tanks and the remaining crewmen.

"A group of us stopped, and there was an old [Staff] Sergeant we called "Slope Plate MacDonald," continued Bennett. MacDonald was the Platoon Sergeant of 2nd Platoon, and responsible for some of the trapped tank crews.[56] "He said, 'We gotta go back up and save those guys.' Six or seven of us followed MacDonald back up the mountain." Others, apparently, continued down the road and reported to Captain Williams that the rear of the column had been overrun.[57]

The group that headed back had reached an unspoken agreement that they would salvage any armor they could squeak past the crippled tank. "MacDonald took a few men on up. Two guys jumped in the first tank [B-12] . . . and I jumped in my tank [B-13]. . . . Some kid jumped in the tank. His name was [USMC Reserve Cpl. C. P.] Lett. What I didn't know at the time, he had never driven a tank. He was a replacement, and he had been made the assistant driver. He knew how to start it, but he had never driven it. I get up in the tank commander's hatch, and put my helmet on," continued Bennett. "I don't have anybody else, but I'm talkin' to him. He seemed to have a problem getting it started."

Rather than try and free the stuck tank, some other Marine drove it "forward as far as the tank would go up the side of the cliff. Finally we were able to get two tanks by this disabled vehicle. And I mean we scraped our fenders off and everything else getting by. The first tank got by. I started and got my tank by, and we were all milling around waiting for another tank to come around when . . . a lot of shooting [broke out.]."[58]

A small group of Chinese had emerged from the group of refugees pressing against the rear of the stalled column and offered to surrender. It was a ruse. The Chinese pulled out weapons and opened fire on the Recon Company men, while others rushed down from the high side of the road in a coordinated attack. A grenade sailed through the air and exploded, setting the last tank in line on fire. The crew of the next to last tank in line slammed shut their hatches when the shooting began. The Recon men screamed and hammered with rifle butts on the armor, but the crew refused to open up. Bennett believes that MacDonald also tried to get the crew to open up, without success.[59] Even though surprised, the Recon men managed to cut down the attacking Chinese and fell back down the road.

The crews who had gotten past the jammed tank took off down toward the bridge, still unaware whether or not it was still standing. Bennett, meanwhile, was struggling with his neophyte driver on a harrowing ride to safety. "Once he [Lett] got it started, the other tank, we can't even see his red [tail] lights. It's gone," explained Bennett. "As we went down the mountain, he keeps hitting the left side of the tank . . . keeps running into the bank on the left side. . . . I kept saying, 'Hey! Take it easy! Just a little more to the right.' Trying to help him out." Somehow Bennett and Lett managed to get the tank safely across the bridge. "Everybody was surprised we got those two tanks. We stayed there. The rest of the column had already gone. I think we ran into Captain Williams at that point."

As it turned out, Bennett's tank was "the last vehicle—B-13—that made it out of the reservoir trap." The crew who pulled their hatches shut on the road north of the bridge during the Chinese surprise attack were not so fortunate. Instead of escaping, they went down in history as the last Marines captured during the Chosin Reservoir campaign. They were taken prisoner the next morning, and watched from afar as an air strike napalmed the abandoned tanks.

Bennett wrote about their plight:

These last two tanks stayed with the Recon Platoon and engineers until long after daylight as we came down the road. We must have passed Chinhung-ni around 9:00 AM. As we proceeded on, there was evidence of many ambushes that had happened during the night. Burned trucks, dead Chinese littered the area as we headed for Hamhung to rejoin the company. The Treadway bridge was blown about 2:30-3:00 AM after stragglers from the Recon and tanks crews ceased to appear.[60]

The last tanks paused only long enough to fire an occasional round into masonry road fill embankments in an attempt to collapse them.[61]

The need to keep moving at all costs meant that the tanks were not properly maintained. As Ben Busch explained it, "The panel board in the driver's compartment was—Christ!—high oil pressure, low oil pressure, overheating engine, these lights were flashing on and off, and we just kept moving."

Below the Funchilin Pass the Chinese attacks were isolated, less effective, and delivered with less enthusiasm. "The danged line stopped. I could hear gunfire, small weapons. It stopped, so I just got the tanks I had and went around," said Paul Sanders.

South of the pass the road crossed a broad open flat where a group of Chinese had the road under fire. "They must have been four or five hundred yards from the road," continued Sanders. "A platoon of British Royal Marines was going to make an attack. I sat there in my tank watching, and it was just like a textbook. They were off to the right, fire, and maneuver. I was sitting right there where I could see the Chinamen, so I had a couple of tanks open fire on them. Then I saw a figure detach itself from the platoon, and start back my way. It was a tall corporal, nice-looking fellow."

"Are you Leftenant Sanders?" the man inquired.

"That's right."

"I came back to tell you that our platoon leader says that this is our fight, and we don't need you're damned tanks. Kindly quit firing."

As Sanders put it, "Big ol' stiff upper lip."

Harry Smith and the rest of 3rd Platoon, A Company, watched the column pass through. "It was horrifying to watch them. I remember seeing an infantry guy walking along, and all of a sudden he just dropped to his knees. He just kept walking on his knees. He was asleep. One of his buddies helped him get up. When the ambulances went by, you could see right through them, they were so full of bullet holes," continued Smith. "Goddamn it! Wounded just hanging on the trucks. They were indescribable."

When the last units passed through the Army lines a few miles below Sudong at Majon-dong, Able Company was released from guarding its lonely bridge and rejoined its parent organization on December 11.[62] According to Morell, Able Company tanks "formed up behind us . . . and we all continued to march, never stopped. From the time the column started by you, it was fifty-four hours 'til the last guy came down. There was no fighting once we got halfway down the hill." Morell recalls an incident that still lingers in his mind. "At one point . . . I looked over, and there was guy in a firing position, and there was snow on his uniform. I had a couple of the tankers go up around behind him. They just pushed on him . . . he was frozen, in a firing position. He was a Chinese, or North Korean, I don't know which."

O'Sullivan and his crew mates finally turned D-23 back over to D Company in Majon-dong and returned to Charlie Company. "Those fellows had hot water and showers, and clean shaves and everything else. We looked like derelicts who had lived out in the garbage dump for a month and a half. . . . Did you ever try not to go to the bathroom for a week? You didn't want to take your pants down to go to the bathroom, because your rear end would freeze. I had on my fatigues, and then . . . my tank coveralls, and then . . . a pair of winter pants over them. By the time I got through all the damn pants, it was too late. And it felt good. It was nice and warm, anyway."

Men were simply lost in the bloody fighting and the reorganization shuffle that followed. When Tanker Basilo Chavarria returned from his convalescence in Japan, he was assigned to another company.[63] Others survived the ordeal in the pass, only to be stricken by mundane hazards. Ben Busch: "Our driver had pneumonia, so they evacuated him. He made that drive all the way down with pneumonia."

Jim Edwards's M4A3 dozer tank was disabled by engine trouble. "They were towing the tank. We were sitting in the tank, and had wrapped towels around our faces. The exhaust from the tank that was towing us just filled the tank. Three of us just passed out. I never thought about it. The hatches were open. You could smell it, but I thought it was dissipating as it was coming back, anyway. Never thought there was enough of it to get to us. When I woke up, I was on a stretcher laying down on the beach."

George Duncan finally caught up with the D Company tanks in Hungnam. Paul Sanders promptly berated him, telling him he had been reported Missing In Action. Duncan showed him his wounds and explained the situation, and Sanders took him to sick bay for the medical attention he required.[64]

The Marines had bought priceless time for the 3rd Division to prepare for the defense of Hungnam, through which X Corps could be evacuated. Between November 28 and December 11, the Marines and survivors of the 32nd Infantry—together with the savage winter weather—inflicted 37,000 enemy casualties, rendering in the process seven Chinese divisions combat ineffective.

There are many stories about the Marines scavenging abandoned Army equipment, but that knife cut both ways. Sanders said that one of the tanks from B Company was towed up and parked beside his tanks. "I told my two crews to go ahead and go in and get a shower. I was out looking for the tank park, and I came back and the tank was gone! The disabled tank. I thought, 'What the hell, is this?'"

Colonel Milne wondered the same thing. "Where's your tank?" he asked Sanders a short time later.

"I don't know," answered Sanders truthfully.

"You better find it!"

Milne continued the story: "The tank crew got out of the tank, and they left it. The Army 3rd Division, which was supposed to keep the supply lines open, took the tank. They thought the tank was inoperative . . . and sent it to Japan. When the Division asked me about it . . . I called the lieutenant in, and I said, 'You better go find that tank! Get a jeep and find it!'"

"It was just getting daylight," remembered the chastised Sanders. "I got a friend of mine who drove a jeep, and we drove all over that area looking for that damn tank. Milne was pretty pissed off, and I don't blame him. [We] found the tank about two months later. The Army people who were dragging the equipment off the beach and loading it aboard ship, they came along and they couldn't get it started. They just hauled that sucker on board one of the ships, and hauled it to Japan, where the Marine

Corps finally found it. Colonel Milne was a little upset," he added. "He was damn near going to make me pay for it!"

As far as Milne was concerned, turnabout was fair play. "We and the infantry, and everybody else in the Marines . . . picked up whatever they could find from the Army, and put it aboard the ships. We had one Army truck—which later Division made us take 'em all back—on the LST.

When an Army sergeant discovered the Marines had his truck on the LST, he hollered up, "That's my truck!."

"That's too bad!" yelled back one of Milne's men.

"Well, at least give me my coat!" yelled back the soldier.

"We kept his truck," chuckled Milne, "but gave the coat back because we were nice guys."

Leon Mullins recalls boarding the ship and receiving fresh clean clothes. "We hadn't shaved in a month. They had boxes of clothes at Hungnam. Several of us just went and picked out clothes our size. . . . My closest buddy and I went aboard a Navy ship, shaved and showered, and threw away our old clothes. We had to.[65]

Mullins continued describing his return to civilization:

> When we were evac'ed out of there—I don't remember what ship we were on—it was a Navy ship. The next morning after we boarded it, we [started] for breakfast. What we couldn't see was that the line went 'round and 'round, and by the time we got there to eat there were [medical] corpsmen on either side. Before we could pick up a tray we had to take a shot in each arm. We ate one meal a day, because we were too tired to get back in line. Guys were sleeping wherever they could find a spot to sit down, let alone lie down. Some guys were down in the boiler room, we went down there, and guys were spread out everywhere.
>
> We all had bad colds. The corpsman said "Pneumonia" or "Light case of pneumonia," and we were given more shots. About everyone had various stages of frostbite.

Harry Smith experienced much the same thing: "First thing I did I went and took a shower. . . . I took off my dungarees, and the long underwear I had on was black, just like I'd been in a grease pit. After I had the shower, I looked at them . . . and I just took the long johns to the side, and threw 'em over."

* * *

Between December 11 and 14, every major elements of the Marine Division was evacuated by sea. Heavy equipment was divided piecemeal among several ships, and the tank battalion was split up among two LSDs (*Fort Marion* and *Colonial*) and three of the Japanese LSTs (*Q009, Q058,* and *Q085*). On Christmas Eve afternoon Sunday, December 24, Marine Corps LVTs lifted the last three platoons of the 3rd Division off the beach at Hungnam, while huge explosions rocked the abandoned city. General Smith and the men who comprised his grand division had executed one of the classic fighting withdrawals in all of military history.

Their reward would be more hard fighting on familiar ground.

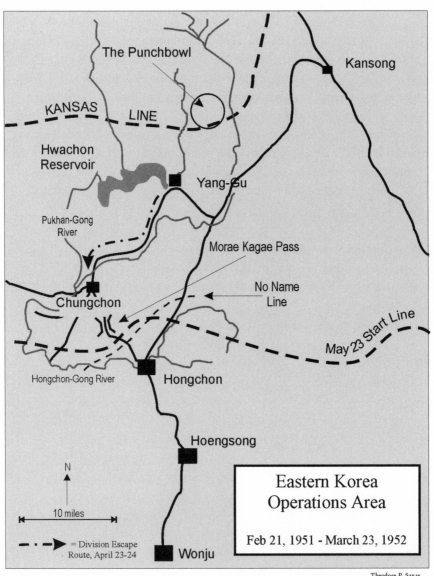

The Punchbowl

Kansong

KANSAS LINE

Hwachon
Reservoir

Yang-Gu

Pukhan-Gong
River

Morae Kagae Pass

No Name
Line

Chungchon

May 23 Start Line

Hongchon-Gong River

Hongchon

Hoengsong

N

10 miles

= Division Escape
Route, April 23-24

Wonju

Eastern Korea
Operations Area

Feb 21, 1951 - March 23, 1952

Theodore P. Savas

"Nothing except a battle lost can be so melancholy as a battle won."

— Arthur Wellesley, Duke of Wellington

Chapter Six

Lives for Real Estate

Offensives and Counteroffensives, 1951-1952

The 1st Marine Division disembarked where the Marine Brigade had begun the Korean odyssey. The tank battalion and the regimental anti-tank companies landed at Pusan between December 15 and 17, 1950.[1]

Don Bennett's tank had somehow survived the rigors of the Chosin campaign, but the Pusan docks were another story altogether. "The Navy kinda dropped it," he recalled. "The crane driver, as he was lowering it down, he lowered it down a little bit too fast. When it hit the dock . . . to everybody's great amazement, the [drive] sprocket in the rear fell off. On the left side. Hitting that bank all the way down that mountain in that pass . . . had done a lot of damage. We [took] that tank, and several of our other tanks, over to the Army repair unit."

According to Phil Morell, "Milne and I went over to a barracks, where there was an Army tank battalion.[2] We needed some tank parts, and it was about two in the morning or something, but they got up and they helped us."

The accommodations at Pusan were familiar to the Marines. The Division was gathered at Camp Lopez, otherwise known as The Bean

Patch, the same area on the outskirts of Masan the Brigade had occupied after the First Battle of the Naktong. The welcome period of rest and recuperation lasted through Christmas,[3] but the Marines lost most of the accumulated Army gear they had picked up on the Chosin withdrawal. Explained Harry Milne, "Division, when we got to Masan, told us, 'Alright, you turn all this Army equipment back,' which we did of course."

The tank battalion reorganized and absorbed replacements for its casualties. Paul Sanders took over as the executive officer of D Company, while Vaughn Stuart took over his old platoon.[4] Captain Joe Malcolm assumed command of the company.[5] Ben Busch's wounded tank commander was replaced by a new staff sergeant, so Busch was made a driver and promoted. The man who had somehow always managed to look relatively neat and clean regardless of the circumstances finally had his own tank.[6] All of these promotions were well deserved.

Darell Snideman, who had been undergoing training in tank lubrication when the Chinese attacked at the Chosin Reservoir, fortunately sat out the battle at the lower end of the Funchilin Pass.[7] At Masan, he was reassigned as tank commander for a Platoon Leader's tank in B Company. "It was his tank. He would function as the tank commander if we were under fire or on an objective. All the rest of the time, the tank commander takes care of the tank, makes sure it's in repair, and everything else taken care of. Naturally the lieutenant's not going to have to do that." When the officer took over the tank, he continued, "I could either go and join some other tank, or maybe someone didn't want to go on the run, then you could fill in for them. Most of the time we just sat in camp."

As one might easily imagine, immediately following the Chosin Campaign the Division found itself desperately short of equipment and trained personnel. The M26 tanks had proven sturdier than the old M4A3s, but losses in both types had been severe. The tank battalion was authorized 85 M26s and 12 M4A3s, but was reduced to 69 M26s and only five M4A3s.[8] Worse for the division as a whole, General Smith's decision to fight his way out with all his heavy equipment meant that Eighth Army divisions that had abandoned their equipment in the long retreat had first call on replacement trucks and other heavy gear.[9]

Just days after the return from Chosin, Harry Milne was designated Coordinator Southern Defense Sector on December 18. The battalion absorbed trucks to replace those lost in Hellfire Pass, as well as seven tanks rebuilt by Army ordnance repair units.[10]

The autonomous X Corps ceased to exist, and the 1st Marine Division was put under operational control of Eighth Army as part of the EUSAK (Eighth U. S. Army Korea) Reserve. On December 23, the commander of Eighth Army, Lt. Gen. Walton Walker, was killed in a traffic accident, and on Christmas Day Lt. Gen. Matthew Ridgway arrived to replace him.

*   *   *

The rest and relaxation period ended abruptly on New Year's Eve 1950, when the Chinese opened their winter offensive with heavy attacks along the peninsula's western coast. By January 3, 1951, United Nations forces were again driven out of Seoul.

The 1st Marine Division remained in reserve throughout this new crisis. On January 8, the division was assigned to provide internal security against NKPA units that were functioning as guerrillas. The division's primary task was to protect the Main Supply Route (MSR) from Pohang, a small port north of Pusan, along its western route to the important road center at Andong. This deployment also placed the division in position to backstop Army divisions holding the Main Line of Resistance (or MLR). Once again, the division found itself strung out over 1,600 square miles. On January 19, the 1st Tank Battalion was assigned the task of securing the area south of Pohang, a job Roger Chaput jokingly referred to as "the Pohang guerilla hunt. Didn't see a damn one."

While Eighth Army launched counteroffensives Operations Thunderbolt and Roundup, the Marines conducted mechanized patrols along the roads to the rear—usually a single tank escorting truck-mounted infantry—and dismounted patrols in the hills. Remnants of the NKPA *10th Division* seldom made serious contact with the Marines. Contact usually came about as a result of the NKPA's ineptness as guerrillas. The total lack of support of the indigenous civilian population deprived them of supply, communications, and intelligence on U.N. counter-guerrilla operations, and even their base areas in the rugged hills were not secure from American raids. Still, any action against guerrillas was, by its very nature, enervating and dangerous.

"We chased guerillas," said Vaughn Stuart. "We had an airstrip there. We had at least two tank companies there. We'd go out and have some pretty good encounters with guerillas." Stuart was working at this time with the First Battalion, 5th Marines. "We did a lot of fighting up in the back areas there. The regular [North Korean] Army had just gone into guerilla bands. They were just harassing the units." Stuart recalled their tactics: "They would hit us on their own ground, on ground they selected, and then fade back away. We'd see bloody bandages, and evidences of wounds. We never saw any dead. They took them all away. That was really disheartening to us. We were taking casualties as well."

The biggest engagement incident came about on February 7, when a tank returning from a patrol blundered into an NKPA roadblock. The enemy was as surprised as the tank crew. The confused exchange of gunfire that followed killed two enemy soldiers and demolished the roadblock.[11]

The period of relative quiet gave the 1st Marine Division time to integrate the massive influx of the First Replacement Draft. One of the new arrivals was Corporal Robert Mack, a tall and thin man with a full head of wavy black hair. He was also an experienced tanker and good teacher who had enlisted in 1945 at age at seventeen and attended the basic tank school with tanker Don Gagnon. "I was an M4 man," explained Mack. "When I got there I had to learn about M26s. They had a hard time even getting uniforms for us. We weren't prepared for nothin.'" Instead of training on the new M26s, "We walked around with tommy guns and M2s. Went through little villages, and around the countryside."

Throughout late January and early February, the CCF exerted continuous pressure on the U.N. forces, and on February 11 a massive Chinese offensive drove the U.N. forces back. Eight days later the 1st Marine Division was reassigned to IX Corps for Operation Killer, Ridgway's counterstroke against the encroaching enemy. Part of the plan included shifting the division north to protect the town of Wonju, a critical road junction.

This redeployment tested the tanks to their limit; in return, American emphasis on mechanical reliability in tank design was rewarded.

A shortage of railway flatcars forced Baker, Headquarters, and Services Companies to undertake a hasty 120-mile (193 km.) road march. The lengthy march along the narrow twisting roads was an ordeal for both the tanks and their crews—particularly the drivers. In slightly warmer, near-freezing temperatures, the poorly-constructed and maintained roads disintegrated into icy mud slush, and vehicles of every description were hard-pressed to keep up with the slogging footsore infantry. For the big tanks, negotiating the narrow mountain roads was a nightmare. "Nobody would ride in the tank except the driver," said Harry Bruce. "The road would cave away. You could stand on the side and watch the side of the road being caved away."

The other companies moved by rail, but their journey proved almost as difficult. The steep gradients, small railway locomotives, and narrow, twisting tunnels were not designed to allow the passage of the huge American tanks as cargo. Harry Smith recalled that en route from Andong to Chunchon, A Company was loaded onto five separate trains. Each train had "five tanks [on flatcars], an engine, and a boxcar with straw in it. Our train was the first one. They kept adding cars to it—Army guys going back to the front. We got in a tunnel, and . . . the engine stalled. Just sitting there. It was dark, pitch [black] in that tunnel." The tunnel began to fill with smoke and fumes from the engine, and the men dismounted and starting stumbling about in the darkness. "Mister Sweet says 'Everybody stays in this car, nobody gets out. Get down on the floor and get your head under a blanket or whatever so the smoke doesn't get you so much.' All of a sudden the train lurched, and it started going backwards. It was going full speed. Whoever started it up, they had the throttle wide open, 'cause it was roaring past."

Despite fears that the train would crash into another running only fifteen minutes behind it, the men made it safely out of the tunnel. The appearance of a second locomotive enabled the train to proceed on its journey.[12] By the morning of February 21, only four rifle battalions, supported by a company of tanks and two battalions of artillery, were in position to begin the counteroffensive.

Like much of Korea, this ground had been fought over before. The evidence of past horrors in what the Marines called Massacre Valley appalled Mike Wiggins. "There were a lot of dead Army troops," he began. "They were frozen there. We took that ground, and they got the bodies out. . . . They were frozen. A lot of them were black troops. It was segregated at that time.[13] Not all the people we saw were black—there were a lot of Caucasians—they just got overran, and they never recuperated until we took that ground again, back in the Spring." Robert Mack agreed, adding: "There were a lot of dead horses, dead people. . . . Stunk terrible. Worst smell I ever smelled in my life." Acccording to Harry Smith, "Army ordnance came and started trying to remove the vehicles. There was a lot of upset Marines, and [we] finally said, 'You ain't getting your vehicles until you get the bodies out of there.'"

When the Marines received word that there were survivors of Army units hiding in Hoengsong, Harry Smith was dubious. "A little . . . kid came out, and said there was a doctor in there with wounded. Nobody wanted to believe him. He was talking to the interpreter, Murphy.[14] The kid added, 'The doctor said if you didn't believe me to give you this.' He gave the guy a dog tag from a doctor."

On February 24, the Marines attacked Hoengsong. "The next morning we [Sleger's section from 3rd Platoon] started firing in preparation for the assault," recalled Smith. "We had made arrangements with the infantry, and a guy was on the telephone directing some of our fire. We had spotted a pillbox. We fired, and we thought we had missed. Joe had Harry Roth fire another round. The guy on the telephone there with us said, 'Christ! He put both of 'em right through the slot of the pillbox without touching anything else!'"

A patrol consisting of Charlie Company 1/1 and Gunner Mac McMillian's 2nd Platoon of A Company tanks tried to enter Hoengsong proper. The two sections split up, moving through the narrow streets of the small town.[15] The effort proved to be difficult. CCF fire was so intense that the radio antennae were sheared off the tanks. Robert Mack remembers losing "a tank going into Hoengsong. . . . They had been in the day before, and decided they were trying to ambush 'em, so they pulled 'em back out. When we went in the next day, we went in line."

Mack was in Platoon Sergeant Don Gagnon's tank, A-24. "Two tanks went over [a mine] and we went over it all the way to the last bogey wheel. All of a sudden it's this huge explosion, picked the tank up and set it back down."

"Castor!,[16] get this thing in gear!" yelled Gagnon.

"It is in gear, Sarge!" Castor hollered back. "It ain't goin' nowhere!"

"We thought we'd been hit by something," explained Mack. "We didn't think of a mine right away. Nobody got seriously hurt, we were just sort of stunned." Mack recalled that Gunner McMillian's reaction was typical. "I wasn't out of the hatch two minutes and he hopped up on my tank. . . . He asked each one of us. 'You all right? Everything okay?' "That's when I realized that he was thoroughly interested in our well being."

The explosion wrecked the engine and transmission, so the crew of A-24 tagged along with the other tanks. That night Gagnon assigned the members of his crew to take the first two-hour watch of the night guard to give the other exhausted crews additional rest.[17] It was cold that night, Mack remembered. "I was standing . . . on a ration box, trying to keep from freezing to death. Finally our stuff came, and we got hot coffee, sleeping bags and such. I threw my sleeping bag on the sponson behind, I forget which tank, Buford was the assistant driver. . . . This was about two o'clock in the morning."

A short time later, Buford shook Mack awake. Mack saw the hatch was open. "Sarge, you better get inside. There's incoming."

"How close are they?" asked Mack, who wanted more than anything to roll back over and go to sleep.

"Oh, about fifty yards."

"If they get any closer, wake me up."

Mack did not remember the exchange, and did not find out about it until Buford recounted it forty years later. "I don't remember him waking me up, or anything. I was, I suppose, dead-tired and finally warm."[18]

As it turned out, the small Korean boy was correct about the doctor in Hoengsong. When the Marines swept into the town, they recovered the survivors of an Army medical unit. McMillian remembers rescuing the hurt soldiers: "They told us to haul them out . . . on the backs of the tanks. Seems like there was about a dozen. They were in bad shape. There wasn't any walking [wounded] amongst them."

On March 1, the second phase of Operation Killer commenced, which meant the Marines would have to cross the flat, water-sodden plain north of Hoengsong. Rain-swollen streams blocked the advance, and the Marine Division took three days to reach its objective.

On March 4, Maj. Gen. William Hoge, U.S. Army, arrived at Yoju to take command of IX Corps. This, in turn, relieved Maj. Gen. Oliver P.

Smith, who returned to lead the 1st Marine Division. A new course of action, this one named Operation Ripper, was set for early on the morning of March 7. The operation was designed to thrust IX and X Corps toward the 38th Parallel along the central front. The cities of Hongchon and Chunchon rested directly in the path of the IX Corps line of advance. The purpose of Ripper was to inflict as many casualties as possible on the enemy, which in turn would hopefully disrupt their plans for a new offensive. At this time, Allied forces held a line extending across the peninsula from the western coastal city of Inchon, through the recently captured Hoengsong, and east to the coast at Chumunjin.

Unlike Operation Killer, however, Operation Ripper was a throwback to World War I, presaging the war of attrition about to ensue on the Korean peninsula. Maximizing CCF casualties was a worthy goal—but it did not include a coherent strategy to achieve a decisive military victory over the Communist enemy. Although it was not yet readily obvious to many contemporaneous observers or participants, the war in Korea had irrevocably changed.

For the men of the 1st Marine Division, the transformation was more obvious. The division was no longer acting, in any independent sense, as a mobile unit shipped wherever it was needed to launch an attack or defend a piece of valuable terrain. Instead, it was now only one of several divisions holding a continuous front stretching across the width of Korea. The Marine Division's orders were clear: stay in contact with the 1st Cavalry Division on its left, and the 2nd Infantry Division on its right.

Ripper got underway about 800 a.m. on a cold and clear March 7 when 3/1, supported by the tanks of A Company, advanced into a roadless timber-covered maze of steep ridges and narrow valleys. In the mud and snow the tanks were restricted to the floors of the valleys, utilizing the rocky streambeds as paths. As the tankers quickly discovered, however, these relatively easy pathways were hazardous. When large rocks got caught in the center guide of the rear sprocket, they would push the track off the sprocket, bringing the armored vehicle to a halt. Or, as Harry Bruce described it: "You'd pick up rocks when you made a hard turn. It would scoop the rocks up on the track, and it would walk the track off. You had to break the track up and put it back on. . . . It would take at least two hours of good hard work."

The flat trajectory fire of the tank cannons could reach into areas inaccessible to artillery and heavy mortars. By the time Phase Two of Ripper began on March 14, the spring thaw had set in and vehicles were hampered by even deeper mud and the flash floods that swept the narrow valleys after the sudden torrential downpours. Infantry units had to be supported by hundreds of Korean porters with packframes.

The most serious impediment to the tanks was the plethora of mines seeded in the region. The mines were of several varieties, including Soviet-made anti-tank mines, captured American M6 Anti-Tank mines, locally manufactured box mines, and artillery shells buried nose-up in the ground. Some mines were stacked, with multiple mines in the same hole. In all, thirteen tanks struck mines, four of them on March 27. Only one of these tanks was deemed a total loss, an M4A3 that struck an American M6 mine buried atop a box mine.[19]

When the weather finally cleared on March 21, the Marines were advancing against sporadic opposition when the 6th ROK Division on their left stalled. As the Americans began to pull ahead, a gap opened on their flank, a problem that would soon produce serious consequences.

Experienced personnel were shuffled about among the companies. Harry Bruce found himself a gunner, and then a tank commander on an M26 in Able Company. Another tanker, a skinny, talkative, red-haired Tennessean named George Saunders, rejoined the 1st Tank Battalion in April of 1951 and was assigned to the 1st Platoon of A Company.[20] "Red" Saunders had enlisted in the Marine Corps during World War II because he wanted to be in a Raider Battalion. When the Raiders were disbanded before he went overseas, he ended up as a dismounted reconnaissance man in a tank battalion. After the war, he transferred into tanks as a platoon sergeant, although he had no actual experience with tanks. As Saunders put it, "[I] fell in love with the damn things." He transferred out of Able Company the week before the Korean War began, to duty at a depot in Arkansas.[21]

"When I got into the company area, the tank I was assigned to was the tank of a very good friend of mine[22] who was being rotated [home], and the tank was in maintenance," explained Saunders. "I checked into maintenance, and they said, 'Okay, your tank is ready. Go down this road so far and you'll see another road and you'll turn right and you'll go down to a river.' I hadn't been off the boat seventy-two hours. I've just met this tank crew. I'm going down this road and I see this river—a little stream two or three feet deep, fifty or seventy-five yards wide. I had the driver pull about halfway out into this creek." As far as Saunders was concerned, however, something did not seem quite right. He ordered the driver to stop the tank. "I started looking around. I should have seen some tanks by then. Back on the other side, I could see a gun tube sticking out of some bushes. I said, 'Back this thing down!' The Chinese were sitting right on the other side of the river. In fact we got hit that night."

On the morning of April 22, Maj. Holly Evans, a reservist and schoolteacher from Texas, replaced Harry Milne as commander of the tank battalion.[23]   That same day, advancing Allied forces collided head-on with the CCF's Fifth Phase Offensive. The Reconnaissance Company of the Marine division, supported by tanks, was warned by aerial observers of a mass of Chinese on the march, and managed to extricate its members under the protection of the tanks' guns. The Korean Marine Corps Regiment attached to the division encountered fierce resistance to its advance on Hwachon. The ROK 6th Division, however, which had lagged far behind the advanced left flank of the Marines, was under heavy attack.

Throughout the day the Chinese attacks increased in ferocity, with the heaviest blows at first falling upon the right of the division in the sector held by the KMC Regiment and the 5th Marines. By 2300 hours, the 6th ROK Division had collapsed under the onslaught, leaving the 7th Marines and the entire left of the division dangling in a flood of victorious Chinese troops. The 7th Marines refused their flank, folding back to prevent the CCF from getting into the division's rear, while extricating two battalions of US Army artillery left isolated by the collapse of the South Korean troops.

Red Saunders: "We had just got there, my goodness! One friend I was with got hit that night, and evacuated."[24] The man had lasted only a few hours in combat.

On April 24, the IX Corps was ordered to pull back across the Pukhan River, and for the Marines the battle devolved into a desperate struggle to screen the bridges. If the Chinese penetrated the thin line held by the 7th Marines and seized the river crossings, IX Corps would be trapped north of the river. The maneuver to refuse their flank, while essential to preserve the integrity of the line, left the men of the 7th Marines dangerously extended, holding only essential hill positions. The tanks of A and B Companies were thrown into the melee, where liberal use of their 90mm. guns and heavy machine guns flooded the gaps between the hill positions with fire.

The CCF continued to probe the 7th Marine positions throughout the night of 24-25 April. "They just hit with the idea that they could overrun you. You'd just stack them up, was about the size of it," said Red Saunders, who was not particularly impressed with the enemy's tactics. The Marine units were very careful to tie in adequate night defenses. "You'd take your tanks, and if it's still daylight, you can lay out your instruments, your field of fire, overlapping. I actually stood up in a tank and watched the tracers firing. I thought, 'My God, a mosquito couldn't get through this.' They just came in mass, and hoped they'd get through."

Harry Bruce had driven his tank to the rear for repairs. "I was supposed to go back up to the company the next day, but they put me in a line with infantry and told us that that's the way the Chinese should be coming. We sat there and waited. . . . We were holding that pass open so the rest of the division could get back down. There again we were trapped up in there on a damn one-way road. They cut that road, and they were gonna be trapped up there in those mountains again."

The last gasp of the Chinese onslaught began against the positions held by 1/1, which were supported by three tanks from A Company, at 1350 hours on April 25. The struggle continued until the Chinese broke off the assault at 1645, and the Marines withdrew with their wounded aboard tanks.

Harry Smith was the tank commander for a new crew in 3rd Platoon of A Company. After the Chinese attack ended, the Marines sent tanks out to assist the infantry. "They sent a patrol up this nose, and it got ambushed. I remember those guys running down like crazy, bringing one wounded and one dead guy with 'em. We fired machine guns. They loaded the dead guy on my tank. The corpsman flipped out. He was in another tank."

The following day, Smith's tank was covering a bridge and the withdrawal of the ROK Marines. "Some Army engineers came up to blow the bridge, but they forgot their explosives."

"Hell, we'll knock it down," Smith told the engineer.

The engineer readily accepted the offer, but seemed to doubt whether it could be done. "In Germany I watched tanks trying to blow a bridge." "Well, they weren't Marines, you know," Smith replied.

Smith and his crew fired "hyper[shot] at it, and it was going through it like spaghetti. Then we used some HE, and finally we did knock a span down. We wanted to knock the whole thing down, but they kept saying no, just knock one span down."

Bill Robinson's 2nd Platoon was assigned to hold the last bridge.[25] "We had to hold that bridge until they all got through. . . . After Gunner Mac [McMillian] left, this lieutenant took over, and he got hit that one night with a mortar round, and paralyzed.[26] He was sent back to the States." Robinson's platoon had set up at the base of a hill, with the Chinese massed on the opposite side trying to destroy the bridge to prevent the withdrawal of the Army units. The Marines used rocket artillery to break up the Chinese attacks.[27]

Robinson described his experiences: "We set up a perimeter, and they sent aircraft over all night long, illuminating the area. We started receiving fire, and [they] threw some mortar rounds in. [The lieutenant] was standing on the back of the tank. He was the only one hurt. We got a corpsman up there with a stretcher, and got him back to the rear. The next day they sent Lieutenant Snell up to take over the platoon."

Robert Mack remembered that two of the last Army soldiers to cross the bridge were carrying a pole with two five-gallon cans suspended from it. "This one guy dropped the pole, and said, 'I ain't carryin' this no more.' They argued for a little while." Finally, one of the men approached the tank.

"You guys want some raisin jack? It's not quite done yet."[28]

"What the hell, sure!" answered Mack. He would soon have reason to regret his response.

The tankers took the two cans of fermenting fruit and alcohol and hung them on hooks from the turret, pulled across the bridge, closed the hatched, and headed down the road. They had only traveled a short distance when a terrible smell filled the inside of the tank. Mack: "We had taken some fire that punctured those cans, and that mash ran down into the turret ring. Ohhhh. We had to go down to the river three times before we got the smell out. Took about two months to get the smell out." The stinky raisin jack notwithstanding, Able Company tanks and the 1st

Marines successfully covered the withdrawal, destroying abandoned ammunition and fuel dumps.

By April 30, IX Corps was established along a new line twenty-five miles to the south. The fighting had been bloody indeed. The Chinese alone had suffered as many as 100,000 casualties, but U.N. forces had given up a broad swath of ground.

The Americans were using their superiority in artillery to savage the stalled Chinese, with the tanks called upon to add their fire to the long-range barrage. This tactic did not please Major Holly Evans, who vigorously protested the use of the tanks as artillery. This practice wore out the 90mm. guns, he argued, and there were no replacements available.[29] Evans prevailed, and two Army artillery battalions were seconded to the division.

In the spring of 1951, the American military began a policy of rotation, sending home the men with six months or more of Korean service. The policy was designed to assure that the brunt of the war was not borne by a handful of men, but an unintended (though predictable) effect was to rob the units of the most experienced veterans.

Harry Smith's experience was typical. "My tank crapped out, and they pulled it back to the CP. The first sergeant came and said, 'Smith. Pack your gear. You're goin' home.'"

Paul Sanders was among the first to be rotated back to the states because of time previously spent on the Mediterranean cruises. Once aboard ship he was assigned as the mess officer, and some Marines were assigned to the ship's galley. Sanders found the ship's civilian crew overbearing and brutish. "The head cook . . . this guy was the supervisor. He didn't understand Marines, and what they went through. He'd never come up to see me. If I wanted to see him, I had to go down there. I figured that was the way to do it, so I went down and talked to him," explained Sanders. "When they got in line, he started pulling those Marines around—'Over here, bud. Over there.' They were pissed."

One day Sanders called the cook aside and said, "'I just want to tell you something. When you go on deck at night, better not go alone, because the Marines down there in the galley, it's been rumored they're gonna throw your ass off the ship.' Boy, his attitude changed!"

The massive influx of new men placed a premium on experience. Red Saunders was jumped up from corporal to Platoon Sergeant of 1st

Platoon, a position he described as "the best job I ever had in the Marine Corps." The Platoon Sergeant was responsible for training the platoon. "If you got a new man in . . . he could have been shipped in from and infantry outfit, or just out of boot camp. If they're in a hurry they don't send you to too much school. Your job is to make sure he's schooled properly, and that every tank commander knows what the hell he's doing . . . You know a kid eighteen years old, he wants to look for souvenirs and all that crap, and they get shot, and booby-trapped, and everything else."

Many of the replacements had not been trained in any military specialty. Reservist Bart Clendenen was working for the U. S. Forest Service in 1951 when, as he put it, "I got my letter inviting me to the fun." Clendenen arrived in Korea at the end of April 1951, and was immediately assigned to the Tank Platoon of the Anti-Tank Company, 7th Marines "because they were desperate for people. All of the rates were practically wide open, and nobody higher than PFCs in the tanks."

Clendenen was given a choice between tanks and a line infantry company, "So I figured what the heck. I had never seen a tank, except in pictures, until Korea. It was on the job training. That worked out. Actually some of the guys who were still PFCs and tank commanders were ones that had been with them, some of them through the Chosin. We had a few higher NCOs, gunny sergeants who had been in the tanks." Clendenen started out as a loader, and about a month later became gunner.[30]

The 7th Marines was left as a regimental-sized outpost in front of the main Allied line, along with companies B and D of the tanks. Baker Company tanks provided indirect fire support to augment an artillery battalion attached to the outpost, while D Company conducted long-range patrols with the infantry.[31] "The Army thought that was a great idea" said Vaughn Stuart, talking about using a regiment for outpost duty. "We didn't really have much confidence in it."

Stuart's lack of faith in the general overall plan was well placed. Unlike the earlier phases of the war, it was now planned that the front would be held as a continuous line, with squads or platoons outposted hundreds of yards to the front to serve as trip wires for an enemy offensive—and sacrificed, if need be, in order to give warning to the Main Line of Resistance (MLR) in the rear. Someone at Army corps level came up with the idea of sticking an entire regiment—as it turned out, the 7th Marines—several miles in advance into no-man's land, where it would serve as an extraordinarily large "outpost." The risks were obvious and great, as Stuart and other Marines readily realized.

When patrols reported that the Chinese were flowing into the unoccupied ground behind the isolated rifle 7th Marine Regiment (which threatened to sever the Hongchon-Chunchon Road, the regiment's logistical lifeline), the wisdom of using large outposts was put to the test. On the night of May 16-17, the CCF again struck US Army and ROK divisions along a thirty-mile front in eastern Korea. Stuart: "The Chinese tried to come in around behind us, to set up a defense on an outpost before their Spring Offensive in 1951."

The single lane road provided the only link to the regiment's rear. On the afternoon of May 16, an emergency force consisting of 3/7 and tanks was dispatched to occupy the critical Morae-Kagae Pass a few miles below Chungchon. "They sent one battalion and our tank company [Dog Company], and the Seventh Marines Anti-Tank Platoon, which was five M26 tanks, back to this pass," explained Stuart. "It was very mountainous. If we had not moved back there, and the Chinese had occupied it, it would have been difficult. It was the only road, the only way we could get vehicles out through there. They came in the night, probably five hours after we had set up."

At 0245 hours, a battalion of the CCF struck the roadblock position. Although the Chinese had scouted the ground, they were thwarted by a quick-thinking rifleman on a listening post. He gave the alarm, disconnected his field telephone, and settled into hiding.[32] Stuart speculated that the Chinese commander was killed in the first exchange of fire because the attacks were launched without the usual audible signals and seemed to come in blindly.[33] "They hit the tanks first, and then tried to spread into the infantry. We had artillery and everything, the next morning some air [support]."

The Chinese threw wave after wave of men at the American positions while U.S. artillery boxed in the Chinese formations and prevented reinforcement. The fighting was heavy, bloody, and waged in close proximity. Some Chinese infantry managed to get in amongst the tanks and disabled one with a grenade thrown into the engine. A 7th Anti-Tank Platoon vehicle was crippled by a satchel charge shoved into the drive sprocket, and two of its crew killed when they dismounted. Other Chinese swarmed over the tanks. According to the official history, "CCF troops, dressed in U. S. uniforms, climbed onto the tanks, pounded on the hatches and called out in English: 'Hey tank. Let me in.'"[34] The Chinese attempted to destroy another tank by rolling a burning barrel of gasoline down a hill onto the vehicle.[35]

The next morning revealed a charnel house. The always observant Vaughn Stuart recorded what he saw:

> Almost six hundred of them were killed near the roadblock and in a depression running parallel to the main line of resistance. The depression and the hill just across from the Marines had been totally blackened by cannon fire, and the vegetation was gone, attesting to the intensity of the defensive fire.
>
> With a bulldozer, we dug a trench along the long axis of the depression. A Korean labor crew, usually employed to carry rations and ammunition into the hills to the infantry, gleefully dragged the bodies into the trench. We noted that the Chinese were dressed in new summer uniforms and sneakers and carried a spare uniform and extra shoes in their packs, and the laborers outfitted themselves with new clothes and shoes.[36]

When full daylight arrived at 1030 hours, Marine aircraft joined in the slaughter of the fleeing enemy, who left behind 82 prisoners and heavy weapons, including Soviet-made ZiS-3 76.2mm. field guns.[37] That afternoon, the Marine tanks encountered another enemy column in company strength. According to Stuart, the enemy soldiers were "marching down the road four abreast." The tanks virtually annihilated this hapless column.[38]

If Allied forces believed they had thrown back the full weight of the enemy attack, they were disabused of that notion the next day, when the full power of the Chinese offensive struck home. In some places the Chinese drove as deep as thirty miles into the U.N. lines. One of the ruptured formations was the U.S. 2nd Division, which was fighting on the right flank of the Marines. The IX Corps began a retrograde movement to the No-Name Line, a series of defensive positions athwart the Hongchon River. For the remainder of the month, the Marine Division held its position while other U.N. units worked to restore the original line.

More aggressive operations were generally stymied by the terrain and weather. At noon on May 30, Captain "Roughhouse" Taylor mounted B/1/7 on his C Company tanks and attempted to force a passage into Yang-gu. When the column plowed into an unreported mine field seeded by the U.S. Army, it fell back to safer terrain.[39]

In late May, eighteen Americans captured months before during the Chosin Campaign accomplished the only mass escape of the Korean War. In early April, sixty captured soldiers had been brought south to the vicinity of Chorwon, a town about ten miles south-southwest of the North Korean capitol of Pyongyang. According to some official sources, these men were sent south as work details. Marine tanker Len Maffioli, one of the captives, disputes this, claiming the move was nothing more than a measure designed to demoralize the POWs. He recalled that after their capture in December of 1950, they were . . .

> herded up into the hills, and spent that night . . . in some log cabins they had built in the pines, and the Americans didn't even know those cabins were there. Early the next morning we started our trek. It was actually sixty air miles from where we were captured to the prison camp at Kanggye, but it took us fifteen days of walking all night and hiding in a village during the day so the aircraft couldn't see us, on good days. We walked at least a hundred and fifty miles.
>
> There were a hundred and twenty three of us that they marched away that morning. Just about one hundred of us got to the prison camp. Twenty-three died along the way from wounds that weren't treated, or from frostbite that turned to gangrene within a few days. There were no medical facilities on the march; no towns . . . and the Chinese did not have the medical supplies. We tried carrying some of our own buddies on stretchers, but after the third or fourth day of a potato a day or something like that, we were so weak we couldn't even carry a stretcher any more . . .
>
> It took us twenty-one days to get to the camp, but fifteen of it was walking every day, and then they gave us a six-day rest about three-quarters of the way. That's about it, except for the five more months as a prisoner of war.

From December 21 until early March of 1951, the prisoners marked time in the camp in extreme northwestern Korea. "We underwent three or four hours a day, every day, of lectures and study periods for the indoctrination course, re-education course," remembered Maffioli. "Some people call it a low-powered brainwashing. It was actually a high-powered political indoctrination course was what it was. Three or four hours a day, every day for months and months, is more comprehensive than some college courses."

In early March, a large contingent of POWs was suddenly pulled out of the camp and shipped by train into north-central Korea. Just as suddenly, most were shipped back. Maffioli continued: "I was one of the sixty chosen to continue. We set up a prison camp. They brought three hundred soldiers they had just captured, all Army, all from the same regiment, and we helped set up the prison camp for them." After this work detail ended, he continued, "they grabbed thirty out of the sixty and said, 'We're gonna turn you loose.' They took 'em all the way down to the front lines—I was not part of this thirty—and said, 'Oops! Too dangerous to set you loose!' and brought them all the way back. It was one of those morale-busting deals, just to keep you off guard, off balance, to keep your morale down."

The Chinese selected nineteen prisoners, eighteen Marines and a Nisei interpreter/translator, Cpl. Saburo "Sam" Shimamura, to continue the bizarre odyssey.[40]

Simamura, Maffioli explained . . .

> was an Army intelligence man, but he spoke fluent Japanese and of course all Koreans of any age spoke Japanese. It was a mandatory language [during the Japanese colonial period]. They . . . took us down toward the lines because they thought they were gonna capture some Marines, and we would set up a camp. They took us too close to the front lines. Artillery was registering in the area,[41] and our guards panicked and ran away from the sound of it.
>
> We ran toward it, and were able to hide out that night when they came back looking for us. The next morning we signaled an airplane.

The men stripped wallpaper from a wrecked house and laid it on the ground to spell out "POWS—19 RESCUE." Fortunately, an observation plane spotted the sign and a patrol of three Army tanks was dispatched to the area.[42] It was one of the happiest days of Maffioli's life:

> It was after exactly six months. It turned out to be the only group escape ever made from the Chinese or North Koreans. Very lucky. Just like the Marine Corps history book says, 'Through a series of fortuitous events and quick thinking, [we] were able to get out.'

It was over for all of us. I weighed a hundred pounds.[43] I had been really troubled with amoebic dysentery, which was the biggest killer. A lot of people don't realize . . . we had the highest death rate, in captivity in Korea, of American prisoners than we've ever had in any war, before or since. Four out of every ten Americans known to have been captured died in captivity. . . . . The biggest killer was amoebic dysentery."

*   *   *

The early summer of 1951 introduced the seesaw fighting that characterized the rest of the undeclared Korean War. Don Bennett described it thusly: "We attacked and took maybe thirty miles or so from the Chinese. After they built up enough men and supplies, they attacked us and pushed us back twenty. That's what it seemed like to me. It was a war of attrition, to make the Chinese pay very heavily for their gains. We didn't stand and try to hold some location for a long, long time like they did later on."

To the men at battalion level, the back-and-forth fighting seemed senseless. "We had a pretty good fight to get to this one ridge," explained Phil Morell. "We had cleared it and everything else, and . . . we even had a couple of volleyball courts behind the front lines. We were in good shape. And then the Security Council from the United Nations said, 'Oh, we made a mistake. That isn't gonna be the line. You gotta go to that next ridge up there.' There were a number of infantry guys killed getting up to that next ridge, which was maybe two, three miles away. We were in good defensive positions where we were, and they moved us on up there."

On the whole, enlisted Marines seem to have given the situation less thought. "You don't get involved in that," said Red Saunders. "You're a tank platoon, and you live in your own little niche. You don't even know the people in the company, hardly. You're attached to a different battalion of infantry, and the only time you get together is when you pull back. You may be back for a month or so, but still . . . you're in your own little world."

In the last week of May 1951, U.N. forces launched an offensive to push the Chinese north toward the town of Yang-gu and the large Hwachon Reservoir. Red Saunders experienced the same heartbreaking frustrations as other veteran tankers in dealing with infantry officers who did not know how to use tanks in combat. "We ran into a box canyon. You could see the infantry in hand-to-hand combat with the gooks there. I jumped off the tank, this [infantry] company commander was there, and I said '*Please* let me give you overhead fire support!' [The infantry officer replied] 'Ah, bullshit.' I'm standing there *begging* him, and what does he do? He calls in airplanes, shooting rockets! That's like shooting shotguns, you know." The refusal gripped Saunders emotionally. "I'm sitting there, with a gun that'll blow your head off at fifteen hundred yards, and I'm crying. I'm literally just emotionally ripped up, 'cause I'm watching Marines die, and this dumb sonofabitch, he's calling airplanes in, probably killing other Marines. We just sat there with five tanks. Couldn't fire."

By May 31, the Marines were embroiled in bitter fighting for the rugged hills east of the Hwachon Reservoir. The Chinese were in carefully concealed positions overlooking the road, from which they could pour down heavy fire upon the advancing troops. The tanks of C Company that led the advance up the narrow road were an unfailing provocation to the Chinese, who poured heavy fire onto the rolling armor, revealing their positions in the process.

The tanks were not seriously threatened, however, because the Chinese were still using relatively light mortars and artillery. Cecil Fullerton remembers that they used 82mm. mortars extensively, and "we could hear them clanging off the top of the turret, on the armor plate. They weren't doing anything except making a loud noise. One sergeant got hit in the engine compartment. It must have been a 120mm. The engine compartment doors caved in, and stopped him. I remember his famous radio transmission to his lieutenant. Have to excuse the language. He said: 'Out of gas, shot in the ass. Request instructions.' That was [Doyle] Brummitt. He was in B Company."

The fighting around the east end of the Hwachon Reservoir was "pretty bad," said Ben Busch, "especially for the infantry. We were most of the time road bound, and fired long-range support missions for the infantry." By the evening of May 31, the Marines controlled the town of Yang-gu.

About this time, the 2nd Platoon of A Company acquired a "washee-washee" boy. Corporal Robert Mack: "His folks had been shot up in Yang-gu, and the GIs, they felt sorry for him. When Murphy asked him if he had any relatives, he said no. He was a kid kind of left on his own, so they took him with 'em. [He did] Little errands. Wash clothes for you, and stuff like that. He didn't do an awful lot of washing clothes. I don't know what the other guys would call him. Houseboy, but we didn't have a house or anything, but he traveled with us. His name was Ski."

The terrain northeast of Yang-gu was ideal for defensive warfare, with the tanks restricted to a few poor roads. The American advance was blocked by high ridges with right-angle spurs to the main ridge lines. By digging in along these spurs, the Chinese were able to unleash a devastating fire into each flank of the advancing Marines, turning each of these blind valleys into a huge U-shaped ambush.

The task of clearing the steep wooded ridges fell as usual to the infantry, but the tanks were the key to breaking through this stubborn enemy defense. The armor advanced into the mouth of the ambush and lay down suppressive fire to both flanks, giving the rifle companies an opportunity to assault the Chinese positions.

Moving up onto the ridges, however, was treacherous work for the tanks. Corporal Mack remembered how Korean burial practices interfered with the advance: "The Koreans would bury people above ground. They'd take them up the hill, and bury them on the ridge crests." The traditional graves were raised mounds, several feet high. "We'd get almost up to where we want, and there'd be one of those damn graves. You either had to try and go around it, and risk tipping over, or try to go over it and risk getting high-centered."

Novice tanker Bart Clendenen quickly learned that the tanks in the rifle regiment Anti-Tank Platoons "were kind of a loose cannon. It was a strange setup. They had the two sections of seventy-five millimeter recoilless, and then we had this one platoon of five tanks. We operated pretty much as lone wolves, so to speak. Quite often we were put into action as a platoon, five tanks together, but when it came to working with a line company it was often on a single tank basis."

Clendenen recalled moving out one afternoon "and we were getting fire from machine guns, rifles and stuff all the time. On one of the tanks, [the tank commander] jumped out to check on something because the radio conked, and ran up to the platoon leader's tank. Coming back, he got up on his tank, stepped on the deck where a machine gun had hit the spare oilcan on the side of the turret. He went skating off the tank. Result – one very mad TC."

Although the South Korean divisions were taking heavy casualties, continued Clendenen, "The Chinese, by that time, were the ones that were gettin' it. God. Go through those valleys along those roads, and it was one of those things—you didn't want to see it. Our planes were coming through strafing. . . . It was just long stretches of bodies along the side of the road." Clendenen recalls seeing what he described as "occasional weird stuff," in the operation through the ridged terrain. "I saw a couple of Corsairs collide over on the ridge when we were moving up," he said. "Happened to look up and they were strafing. Somehow or other I guess they got their signals mixed up, and two of them came up from opposite sides. All I saw was wings and tails flying. They collided in mid-air, right over that ridge."

Many vehicles competed for the limited road space. Wheeled vehicles were under strict instructions not to break into the tank columns because the tank drivers had such poor visibility. One day, Robert Mack's platoon was bypassing a bridge by driving through the stream bed when a loaded truck raced up from behind, crossed the bridge, and broke into the tank column. Mack was leaning against the front of the turret behind the driver's hatch when he caught sight of the speeding truck.

"I knew Castor wouldn't see it with that damn hatch blocking [his view]," Mack explained. "I hollered. I kicked him in the back of the helmet the old, old style [signal] to stop.[44] The tank stopped just in time. "We just barely missed him."

A furious Castor, meanwhile, yelled back, "Sarge, call up Robbie in the next tank and tell him to slow down. I'm gonna put his tit in a wringer!"

"He slowed down and gosh, we crawled up and started just chewing the track on the back of his tailgate," said Mack. "It was just a six-by." It did not take Mack long to realize there was a bit of danger in that action. The truck did not have a canvas top, and visible inside were barrels of aviation gasoline.

"Back off before you blow that thing up!" he yelled at his driver.

He did, and the truck quickly found room and pulled off. "I bet you he sat there and never got in another tank column again," laughed Mack. As for Castor, "[He] was kind of crazy like that. We'd have had a hell of an explosion if he got enough sparks to set it off."

The last phase of the spring offensive arrived when the Marines broke out into the So-chon River valley, but the tanks found this terrain more dangerous than the hills they had just left behind them. The Chinese had liberally sown the valley with mines, and ten tanks were quickly crippled by the dangerous explosions.

Red Saunders admired the quality of the junior officers who had replaced the old hands. "Most of them were all young second lieutenants. Every one I served with I called them Superman, because they listened to you, stuck their head out. We hit lots of mines over there. The Platoon Leader I had . . . he would take the point, because he wouldn't let any other of his troops go out there. I'm pretty sure he hit five mines within a period of three months. That was the lead tank, and then he'd jump off and go get in another one. The concussion a man goes through when you do hit a mine is pretty severe."

Not all of the officers were green. Charles Sooter, who enlisted in 1942, served as a sergeant in Ed Bale's tank company at Tarawa and Saipan during World War II. After Saipan, Sooter was given a field commission and was shipped to Korea as a first lieutenant. Three weeks later he was promoted to captain and became the CO of Dog Company.[45]

By June of 1951, the enemy artillery had become "annoyingly accurate," but the greatest threat was still from the lowly land mine. These subterranean explosives disabled twenty-six tanks, and most tank platoons were makeshift affairs as the units were combined to comprise full-strength outfits.[46] The unit diary records the events of June 14, when one such under strength composite platoon of four tanks moved toward an objective known as Hill 500:

> At [map coordinates] (TA-1628-R) one tank hit a mine. The platoon continued to move forward to the RJ where heavy mortar and artillery fire forced the accompanying engineers to cover. The tanks continued to move forward for approximately 300 yards without engineer assistance in order to be masked from artillery fire. The engineers rejoined the tanks and this team moved forward to (TA-1629-M) where a second tank hit a mine.
>
> Engineers cleared a path around this tank and the following tanks started through. The first to try it hit a mine. All tanks delivered fire on objective 10 (TA-1628-R) supporting 1/7. In preparations for

recovering the knocked out tanks the engineers rechecked and probed the road back south to the RJ at (TA-1628-H). The last operative tank in the platoon, having completed its mission, turned around and began to retrace its route. At (TA-1629-R) this tank hit a mine, making a total of four for the day. All tanks were disarmed and disabled. The first tank which hit a mine at (TA-1628-R) was retrieved and the three remaining were left in place. An infantry outpost remained forward of the tanks during the night.[47]

Chinese mines were simple affairs—wooden boxes filled with picric acid and rigged with a pressure detonator. The rounded lower hull of the M26 made it far more resistant to mine explosions than the older M4 tanks, and the typical damage that resulted from such an explosion was a broken track and road wheel damage. On one occasion, Vaughn Stuart's tank hit two mines at once, which left "both tracks . . . destroyed, the left escape hatch blown into the bottom of the tank, and one complete set of road wheels blown off of the tank, bounding about a hundred feet or so out to one side."[48]

The escape hatches in the bellies of the M26s were particularly vulnerable, as Harry Bruce noted: "It was more hazardous to the driver and assistant driver than it was to anybody else, because the escape hatches were right under their feet. . . . We sandbagged the hatches. We put about four sandbags on top of those hatches to add more weight to it, and take the brunt of the blast."

Bart Clendenen elaborated, explaining that "Quite often you had drivers killed, or assistant drivers, from the [escape] hatches blowing up through [the opening] when you hit a mine. One of them, sad to say, was not even in action. We had been pulled back and were doing some reserve training. . . . We drove into an area that they supposedly had cleared [of mines], and we found one. Killed the driver. Fortunately he was the only one."

It didn't take much," said Clendenen. "If it hit the outside of the track you were okay. If it hit underneath, on the inside of the track, it was pretty much a given that it was gonna hit that hatch."

The platoon's mechanic improvised a better remedy than heavy sandbags. "They just got some heavy [steel] bar, cut off chunks, and welded them to the opposite sides of the hatch cover," continued Clendenen. "You could still release the lever and drop the thing, but it wouldn't blow up through. That was a real godsend. So simple it was amazing that they hadn't come up with it before."

The tank battalion also experimented with heavy rollers and scarifier teeth [rakes] to help disinter or detonate mines.[49]

The Porcupine communications tank was increasingly used as a forward support coordination vehicle.[50] Artillery was very quickly becoming a dominant arm in the struggle amid the steep mountains, so the tanks again found themselves used to augment the division artillery. Although this misuse of the tank's mobility and firepower drove the higher-level officers to despair, junior officers like Vaughn Stuart found their skills at this secondary mission a point of pride.

According to Stuart, the platoon he inherited from Paul Sanders was a good one. . .

> the best-trained tank platoon I ever saw. They could do anything I asked them to do. Periodically, on our movement up to the KANSAS Line, Colonel [Homer] Litzenburg, the commander of the Seventh Marines, would call my company commander and say. 'I want a tank platoon to fire a mission to this point.' He would just give a point on the map. When I was enlisted I had gone through an artillery school for using the one-oh-fives for indirect fire. I knew all about the aiming circle[51] and all that good stuff.
>
> So the Old Man says, "Okay, which one of you lieutenants think you can do this?"
>
> I said, "Well, I think I can do it alright."
>
> It was all by inspection on the ground, find your location, so I don't know how good these first rounds were.
>
> We got lined up, and all laid parallel. I conducted the fire from my tank by radio. From then on, every night when we set up, I'd set my platoon up for indirect fire.
>
> When we got to the KANSAS Line, we just set up right on the front lines, on a line with the infantry. I had all five of my tanks on line. Artillery dug us some holes so we could go hull-defilade, just have the turret exposed. There was a bridge abutment nearby, so they were able to survey me in precisely.[52]
>
> Once I got the guns laid, they put up an OE just to see what I could do.
>
> This OE started firing in our base piece, and then we got a fire for effect. He said, "Mission successful and complete" Later on we found out that we were right on with those nineties. They were very accurate.

From there we fired a lot of harassing fire. . . . We stayed there for quite some time. We got missions from the artillery, so we fired periodically every night.

Stuart continued:

I was out, must have been about midnight one night, watching what the tanks were doing. I saw this tremendous explosion, never heard the sound, it was so far away. We know we hit something, we thought maybe a truck, because we were firing at a crossroads, more the harassing and interdiction type fire.

There were times when we dug parapets, and we would put the tanks up at an angle. Well, you can imagine the deflection was horrible! You deflect three mils;[53] no telling how many yards that would take you off to the side (of the target). But the artillery regiment had that pretty well figured out what it would be."

*   *   *

In early July, the 1st Marine Division passed into corps reserve, where it remained through August 26. The tank battalion continued to receive influxes of new men, most of whom had no experience with tanks. By the end of the summer, the last of the division's original personnel were in the process of leaving Korea. Over the years, a myth has grown about how the returning warriors were welcomed home. "Nobody gave me a parade," Harry Bruce said simply.

Like many of the returning men, Bruce touched U.S. soil in a state of shock. "To be honest with you, I don't even remember coming home. They hauled us to an airfield in a truck, and I remember the big [Lockheed] Constellation, that big four-engine job with the three tails on it, I remember it coming in for a landing. I will never forgive the Red Cross, because they charged me for coffee and donuts, and I was still in a what was considered a combat zone. I could not tell you where they flew me to. I can remember being in Kobe. . . . But I don't remember anything else about it."

The replacements included men like Pete Flournoy, a college athlete in the Navy Reserve who got mad and quit school. He tried to join the Army and the Air Force, and was finally accepted by the Marine Corps. "The next morning I was on my way to Parris Island," he said. Flournoy went to Korea as an automatic rifleman in the 5th Marines, and transferred into C Company tanks. He joined while the company was on a small island called Taylor's Island, named after the company commander.

"Captain Taylor left and Walter 'Mu-Mu' Moore came in and took over the company then," remembered Flournoy. "We were in corps reserve. . . . Before I got there, in the early spring of that year, the tanks had a bad time. They really got clobbered." Flournoy had "absolutely no tank training at all. It was all on-the-job training. They had me drive around the island. . . . Learn how to drive the darn thing. I caught the usual flak, where they send you over to get a road wheel pump, the comedy things they always do to you. Get a bucket of muzzle blast . . . garbage like that. Course being a dumb, ignorant ol' grunt like I was, I didn't know any better anyway." Within a few months Flournoy could perform any task in the tank. "We switched positions all the time. If you were a driver one day, next day you might be the loader, next day you might be tank commander. It was just a constant evolution." Generous to a fault, Flournoy would demonstrate considerable personal bravery on the field—even for a Marine leader.

Walter Moore, the new "hands-on" company commander, was another mustang who received a field commission in the 3rd Raider Battalion in 1943. After recovering from malaria and filariasis, he switched over to tanks in 1944 and served with 1st Tank Battalion in the savage fighting on Peleliu and Okinawa, and then on occupation duty in China. In the summer of 1951, Moore rejoined Charlie Company, his old outfit from World War II.

"At that time," explained Moore, "Captain Richard 'Roughhouse' Taylor's company was supporting the Fifth Marines in a blocking position at Inji. This was south of the Punchbowl."[54]

On August 27, the Marine Division moved up to replace the 2nd Division and the 8th ROK Division in the line, in preparation for an attack following the expiration of the truce talks. On August 31, the division attacked north toward the hills on the eastern side of The Punchbowl, a vast circular valley northeast of the Hwachon Reservoir and just north of the Kansas Line. The enemy was ensconced in clusters of sturdy log and earthen bunkers that resisted all but direct hits by artillery. Even when the infantry cleared these structures they could not always destroy them, and enemy artillery observers often hid in the rubble.

Bart Clendenen reported that one unlucky day, the men "had parked the tanks pretty much crowded together because of the terrain. The guys had built a little fire up near the tanks and were standing around. . . . Luckily I was somewhere else. Two artillery rounds came in. One hit the engine hatch on the back of one tank. The other landed right in the middle of the fire. I don't know why they weren't all killed. It was big artillery, similar to our one-five-fives. One was killed, two were pretty badly wounded, but they survived okay. The rest of the men had sort of deaf ears. That blast of course shook 'em up good."

The casualties that were accumulating, continued Clendenen, "made it real tough to fill in, because you didn't have any spare people around. In some cases we were running one short. Actually, you could operate with just the driver down in front, and the assistant driver could come up and act as loader for the gun."

From Sept 11-22, 1951, Walter Moore's company participated in the 1st Marine Division's contribution to the final offensive operation of the war on the northeastern front. His recollection follows:

> The Division attacked the North Korean hill/ridge positions of 673, 749 and 812 in a column of Regiments. 1/7 led the way capturing Hill 673, then it was 2/1's turn on the fortified slopes of Hill 749. The next final objective was Hill 812, where after another tough fight, 2/5 won a victory over the NKPA forces. This ridge line running roughly in a NW direction was heavily defended by the NKPA. They fought very much like their old Japanese mentors, giving no quarter and not expecting any.
>
> My tanks were in the fight continually (not eventually). We initially supported 1/7 in the attack on 673. I had tank liaison teams situated with the forward elements. These liaison teams were the reason we could shoot over the heads of infantry marines without causing casualties. Unlike Hills 749 and 812, 673 was pretty well exposed to the 90mm. flat trajectory fire of the tank guns. Distances from my tanks in the valley to the impact area varied from 400 to 900 yards. One must remember that a high velocity 90mm. tank gun was a very accurate weapon at the shorter ranges. Thanks to a stash of light combat wire and sound power phones, I was able to keep in touch with my liaison teams up front. Radio communications went out on a regular basis so this scheme worked pretty well. The light wire we used was very vulnerable to tank treads and mortar fire.

This meant people under my command, like the intrepid Sgt. C. B. Ash, were personally laying wire under fire to keep communications open.[55]

Although Moore's armor played a key role in several of the hill engagements, most were largely infantry fights, and in most areas the tanks simply could not get into position to assist the riflemen. One exception was the protracted struggle for Hill 749 that began on September 13.

The NKPA had burrowed deeply into the slopes of Hill 749. When 2/1 launched a series of attacks, the enemy called down their own artillery upon the exposed Marines, inflicting severe casualties. C Company tanks were brought into position and fired 720 rounds of 90mm. ammunition at six large bunkers. On September 15, the enemy launched a series of savage counterattacks under heavy artillery and mortar fire. These bloody attacks continued—in vain—until late on the afternoon of September 16. One this final day of the attacks, 2/5 and 3/5 assaulted and captured nearby Hill 812, a dominating terrain feature that was to prove important to the future tank operations.

Moore explains:

> In order to keep constant pressure on the enemy, we used the "processing" system developed in fighting the Japanese defensive system on Okinawa. "Processing" meant shooting in relays. This kept at least one tank platoon on station firing on call during the daylight hours. Due to the good relationship we maintained with the regimental commanders, I was to [have] the three tank platoons, from each of the infantry regiment AT Companies, under my Op Con (Operational Control). Small wonder we expended from 70 to 100 rounds [per day].
>
> Mainly because of the intervening terrain, it became difficult for my tanks to support 2/5 on Hill 812. Thanks to the initiative of my men, we solved that problem . . . by using the two Company Headquarters dozers and an armored TD-18 bulldozer from the engineers to cut a tank trail that traversed up the side of the ridge. Later in the winter months this technique became standard operating procedure....
>
> Accomplishing this tricky feat was done in the face of the "it can't be done" nay sayers who referred to the tanks as "the sick beasts of Korea." How wrong they were.[56]

Pete Flournoy described the difficulties faced by the tankers: "You had to be so careful . . . we were on ridge lines, straddling ridge lines. At times, even under fire, you had to get a man to dismount and walk the driver up, ground guide him, to keep him from throwing track. Most of the time it seemed that the really steepest spot was on the frontal slope, where the gooks could see you. They started throwing mortars and stuff."

The next day the Marines found more bunkers on the reverse slope, and the tanks expended another 400 rounds on these stubborn positions. When firing against enemy timber and earth bunkers, it was more effective to fire the HE rounds in delayed-action mode.

By now, most of the tank companies had also adopted the practice of carrying extra ammunition for the infantry. "We would carry a ton of ammo," explained Flournoy. "Thirty caliber, and fifty. The grunts would get in a bind, reach up on the fender, and grab a box of ammo off. We had what they called fender shields that went down over the edge of the track. We . . . turned 'em upside-down, put 'em back on, and it was the perfect spot to store ammo. If you need a gun, grab a gun. Tripod . . . a thirty caliber [machine gun], all just lying wrapped up, usually in a sweatshirt coated with oil."

Heavy enemy counterattacks aimed at recapturing Hill 812 continued through the evening of September 18. The tanks played havoc with the enemy. On September 20, the Marines captured one NKPA soldier and killed several more operating behind American lines. Interrogation of the prisoner revealed that he was a member of one of several special infiltration teams, numbering about fifty men in all, whose task was to plant mines along trails used by the tanks, and to scout the positions of the tanks for attack by artillery.[57]

With the U.N. forces in possession of ground that dominated the enemy-held hills, the corps commander ordered a consolidation of positions, with no more advances after September 20.[58] The division launched several innovative operations during the balance of the month. During Operation Summit, which began on September 21, helicopter squadron HMR-161 inserted 224 men and 36 tons of cargo onto the crest of rugged and inaccessible Hill 884—the first such operation in history. Operation Blackbird, on September 27, was the first nocturnal helicopter-borne assault.[59] Other than these unique operations, however, the war quickly settled into a war of position—a euphemism for trench warfare and general stalemate.

The tanks spent much of October supporting long-range raids by both the American and South Korean Marines. Like the trench raids of the First World War, these small scale operations were designed solely to inflict maximum casualties upon the enemy, although the raiders, too suffered losses.

Roger Baker wrote about one such raid that went horribly wrong. On October 16, the 3rd Platoon of A Company was ordered to support a company-sized operation by the 7th Marines, but was halted by a minefield. As more and more engineers were dragged back, dead or wounded, GYSGT Robert "Red" Wheeler dismounted and walked from tank to tank to calm his men. Wheeler, who had succeeded Joe Sleger as Platoon Sergeant of 3rd Platoon, Able Company, was a World War II veteran who had come back into service from the Reserves. He was on his last combat mission before going home.

When it was time to move out, Wheeler climbed back into his tank and the armor at last lurched forward. After a short time a titanic explosion racked the tank in front of Roger Baker's tank. He watched while several men struggled to escape from the tank. To his dismay, he soon discovered that Wheeler had been hit in the skull by a hot piece of shrapnel. "It was hard to see through the cupola, so he had it cracked open, looking out," explained Roger Chaput. "There was kind of a knoll on the side. A round landed there, and shrapnel flew. Just through that little opening, he got it right through the side of the head. When the corpsman got there, he didn't think it was that bad, just a little [splinter]. Then when he pulled it out. . . ." Wheeler later died of his wounds.[60] "He had the hatch cracked open, but he wasn't wearing a steel pot. If he had," Chaput added, "it would probably have saved his life."

Even though Wheeler was down, the battle was still being waged. As the remaining tanks moved forward about 500 yards to be in a position to support the riflemen, two more struck mines and stopped in their tracks.

With his ammunition nearly exhausted, Roger Baker turned his tank to withdraw and threw a track in the muddy rice paddy. Deluged by artillery and mortar fire, the officer on the scene decided to temporarily abandon the vehicle, and the crew crawled out of the crippled tank into the stinking mud. A timely air strike provided some cover while the Platoon Leader, Lieutenant Muser, picked up Baker's crew.[61]

The shelling that poured in the next morning wounded another man in the platoon, and a friend of Baker's from another platoon invited him over to share a food package from home. As they started toward the other platoon's position, remembered Baker, "the last thing I saw was the ground heaving up, like in slow motion, directly in front of us."[62]

Baker regained consciousness amid the sounds of exploding shells, men crying out in agony, and frantic calls for medical corpsmen. When the shelling finally ceased, Baker emerged from his temporary shelter and staggered a few steps. Something caught his attention, and he stooped to pick up the unfamiliar object. A headless body was lying nearby. The bloody corpse turned out be his friend, and the object he had picked up was a large piece of his friend's skull. "I went into further shock, and was unable to speak or cry," he said.[63]

In their ongoing efforts to destroy one another, both sides had first to overcome the difficult terrain. Walter Moore: "Contending with snow and ice, we actually cut roads up to the top of these ridge lines, at a thousand meters in elevation, to use tanks to help the infantry kill or destroy the enemy.[64]

Random death was never very far away, as Bart Clendenen easily remembered: "We're up on a wooded ridge on this rough road and stuff was whistling through the brush. All kinds of machine gun and rifle fire going. The tank commander wanted something, and I just dropped down the hatch to grab a pair of pliers or something out of the toolbox behind the gun. Just as I dropped through the hatch, a slug hit the ammo box on the fifty right above my head. Sprayed me all over the place with little tiny particles off of the strap and the slug itself. I kept [the peeled metal jacket] for a souvenir. Needless to say," added Clendenen, "I didn't come out of that hole for a few minutes."

One of the most difficult targeting tasks was to get plunging artillery fire to precisely land on targets situated on ridge crests. Under such conditions, even a minor adjustment would drop the rounds far down the slope. To deal with these specific targets, tanks were laboriously positioned on Hills 812 and 854. From these positions, the tankers "sniped at the enemy both day and night."[65] The Army's 92nd

Searchlight Company turned spotlights directly onto targets to allow night firing.

The enemy was by no means impotent in these exchanges of artillery fire, as the return artillery and heavy mortar rounds that routinely slammed into the tank positions attested. On October 17, Able Company command post was hit, leaving three dead and four wounded when the smoke cleared. On the last day in October, a mine disabled one tank in no-man's land; the dozer tank and both of the VTRs sent to recover it were likewise incapacitated. All four vehicles sat abandoned between the lines until they could be recovered the next day.

As an eleven-year old, Donald Boyer had been fascinated by the story of the men who survived being pulled from their tank and beaten by the Japanese on Tanambogo in 1942. "I thought, 'Geez, someday I'd like to be in tanks.'" At Parris Island, he requested to be trained as a tank crewman, and was sent to tank school. Boyer went to Korea at the end of October as part of the Thirteenth Replacement Draft.[66]

"When I went overseas a lot of the guys who trained with me, they ended up in the infantry, because that's where the casualties are," Boyer explained. A few men were assigned to the tank battalion, but "A guy pulled us aside and said, 'You're going into the AT Company.' He said, 'It's a good outfit. You don't have all this spit-and-polish the tank battalion had.' When they were in reserve, they put painted rocks around their tents, and that kind of stuff. We never had that kind of spit-and-polish."

Boyer's first impression of Korea, like that offered by so many veterans of the war, was of the weather and terrain. The first time he went up into the lines, "There was an ice storm came up. We were going around this sheer cliff wall, and if the tank started to slip a little bit, there was quite a drop off. The lieutenant says, 'Everybody get off the tanks, but the driver.' It was real precarious going around that cliff face. They'd start to slide. . . . It was very hairy there. It was in the dark, too, and that didn't help."

The old M26 tanks were worn beyond repair, and between July and November of 1951 they were gradually replaced by the improved M46.[67] The Anti-Tank Platoon did not receive new vehicles until later, around late December.[68] In many respects the new tank was an improvement over the M26, with a more powerful V-12 engine and Hydramatic automatic transmission, a bore evacuator to reduce the backflow of gasses through the main gun breech, and other minor changes. However, there were problems with the new model.

According to the official Marine Corps history, the new tanks suffered engine problems from faulty oil cooler fans,[69] but for the crews the new vehicles had other, terrifying, quirks. Pete Flournoy expounded on one of its more serious defects: "The forty-six had a bad flaw, particularly in that kind of terrain. . . . As long as you kept it revved up you had good steering. You started backing off the gas pedal going downhill, and your engine slows down, you lose your steering. You had to keep it revved. We banged up a lot of tanks over there, doing that. You couldn't steer 'em. You run into embankments, damn near off the road down in the valleys. Hit some truck and knock him off the road trying to stop the damn thing."

And the Marines operated in ghastly terrain. Bart Clendenen's platoon leader led his men on conditioning hikes—both physical and mental. "You could still see where bodies were around some of these gun positions and trenches." The bodies were not yet skeletons, because "they hadn't quite gotten that far yet, unfortunately. It was not pleasant."

Amid the bitter cold and mud of another winter the tanks were dug into tank slots—revetments—in the front lines. The tanks were often immobilized by deep mud and were vulnerable to attack by infiltrators.[70]

"Mostly we fired at fortified bunkers," explained Donald Boyer. "We would use high-explosive. They had a little screw slot in the nose [of the projectile]. You just turn that and set it on delay. I don't know how many tenths of a second that was or whatever. . . . It would penetrate into the bunker and then explode."

To Boyer's dismay, the tankers seldom saw the effects of their fire:

> It was pretty hard, really. You'd be buttoned up, receiving mortar fire, and small arms fire. The Chinese could drop a mortar round right through your hatch. Those guys were good. One time they shot at us with a bazooka, and we weren't very far from 'em. I saw it go by, and I thought, 'My God, what's a bird doing out here?' The infantry guys later said, 'We couldn't even see your tank. I'm glad I'm in the infantry.' It was all covered from dirt, and dust, and smoke from all the mortars hitting all over it.
>
> The rocket went by us, [and] hit the tank behind us. He had the turret turned with the gun to the rear. The rocket hit right in the

corner where the armor is cast real thick, and it didn't penetrate. It was only about the size of my finger, the hole, but it cut the fifty caliber spare barrel right in half. . . . It looked like a small round hole, like it was cut with acetylene."

Even in midwinter when the ground was frozen rock hard, moving the tanks was often an exhausting ordeal. Charles Sooter described moving a platoon of his tanks up to a new firing position that required the armor to climb a steep slope before making a right angle turn. "I had to send the retriever up to one corner, and winch these tanks up because it was so slick," he explained. The retriever crew first had to drag the heavy steel tow cable up the slope by hand and attach it to an immovable object, then drag the VTR up the slope using its own winch. Once the VTR was emplaced, it pulled the other tanks up the icy slope.[71] "When we got them up to that corner, they could drive on up. . . ."

The grinding positional warfare aggravated other problems that had long plagued the tankers. When 90mm. ammunition was stacked outside in the bitter cold, the rounds accumulated water vapor inside the shell casing, and the propellant would not properly burn. Bart Clendenen commented on this problem: "These things (the powder pellets) were about the size of shotgun wads. [When the main gun fired], it would leave a trail of those darn pellets out the full length of that hot barrel. Then the pellets would catch fire, and it was just like a back draft. That breech would drop, and there would be a two-foot flame coming out of that thing."

The tongue of flame could also be dangerous. "I got the side of my head singed quite a few times, until I finally got wise," said Clendenen. "I could hear it coming, just like a freight train. Lean way over to the right [in the gunner's seat] and get out of the road. The loader had to watch it, too. He'd lean over trying to grab a casing, and get in the way of that flame coming out. It was just like a flamethrower when the flame came roaring out of that breech."

In the bitter cold, continued Clendenen, "We had to run the tanks every hour at night. The guys on guard duty had to come around and crank them up. When we first pulled in there was no place to sleep, so I just slept on the floor of the tank, in the turret. This guy came along on guard duty while I was sleeping, and cranked up the auxiliary engine,[72] which we later found had faulty exhaust systems. I just happened to wake up, and was able to get myself up and flip the hatch open. Next thing I knew I was back down, my back on the floor looking up at that hole. It took me about two or three days to get over that experience. I was sicker than a dog."

The tedium along the static front also inspired experimentation with weapons. Some efforts were distinctly more ill advised than others. "We had this one older lieutenant," remembered Don Boyer. "He had a real brainstorm. He said, 'I'm gonna put that fifty, coax mount it in the turret where the thirty is,' so he can bore-sight it in with the big gun. It [the fifty caliber] reaches out farther, and if he gets on target with that, he knows he's on target with the big gun."[73] It did not work out as the lieutenant had anticipated. "We couldn't handle it in there!" Boyer explained. "It was so noisy, it just rattled your brains. And the [metal ammo belt] links were huge. They would get down in the floor, and almost jam your turret when you tried to turn it. We took that thing out of there. It didn't last very long."

More pragmatic ideas included jury-rigged stoves that heated small two- to five-man bunkers. A firebox was made from a mortar ammunition box, and the stack from the packing tubes for artillery rounds. A valve improvised from rubber tubing and a pair of vise-grip pliers dripped diesel fuel into the firebox.[74]

*   *   *

In December 1951, Walter Moore moved up to become the tank battalion's operations officer. The S-3's job was far different from what he was used to, as Moore explained: "In relationships a successful tank unit leader has to be tactful, but persistent, much like a traveling salesman. It means traveling to see infantry commanders on almost a daily basis, selling your wares."[75]

The winter war was not without moments of perverse humor, even between such different foes as the Americans and the Chinese. Red Saunders occupied a piece of high ground facing Chinese positions on Hill 1052, about 400 yards away.[76] "Christmas Day, we woke up and there were big block letters 'MERRY CHRISTMAS MARINES,' that the Chinese had put out. We just blew them away, one by one," he said.

That same morning, Roger Baker's section moved up into a firing slot, where the men found a hand-lettered sign reading: "SCENIC VIEW OF PUNCHBOWL—PARKING 25 CENTS."[77]

Next to the enemy, perhaps the greater danger faced by the men were the fires caused by the improvised and government-issue stoves. One night in early March, a bunker occupied by one of Platoon Sergeant C. B Ash's tank crews from the 1st Platoon of B Company caught fire. Ash, a veteran of the tank fighting on Roi-Namur, Saipan, Tinian, and Iwo Jima in World War II, organized the fire fighting effort. Just as he approached the flaming bunker a grenade stored inside exploded. When he inquired, the stunned Ash was told that there were three grenades inside. He waited until two more exploded, and approached the bunker, only to be showered with sparks by a fourth explosion. The irate Platoon Sergeant's orders were to "let the son of a bitch burn."[78]

The tanks often acted as long-range snipers, and Ash described one such effort. The Chinese were constructing a tunnel through a hill 5,010 yards away, beyond the effective range of the tank's gun. Two Chinese would use a stretcher-like tray to carry the dirt out and dump it along the skyline of the ridge. The tankers carefully weighed 90mm. rounds to select those with similar ballistics, and manned a spotter scope during the daylight hours. Patiently, the tankers sniped at the construction workers, their rounds either flying over their heads and striking far to the rear, or landing closer and showering them with snow. Finally, on the sixth day, the tank gunner loosed a round on its five-second flight to the target. According to one witness, there was "a little burst of red flame, no snow . . . no dirt, they got a direct hit on one of the two chinks." Ash noted that the next morning the ridge was covered with a light fall of snow, and thousands of black birds feasting on the scattered remains of the two Chinese.[79]

Elaborate raids were mounted to inflict casualties and destroy enemy positions. The costs of these operations included the inevitable infantry casualties and wrecked tanks. Walter Moore picked up the story:

> Once the 1st Marine Division front settled down, it was Maj Gen John T. Selden, the 1st Marine Division Commander's policy to constantly keep the enemy of balance. A procedure that was continually followed even after we moved to the western front, along the Imjin River north of Seoul, in March 1952.

One such example was the "Pinnacle Raid" in late January. The "Pinnacle" operation took place up the same ridge about 400 meters northwest of the front line on Hill 812, the scene of bitter fighting the past September 1951. The "Pinnacle" was a terrain feature that blocked our forces on Hill 812, with the ridge line dominating the terrain feature [called] Hill 1052. Nearest we could tell, the NKPA developed [it] into a defensive position much like a chunk of Swiss cheese, holes and all.

3/1, currently the tenants of Hill 812, were ordered to pull a raid on this objective. Now remember 3/1's front lines were located only about 300 meters from this enemy position. Both gun and a platoon of flame tanks were put in direct support. The flame tank's mission was to burn and destroy the innards of this piece of Swiss cheese. Purpose: to force the enemy out and let the marines occupy it. The gun tanks were given the task of supporting this effort by fire.

The Battalion S-3, you gotta know what the hell's going on. Curiosity kills the cat sometimes. Guess I was still a company commander at heart. Charlie Company (now commanded by the fearless Captain Tom Clarke) was the tank company selected to support elements of 3/1 in their raid on The Pinnacle. We had a platoon of flames, and I was up there every day to coordinate ... with other supporting arms, [and] with the infantry battalion and regimental commanders.

Everything went well up to a point. Our flame tanks went out on that cold, narrow icy ridge, close enough to burn the objective. In backing out, the lead flame tank hit a mine, blowing a track. In the ensuing fracas, it turned into a rescue operation to evacuate the crews and the tanks.

I went on a reconnaissance to look right on the ground where the tanks were knocked out, some fifty meters at most from The Pinnacle. From that close, it stuck straight up in the air. You could see the heat emanating from the inside. They had a pretty cozy place in there until we wrecked it for them. Well, temporarily at least.[80]

While supervising the recovery of the flame tank, Moore was hit in the face by fragments from a mortar burst. "I was evacuated for a day or two, and when they saw it wasn't infected, they took a piece out of my eyebrow, and just below [it]. They thought it had hit the eye, it bled so much," he continued. "[It was] something I could live with." Moore soon returned to duty.

In late March of 1952, the Marine Division was ordered to prepare for redeployment to western Korea. In the horrific Korean winter, a major logistical move like the one in the works was a nightmare. The division was to march over 140 miles west, crossing through the main traffic arteries used by the other divisions of the U.N. army, a difficult feat even in ideal weather. Wheeled vehicles went by road, but the division's heavy trucks and tracked vehicles were shipped by sea.[81]

Between March 20 and 23, the tank companies were pulled out of the line.[82] Pete Flournoy remembered the beginning of the movement: "On Saint Pat's day of fifty-two, we [began] a fifty-mile road march. That was the worst road march I ever made in my life. Fifty miles, in the mountains, to Sojo-ri. It took fifty hours to get there." Flournoy remembers the tanks "sliding . . . on the ice and snow, slamming into each other. Move twenty feet and stop, move twenty feet and stop. Then we'd get asphyxiated from the exhaust of the tank in front of you. It took us more than two days to make that fifty miles. It was miserable. You'd almost have blood in the palms of your hands from pulling back on those damn laterals [steering levers]."

Despite the freezing cold and driving snow, the tank drivers had to keep their hatches open and heads exposed in order to see. "I must have had a foot of snow in my lap," recalled Don Boyer. "We had to keep moving, and it was kind of tricky." During the crossing of one stream bed to bypass a bridge, Boyer remembered "a big boulder there. I hit this boulder and the tank just went airborne. The guys were sleeping on the deck inside, and boy, that shook 'em up! I remember they chewed me out!" He had a good excuse: "The snow was hitting me in the face, and I could hardly see. All I could see was two little red dots up ahead of me [the taillights of the tank ahead]. The snow was pelting me because you couldn't wear goggles."

Bart Clendenen remembered the same thing: "It was raining, and half snow. . . . I was running a fever by the time we got out there, on the LSTs. Spent the whole trip around the peninsula in the bunk taking antibiotics. It was cold, and it was nasty." Journeys on LSTs were not comfortable by any stretch of the imagination: "It was a rough and wild ride. LSTs were flat-bottomed, and after we cleared the peninsula and went up into the Yellow Sea, whoa! That thing got wild. The Navy was having trouble keeping the tanks cleated down." Tank crews worked around the clock, continually checking and adjusting the lashings. "Forty-six tons skating around loose is nothing to get tangled up with."

Walter Moore led the convoy of wheeled vehicles, and recorded his recollections in a letter:

> We took off in a snowstorm. The first hour or two we were down to about three miles an hour. We had [tire] chains on the vehicles.
>
> We went through some places that were not considered secure. The South Korean military . . . said they had positions somewhere, [but] hell, they were nowhere to be seen. The more we got over to the western side of the peninsula, the more people we'd see.
>
> It was kind of sad. You'd see more hungry children pathetically asking for food, wearing these damn rubber slippers with socks on, their feet almost blue.
>
> I hunted down the Army tank battalion commander and his staff. I had served with Army tankers before. They're a good lot! Believe me I was impressed with their clean, squared away uniforms, shined boots and all.
>
> This was a far cry from the "mix & not match" uniforms we were wearing. In contrast our "tailor shop" was the aftermath of our field shower system. It could be a jacket with PFC stripes painted on the sleeves, and some baggy pants, and a venerable pair of USMC field shoes.[83] We'd go through these organized showers, and they'd give you a PFC jacket and God knows what kind of pants, and an old pair of shoes. We didn't even have boots yet. It was a big contrast in the way we dressed.[84]

When Moore visited the forward positions and was briefed by the Army tankers, he discovered that "They had a by-the-book school solution. I remember their S-Three handed me a booklet of overlays . . . the kind of thing you'd turn in at a staff college. How you do a counterattack here, what you do here, what you do there, et cetera. I could see me, in the middle of the night, whipping one of these things out and saying, 'A counterattack here. That looks good,'" joked Moore, who worked to "change all that. I just simplified it down to maybe four different approaches, four different techniques to use. You can pre-plan, you should be thinking about it, but you shouldn't be lockin' it in concrete, 'cause it ain't gonna work. The Germans found that out [in World War II]. A lot of pre-planned stuff that didn't work."

The tanks eventually went ashore at Inchon, and by rail to Munsan-ni. Flournoy: "Typical thing. We had already turned in our cold-weather gear 'cause it was in March, first of April. Damned if it didn't come a big snowstorm over on the west coast. Summer sleeping bags, no cold-weather gear. It had all gone to the rear. We all damn near froze to death."

As the men soon discovered, the massive movement was part of Operation Mixmaster, a shuffling of U.N. units that involved the relocation of over 200,000 troops.

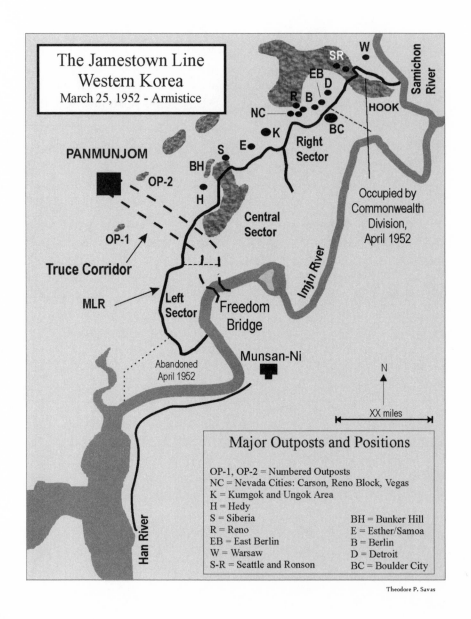

The Jamestown Line
Western Korea
March 25, 1952 - Armistice

SR
W
EB
D
R B
NC
HOOK
K
BC
S E
Right
Sector

PANMUNJOM
BH
OP-2
H
Central
Sector

Occupied by
Commonwealth
Division,
April 1952

OP-1

Imjin River

Truce Corridor

MLR
Left
Sector
Freedom
Bridge

Munsan-Ni

Abandoned
April 1952

N

XX miles

Samichon River

Han River

Major Outposts and Positions

OP-1, OP-2 = Numbered Outposts
NC = Nevada Cities: Carson, Reno Block, Vegas
K = Kumgok and Ungok Area
H = Hedy
S = Siberia   BH = Bunker Hill
R = Reno   E = Esther/Samoa
EB = East Berlin   B = Berlin
W = Warsaw   D = Detroit
S-R = Seattle and Ronson   BC = Boulder City

Theodore P. Savas

Chapter Seven

Backs to the River

Battles for the Jamestown Line, 1952-1953

In a time-honored tradition, the 1st Marine Division's reward for a
job well done was to be given an even more difficult and critical
responsibility. On March 25, 1952, the division assumed responsibility
for the defense of the Kimpo Peninsula northwest of Seoul, as well as the
adjacent mainland.

For centuries the western coastal plain was the route of choice for
armies moving north and south along the peninsula. The main thrust of
the North Korean invasion of 1950 followed this course, and
MacArthur's counterstroke later that same year traversed the same
ground. This narrow zone contained Seoul, the capital and most populous
city in South Korea, the major port of Inchon, major communications
centers, and the most valuable agricultural land in the country. This
coastal plain was the most critical piece of real estate in southern Korea,
and it had to be held at all costs. The orders delivered to the Marines were

not to simply delay a Communist offensive, but to "aggressively defend" their positions.[1]

The Jamestown Line stood along good but awkward ground. The hills were steep and generally barren except for small trees. Along much of its length the line stood with its back to the broad valley of the Imjin River, the scene of ghastly fighting during the Chinese offensives of 1951. The valley itself was low and swampy, and when the river was in flood, two of the three bridges across the river were rendered unusable. There was a mile-wide gap in the line of defensible hills at the confluence where the broad Han River flowed north from the vicinity of Seoul, and another where the Samichon River flowed south through a gap in the hills to meet the Imjin. The capital itself lay only twenty-six miles behind the defensive line at its closest point. Isolated outposts were situated as much as a mile forward of the main line of resistance (MLR).[2]

Offshore, several huge islands and their intervening waterways provided natural routes for amphibious infiltration. These islands were defended by the Kimpo Provisional Regiment, made up of a battalion of the Korean Marine Corps, a battalion of ROK security troops, with US Marine advisors and combat support units.[3]

Further complicating the defensive situation was the Truce Corridor. Since October 1951, both sides had maintained a narrow neutral zone that ran along a road from the United Nations MLR, northwest to the town of Kaesong and the insignificant village of Panmunjom, deep inside Communist territory. The village was to become famous as the negotiating site for the off and on talks which, in U.N.'s eyes, were designed to end the conflict; the Communists, however, manipulated the discussions as a means of improving their military stance. The I Corps commander further designated an arc-shaped no-fire zone that included the area of the village and road. The Communists took full advantage of the corridor to move troops and emplace their own artillery, free from U.N. attack.

Fearful the enemy might manufacture an incident that would result in a massacre of the unarmed negotiators, the Marine Division was tasked with the responsibility of providing security for the diplomats, who conducted their business deep inside enemy territory. This obligation was vested in the 1st Tank Battalion.

The tank battalion maintained the Everready Rescue Force—a platoon of five tanks and a 245-man rifle company, supported by heavy mortars and artillery—on continuous standby whenever talks were in progress. The Everready Force was based at Combat Outpost Two, on a hill about a half-mile east of the Panmunjom corridor.

The Everready Force was on standby to race to Panmunjom, snatch the negotiators, and fight their way to safety along the narrow road, should such a thing become necessary. The task force consisted of the Forward Covering Force of tanks and infantry who would secure the area and protect the delegates until the arrival of the Pickup Force. A Rear Covering Force of tanks and infantry would move to secure the road south from Panmunjom, and act as a rear guard during any withdrawal.[4] The tankers did not seem to have much faith in this plan. Indeed, they called it Operation Abortion because, in their minds, "it would be a bloody mess."[5]

Charles Sooter's Dog Company took a turn at providing the tanks for this rescue force. "It was to rescue the men if they sent a flare up," he said. "I had twenty-one personnel carriers and twenty-one tanks. I was in charge of all of it, but I don't remember the name of the lieutenant who was in charge of the personnel carriers."

The Pickup Force included a platoon from the tank battalion's Headquarters Company equipped with M39 Armored Utility Vehicles. These open-topped tracked vehicles were derived from the thinly armored M-18 tank destroyer of World War II vintage. Although the Marines referred to them as Armored Personnel Carriers, they were designed as tow tractors for light guns or carriers for heavy weapons. They were simply open-topped boxes on tracks, and thus not designed to be fighting vehicles. Their cross-country mobility was, however, vastly superior to trucks, and "in many instances provided the only means of resupply and [casualty] evacuation for MLR units."[6]

Sooter liked the M39s, even though they had an obvious weakness: "Very nice, I thought. At that time the best we had. They were very reliable. . . . I don't know how worried those guys were, but just drop a hand grenade in one of them you'd kill several people. [With] mortar fire, they could have killed a lot of people."

The primary responsibility of the tank battalion was to support the infantry. The usual deployment was for two rifle regiments to be on the

MLR at any particular time, with one in reserve. Similarly, two tank companies were usually in the line, with one in immediate reserve. The fourth company, in division reserve, was used to train the constant influx of replacements from the rotation policy, and to occasionally supplement the division artillery, a continuing, if unwelcome, task.[7]

The Chinese, as the Marines soon discovered, were a different foe from the NKPA they had faced on the eastern fields of battle. "The North Koreans were a lot like the Japanese [in World War II]," explained Walter Moore. "They gave no quarter, and expected no quarter. The Chinese . . . they're hot and cold. They'd fight like mad one day, and the next day put their hands up and surrender. Maybe because their officers were shot, I don't know."

In the zone where the 1st Marine Division replaced an ROK division, the opponents had settled into a live-and-let-live routine. "The South Koreans," Moore explained, "even had their families out on the out-post line of resistance (OPLR). The Koreans had laundry drying in the sun, kids playing soccer, etc. Seemed as if everybody had a nice quiet life. The Chinese on the other side had their laundry hanging out—no pun intended. The Koreans and Chinese even divided up the rice paddies. They had an unwritten understanding: we don't touch you, you don't touch me."

Still, the Marines were there to fight, and fight they did. Moore: "In keeping with the aggressive policy ordered by the Division CG, we started immediately with a series of tank-infantry attacks on the Chinese positions. It made them madder than hell. Captured prisoners would ask, 'Who are you people that are in there now? What are you tryin' to prove? What are you trying to prove?'" Although Moore and his men had been exposed to heavy artillery before, the furious Chinese response "shocked" them. "I recalled those WW II newsreels where the Russian artillery (was) shooting hub to hub, firing a thousand rounds a minute," Moore said. "They literally would just smother our positions with artillery fire. The Chinese learned well from their Soviet masters. On the other hand the 8th Army policy at the time was to ration our daily ammo expenditures. It didn't take long for our enemy to realize they were facing the mean–ass First Marine Division."[8]

On April 1, Chinese forces launched their own assaults against the Marines, attacking the left flank of the division positions north of the

Imjin River, briefly threatening the critical Freedom Bridge between Munsan-ni and Panmunjom in the process.

Tank slots (revetments) were built into the front-line trenches, from which the flat-trajectory tank gun fire could be directed against specific enemy positions. The Chinese invariably brought down heavy artillery fire upon the tanks, and it was impractical to permanently entrench the vehicles. Instead, the tanks would move up from their rear assembly areas, execute their missions, and withdraw. The tanks also participated in patrols north of the MLR, but the Chinese often chose not to engage these heavy forces.[9]

Because the tank units could not be employed *en mass* on the hilltops, the companies were split up, with platoons from the same company sometimes supporting battalions from different rifle regiments. Tank units were not tied to specific units, and when rifle battalions rotated out of the line for recuperation, the tanks would usually stay behind to support their replacements.[10] Unit cohesion inevitably suffered, as Pete Flournoy explained: "I didn't see the company CP but one time. I went back one time to get a Purple Heart at battalion, and the rest of the time I didn't see anybody. You'd have guys in your own platoon that you didn't know. You put a heavy section on one hill, a light section a few hundred yards over on another hill. Lots of times there was [enemy] between them. No grunts. You belonged there, so you stayed there."

Facing the division was a veteran Chinese force of fifty-seven infantry battalions, supported by at least forty tanks and self-propelled artillery pieces, and twelve battalions of towed artillery.[11] The main body of the Chinese tank regiment was reported to be in the vicinity of Sibyon-ni, forty miles north of Pyongyang. On April 4, Able Company reported firing at a moving tank at long range, and sighting another two days later. Aerial reconnaissance, however, disputed the presence of the enemy tanks.[12]

Another ongoing plan called Operation Clobber involved area artillery bombardments in late April. The D Company tanks and the nine M4A3 POA-CWS-H5 flame tanks of the battalion participated in Clobber, the latter vehicles using their 105mm. howitzers to good effect. The fire was not intended for specific targets, but H&I—firing random shots or salvos at specific points on the map, like road junctions or bridges, in the hope of catching an unlucky enemy.[13]

The two sides quickly settled into something that combined aspects of the Western Front of World War I and the classic sieges of antiquity. The Chinese would gradually encroach upon the American positions using saps and approach trenches. At night, they would dig entrenchments and build positions, then withdraw before daylight and observation by American artillery. During the day the Americans would try to shell the new positions to rubble, but the Chinese would return at dusk, and over the course of weeks would inevitably construct new positions that could withstand American bombardments.

The typical American countermeasure was a variation on the trench raid of World War I. Company-scale patrols attacked Chinese positions, sometimes to capture specific posts, at other times with little intent other than to inflict casualties and take prisoners. Tanks often supported these raids, moving into the low ground between the ridges and supporting the infantry with direct fire.

These raids were both rewarding and frustrating for the troops involved at all levels. A good example of this involved a limited attack on a Chinese outpost line of resistance, launched by elements of the 7th Marines in April 1951. The battle started at 0200, "supported by a company of our tanks," Walter Moore explained in a detailed letter on the engagement:

> In the darkness, the Marine infantry caught the enemy by surprise. At first light the Chinese launched a counter attack that almost drove our Marines out of the captured trench line. One of the more Gung Ho tank platoon leaders could not stand it any longer and took his five tanks up this hill. Some of his tanks straddled the trench line and fired into some bunkers and parts of trench line still occupied by the Chinese. All this is not the way to use tanks, but it did the job!
>
> During this time I was on the OP with the infantry Bn. CO. Suddenly I looked behind. On a hill some two thousand meters behind me . . . were all these radio jeeps, and antennas sticking up in the air. It didn't take a genius to see it was a group of VIP observers from probably I Corps and Eighth Army. All up there watching this Roman circus.
>
> The Chinese saw them too, and they started firing direct fire weapons at this cluster of men and vehicles. You could hear the high velocity rounds whiz over us. Then after a short interval a "Crunch" of a round going off behind us. I felt a bit guilty but it made me feel good to see those people get fired at! I said, "What are those guys doing back there? Why don't they come up here and join the fight?"

Was this a form of entertainment? There wasn't anything tactical about that OP whatsoever.

I guess maybe my mentality made me feel maybe that's a good way to keep those guys at the upper level a little bit honest. Learning the real side of war. . . . Terror and close calls for starters!

At dusk, the Marines on the Chinese outpost objective were ordered to pull back. Collecting the wounded and dead proved "a nightmare." The tankers covered the withdrawal and carried the casualties to the rear. Moore remembers that sad night well:

> About dusk I remember a group of dead Marines laying next to this Battalion Aid Station tent. These men were wrapped in ponchos, with their feet sticking out. I saw a couple of chaplains and a Company First Sergeant slowly going down the line, pulling back the ponchos. They had the depressing task of removing dog tags and peering at their very young looking faces. I didn't count how many men, but it looked like about fifty men.
>
> Many years later, during my service in Vietnam, I saw this giving back hard fought terrain many a time. Was Korea a rehearsal for what occurred in Vietnam? To many of us it seemed so.
>
> The 1st Tank Battalion did its job in a fearless way. Even in breaking accepted tank employment practices by going up that hill to help fellow Marines in a deadly spot. The years have blotted out the name of that young officer who took his platoon up that nameless hill. I do know he earned a well-deserved Navy Cross.[14]

Another typical episode in this protracted struggle for the small hills occurred on May 9, 1952. Able/1/5 was assigned to seize several modest hills in order to deny their use to the Chinese, to inflict casualties, and to capture prisoners. The assault force moved out at 0430 and quickly captured several patches of high ground. The tanks from the Anti-Tank Platoon did not fire their weapons, but watched a flame tank in the valley below. Don Boyer was involved in the action. "We went out at midnight on an operation. Most of the time you didn't even know what the heck was going on," he said. "They'd pop out there about a hundred yards. . . . They were going over to capture some people for interrogation, and they stumbled in on top of the Chinese or something, and a big firefight went on."

When a rifle platoon attempted to seize another hill designated as Objective X, a strong Chinese counterattack drove it back, and then deluged the exposed assault force with artillery fire. The supporting platoon of tanks from B Company covered the withdrawal of the attacking infantry. By 1730 the attackers were back inside friendly lines. They inflicted 88 enemy casualties and captured one prisoner, at a loss of seven Marines killed and 66 wounded.[15]

Most of the veterans of the Pusan campaign were gone by late spring and summer 1952, and shortages had developed in specific skill areas, particularly artillery and tank crewmen. The combination of the replacement and rotation policy and the influx of new M46 tanks presented unique problems to the tank battalion, which had received huge influxes of inadequately trained replacements. Although the 1st Tank Battalion was equipped with the new M46, the Marine Corps had few of these vehicles in the United States. The Training and Replacement Command in California had M46 tank engines that could be used to train maintenance personnel, but no vehicles for training in the key skills of driving and gunnery. General Lemuel Shepherd ordered the 7th Tank Battalion at Camp Pendleton to transfer five complete vehicles to the training facility, and authorized an increase in the number of men being trained as tankers.[16]

Dealing with the replacements became the problem of Lt. Col. John I. Williamson, who assumed command of the tank battalion on May 20. Another problem that attracted Williamson's eye was the hazardous task of recovering tanks disabled in the broad expanse of no-man's land. Within the month, Williamson had his maintenance men construct a device that could be used to hook onto a disabled tank without the crew dismounting the vehicle.[17]

The low-level static warfare persisted into the summer months of 1952. Infantry and artillery actions became increasingly more grisly as each opponent tried to bleed the other dry. The Korean War had evolved from one of mobility to one of simple static attrition.

For their part, the Chinese continued to augment their heavy weapons far above the levels of the previous six months. There was evidence that Soviet-made tanks and self-propelled guns previously observed by aerial reconnaissance were being used for direct fire missions against Marine positions.[18] The Chinese also introduced rocket artillery, the Soviet-made BM-13 *Katyusha* ("Cathy"), sixteen launch rails for 132mm. rockets mounted on a medium truck chassis. This fearsome weapon was not as accurate as tube artillery, but a battery of them could dump 4.35 tons of explosive onto a target in a ten-second salvo.[19] One prisoner reported that there were two regiments of these launchers deployed against the American positions.[20]

Of more direct concern to the tankers were the smaller 82mm. M-30 rockets, launched from single- or multiple-rocket frame launchers, which were used to snipe at individual American tanks.

Lieutenant Colonel Williamson's concern over the recovery of disabled tanks was justified by an episode that occurred on July 6. As Williamson watched a platoon of gun tanks and the flame tanks on a raid, one of his tanks ran over a mine and was disabled. Two more threw tracks maneuvering back down the enemy-held hill. Williamson recorded that when the VTRs went out to help, "the whole operation became a bitched-up mélange of disabled tanks and others trying to assist them."[21]

Without the aid of friendly infantry, the tankers established a defensive perimeter and went to work, but the situation steadily deteriorated. Williamson described what he observed:

> The company commander later reported to me that some of them did amazingly foolish things. A combat movie cameraman went out in one of the retrievers, which inspired all sorts of hammy things from the tankers. One of them stood up in the midst of machine gun fire and squeezed off a bazooka round just as though he were on the range. Others stalked behind moving tanks in attitudes of crouched readiness. One man was wounded and fell, clutching the retriever boom with one hand in exaggerated theatricality. Some posed in various attitudes about the tanks. Throughout all this, and despite the fact that they were under fire in enemy territory, the corporal cameraman was grinding away.
>
> Later in the day an enemy gun opened up and disabled a retriever, wounding two men. It was quickly silenced by the tanks. I left in the early afternoon and missed most of this. Coming back shortly before dark I found the operation still in progress. I ordered it secured, and told them to strip the tanks, cover them with tanks and artillery through the night, and we would resume recovery the next day. All operating tanks withdrew, and three disabled ones were left out in front.
>
> I left at 2045 and went to another sector where we were to have another operation that night.[22]

To his consternation, Williamson arrived back at the CP at dawn only to find that the junior officer in charge had ordered two of the disabled tanks destroyed. "On the surface, this is normal and accepted procedure for tanks disabled beyond recovery in enemy-held territory," Williamson explained. "However, it is practically never done by Marines, and was a case of horribly bad judgment on someone's part . . . " The undamaged vehicle and one of the hulks was recovered the next day, but the following night the remaining vehicle began to burn again, and was eventually abandoned as a total loss.[23]

On July 9, another raid by a platoon of tanks fell victim to faulty reconnaissance. The tanks moved down an unusually steep slope from the MLR, and stumbled into a hornet's nest of Chinese. Several tanks threw tracks maneuvering in the soft ground, and a second platoon accompanied by VTRs was committed. The steep slope blocked return by the original route, and swamps and rice paddies prevented the tanks from moving along the valley parallel to the MLR to find negotiable slopes. A tank dozer assigned to cut a path through to the tanks became stuck, and by dusk eleven tanks were trapped in no-man's land.

Williamson had to personally intervene to salvage the situation. Under bright moonlight, infantry moved out to screen the trapped armor while VTRs and dozers helped the company extricate the vehicles. One man was killed and five wounded during the operation.[24]

Torrential rains at the end of July put a stop to much of the fighting, and three bridges over the Imjin were closed or destroyed by flood waters. The dry weather of August, however, brought with it a bitter struggle for possession of patches of high ground called Siberia (Hill 58A) and Bunker Hill (Hill 122), several miles east of Panmunjom in the central sector of the division line. This vicious and bloody battle was fought solely for possession of high ground that offered little more than improved artillery observation posts.

Siberia was a squad outpost about a quarter of a mile forward of the American MLR. At 0100 hours on August 9, the Chinese precipitated a nineteen-day bloodbath when they drove the Marines off the hill. The hill changed hands twice after the initial Chinese victory, deadly fighting that took place under torrents of artillery and mortar fire. By 1130 hours the Marines were again in nominal control of Siberia, but enemy fire directed against the northern slope and crest was so heavy that the Americans

The Battles of Eastern Korea

Battered and burdened tanks plow through deep mud during the advance on Hwachon in April 1951. The left fender is held on by communications wire attached to the lifting ring, and the cargo frame on the right side appears to be made from an artillery aiming stake. (Marine Corps)

Above: Don Gagnon and a small fuzzy puppy saved from the cooking pot pose atop his heavily loaded tank as the battalion prepares to displace north in support of Operation Killer. The practice of eating dogs is dying out in modern Korea, but older Koreans still eat them as a way to remember the "starving time." (Don Gagnon)

Below: Marine infantry and tanks advance gingerly through Massacre Valley in February 1951. The partially frozen crust overlying deep mud limited the off-road mobility of the tanks. (National Archives)

Above: The scenes that greeted the Marines in Massacre Valley were grim indeed. Many Marines were enraged at Army ordnance units, which salvaged vehicles before the dead had been recovered. (National Archives)

Below: Lieutenant Vaughn Stuart fires the .50 caliber anti-aircraft machine gun from the back of his tank in February 1951. The awkward position of the weapon mount made it virtually impossible to use it effectively from inside the tank. Note the battered fenders and the open engine deck grill. (National Archives)

Above: An M4A3 disabled by a mine on the Hungchon-Chunchon Road. The tank continued to fight, as indicated by the discarded 105mm shell casings. The tank battalion insignia on the side is a yellow "TK," followed by a yellow diamond with red upper and lower points, and a superimposed "2" in red. (National Archives)

Below: The POA-CWS-H5 flame tank mounted the flame gun to the right of the 105mm. howitzer. By this time, the improvised ammunition racks on the fenders were a common feature. (National Archives)

Above: This Company B M26 was one of ten disabled by mines in the So-chon River valley in June 1951. The damage is typical: broken track, damaged wheels and return rollers, and a bent suspension arm. The battalion symbol was common only on Company B tanks. (National Archives)

Below: With few roads northeast of Hoengsong, tanks and infantry advance along a stream bed toward Hill 505. Note the smoke- and fog-filled valley and charred areas at left, where the flame tanks had been in action. (National Archives)

Above: The rains of April 1951 turned eastern Korea into a vast morass. This tank from Dog Company slipped off a hillside trail during Operation Ripper. The white star and large serial number are obvious. The stenciled "Lift Here" marking by the sling point is unusual. (National Archives)

Below: "Bunker busting" consumed ever-increasing amounts of the tanks's time when the fighting fronts stabilized in 1951. The puff of smoke from the impact of the HE round is visible on the far left, below the crest of the ridge. (National Archives)

Above: Despite the heavy damage, the crew of B34 was lucky. Anti-tank mines were often stacked several to a hole, and the powerful explosion under the front of the hull could be fatal for the driver and bow gunner. (Marine Corps)

Below: Marine tanks in the Morae-Kagae Pass after the failed Chinese attempt to isolate the 7th Marines on the night of May 16-17, 1951. The charred area in the left foreground is where the Chinese attempted to set fire to a tank by rolling a barrel of burning gasoline down the hillside. (National Archives)

Vaughn Stuart's platoon firing as artillery. Although effective, the practice prematurely wore out the gun tubes and could damage the traversing gear. The gout of flame on the tank on the left is the result of partially burned propellant, a constant hazard for the turret crew. Note the stacked ammunition. (National Archives)

As the war of movement ground to a stop for the winter, many tanks were placed in revetments on ridges overlooking the front lines. Note the ammunition stacked on the ground, and the men preparing to refuel from a fifty-five gallon drum. (National Archives)

Above: The old M32B3s were less able to cope with the weight of the M26 tanks. This Headquarters Company VTR is attempting to lift and turn a mine-damaged tank. Note the track rolled on the rear deck of the tank—they could not be towed across soft ground with the tracks on. (National Archives)

Below: This remarkable photo shows a POA-CWS-H5 flame tank from the Headquarters Company Flame Platoon directing a "rod" of flame at an enemy position on a frozen hillside, February 1952. (National Archives)

Stalemate—The Jamestown Line

A view of some typical positions along the rear slope of a hill in the Jamestown Line. Unlike the rear-slope bunker in the center, most such positions were dug in flush to the earth. Note the debris and the hill, which was denuded of vegetation by heavy shellfire. (National Archives)

Above: In the rugged hills along the Jamestown Line, getting the tanks into position was often a large part of the battle. Here M46s of C Company churn their way up through the snow and soft mud of a steep hillside. Field telephone lines strung through the blasted trees are barely visible at right. (National Archives)

Below: "Junk on the bunk," tank style. This crew from the Anti-Tank Platoon, 5th Marines, has their gear laid out for inspection. Note the water and fuel cans, huge wrenches, and four .30 caliber and one .50 caliber machine guns at right. (Robert Schmitz)

Left: The auto-coupler device described by Lt. Colonel John Williamson, fitted to the front of an M46 tank. This allowed another tank to hook onto a disabled vehicle without exposing the crew. The tank was issued from Army stocks, and still carries Army markings. (National Archives)

Right: This recovery hook fitted to another M46 tank could latch onto the auto-coupler (see photo above). Note that on this tank, also issued from Army stocks, the identity-conscious Marines have simply painted out the "A" in USA. (National Archives)

Right: Major repairs were often conducted in the field, and under very primitive working conditions. These mechanics are working on the power pack (combined engine and transmission) of an M46 tank. (Harry Regan)

During the latter stages of the war, the older M4A3 tanks proved to be distressingly vulnerable to new Communist anti-tank weapons, as well as captured American weapons and ordnance. These flame tanks have track blocks welded to the sponsons and turret sides. (Harry Regan)

Above: Damage to Lt. Michael McAdams's POA-CWS-H5 flame tank, inflicted during the ill-fated Operation Clambake. Shaped-charge explosions would bore through the armor and spray the interior with molten metal. (Marine Corps)

Below: A Baker Company tank replenishes main gun ammunition from an M39 Armored Utility Vehicle during the battle for Outpost Vegas, May 29, 1953. The markings on the vehicle are "APC 13 USMC," painted in yellow on the aft storage hatch. (National Archives)

Above: The Headquarters Company "Porcupine" communications and liaison vehicle sported numerous radio antennae and a dummy main gun. It is parked at Combat Outpost Two. The helicopter in the background is outbound from the Peace Village at Panmunjom. (National Archives)

Below: M39s of the Carrier Platoon wait at a forward ammunition dump during a lull in the Berlin Battles, July 25, 1953. The closest vehicle is marked "APC 11 USMC," probably in white letters. (National Archives)

Marines relax around a Charlie Company M46 tank at the Boulder City combat outpost on July 29, 1953. The armistice was only two days old. (National Archives)

were able to reoccupy only the southern slope. The seesaw action continued that afternoon, when a powerful Chinese attack inflicted heavy casualties on the defenders and once again drove E/2/1 from the hill. That night a fresh rifle company, C/1/1, recaptured the terrain, only to be driven off yet again by enemy artillery at dawn on August 10.[25]

Following this costly reversal, the division decided to take higher, more rugged, but more desirable Bunker Hill to the southwest. Chinese artillery and mortar observation from Bunker Hill had been a deciding factor in the Siberia struggle. American control over it would neutralize this advantage and allow observation of the enemy's routes to and from Siberia. It would also extend artillery observation as far north as the next range of hills about 3,000 yards to the northwest, and allow American artillery to dominate a broad lowland to the north and northeast.

The struggle for Siberia became a secondary part of the battle. The next assault against it was designed to serve as a diversion, and the highly visible tanks provided the major diversionary element. The Chinese force on Siberia, a reinforced platoon, was inundated with fire from artillery and tank guns, while enemy positions on Bunker Hill and other positions to the north and east were similarly bombarded.

At dusk on August 11, four M46s from Captain Gene McCain's C Company and four M4A3 flame tanks moved toward Siberia to support the night assault. The M46s opened fire on the hill at 2100 hours. Two of the flame tanks threaded their way along a rocky stream bed to the base of Siberia. They moved cautiously up the southern slope of Siberia, and then partially down the northern side of the hill, burning off dense vegetation as they drove forward. When the two tanks exhausted their flame fuel, they returned to the MLR and a second section followed, completing the work of the first pair of flame tanks and working their way down the reverse slope of the hill.

Infantrymen followed the tanks, rooting out the last of the defenders and consolidating a hasty defense. After exhausting their limited supply of flame fuel, the flame tanks withdrew. The M46s remained to support the infantry, blasting away at both Siberia and Hill 110 to the northeast, covering the movement of an assault team from D/2/1. The low ground between the hills was exposed to fire and swarming with enemy infantry, and M39s were used to resupply the beleaguered outposts.[26]

Much of the fighting took place at night, but in those days before the appearance of thermal imaging systems, the tanks were virtually blind in the darkness. The only way to effectively control the actions of the tank was for the tank commander and driver to expose their heads to enemy fire, and this practice resulted in heavy losses among experienced men. The M46s were equipped with the new fighting light, a powerful incandescent spotlight mounted above the main gun so that it traversed and elevated with the tube. The light was mounted in a thinly armored box. Steel shutters that provided some protection for the lens and screened the glow of the lamp could be controlled from inside the tank. This device provided enough light to reveal and target enemy positions, while temporarily blinding an enemy who looked directly at the tank.

On Siberia, the M46s took full advantage of the new fighting lights, flicking the shutters open and shut. All night the tank-infantry force blasted away at desperate Chinese counterattacks until ammunition was exhausted. The D Company riflemen fought off one last fierce Chinese counterattack and then withdrew, the diversion completed.

While the Chinese were preoccupied with these provocative actions on Siberia, B/1/1 (under the operational control of 2/1) assaulted nearby Bunker Hill, which was the primary objective of the entire action. By 0230 hours, American forces were in possession of the crest. American and South Korean Marines hauled tools and building materials through a storm of enemy fire to construct defensive positions on the precious ground.

All day on August 12 the Marines burrowed into the crest and south slope of Bunker Hill, while the M39s evacuated the wounded. The Chinese still occupied the low ground below the northern side of the hill. At 1600 hours, the Chinese launched their strongest effort to recapture Bunker Hill. Wave after wave of CCF infantry surged up the northern slope. By 1740, the enemy controlled the northern slope and were trying to push the Marines off the southern slope. Neither side could hold the open ground on the rounded crest, swept clean by deadly fire from both sides.

The tanks of C Company replenished their ammunition and continued to flail away at the Chinese on the nearby slopes. More tanks—the rest of C Company, five M46s of the Anti-Tank Platoon of 5th

Marines, and five from the division reserve—were brought forward to subdue the enemy positions on nearby hills.

The war in Korea was evolving into one of increasingly lavish use of firepower. At Bunker Hill alone the tank force expended 817 rounds of 90mm. ammunition and 32,000 rounds of machine gun ammo during the two days of heaviest action.[27]

The contest for Bunker Hill inevitably spread to nearby hills as each side strove for any advantage to be gained. The direct fire capability of the tanks again proved useful, eliminating enemy heavy machine guns that opened fire from any adjacent high ground. The fighting was particularly heavy on a small outpost, appropriately code-named Stromboli, about 2,500 yards east of Bunker Hill. It was originally believed that the squad occupying Stromboli had been overrun, but the Marines trapped there eventually managed to communicate with their parent unit. The tanks took the slopes of the hill under fire from the MLR, and helped the isolated squad hold out against repeated enemy assaults.

Night combat still presented problems for the tank gunners. The gunner could illuminate the target with the fighting light and fire, but light reflected back from dust raised by the muzzle blast obscured his vision. Waiting for the dust to settle before reacquiring the target meant that considerable time was required to adjust fire for following shots. An aggressive enemy wisely used this interval to rain down a deluge of artillery and mortar fire upon the tank, which was easy to spot because of its glaring spotlight.

One solution was to work the tanks in pairs. When a machine gun position was spotted, one of the tanks would illuminate it while a second tank, hidden in the darkness, took it under fire. This allowed the second tank gunner to fire several rounds in rapid succession, thus minimizing the exposure of the illumination tank.

Like most actions during the latter part of the war, Bunker Hill degenerated into a bloody inch-by-inch infantry dogfight. When the tanks became less useful, they were withdrawn on August 16. The heavy rains that followed a week later eventually brought a halt to the futile struggle, flooding positions and disrupting logistics for both antagonists. The prolonged battle had resulted in the capture of Bunker Hill and the abandonment of Siberia, but at a steep price: the Marines suffered 48 killed and 313 seriously wounded. Exact Chinese casualties are not known, but are estimated to be 3,200.[28]

Although the serious fighting had ended, small unit actions and firefights on and around Bunker Hill dragged on well into October. On September 5, Chinese tanks put in one of their few appearances on the battlefield, blasting away at an American outpost on one of the nearby hills. For their part, the Marine tanks moved forward on occasion at Bunker Hill, rumbling through the valleys below to support raids against the enemy positions on the northern slopes of the hill mass.

One of the tasks undertaken during this period was the training of a tank company for the Korean Marine Corps. This unit was equipped with the M4A3, which mounted a 76mm. gun. American Marines never used this version in combat, but retired Col. Elliot Laine, who was then a second lieutenant, says that they maintained a training platoon of five of these vehicles to train mechanics and tank crewmen who were then seconded to the KMC Tank Company.[29]

The heavy rains of late August continued well into September, further reducing the mobility of the tanks. With the lines in such close proximity, any movement was likely to bring down a shower of artillery and mortar rounds. In all, more than 4,000 rounds fell on or around the tanks during the month. On September 20, a direct hit by a 122mm. howitzer round tore off the front of an M4A3 and wrecked the main gun. A week later a direct hit by an impact-fused 105mm. howitzer round on tank A-14 caved in the roof of the turret and drove the periscope into the gunner's head, killing him. According to John Williamson, this was his first man killed while inside a tank.[30]

The increase in power behind the recent Chinese artillery attacks was due, at least in part, to the expanded use of tanks to extend defensive works into no-man's land. To counter this, American tank dozers worked day after day during the twilight hours—when artillery observation is most difficult—to build tank trails toward hill outposts. Flame tanks moved behind the dozers to burn away underbrush that might shelter enemy attackers. On the MLR, M46s stood watch to lay smoke screens and fire upon any enemy who threatened the tanks working in the valley below.[31]

In October, Chinese attention—and the activities of the Marine tanks—shifted east to the extreme right of the Division zone near the

Samichon River, which flows from the north to join the Imjin. The valley at the junction forms a broad gap in the range of hills that anchored the Jamestown Line. The Samichon also formed the boundary between the 1st Marine Division and the British Commonwealth Division, the latter a composite force from several nations.

Neighboring units often visited one another and showed off their hardware, as Don Boyer recalled: "The British came into our area, and they had those Centurion tanks. They were a wonderful tank! I think their armor was thicker, and they had about a six hundred horsepower Rolls-Royce engine in 'em. They weren't real maneuverable, but they would really climb those hills. Our chevrons on our tracks were roughly an inch thick. They had a deeper chevron, and they could really climb the hills. We got 'em both out there on a real steep hill. We had way more power than they did, and they had a little more weight. We'd sit there where it got steep and we'd spin, where that British Centurion would climb right up."

Military boundaries like the one between the Marines and the Commonwealth Division are by nature weak points in any military line, because actions that occur there must be coordinated through separate headquarters. The Chinese command was smart enough realize that a penetration in that vicinity would be difficult for U.N. forces to contain. The low ground behind the units also offered easy access to the Imjin River—and a clear path to Seoul.

CCF forces hammered at the American outposts west of the Samichon throughout October, softening the positions in preparation for a large-scale attack. The two most exposed outposts immediately west of the Samichon, Warsaw and Seattle, fell in the pre-dawn hours of October 2. For several days both sides sought to take and hold the isolated hilltops. On the night of October 6-7, the Chinese enlarged the scope of action, attacking outposts all along the four-mile front held by the 7th Marines. The heaviest attacks fell upon squad outposts Frisco and Detroit. In all, the division was forced to cede control of three minor and three major outposts. The latter positions—Seattle, Frisco, and Detroit—all lay to the west of a topographic salient called The Hook, where the MLR extended north of an otherwise smooth line. It was in this vicinity that the next major action took place.[32]

The opening stages of the CCF offensive against the 1st Marine Division in The Hook sector closely followed the fighting of early October. The Chinese tipped their hand when their artillery fire steadily intensified in this area later in the month. American and Commonwealth artillery opened in reply, a counter-bombardment intended to throw enemy preparations off balance. Able Company tanks, supporting the 5th Marines in the division's center sector, were used to snipe at enemy positions around the clock. This artillery duel reached a crescendo on October 24.

The Hook, which got it nickname because of its fancied resemblance to an inverted fishhook, was a curved ridge line that extended the American MLR some 250 yards into Chinese-held ground. Infantry outposts like Warsaw and Ronson extended another 500 yards in front of the MLR. The high ground of The Hook offered clear observation of the adjacent Samichon valley to artillery observers stationed there, and in American hands constituted a strong shoulder from which to pinch off any Chinese penetration down the river valley. Thus, its elimination by the CCF was an essential preliminary to any Chinese breakthrough.

The vicious outpost battles of early October had already forced the 7th Marines to put all three battalions into the line. The total reserve component was but one company from 3/7 and the so-called "clutch platoons" made up of cooks, clerks, truck drivers, and headquarters personnel.[33]

All told, an estimated 120 enemy guns shelled the forward positions of the 7th Marines. In addition to the usual 76.2mm. field guns used during the intensified artillery preparation, the enemy also employed 122mm. howitzers, which outranged American artillery. The Americans were justifiably concerned about the power of that weapon. When tanks from the 7th Anti-Tank Platoon moved out onto a ridge line in no-man's land as part of a raid, word passed through the tankers that the Chinese were going to fire at them with a 122mm. weapon that would "crack the turrets open, or some damn thing," recalled Don Boyer. "Our old sergeant, who was a World War II vet, said, 'You better back down off here.'" Boyer was in the act of accepting that good advice when " . . . the tank shook, and it spun my periscope around. I saw a huge geyser of dirt fly up just off the right side of the tank. I think one of those big rounds hit there, because it would take a lot to make the tank move."

With the ground exploding around them, the tanks worked their way into low ground in defilade from the big guns, but quickly found themselves trapped. Boyer: "We couldn't get out of this valley. We'd start to move. Every time we'd move a little bit, they'd pop a mortar on us. We'd stop and they wouldn't fire any more. Then we'd move, and they'd fire again, just load us down with mortar rounds." Matters went from bad to worse when one of the tanks broke a track and blocked the escape route. "We had to get the heck out of the tanks and run. Good friend of mine, he got shot right through the rear end. It went through one cheek and came out the other side and he yelled, 'It didn't hit anything vital!' Infantry were back on the hills behind us. This one infantryman, when we came back, he said, 'Boy, I'm glad I'm in the infantry! I couldn't even see the tanks.'" As far as Boyer was concerned, it was just as rough going for the infantry and retriever crews who had to recover the abandoned tanks. "Those poor guys were sittin' ducks, too. They just sat there and waited for those guys to get outside. I had a buddy of mine who had six Purple Hearts, for cryin' out loud."

The loss of the tanks proved a temporary setback; the VTRs recovered the abandoned armor the next day.[34] Recovering damaged or abandoned tanks was a lengthy and arduous task, in part because in soft ground the tracks had to be removed. Boyer's tank could not be restarted because, in his words, he had gotten "so flustered, I left the ignition on . . . the battery was dead. They used to take little blocks of TNT . . . and they would put a half-pound or quarter-pound block on the track connectors, and blow them off. Then they had to drag the tank out, because they couldn't drag it with the tracks [on]; it's impossible. We had to pull the tracks off, where the ends were all bent to heck, the [connector] pins, and put new sections in."

Artillery analysis teams and intelligence reported the probable presence of two more batteries of self-propelled 152mm. howitzers.[35] This formidable force rained fire on the American positions even as the Chinese continued their slow encroachment by saps and trenches. The intensity of the bombardment made life so hazardous for carrying parties that six of the M39 Armored Utility Vehicles were placed at the disposal of the 7th Marines for resupply and casualty evacuation.[36]

The contrast between the number of American and Chinese guns at work around The Hook was stark. The Marines enjoyed the direct support of only thirty-eight guns, and there were shortages of mortar and 105mm. howitzer ammunition. To help make up the shortfall, they fell back on the World War I tactic of "beating" ground with massed machine gun fire, particularly at night. The tanks of A Company were called upon for fifty-four separate direct fire missions, and the division's 4.5-inch rocket artillery batteries were also called into action.[37]

On October 23, the Chinese began a systematic program of bombardment designed to wreck specific defensive positions, and were able to destroy positions faster than the Marines could rebuild them.[38] Three days later at 1800 hours, the CCF launched their expected offensive with assaults on Ronson and Warsaw. Ronson fell in little more than half an hour of heavy fighting. By 1910 Warsaw was also overrun, and at 1944 hours the Marines there called down artillery upon their own position. One section of Able Company tanks pounded enemy positions on the nearby hills, and at 2000 hours a second section joined them. The Chinese penetrated the lines of C/1/7, forcing the rifle companies back along the ridges to either side. A series of relentless infantry assaults that lasted through the night drove 1/7 off The Hook and into the ridge lines behind.

By 0530 on October 27, the Chinese had achieved their maximum penetration, but never managed to sever the critical Tank Road, a winding path running parallel to the MLR that allowed the Americans to move troops and vehicles along the front. That same day, 1/7 and 3/7 launched a counterattack from the ridge southeast of the Chinese penetration, and the savage fighting continued through the night. By 0600 hours on October 28, the Marines had pushed the enemy off The Hook and within a few hours had also driven them off both Ronson and Warsaw, reestablishing the outpost line. Heavy fighting, solid tactics, and countless acts of bravery that will never be retold had stopped and then thrown back the major Chinese offensive in its tracks.

Thwarted in the east, the Chinese cast their eyes along the western end of the division line where, on October 31, they fell upon the outposts and seized temporary control of several positions. Intense fighting followed, and the enemy was thrown back with heavy loss.

Throughout the combat the Marines had anticipated a Chinese tank attack. This nagging threat of an enemy armor assault still confronted them. During November, Chinese tanks were spotted moving about, and aerial reconnaissance revealed the construction of tank trails and bypasses. Enemy tanks, however, refused to reveal themselves.[39]

During this period a Provisional Platoon was detached from C Company and sent to Khangwa-do island in the Han River to support operations by U.N. forces occupying the island.[40] For the remainder of the war these orphaned tankers would carry on their lonely task, sniping at enemy positions along the other side of the broad river.

For those that remained along the Jamestown Line, however, the, grinding war of attrition continued. Both sides settled in to harass each other through another bitter winter of suffering and death. The last two months of 1952 saw Chinese company-sized assaults against several outposts, and one battalion-scale assault against the Commonwealth Division troops who now occupied The Hook, but none of the fighting matched the scale of the October offensive. U.N. forces launched powerful raids, including tanks, into the disputed no-man's land. The Chinese countered with increased activity by infiltrator teams that slipped in at night to emplace mines along tank trails, and fire clouds of 57mm. recoilless rifle rounds at the tanks.

In addition to supporting raids, the tanks helped relieve combat engineers and infantry of some of their more hazardous tasks. John Williamson: "Yesterday, we succeeded in carrying a pre-built bunker out to one of the infantry outposts with a tank retriever, dug a position for it with a tank dozer, placed it in position with the retriever, and then dozed dirt up around it, completely installing the thing without exposing a man.[41]

The United States had begun the war with adequate stocks of 90mm. ammunition for the tank guns, but the enormous expenditures produced a shortage. The battalion drew its logistical support from the much larger Army system, which eventually led to many complaints. In late December, Williamson complained that the Army was refusing to issue 90mm. ammo unless a certain amount of expended brass shell casings was returned. "To my mind this is the absolute end in asininity, capping the climax of a veritable torrent of administrative harassment that has burgeoned as the activity to our front has decreased," explained Williamson. "When not assailed by the enemy from the front, we are eternally harassed by supposedly friendly echelons to the rear!"[42]

There was equal grumbling at the platoon level, where Red Saunders served: "We received an order, supposed to come down from Washington D. C., that we couldn't fire the ninety millimeter unless it was at two or more [enemy]. I told my Platoon Leader they all looked like Siamese twins to me. You could take one sniper to take out one Marine, and that would be one too many." The response Saunders received was purely economic in nature. "We were told a ninety millimeter shell cost a hundred dollars. They expected us to live by that order, I guess. I don't know. We took some of [the brass casings] back, I guess to make everybody happy, but there was nobody there to count 'em, or anything like that."

In an attempt to satisfy Washington, D. C., tanks were fitted with steel cages on the left side of the turret to catch brass tossed out by the loader.[43] When the tanks were firing furiously the loader had no time to try and shove the brass out the pistol port. He usually left his hatch open, and simply tossed it out straight overhead.[44]

The sporadic raiding operations across no-man's land became increasingly more complex after the turn of the year. Early on the bitterly cold morning of January 8, ten tanks from Capt. Gene M. 'Jinks' McCain's C Company moved out into prepared firing positions in no-man's land, covered by fire from four more tanks from the Anti-Tank Platoon, 7th Marines. At 0815, the infantry moved forward supported by two flame tanks from Lt. Michael McAdams's Flame Platoon. The tanks were able to shrug off the heavy mortar fire that temporarily pinned the infantry in place, but continuous Chinese assaults with mortars, grenades, and small arms fire grew so intense that the concussion of explosions temporarily disabled the flame guns. After the tanks recovered and cleared the enemy trenches, the main infantry assault group moved in to blast out the Chinese positions. A special "cleanup group" mounted in M39s moved in to recover the dead and wounded.[45]

In mid-January, U.N. forces undertook Operation Bimbo, an attempt to trick the Chinese into preparing to receive an attack and thereby expose themselves to artillery and air attack. The Americans opened with artillery and tank fires, and launched air strikes with napalm in their effort to goad the Chinese into moving infantry reserves forward. Although some enemy infantry was spotted and fired upon by artillery, the wary

Chinese refused to swallow the bait. Operation Bimbo lasted a grand total of ninety minutes.[46]

As the war passed its third Korean winter, the struggle's popularity at home waned. President-Elect Dwight Eisenhower toured the battlefield and actively sought some way to extricate the United States from the Korean morass. Peace talks stalled, largely because of Communist intransigence—particularly on the issue of prisoner exchange. The grinding war continued.

Just as soldiers had done in other similar wars, those fighting in Korea devised ingenious ways to make life in the dirt and bitter cold a little more bearable. Pete Flournoy explained that although the tank itself provided protection, the tankers did not dig in under the tank as in times past. "The weather was so damn bad we'd build bunkers. Just get in a bunker, just have two or three candles . . . you'd be surprised how much heat those candles give off." The tankers made the improvised heaters a bit more sophisticated. "We managed to get us a fifty-five gallon drum of diesel fuel. Ran a line down the side of this hill to a tarp we had over bushes and trees there—stumps. Got us a little valve and a mortar [ammo] box, set it down inside, with a bigger box on top." The valve was set to slowly drip diesel fuel, which was set on fire inside the closed box. The device, proclaimed Flournoy, "gave off pretty good heat."

Food was also subject to improvisation, since victuals on the hill posts were mostly frozen C-rations.[47] "Ol' Harry S. Truman said everybody's gonna get a hot meal for Thanksgiving, and for Christmas," remembered Flournoy. "I think for Thanksgiving we had a can of corned beef hash. The outside was burnt, the inside was still frozen." In an attempt to alter and improve their diet, Flournoy shot a pheasant, which he said were "common as sparrows or pigeons." Cooking it proved more difficult than anyone imagined. He and his fellow tankers melted enough snow to stew the bird whole in a large can. "We boiled that damn pheasant all day long. About noontime we tried to eat some, and couldn't. We boiled him until dark. Finally took him out of the pot, laid him up on the fender of the tank, and took a hatchet, and chopped him into chunks." [We] spent all night chewin' on that thing. Tasted good, though."

Replenishing the few supplies the occupants of the hills enjoyed was always a problem. Flournoy recalled that porters of the Korean Service Corps used A-frame backpacks to resupply the units on the hills.[48] "They would come up and bring us ammo," he explained. "Don't know why they never brought us any water. What water we got was melted snow. They would bring us cans of gasoline, 'cause we would move those vehicles every thirty minutes sometimes." The moving was simply back and forth two or three feet, to keep the tracks from freezing into the mud. Unless this was done "You try to move it, and you would bust your final drive." Stewed semi-cooked pheasant aside, it was a miserable time to be in Korea. Flournoy and others spent "weeks and weeks up there, no water, no baths. No change of clothes. I went to pull my socks up, and pulled the tops off of them. They had rotted on my feet."

Food and cold were not the only problems. The defense of Outpost Hedy, at the end of a ridge protruding forward of the MLR, offered an ongoing dilemma. A constant threat was posed by the Chinese who occupied the low ground in defilade below the face of the ridge. Captain McCain wanted to try to dislodge them by hosing the area with flame, so dozer tank A-42 spent several days scraping a track to the forward edge of the position. Chinese artillery constantly harassed it, and eventually succeeded in damaging it.

On February 1, Sgt. Ken Miller's flame tank F-22 moved out onto the nose of the ridge. While maneuvering on the uneven ground under heavy mortar and artillery fire, the tank blundered off the side of the narrow track, slid slowly and majestically down the muddy slope, and rolled ponderously over onto one side. The crew emerged and ran for safety; Miller stayed to disable the tank and then followed them, limping along on an injured leg. Colonel Williamson decided that a complex recovery operation only "tens of yards" from the enemy was out of the question, and ordered the tank destroyed.[49]

While the ill-fated tank action at Hedy was playing out, the Marine Division was planning Operation Clambake, a major raid that would involve all three battalions of the 5th Marines. Its primary intent was to capture prisoners by simultaneously assaulting and neutralizing three of the enemy's combat outposts—Hill 104, Ungok, and Red Hill, about two miles west of the old Detroit outpost. Sixteen Able Company tanks and four flame tanks were to launch a purely diversionary raid, unsupported by infantry, on nearby Kumgok. Captain Clyde Hunter of A Company objected to the lack of infantry protection for his tanks, but was overruled. He attempted to compensate for this lack of ground support by arranging pre-registered artillery fire to help protect his vulnerable tanks. Patrols of men from the division Recon Company, the tank recon party, and engineers searched the area forward of the MLR for mines and suitable routes for the tanks.

On January 30, John Williamson recorded the death of one of the original Brigade tankers. Master Sergeant Charles J. 'Tiny' Rhoades, who had fought so magnificently with Lieutenant Sweet earlier in the war, was killed on a night reconnaissance. Rhoades had requested a second tour in Korea. Unhappy with his administrative job, he had been made chief of the reconnaissance section. The Chinese ambushed the returning patrol, and in the confusion Marines on the MLR also began to fire into the area. One Marine was killed outright and two wounded. Rhoades was shot twice through the chest, and died of his wounds before he reached an aid station.[50] The affair offered an ill omen for Operation Clambake.

Just after dawn on February 3, the tanks moved out on the heels of an artillery barrage and assailed Hill 104. The tank force served both as a feint and directed suppressive fire against enemy outposts that might flank the real assault force. Recognizing the value of the tanks in these raids, the Chinese had now equipped their forward units with 75mm. recoilless guns and captured 3.5-inch rocket launchers.[51] For the unsupported tanks, things began to go terribly awry almost immediately.

The five tanks of 1st Lt. Albert R. Bowman's 1st Platoon were inundated with artillery fire. A direct hit set tank A-15 afire, although the on-board fire extinguishers were able to snuff out the flames. It was just the beginning of nightmare. First Lieutenant James B. McMath Jr.'s 3rd Platoon tanks stumbled over a steep, unmapped paddy dike and smashed their protruding gun tubes against the rock-hard ice. All five were disabled by damaged gun mechanisms. Lieutenant Michael McAdams of the Flame Platoon watched the horror unfold and promptly ordered his tank commanders to dismount and guide their vehicles across the obstacle.

McAdams and his four tanks forged onward into the dust and smoke, unaware that they were now protected only by long-range machine gun fire from two tanks.[52] McAdams discovered that his hatch would not close completely, and that his radio had chosen this, the worst of all possible times, to malfunction. Without any other option, he exposed himself in his hatch to wave his second section under Platoon Sergeant Ken Miller to take the lead.

The Chinese tank-killer teams advanced through trench lines toward the tanks, holding bushes in front of them, a sort of dubious camouflage they hoped would allow them to close the distance for a sure kill. Machine gun fire from the tankers ripped apart the advance, although the effort delayed Miller, leaving McAdams to once again assume the lead position.[53] His section moved up onto the crest, where the tanks exhausted their flame fuel. It was then that disaster arrived in the form of trio of rockets that struck the Platoon Leader's tank, F-31. One round tore through the side of the turret, killing McAdams and wounding the other crewmen inside. Another round hit a track block welded to the side as extra armor, but failed to penetrate, By this time, however, the entire crew was either dead or seriously wounded. Blinded by blood from a serious head wound, Cpl. Charles Craig, the tank's driver, was unable to operate the vehicle. F-31 was stranded and waiting for the final killing shot.[54]

Word of the catastrophe unfolding at the front arrived about this time, remembered John Williamson, who was directing the action from the OP in the rear. He, too, could see little because of the clouds of dust and billowing smoke. But what he heard crackling over the radio that day chilled his bones: "[W]e started to hear alarming transmissions over the radio . . . 'My tank is on fire!' or 'One of the flame tanks is burning!' and 'Tank has been hit!' 'The hatch is open and all I can see is a bloody head sticking out of the turret, but there's at least one man left alive in the tank!' 'The enemy is closing in and within three yards of tank 31!' 'Have them close the hatch and we'll bring VT fire down on them!'"[55]

While Williamson was listening to the action, tankers inside McAdams's F-31 were trying in vain to dislodge the lieutenant's corpse and close the hatch. The shot that had entered the turret had also struck Cpl. Marvin Dennis, the tank's gunner. One of his arms was nearly severed and he was losing blood rapidly. With a cool presence of mind, Dennis picked up his pistol with his one good hand and used it to deadly effect on the swarming Chinese soldiers climbing on the tank who tried to enter through the open commander's hatch, where his lieutenant and friend's corpse was still stuck fast.[56] F-21, the second tank from Miller's section under Cpl. Thomas E. Clawson, maneuvered into position next to McAdams's crippled tank and helped fend off additional Chinese attacks.

Assistant driver Sgt. Charles Foley—normally the TC for F-31, but who had been 'bumped' by Miller—dismounted from F-32 to render aid to the men trapped in the disabled tank. A grenade launched from who knows where landed nearby, showering the area with shrapnel and wounding Foley. Another round penetrated the luckless F-31, smashing gunner Dennis's legs.

Corporal Elmer R. Betts Jr., inside flame tank F-12, had just completed hosing down one of the trench lines with flame when he spotted several wounded Marines on the ground. Betts backed his tank toward the men on the ground until it tumbled into an unseen ditch. Bravely, the corporal dismounted and guided his tank back onto firm ground. When he found that the wounded men he had spotted were from McAdams's crippled tank, he and Clawson from F-21 led Foley and Craig to the cover of Betts's tank.[57]

A Company's Captain Clyde Hunter's worst nightmare was coming true. He had lobbied for infantry support but was overruled. Now, with all these men on the ground, and visibility blocked not only by the smoke and dust of the battle but also an artillery smokescreen drifting over from the main infantry assault on nearby Ungok, the frustrated captain was unable to use either machine gun fire or his carefully plotted artillery fires to protect his men.

While Hunter fumed, unable to render assistance to the trapped tankers, Betts climbed into the immobilized tank with the wounded Corporal Dennis who, despite his grievous wounds, managed to squeeze off bursts from the coaxial machine gun to make the Chinese think the tank was still capable of fighting back. With Dennis on the machine gun, Betts drove the tank to safety. Clawson leapt onto the back of the retreating tank, where he was wounded several times.[58]

Sergeant Miller, meanwhile, requested and was denied permission to withdraw his own tank from the exposed position. As far as his superiors were concerned, he was still valuable as bait to divert Chinese artillery away from the main assault on Ungok. As he marked time in the killing zone, the supporting tanks of McMath's 2nd Platoon were experiencing their own travails. When one tank's electrical system failed, a second pulled alongside and their crews exchanged the heavy batteries under fire, a brave decision that enabled the stalled tank to escape.[59]

After what must have seemed a lifetime of waiting, Miller finally received permission to withdraw. He was about to do so when a strange voice on the radio told him to stop. Without thinking he did so and a round from a 57mm. recoilless gun tore through one of the fuel tanks, setting his tank ablaze. The order had come from a Chinese solder in possession of a captured radio.[60] Somehow Miller and his crew managed to abandon their tank under heavy fire without additional loss, and Captain Hunter ordered it destroyed by gunfire.

Although the tankers had suffered their own hell that day, the main infantry assault on Ungok was a far bloodier affair. Still, Col. Lew Walt of the 5th Marines pronounced the raid a success. Author Lee Ballenger's assessment of the diversionary tank operation could equally apply to the whole Clambake affair: "Success was obvious; the feint drew more enemy than it could handle."[61]

*   *   *

Marine tanks later supported other raids all along the division front, though mostly by offering direct fire from the gun slots along the MLR. One such raid, Operation Dog, occurred on the night of February 23-24. A platoon of tanks screened by infantry moved up onto Hill 90 to support an attack on a position known as The Boot. The result was predictable. One tank struck a mine, and before anyone could react all of them were overrun by repeated Chinese infantry assaults. Within minutes the operation degenerated into an all-out battle for Hill 90. In the hand-to-hand combat that followed, tank commanders were forced to stand upright in their hatches, blasting away at the Chinese with their anti-aircraft machine guns and sidearms. One tank, loaded with wounded, headed down the hill only to be ambushed in a creek bed. The assistant driver, who was helping the wounded infantrymen on the engine deck was wounded, but the tank commander fought off the attackers with a wounded Marine's BAR (Browning Automatic Rifle.).

Back on the hill, the Platoon Leader's radio failed and he was wounded trying to coordinate his tanks by running from vehicle to vehicle. The injured officer was thrown inside a tank and the battle continued. The Chinese finally broke off the action during the early morning hours and the Marines withdrew, leaving one damaged tank for later recovery.

Some of the withdrawing tanks carried extra cargo: American infantry had thrown six Chinese corpses onto the decks for intelligence analysis. "Unfortunately, they were piled over the exhaust mufflers and caught fire, causing the ammunition on their bodies to detonate," remembered John Williamson. "A grenade even cooked off on one, so my men were forced to jettison this grisly cargo."[62]

This late winter period brought yet another influx of new junior officers. One of them was Bob Montgomery, a veteran who had served in half-track tank destroyers in World War II before transferring to tanks in 1950. After stateside service with the 7th Tank Battalion, which he described as "a sort of filter for sending tankers overseas," Montgomery joined B Company as a Platoon Leader while the company was in reserve. "This gave us a chance to fit in a little bit, and then we moved up into what was known as the Forward Reserve Area, just behind two line companies."

Another new junior officer was Charles Rosenfeld, an aerial dive-bomber gunner during World War II. Burly, self-confident and blessed with an easy laugh, he had been commissioned lieutenant in 1950. He, too, was in the 7th Tank Battalion, a Force Troops unit,[63] and thought the training prepared him well for Korea. "Matter of fact, I even went to a school on flame tanks at Camp Del Mar. I never dreamed I would end up in flame tanks," said Rosenfeld, telling a story worth repeating. "I got to Korea, and I had orders to go to the Fifth Marines' Anti-Tank Company. I reported in—I was a First Lieutenant at the time. The Old Man called me in, and he says, 'Well, we're sorry, but we can't use you because our present commander is junior to you, and he's already on his third Purple Heart, and we're not gonna relieve him.' They sent me back to the tank battalion."

There, Colonel Williamson confronted the lieutenant. "What do you want to do?"

"I want to go to B Company with Captain Sherwood."

Williamson listened to Rosenfeld's pitch for a short while before replying. "That's fine, but you're going to the flame tanks. The Platoon Commander was killed a short while ago."

"[And] that's how I ended up in flame tanks," explained Rosenfeld.

Rosenfeld also found himself the proud possessor of a single flail tank.[64] "That was used to flail mines out, although it wasn't too successful at the time. It kept breaking. It was built on an M4. . . . It had a big rig on the front with a bunch of chains on it. We used it a couple of times to get a few mines out, but it kept breaking down. I think probably the terrain had more to do with it than anything else. Difficult to get in where they were supposed to be." The flail tank was an armored orphan, explained Rosenfeld, and "I think they just put it in there to get it out of the battalion."

Rosenfeld's flame tanks, as he explained it, did not play a leading role at that stage of the war: "The flames did very, very little. Mostly we were reserve. We had a section or platoon at Hedy . . . and we made a couple of forays to fire flame over the top of the hill, but never saw anything." As a result, staff officers were kept busy dreaming up tasks for Rosenfeld's underutilized armored platoon. "One time somebody down at I Corps got the bright idea of putting tear gas in place of napalm, to use for prisoner control and what have you," recalled Rosenfeld. "We never even tried that, because you couldn't put tear gas in there under compressed air—there were just too many leaks in the system. The crews would never make it!"

While the lieutenant was acquainting himself with the flame tanks, the bigger M46 tanks were brought forward to replace the old M4A3s as dozers. On March 17, dozer tank D-43 was scraping out new positions on Hill 124, also known as Outpost Hedy, when a single 3.5-inch rocket struck the right front side of the turret. The shaped charge bored through the armor and spewed a deadly jet of gas and molten metal through the turret, killing the gunner and tank commander inside.[65] This deadly incident resulted in the development of a wire cage that was fitted around the vulnerable turret, and rotated with the turret. The flimsy screen would not stop artillery rounds, but it would detonate the shaped-charge rockets at a safe distance from the tank's armor.[66]

*   *   *

Massive Chinese offensives opened the spring of 1953—just as the annual thaw threatened to disrupt critical logistical functions. The fighting proved to be some of the bloodiest in the Korean War when the

Chinese sought to capture a cluster of three Marine outposts located about 1,500 yards north of the MLR. Each of the 'Nevada cities' outposts—Reno, Vegas, and Carson—overlooked Chinese supply routes and was garrisoned by a reinforced rifle platoon from the 5th Marines. A change of possession would reverse the situation, and allow Chinese observation of the American rear areas.

The 5th Marines, with A Company tanks in direct support, bore the brunt of the Nevada city battles. The D Company tanks were supporting the 1st Marines, with B Company as the ready reserve, and C Company in the division reserve for maintenance and training.[67] Maintenance was always a problem, and spare parts were not always available. Don Boyer, by now an old hand in Korea, explained that one trick was to replace a worn sprocket by simply reversing it. As he explained it, "that front edge of it takes up all the wear on it."

On March 26, eleven A Company tanks moved up into their firing slots to support a planned raid by the 5th Marines. The tables were turned, however, when at 1900 hours the Chinese artillery opened a heavy barrage against the positions of 5th Marines. Within ten minutes more than 3,500 enemy infantry of the *358 Regiment, 120 Division* were pouring down on the combat outposts in one of the biggest attacks of the war. The outposts immediately called for "box-me-in" barrages and mortar support.[68] Although the fire inflicted heavy enemy losses, it did not prevent the Chinese from seizing parts of Carson and Reno by 1935 hours, although the former position was yielded a short time later.

Outposts Reno and Vegas, which were more exposed, were simply overrun by the enemy. Realizing the desperate situation they were in, their occupants called down artillery fire upon their position. While artillery fire flooded the area, tanks in position behind Reno blasted away at the exposed Chinese infantry. Attempts to reinforce the outposts were blocked by enemy ambushes, and some units suffered up to 70 per cent losses.[69]

A major struggle also developed at an interim position called the Reno Block, where both sides tried to assemble company-size forces for their own purposes. The direct 90mm. fire from the tanks broke up Chinese formations, while the Marines tried yet again to push through to the beleaguered outposts.

By midnight, both Reno and Vegas had fallen to the enemy and the men there were killed or captured. Although artillery and tank guns had ravaged and continued to pour deadly fire into the Chinese foot soldiers, the survivors flowed south to attack the MLR; attempts to recapture the lost outposts were abandoned. It was a long night, and one in which the artillery and tanks spent hours firing into the determined attackers. At one point, Marine armor ambushed two CCF carrying parties bringing forward timbers to build new fortifications on the captured hills.[70]

On March 27, a morning counterattack by the 5th Marines and 2/7 was delayed—despite support by Marine tank and artillery fire. The assault bogged down in the swampy ground below the hills amid a rain of mortar and artillery fire. Still, by mid-afternoon the infantry was clawing away at the enemy positions on Vegas, and by nightfall F/2/7 and D/2/5 had seized a tenuous foothold there. Several nocturnal enemy counterattacks failed to dislodge them.

The Marines elected to put all their resources into the recapture of Vegas, and on March 28 launched three separate attacks to secure the hill. At 1307 riflemen secured Vegas and set about rooting out the last enemy survivors while artillery and tank fire disrupted Chinese efforts to assemble their own counterattack. By this time, the tanks of A Company had been fighting continuously for more than forty-eight hours.[71]

The night brought with it renewed Chinese attacks, which were driven off by concentrated and well delivered artillery and tank fire. A smaller attack directed against Reno also failed miserably, leaving scores of enemy attackers dead and wounded in its wake. At 0830 the next morning, March 29, the Marines set about refortifying Vegas under cover of a smokescreen. That night the Chinese launched yet another major attack, which was inundated by one of the heaviest artillery barrages of the entire struggle for the Nevada cities.[72] Throughout March 30 the Marines continued to burrow into the hill, despite desultory attacks and shelling. By dawn the next day the Chinese had made the decision to abandon the attempt to retake Vegas.

Red Saunders remembered that the action was heavy for weeks on end, with the attack and defense of the Nevada city positions especially so. His light section of two tanks was positioned during the battle on a small knob, with his Platoon Leader's heavy section on a higher hill nearby. "For a period of six weeks we received an average of a hundred and ten rounds of artillery [each day] on top of that little hill. We never did get a direct hit on the tank. About six feet away was the closest. You couldn't take a shit during the daytime, unless you did it in the tank," he added. "Every time you moved, here came an artillery shell in on us."

In all, the Marine tanks expended more than 7,000 rounds of 90mm. ammunition engaging enemy guns and marking positions with smoke rounds for air attack.[73]

Some stocks of already scarce ammunition had been damaged, and could not be fired. "When you get a 90mm. shell, it comes in a cardboard case," Saunders explained. "[If] the cardboard had been wet, and it sticks to the brass, it's kind of hard to chamber that thing. Like impossible. When it's eight or nine o'clock at night, and you've got ten rounds of ammo left, and you get a load of ammo up there and you can't use it, it kinda discourages you." Stripping away the cardboard was more difficult than the tankers initially imagined it might be. "It's impossible to clean off. You'd have to sit there and pick it off," continued Saunders. "A couple of grains of sand will keep that thing from chambering. You discarded it."

Fortunately for Zan (A. C.) Bryant, he arrived in Korea just as the Nevada Cities battles ended. He had dropped out of college and joined the Marines in early 1951, and had spent most of his time at Camp Lejeune and Vieques, Puerto Rico. In late March, Bryant was transferred to Korea as a brand new sergeant in the wire, or telephone, section of Headquarters Company at Munsan-ni. Bryant: "When I got there the guy that I replaced was gone. I was senior man and a rookie—not the nicest thing—but I was instantly the wire chief, and I didn't know my left foot from first base." Bryant and his men were responsible for maintaining secure telephone communications from a forward switchboard, call sign Weasel Switch, just north of the river to the tank company command posts on the MLR. From there, he explaied, "we ran wire right up to the tank slots." Other lines ran from the tank company CPs to the infantry CPs.

On April 6, the Communists returned to the peace talks at Panmunjom. The 1st Tank Battalion reconstituted its Everready Force and moved back into the position at Outpost Two. This force stood by to protect the units involved in Operation Little Switch, the exchange of 6,670 Communist prisoners for 684 U.N. prisoners, among them 149 Americans.[74]

The prisoner exchange did not preclude Chinese combat operations, including an April 9 assault on Carson and a new outpost called Elko. Artillery and fire from A and B Company tanks drove off the enemy attacks, which continued to probe at Carson and Elko through April 12.

Later that month, Lt. Col. Charles Worth McCoy, who had been the Executive Officer of the 2nd Tank Battalion at Tarawa, assumed command of the tank battalion as plans were finalized for the Army's 25th Division to relieve the 1st Marine Division on the battered Jamestown Line. Between May 1-5, Army units replaced the Marine regiments, but tank and artillery units remained at the front to support the recently arrived 25th Division.[75] Dog Company tanks were attached to the 35th Infantry Regiment, B and C Companies supported the Turkish Brigade,[76] and only A Company was in reserve.

Operations with the Army units resulted in an immediate dispute over how the tanks were to be employed. Bob Montgomery, who had spent only six weeks as a Platoon Leader in B Company before being promoted to Executive Officer, did not like what he heard: "The Turks, I believe, were attached to the Army's Twenty-fifth Division, but we did not operate directly with them. The tank officer of the Army division . . . came over and told us pretty much what he thought we should do. I suppose we were under their operational control," he continued, "but we did have some problems with this guy. He wanted us to move into the front line, and become sort of armored pillboxes. We objected strongly to that."

Robert Post was the commanding officer of Company C. He had served during World War II as an enlisted radio repairman, and after the war as an aerial navigator. Commissioned a 2nd Lieutenant in 1949, in 1950 he transferred from infantry to tanks while stationed at Camp Lejeune, North Carolina.[77] Post explained in some detail the proper deployment of Marine Corps tanks. "The standard procedure for employment," he began . . .

> was to assign one company in support of each of the on-line regiments. The remaining two companies were kept in mobile reserve. After the US Army relieved the Marines the tank battalion remained to support the Army Division. The Army wanted two companies to support each regiment. They also wanted the tanks

deployed in dug-in firing positions along the MLR (Main Line of Resistance).

This was a significant change in the way tanks had previously been employed. When in support of Marine Regiments, the tanks had operated with mobility, firing from a variety of preselected firing slots in the regimental sector. These were chosen in conjunction with the needs and desires of the battalions and companies who occupied the sector. They also were used to accompany patrols forward of the MLR. In order to comply with the requirements of the Army, I had to join B Company on line. I was therefore required to locate a new Company Command Post and move two platoons into fixed firing positions. Because of logistical considerations, it was decided to use B Company's CP facilities. We worked closely together. We set up phone lines from the platoon CPs back to the company CP. We were also in radio contact. In practice, every night I would go to the B Company CP—all the action took place at night, nothing much happened during the day—[and] I would take my radio. The tanks could communicate by phone or radio directly with me. My Executive Officer (Maurice Ashley) would go to the Brigade CP (in the case of the Turks). I could then pass along any pertinent information. I received from the tank positions, to him by radio. One big plus for the tanks was that they could see. We had searchlights mounted on some of the tanks and they could periodically light up the battlefield.

We as tankers, were not comfortable with the "Pillbox" role. I didn't like it and neither did Jim Sherwood, the B Company Commander. We never complained to anyone, except one another, but the Bn. S-3 (Operations Officer) Major Dick Smith pleaded our case with the Army brass. He felt the same way we did—the tanks were more effective in a mobile role. His arguments went unheeded and we did as we were told.[78]

Like the other tankers, Bob Montgomery of B Company also had few good things to about the Army's interference with Marine Corps tank deployment. "It takes away your mobility," he grumbled. "It was very difficult to get them out of position and move them. We felt that by staying behind the lines, if we got an attack in one company sector, we could move very rapidly over to that area, or move to another. In other words, we could mass the tanks in one position."

At 0100 hours on May 15, 1953, the Chinese began anew testing the defensive positions known as Carson, Elko, Vegas, Berlin and East Berlin. Fifteen C Company tanks were already in position. The tanks and the Turkish Brigade on East Berlin inflicted particularly heavy losses on assaulting CCF forces. For the Turks and their supporting units, it was only the beginning of a long and bloody spring and summer, during which the Chinese continued to slam away at their positions.

On the night of May 28-29, the Chinese launched another major assault. Once again, the fifteen tanks of B and C Companies savaged the Chinese on the open ground, but the isolated outposts changed hands several times. When the Chinese attacks grew in intensity, additional resources were committed to the battle until 33 tanks were involved in the fighting.[79]

Robert Post remembers that "When the Chinese tried to penetrate the MLR, the tanks were very effective as a visible rallying point. The tanks mostly fired machine guns, the main armament wasn't used too often. The tanks would occasionally fire at one another when the Chinese attempted to climb up on the tanks and throw grenades in the hatches. The 90mm. was sometimes fired using a canister round which was something like a shotgun shell. The tankers didn't really like to use canister though because it tore up the lands and grooves in the barrel.[80]

When the Chinese subjected the Turkish Brigade to an unusually intense pounding by artillery, the tanks proved an unintentional godsend. The heavy shelling ripped up communications wires, and for protracted periods the powerful tank radios offered the only "generally reliable means of communications with the scene of the action."[81]

During three days and nights of continuous attack the tanks fired around the clock. The resourceful Chinese found a way to partially counter the effectiveness of the superior American artillery in the rough terrain in this part of Korea. According to tanker Bob Montgomery, "They would move directly down the ridge line to avoid artillery fire. That made them ideal targets for the tanks. At that point we had all seventeen tanks in line, and it was sort of a turkey shoot for us. Like shooting fish in a barrel. We were using up HE faster than we could replenish from our company ammo dump."

The Army also contributed its M16 half-tracked machine gun mounts to the fighting. "Those quad fifties did a terrific job," said Robert Post. "They were firing from defilade positions about two hundred fifty [to] three hundred yards behind the MLR. They were firing indirect fire, which I thought was silly, but the Chinese hated them.[82] Another thing everyone hated to see up there were those damned four point five rocket launchers," Post continued. "They had a firing position right behind our CP. Every time they fired they would fire two or three ripples of rockets and bug out of there, and then we'd get the return artillery fire. I don't remember them ever not getting return fire."[83]

The usual employment procedure was for a tank to fire until its ammunition was exhausted, and then retire to replenish ammunition while another tank occupied its firing slot. Under the massive Chinese onslaught, however, the companies decided to keep all their tanks on the line. The M39 Armored Utility Vehicles were used to re-supply the tanks with a basic ammunition load even while the tanks were engaging the enemy.[84]

The fighting along this part of the Jamestown Line is often remembered by participants as one constant artillery barrage. "The estimate was that along the Turkish area they took thirty thousand rounds of fire over a three-day period," said Bob Montgomery. "In behind our CP there was an artillery position where one of the ammo dumps was hit. That made it sort of difficult for us to operate, since we were in range of most of that exploding artillery ammo.[85] During that time," Montgomery recalled, "we were given credit for killing over a thousand Chinese with tank fire."

As long as the steady artillery barrages continued, Zan Bryant's wiremen were never without work. He and his men constantly repaired telephone lines severed by heavy shells. "I never had to worry a whole lot about getting shot with a rifle. I worried a whole lot about getting hit with mortar rounds and artillery, and any infiltration," he explained. "Most of it happened at night. Ours was a really strange job, because I would be out with one or two other guys, three or four at the most. We'd be wandering around by ourselves just putting wire back in, patching it up, and keep everybody so they could communicate." The terrain funneled not only foot traffic, but also telephone lines through certain vulnerable choke points. "They had all these places zeroed in. . . . When they hit at night, they would have all these places pre-determined, and they would just lay barrages in on you. All the CPs would get hit, all these terminal strips."[86]

Locating the breaks in the lines was both tedious and dangerous. "You weren't on the line fighting with guys. You were out in the dark . . . trying to put lines back together," continued Bryant. "Some kid would come up, and you'd put him on a phone at the end of a wire. You'd just say, 'Stay here!' Here you are all by yourself in God's country, and you're going down the road, and keep [tapping into the wire] and ringing wires, trying to get back to him, trying to patch it back up." Specific dangers were never far from Bryant's attention. "They did have infiltration, and they would booby-trap. . . . You had to go along and whip the wire, because they'd hook it to a hand grenade, and if you pulled it you'd pull the pin out, and you'd have a hand grenade go off in your puss. You had to be careful." And Bryant was indeed circumspect in his dangerous work. "I never lost a person," he said proudly. "Guys I'm sure got a little shrapnel in them now and then, but you just didn't turn yourself in for that kind of stuff."

As Bryant soon discovered, the Turks fought with their characteristic ferocity. "Those Turks, they really fought their hearts out. The APCs were running back and forth, taking wounded out and bringing ammunition up to them. God! It was like nothing you've ever seen before." But for the hard-pressed wiremen, the Turks soon proved as troublesome as the Chinese. "They started stealing all our wires [by tapping into them] and we had people on there speaking a foreign language," Bryant complained. "They'd just clip 'em off. They'd get on one side and they'd keep ringing through until they found it and—'click!'—they cut 'em out. They're cutting the wires off to the tanks that are supporting them!" Attaching an interpreter to Bryant's section solved the problem. Someone liked the solution because before long Bryant and his team "got to eat in the officer's quarters there. Silverware, and white plates and dishes. Boy, that was really good! Best food I had when I was there."

The savage and close-range fighting required the tanks to fire into intermixed groups of Turks and Chinese on the featureless hills. One day, Bryant listened in on the communications between a tank captain[87] and one of his men was impressed by what he heard: "He was on the radio talking to a tank commander who was confused. I can remember this guy doing such a super job calming him down. You could hear the anxiety in the guy's voice. . . . . He gave him something to look at. He said, 'You see that?' and he answered, 'Yeah.' He got him oriented, because the guy was scared to death he had the wrong fire mission, He thought he was firing on friendlies, and he wanted to be sure. This guy was so cool, the way he directed him in."

At midday on May 29, U.N. command finally conceded control of the last of the Nevada Cities to the enemy. Chinese positions on Vegas and Carson made Elko untenable, and the Army's 14th Regiment, which had been moved in to reinforce the Turks, reluctantly abandoned Elko.

June brought with it a change in Chinese tactics. Throughout the month the CCF concentrated its attacks against the ROK divisions—apparently for political purposes. And the war continued grinding forward.

On July 7-8, the rejuvenated 1st Marine Division relieved the 25th Division on the MLR. Except, of course, for the tanks; they had never left. The relief took place under a constant heavy rainfall, and the Chinese took the opportunity to launch a major attack against Outposts Berlin and East Berlin, southwest of the old Outpost Detroit. Both were occupied by a joint Marine—Turkish force. By 2345 hours there was hand-to-hand fighting on both hills, and communications were lost soon afterward. The tanks of B Company battered away at Chinese assault troops and positions on the nearby hills, attracting the full fury of the enemy artillery. In less than seven hours the Chinese dropped 2,000 rounds of mortar and artillery fire on the tank positions, without inflicting any significant damage.[88]

The Chinese attacks also surged against the adjacent hills, as Bob Montgomery recalled: "We had some tanks up on line. The Marine infantry was behind, the Chinese were on the front slope, and the tanks were sort of caught in the middle. The infantry was doing their best to keep the Chinese off. They were carrying shaped charges, trying to get underneath the tanks. Fortunately we were able to hose each other off well enough so they were never able to blow up any of the tanks."

At dawn on July 8, the Marines discovered that the Chinese controlled East Berlin, and that only a handful of survivors still held Berlin. At 1000 hours G and H Companies, 2/7, moved out to retake East Berlin. In this assault the tanks were able to utilize their direct fire capability to the fullest, supporting the infantry assault with a rolling wall of fire that advanced only yards ahead of the infantry.[89] By 1233 the Marines were once again in control of East Berlin, and at 1300 a relief force reached Berlin, freeing the last of the Turkish defenders to rejoin their brigade.

That night, five tanks were ordered to relocate out of the front line and onto Hill 126, a higher commanding hill to the rear, from which the flat-trajectory guns could rake enemy positions all along the front. On the following day, July 9, these tanks supported the consolidation on the Berlins, basting away at enemy positions. For more than a week both sides picked and probed at each other, fighting a series of vicious patrol actions in the ground between the two MLRs.

During one such patrol Charles Sooter's tanks were picking up wounded in an area exposed to enemy fire. It was extremely hazardous work, as Sooter recalled: "Take the escape hatch out, go down there and pull these guys up [through] the escape hatch, and take them back to sick bay. I crawled out the escape hatch to get one of these guys, and they dropped a mortar [round] twenty yards from me. . . . I got hit in the back with it. I had the boys pull me right back up in there and [they] took me to sick bay." The wound was a serious, and ended Sooter's tenure in Korea. A series of hospitals in Hawaii and California awaited him.[90]

Karl Fontenot volunteered for tanks in Officer's Basic school, trained at Fort Knox, and was assigned to a school in Japan *en route* to Korea. He arrived on the peninsula after the B Company tanks were withdrawn to the Reserve, and was given a platoon in that company.[91]

The endless pattern of attack and counterattack continued unabated. On the night of July 19-20, the Chinese again fell upon the Berlins, with smaller attacks against the nearby Outposts Ingrid and Dagmar. At 2300 hours the Chinese were on Berlin, and by 0146 both had fallen. At 0700 hours I Corps headquarters canceled an assault planned to recover the lost positions. Instead, the Marines set about completely wrecking the two hills, pounding them with every gun available—including eight-inch and huge 240mm. (9.4 inch) Army howitzers. The tanks illuminated targets on East Berlin and smashed Chinese bunkers and defensive works with direct fire. The seesaw fighting for the Berlin hills was largely over.

Following the fall of the Berlins, members of the Allied high command grew concerned that the next Chinese effort would be against Hill 119. The talks at Panmunjom appeared to be headed for imposition of an armistice, and one of the provisions would be a retreat from existing positions. If the Chinese could seize Hill 119, the cease fire conditions would force U.N. troops back 2,000 yards, denying part of the northern bank of the Imjin River to U.N. forces. This, in turn, would hamper lateral communications along the U.N. line and allow Chinese observers to remain on another height (Hill 126), from which they could see into key road junctions and communications centers behind U.N. lines.[92]

As the Ready Reserve, Baker Company tanks would be the primary reaction force to stem a CCF breakthrough. New platoon leader Karl Fontenot explained: "They were concerned, obviously, about the possibility of Chinese breaking through and coming toward the south. We spent a lot of time going around and looking at blocking positions, and figuring out how long it would take us to get there."

At 2030 hours on July 24, Chinese forces began probing at Hill 111. The fighting soon evolved into the main assault, directed against Hill 119 (also known as Boulder City), which was held by 3/1, plus four tanks from C Company, one from the 7th Marines' Anti-Tank Platoon, and five tanks from the 1st Marines' Anti-Tank Platoon. By midnight, the Marines had been pushed onto the rear slope of the hill, and the tanks were isolated in ground controlled by the enemy. Though surrounded, the tanks continued to batter the Chinese. Telephonic communications were severed, but the tank radios were able to relay critical information to the rifle regiment headquarters. In a vain effort to destroy them, the Chinese fired a staggering total of 2,200 artillery and mortar rounds upon the tanks deployed on Boulder City.[93]

The fighting spread to nearby outposts held by the 5th Marines, so the five tanks of the 5th Marines' Anti-Tank Platoon and a single tank from A Company joined the artillery in punishing the enemy positions on nearby hills. By dawn on July 25, the Marines, aided by lavish artillery support from the 25th Division and Commonwealth Division artillery firing across their boundaries, had driven the Chinese off Boulder City. At 0820 the CCF launched an uncommon daylight assault, but was unable to make significant inroads. At 1335 hours the hill was again considered secure.

The lull was, as usual, temporary. In the early evening hours the Chinese again assaulted Boulder City, this time led by special anti-tank assault teams. Staff Sergeant James Champlin described these as teams of four men, each armed with a dozen or so anti-tank grenades that trailed a white cloth streamer when thrown.[94] These weapons were probably old Soviet RPG-43 shaped-charge grenades, which were rarely used in

Korea. The attack was unsuccessful. The next day was relatively quiet, although Marine artillery sniped away at small groups of Chinese infantry and directed counter battery missions against enemy guns. On the night of July 26, the enemy devoted a few half-hearted attempts to seize Hill 119, and launched sporadic forays against Hill 111.

The Chinese assaults on Boulder City and nearby positions had forced the Marine tanks to set a new record. In four days of fighting, thirty tanks fired 4,845 rounds of main gun ammunition and nearly 55,000 rounds of machine gun ammunition.

Charles Rosenfeld was assigned to lead a platoon of tanks forward on July 26 to support the 1st Marines: "[They] were expecting a big attack on Berlin and East Berlin. I was Headquarters Company commander at that time, and I was sitting back in the rear, fat, dumb, and happy." The colonel wanted Rosenfeld to lead the platoon in person, but "we never got past the battalion CP," he remembered. "He decided not to use us. Very fortunate, because there was no road out to East Berlin. Our tanks would have hit a trench line, and we would have been in deep mud."

Captain Robert Post came to realize that "The Army brass were very appreciative of the role of the tanks in beating off the last futile attempts of the Chinese to reach the Imjin." These attacks and the bloody defensive efforts to beat them back, he explained, took place during "the final stages of the war, and the peace talks were about to be successfully concluded.[95]

For their gallant efforts, B and C Companies were awarded the Army Distinguished Unit Citation.

"There never was a good war or a bad peace."

— Benjamin Franklin

Chapter Eight

The Warriors Depart

Armistice and Withdrawal

At 1000 hours on July 27, 1953, the warring antagonists signed armistice papers at Panmunjom. At 2200 hours, a cease-fire went into effect, effectively ending the three-year "police action." A brief exchange of artillery fire began at nightfall and quickly petered out, a last gasp of war before an eerie calm spread across the scarred Korean landscape.

Zan Bryant remembers the moment and the fear of losing people at the last moment: "When the thing ended there was this sudden silence. Everybody sighed a sigh of relief. Short-timers . . . people were down where they only had a few days to go. I tried to keep my wiremen out from up front. Christ! You hated to have somebody get hurt when they're on their way home."

"You look at some of the folks that you lost in the last three or four days of the war," said Bob Montgomery, echoing Bryant's observations. "I had a very good friend who was an artillery aerial observer [who] was shot down on the day before the cease-fire. We were able to recover the body and the Oh-One he was in from in front of the MLR, but it's sort of hard to reconcile."

In the rear areas, celebration often took the form of shooting guns into the air, but not near the front. "You didn't see many rounds going off up where we were," said Montgomery. "There was celebration, and a few rounds shot off in the air, but when the night came for the cease-fire, it was complete and total silence from that point on." Montgomery explained that there was a good reason for this: "The word was no rounds, because you could start the war all over again, and that was the last thing we wanted. The next day, in the morning after the cease-fire, the Chinese were up picking up bodies. We let them come up to our tanks to pick up the dead bodies that were scattered all around. We ignored each other. They looked at us, went ahead and got the bodies and trotted off with them, and we let them."

One of the most contentious events that followed the armistice was the exchange of prisoners. Special trains were arranged to shuttle POW's from both sides across the lines. In May 1952, North Korean POWs had briefly seized control of the camp on Koje-do, where they had held the American commanding general of the post hostage.[1] There was concern that hard-core Communist prisoners might cause similar problems in the exchange, or even provoke an incident that might cause a resumption of the fighting.

The U.N. forces decided to make a show of force for the prisoner's benefit, to convince them to behave and send the appropriate message when they returned to their own lines, as Karl Fontenot explained: "There was a large displacement of stuff—equipment, companies, Korean units – all along the line where the train had to pass. They got an impression of a tremendous amount of strength there. Which would encourage 'em if they were going to report on things when they got back. They saw a lot more than was normally there. They saw all these people working on tanks. We made sure that the tanks were all visible, in positions on the hills along the sides."

Bob Montgomery took a hand in overseeing the security of the prisoner operations:

> They moved our tank company over near the Freedom Village. We were the Reaction Force, in case there was a problem with the moving of the Chinese prisoners back across into North Korean territory. The trains went by. We were right on the railroad track. As soon as the Chinese got on the train, they yanked all the military

uniforms off that had been issued by the South Koreans and Americans. Some of them were going back just about naked.

Some way they had gotten Chinese flags, and they were waving all those out of the train as they went by. We had a couple flame tanks over there. Every now and then we'd give 'em a squirt of flame right along the edge of the railroad track, just to let 'em know we were there. Really, we never had any trouble.

They said well, maybe some of these guys will change their mind at the last minute, and revolt and want to come back. If they did, we were to protect them. If the Chinese tried to come across and do anything, we were to stop 'em. It was sort of uneventful.

"That was a show of force at Freedom Bridge, when they released the prisoners," said Charles Rosenfeld, confirming Montgomery's report. "Exciting, but no action."

The overall event might have been "uneventful" for Montgomery and his tankers, but he remembers well watching the trains of prisoners slipping past from north to south: "We saw trains coming back [with United Nations POWs], but they didn't stop. They rolled through so rapidly that all we saw was a few of the guys waving out of the windows. What we did see was the ones in pretty bad shape. They picked them up by ambulance, and they came down the road. They had whole convoys of ambulances with these guys."

The Armistice froze force levels, which were monitored by neutral observers. Karl Fontenot saw this first hand when the counting of the tanks began. "They were monitoring replacements to make sure that if one tank went north, one tank came back south . . . ."

Another provision of the armistice was that both sides would pull back to lines rearward of their existing positions, dismantling all fortifications and removing military supplies within seventy-two hours. When this proved patently impossible, a tacit agreement was reached to extend the deadline some forty-five days. The sheer volume of ammunition and construction materials to be removed or destroyed in place was enormous, and the original directive simply did not take into account the difficulties involved, or of disassembling bunkers meant to withstand the heaviest artillery fire.

Tanks had one more peculiar role to play, as Karl Fontenot observed: "The Army brought in some tanks with the guns removed to work in the DMZ. They had dozer blades on the front of them. I went into one place where they were working. . . . There was a train in there . . . just flat on the ground. Wasn't going anywhere, obviously. These dozer tanks were in there trying to grade the roads, remove the mines, and so forth. There was one case where the tank dozed up the road, and then back-bladed,[2] as you call it, to smooth the road. A truck came along right behind it, and blew up right in front of the [tank]. . . . Frequently the tank has less ground pressure per square inch than a truck might, so it didn't explode the mines. But the truck did."

The M4A3 dozer tanks also helped dismantle sturdy bunkers built of massive ten- or twelve-inch square timbers, held together with steel spikes up to two feet long. To dismantle these monstrosities, the engineers hooked a steel cable to the structure and had a tank rip it bodily from the ground. The exhumed box was dragged down a nearby hillside until it fell apart.

Salvaged materials were used to construct new fortifications from which the combatants would scrutinize each other for decades to come. One component of the new defenses was permanent: concealed firing slots for the tanks. As it turned out, the Marines would use these defenses for only another year. Most of the men who had served in Korea returned home, their places taken by men who had been in the replacement pipeline when the cease-fire went into effect.

One of these men was Vernon 'Doc Oz' Osborn, who worked hard to deliberately finagle a way to join his younger brother John in Korea. First, however, he had to suffer the perversities of the military's personnel system. In high school, Osborn had been interested in both medicine and the Marine Corps, so he joined the Navy and became a medical corpsman in 1951. "I was up there [at Camp Pendleton] when they were drafting," he remembered. "They would come in the barracks at night, and take large groups of corpsmen, and they'd be shipped out. In the morning you'd wake up, and their mattresses would be rolled up, their footlockers would be gone, and their standing lockers would be opened and emptied out. I repeatedly went down to the personnel office and requested transfer to the Fleet Marine Force, and put in what's called a special request." To his dismay, it took several requests just to get some attention.

One day, a Navy Lieutenant from the personnel office called Osborn in and asked, "Why do you keep putting in these applications for the Fleet Marine Force?"

"That's where I want to be," he answered.

"Why don't you put in an application for something else?" suggested the Lieutenant.

By the following Monday, Osborn was on his way to the Surgical Technical School in San Diego, California. After completing the school program, Osborn was sent to North Island Naval Air Station as a surgical technician at an isolated dispensary. He was playing cards with a chief petty officer when a Navy Medical Service Corps officer asked for some old surgical instruments to use in building a model airplane.

"I can get you the instruments, but can you do something for me?" he asked, explaining his desire to get a tour with the Marines.

The officer left the room and returned a few minutes later with a Medal of Honor around his neck. Everyone in the room "jumped up, knocked everything on the table over, saluted, came to attention," recalled Osborn.

The Medal of Honor winner had known his award would convey his message as strongly as any words. "I just wanted you to know that if you really want something, I will get it for you, and it *will* happen," he told Osborn. "When I call NavBuPers back in Washington, and ask anything, they'll do it."[3]

The exchange took place on a weekend evening. The next Monday morning when the men fell out for roll call, the Chief Petty Officer walked in front of the men with a piece of paper in his hand and barked out Osborn's name.

"Four steps forward, Osborn. . . . This is a telegram from the Bureau of Navy Personnel notifying you that you are being transferred from the Navy to the Fleet Marine Force, effective Friday. Get your shit packed, and get up to Camp Pendleton."

Osborn was initially assigned to Japan, but convinced a personnel officer to assign him to the tanks in Korea. Once on the peninsula, he saw firsthand further vagaries of the personnel system: the first battalion medical officer he served under was a pediatrician, the next a gynecologist.[4]

"The only time I ever got shot at was one day I decided I was going to go get some pheasants and ducks for the officers mess," recalled Osborn. "I took a shotgun and a jeep, and I went up to the DMZ and went across a creek that was a tributary off the Imjin River. I was over on an island, and shot a bunch of pheasants and ducks. I saw this tidal bore[5] coming down the river, and I'd never seen anything like that." The Chinese were firing at him, "from real long range. I wasn't even concerned. They must have been a mile or two away. They were just dinging around."

Osborn ran down to the creek. "It was full of hundred mile an hour water!" Osborn used the barrel of the shotgun as a crutch to get through the mud and water. Once through it, he "ran across this field. There were a bunch of machine gun parts blown up, and combat gear laying all over the place, and red triangles. I was in a minefield! I figured, hell, I might as well just keep running, and I did. I finally got to a fence, got over and went back to the jeep." Osborn elected not to repeat the expedition.

Life for everyone on the peninsula, including the recently arrived "Doc" Osborn, quickly settled into a peacetime routine. Instead of launching streaks of flames from his tank, Charles Rosenfeld found himself making "a trip to Japan to get dishes for the officer's mess."

According to Zan Bryant, "There was a whole different frame of mind. We had to start falling out for inspections. But that was well-accepted." Bryant was finally granted permission to spare his wiremen the burden of falling out for 0700 inspection after being out until 0500 repairing wires.[6]

The end of the conflict naturally brought about another round of budget slashing. Ed Bale, a veteran of tank fighting on Tarawa, Saipan, Tinian, and Okinawa, came to Korea to take over the 1st Tank Battalion. He found the job "Boring, and a lot of problems." During the fighting, the 1st Tank Battalion had drawn much of its heavy repair and resupply through Army channels. Now that peace had broken out, however, matters had changed. It was almost impossible to get the vehicles properly serviced. Ed Bale set about to change that situation:

> It was extremely difficult to keep your equipment running. The Marine Corps supply system didn't have the spare parts and components you needed. When the Army started to pull out of there, I made a deal with the Eighth Army. We went over to several Army tank battalions . . . selected the best tanks they had, and

moved them over to our place by rail. I almost got relieved and fired. I had all the power packs—engines and transmissions—out of over a hundred tanks, sitting on the ground. The G-Three of the division found out about it, and he went and told the general. I went down to talk to the division commander.

"You've got to maintain a training and readiness status," he told Bale.

"Well, I've got this old equipment. Most of it won't run. I'm trying to swap out components and bring that stuff up to decent condition," Bale replied.

"Don't talk to me about details!" snapped the general.

"General," answered Bale, "when you talk tank maintenance, you've got to talk details!"

As Bale described it, "They were awfully lean times. [We were] totally dependent upon the Army. The Army supply system was totally different, and we didn't know how to make it work."

Physical conditions were no better than during the war, explained Bale, and "Between the mud in the rainy season and the cold in the winter, you had to take wood that had been used as dunnage on ships, and set your tanks up on that to keep them from freezing into the ground." Other problems for units in limbo included the usual plagues of limited training space, black market theft, and fraternization with civilian women that led to a high incidence of venereal disease.[7]

As a late arrival, Vernon Osborn was there until the bitter end. "They would send in a platoon or a bunch of Army guys . . . and we could send an equal number out," he said. "One of the rules they had for the armistice. You couldn't bring in any new equipment, you couldn't increase the size of your force." With no common enemy, friction between the Marines and soldiers came to the fore. "The guys down at the slop chute at night, they would be drinking beer, and pretty soon there's a big-ass fight."[8]

* * *

The last units to return from Korea experienced the welcoming ceremony that figures prominently in American military mythology, but which returning troops seldom actually receive. "When we pulled into San Diego," recalled Osborn, "here were all the women and children, the flags, and the Marine Corps band playing. It was like something you'd see in a 'gung-ho' movie."

"Let him not boast who puts his armor on
As he who puts it off, the battle done."

— Henry Wordsworth Longfellow

Epilogue

In September 2000, fifty years after the battles along the Naktong, the survivors of Lieutenant G. G. Sweet's tank platoon gathered in a hotel suite. There were far fewer of them, ranks thinned by disease and age. Even including the spouses, children, and invited guests, there would have been too few to make up a platoon.

A half century earlier, Sweet had led these same men into battle. On every field he confronted what General Robert E. Lee once said was the most heartbreaking price of the officer's code: he had to be willing to order the death of the thing he loves. Sweet's duty had been clear, and like Spartan commander Leonidas at Thermopylae, he too had blocked a critical defile with living bodies.

When asked why they had been so willing to obey without question, each of the men gave pretty much the same answer. Sweet was an old mustang, a survivor of battles from Pearl Harbor to Iwo Jima. He was the kind of leader you wanted to follow. He just put it to you straight. No threats. No shouting. There's a job here, and this is how it needs to be done. If you want to live to go home, listen up.

These men, many of whom were barely out of their teens, trusted him and his judgment, and he repaid them in the best possible currency: he brought his entire platoon home alive. The men went on to build successful careers as professional military men, businessmen, politicians, policemen, schoolteachers, college professors, ministers, and postal carriers.

Sweet had been financially blessed, and on the last day of the reunion the veterans and guests boarded buses for a visit to his personal memorial park. Constructed to honor the Marines and others with whom he served in two savage wars, it is neither as big nor as showy as many memorial parks. It by no means rivals the elaborate monument recently erected in Washington, D. C. to honor the veterans of America's "forgotten war." But there can be no adequate physical monument for the men who served in Korea. Constructions of stone and concrete can neither atone for, nor adequately commemorate, the lost lives of some, and the youths of all.

My daughter pointed out their true monument. Although it still lives under the shadow of an unfinished war, modern South Korea is a thriving country where the populace no longer routinely starves or freezes to death. High-rises of concrete and glass coexist with ancient stone palaces and gardens, and Buddhist monks carry cell phones beneath their saffron robes. Bright neon lights advertise blue jeans and painted fans, video cameras and ceramics in the ancient styles. You can dine on burgers or squid, *kimchi* or pizza, but ice cream is the universal treat.

Perhaps that is the noblest monument of all.

*   *   *

Ed Bale served on the staff of the 1st Marine Division in Vietnam, and after retirement from the Corps worked in the banking business.

Prentiss Baughman left Korea in May 1951, the last tank officer of the original Provisional Brigade to depart Korea. He was later a tank company commander, and commander of the maintenance company for a tracked anti-aircraft company. A natural Southern gentleman, Prentiss retired in 1960 and became Emergency Management Director for Alabama. He still works for the Defense Department in support of the

These postwar images depict Prentiss Baughman (left) and Donald Bennett (below).
MCTA

Reserve and National Guard, advising personnel who are going on active duty.

Donald Bennett was rotated out of Korea in July 1951. He was later a drill instructor, and while a Master Sergeant served two tours in Vietnam as a temporary or brevet 2nd lieutenant. Approximately once a month he lectures Marine recruits at MCRD San Diego following "The Crucible," the grueling four-day field exercise that gives recruits at least a vague idea of what battle is really like.

Merl Bennett was a career Marine. He spent time as a drill instructor and was severely wounded in Vietnam in 1966. Bennett retired in 1968, became an ironworker, and later operated several VFW clubs.

Donald Boyer worked for a municipal utility company.

Harry Bruce has little memory of his trip home aboard ship, or the train ride from Los Angeles to San Antonio, en route to Florida. "It's a complete blank to me. That's always been something that bothered me . I don't remember anything about that month." He served in a base Guard Company, and later returned to the Reserves. He worked in municipal services, and then in the aircraft and electronics industries.

A. C. Bryant returned to meet his daughter, born while he was in Korea. He took over his father's general store, which evolved into a supermarket, rental property, and real estate business that his son now manages.

Bart Clendenen was rotated out of Korea in late April 1952. He went back to work for the U. S. Forest Service, then went back to school and became a teacher. He retired after twenty-eight years in that profession. Bart spent the last ten years doing public relations work for the U. S. Forest Service.

Ben Busch left Korea in July 1951. Like several others, he related that he simply shut the Chosin experience—especially the stunning cold—out of his mind, and had difficulty consciously remembering it for decades. Ben spent thirty years in the Marine Corps, including a tour in Vietnam. After fifteen years in law enforcement, he is now a juvenile probation officer. "The guys that don't do nothing, they don't live very long after retirement."

Roger Chaput went on recruiting duty. In 1956 he was commissioned as an officer, and retired as a Major.

Roger Chaput—as a young man in his tank in Korea, and a more recent image, discussing a fine point of military operations at a reunion with his Marine comrades. *MCTA*

Basilo Chavarria (right) left Korea in March 1951. He worked for the U. S. Air Force as a civilian employee at one of their primary maintenance and support facilities. Chavarria died in November 2000.

MCTA

Everett D. Dial went on to become a Master Gunnery Sergeant, and served in Vietnam. He retired after twenty-six years service, and worked for the Post Office until his second retirement.

Jim Edwards saw on his discharge papers that his equivalent civilian occupation was truck driver, "so I thought hey, if that's what it says I'll give it a try." He spent over thirty years as a trucker.

G. M. "Max" English retired as a Lieutenant Colonel, and went into the lumber business in California with his old company commander from World War II. He later moved to Louisiana. Max died in November 1998.

Pete Flournoy stayed in the Marine Reserve for twenty-two years and reached the rank of Captain. He served one tour in Vietnam as a maintenance officer with amtracs, tanks, and the Ontos tank destroyer.

MCTA

Karl Fontenot spent 24 years in the Marine Corps and served as a tank battalion commander in Vietnam.

Harvey "Nik" Frye (left, 1951) was assigned another tour in Korea but the war ended before his return. He served in a variety of posts, and was medically retired after 22 years of service. Thereafter, he earned a Master's degree, taught high school, and started a glass business with his son. Nik died in September 2002.

MCTA

Cecil Fullerton left the war behind in Korea in May 1951. He served another fourteen years before retiring from the Marine Corps in 1965. Cecil worked for the U.S. Post Office for twenty-four years, after which he dedicated himself to serving as a youth pastor.

Don Gagnon (below, right) in a wartime photo, and another more recent image (below, left). He retired from the Marine Corps after serving in tanks in Vietnam. Don is the editor of the *Marine Corps Tanker's Association Magazine*, and in that capacity readily assisted this project by supplying the photographs that appear in this Epilogue.

MCTA

MCTA

John Haynie was married two weeks after his return to the Unites States. He worked as an upholsterer and for a book bindery until he and his wife bought the bindery company. John's son and daughter-in-law now own the bindery.

Robert Mack (right) finished his degree and became a college intramural athletics director, a high school football coach, and principal.

MCTA

Len Maffioli (below) spent three months in naval hospitals in attempt to "fatten him up" after his experiences as a POW, and to cure his gastrointestinal problems.

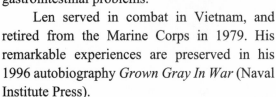

MCTA

Len served in combat in Vietnam, and retired from the Marine Corps in 1979. His remarkable experiences are preserved in his 1996 autobiography *Grown Gray In War* (Naval Institute Press).

William F. McMillian served several terms in the Louisiana State Legislature and was active in politics and cattle ranching, among many other things, until well into his eighties. Mac died in December 2002. Asked by one of his nurses, a former Navy corpsman, how long he was in the Marines, Mac replied "seventy years."

J. A. Merlino left the Marine Corps in 1952 and became a community and university campus policeman.

Robert Miller left Korea in May 1951. He gained a commission and retired as a Major. He served aboard ship and in a variety of other assignments. After retirement, he sold cars until his second retirement.

MCTA

Harry Milne (right) left Korea in April 1951. He served in the Pentagon in a Joint Weapons Systems Evaluation Group that included a "high-priced group of civilians, Ph. D's, Army, two Marines" and Navy personnel. He retired in 1960 and worked as a stockbroker for twenty-four years—"longer than I actively served in the Marine Corps."

Bob Montgomery (left) served in the Marine Corps until 1971, and retired as a Lieutenant Colonel. "Ed Bale . . . suggested I come down and try the banking business, and I did." He retired as a vice-president of a major banking firm.

MCTA

MCTA

MCTA

Walter Moore (right) spent thirty-three years in the Corps, commanded tanks and tank destroyers in Vietnam, and retired as a Colonel.

Phil Morell (left) left Korea on September 17, 1951 after 367 days in action.

C. J. Moss left Korea in March 1951. He did thirty years in the Marine Corps, including one tour in Vietnam as a Company Gunnery Sergeant in tanks, and retired in 1970.

MCTA

Leon Mullins worked at several jobs before entering law school. "A law professor said one day, 'If any of you are naive enough to believe that law is fair and just, you're going into the wrong profession.' I stayed after class . . . and we talked for about forty-five minutes. . . . I said, 'I believe in fairness and justice.' He said 'Leon, you won't find it in law. Law is written by men, and interpreted by men.'" Mullins ended up in international sales.

Vernon "Doc Oz" Osborn returned to Kansas, went to college, and eventually became a dentist. While a student, he joined the Naval Reserve and taught combat medicine to Reserve corpsmen. "I wanted these guys to be interested in the potential, the possibility, of where their lives might end up, and what they might have to be doing."

Michael O'Sullivan got out of the Marine Corps in December 1952. He worked for Republic Aviation, and later was chairman of a local Board of Education in Connecticut. He was program manager for several aircraft, and retired to California because he could not stand the cold weather. Michael went back to work for Ford Aerospace, building the turret for the Sergeant York air defense gun. "They all thought I was a whiz-kid. How did this guy know so much about tanks?"

Robert Post "retired on thirty," and served in tanks, staff positions, and other commands. He did one tour in Vietnam.

Bill Robinson left Korea in May 1951. He retired from the Corps in 1967, and worked for the Bureau of Land Management, for the Oregon State Prison system, and then seventeen years for the Post Office.

Charles Rosenfeld served in a variety of other posts, including advisor to the Nationalist Chinese Marine Corps, commander of a divisional Anti-Tank Battalion, and as a Motor Transport officer in Vietnam. After retirement he worked for a fire protection service for ten years. In one of life's strange coincidences, he lived next door to the author's wife's family when he was on recruiting duty in Alabama immediately after his return from Korea.

Paul Sanders retired from the Marine Corps in 1963, and spent thirty years in the insurance business. Like many others, Sanders said of his experiences on Guadalcanal and in Korea: "I always tried to forget it. I never told my family anything about it. You can't talk to anybody unless they've been there."

George "Red" Saunders retired from the Marine Corps in 1966, and spent another five years overseas as a product broker for American firms in Asia. He purchased a bar, where he hosted the first meetings of the Marine Corps Tanker's Association.

Joseph Sleger (right) as a soldier in
1950 Korea, and as a Colonel 25
years later (below). *MCTA*

Joe Sleger rose rapidly to the rank
of Master Sergeant by late 1951, and
was commissioned as an officer in February 1952. He served for
thirty-three years, and retired as a Colonel in 1978. Joe worked in the
nuclear power industry before retiring again in 1990.

Harry Smith worked his way through undergraduate school as a
bartender. After earning a Ph. D. he served as a college professor, school
principal ("a lot more money than an associate professor") and
superintendent, and school psychologist. He retired from private practice
as a psychologist.

Darrell Snideman spent a year in Korea. He stayed in the Marine
Reserve, worked in public utilities, and spent twenty years in law
enforcement.

Charles Sooter endured a lengthy hospitalization before being given
a medical discharge. He worked for McDonnell-Douglas and
Engineering Research Corporation, and eventually returned to his
pre-World War II trade of barber. He still cuts hair.

Vaughn Stuart left Korea in August 1951 and transferred to the Tank School. He stayed in the Marine Corps for 31 years. Among other assignments he commanded tank and rifle companies, taught at Marine Corps Schools, worked in intelligence and as a military attaché, commanded a rifle regiment in Vietnam, and eventually retired as a Colonel.

MCTA

Granville G. Sweet, the man who had once boldly moved forward with a handful of tanks to block a crucial road cut, retired from the Marine Corps and became a highly successful businessman.

G. G. Sweet (above) in 1945, and 55 years later (left) at a reunion with his men. *MCTA*

MCTA

MCTA

Eugene Viveiros (right) was a tank gunnery instructor, First Sergeant of a tank company, and Sergeant Major of an artillery battalion. He retired in 1959, worked as a firefighter, and retired again in 1975.

N.E. MA-JONG DONG, NORTH KOREA DEC 1950

1st Row Freeby, Trofholz, Eickman, Tarnowski, Roth, Beltran, Blandford, Dial, Miller, Chaput
2nd Row Mr.Sweet, Swinicke, Hoffman, Bloom, Fullerton, Smith, Lindsey, Moreno, Caparazzo, Flippo,Sleger
3rd Row Stedina, Peralta, Oberle, Merline, Amaro, Anderson, Dorman 4th Row Thompson, Haynie

Granville G. Sweet's 3rd Platoon,
Korea, winter 1951. *MCTA*

Mike Wiggins served twenty-four years in the Marine Corps and served in the tanks in Vietnam. He later worked for the State of California, and retired again in 1999.

John Williamson was transferred from Korea to the Inspector General's office, and retired from the Marine Corps some years later. He says that he had resolved never to get in a tank if they sent him to Korea, and he kept this personal vow. He wrote that after he left Korea, "I never got near another tank."

Chapter Notes

Chapter 1: The Unexpected War

1. Millett, *Semper Fidelis*, p. 457.
2. Ibid., p. 412.
3. Ibid., p. 464.
4. Ibid., pp. 453-454; Ken Estes, personal communication.
5. Estes, *Marines Under Armor*, pp. 118-129.
6. Millett, *Semper Fidelis*, p. 466.
7. Estes, *Marines Under Armor*, p. 112.
8. Millett, *Semper Fidelis*, pp. 467- 468.
9. The Vehicle, Tank Recovery, or M32B3, was a tank chassis rigged with a boom, powerful winch, and a variety of repair tools. Its task was to recover, tow, and do minor repairs on damaged or crippled tanks; Estes, *Marines Under Armor*, p. 112.
10. This standardization was to have been effective in 1945, when production and Army logistical support for the 75mm. gun M4 ceased. Because of fiscal limitations, the Corps continued to use the older tanks with the 75mm gun into the late 1940s. Estes, *Marines Under Armor*, pp. 111, 117, 134; Ken Estes, personal communication.
11. Names for tanks—like Sherman, Pershing, and Chaffee—were originally a British practice, and the names were not typically used by American troops either in World War II or Korea. Although the names have crept into the American vocabulary, they are generally avoided here.
12. Estes, *Marines Under Armor*, p. 114.

13. Estes, *Marines Under Armor*, p. 115. However, most or at least some deployments apparently utilized M4A3s—Paul Sanders telephone interview, December 5, 2000, and Ken Estes, personal communication.

14. Ibid., p. 117.

15. Everett Dial interview, Las Vegas, NV, September 24, 2000; Basilo Chavarria interview, Las Vegas, NV, September 24, 2000.

16. Even Moss does not know the origin of this unusual nickname. He recalls only that a maintenance chief in China stuck it on him. C. J. Moss telephone interview, November 22, 2000.

17. Ibid

18. Marines called combat uniforms "utility uniforms" because they were originally issued as a work uniform.

19. Millett, *Semper Fidelis*, p. 476; Utz, *Assault From The Sea: The Amphibious Landing At Inchon*, pp. 7-8.

20. Ridgway, *The Korean War*, p. 10.

21. McCullough, *Truman*, p. 777.

22. Ridgway, *The Korean War*, pp. 13-14.

23. Montross and Canzona, *U. S. Marine Corps Operations in Korea, 1950-1953*: Volume I, *The Pusan Perimeter*, p. 29.

24. Ibid., p. 33.

25. Ridgway, *The Korean War*, pp. 19 – 20.

26. McCullough, *Truman*, pp. 777-779.

27. Simmons, *Over The Seawall—U. S. Marines At Inchon*, p. 2.

28. Montross and Canzona, *U. S. Marine Corps Operations in Korea, 1950-1953*: Volume I, *The Pusan Perimeter*, p. 43.

29. Ridgway, *The Korean War*, p. 34.

30. The artillery was not present in the initial battles fought by the Task Force because of its limited mobility.

31. Ibid., pp. 25-26.

32. Montross and Canzona, *U. S. Marine Corps Operations in Korea*, Vol. I, *The Pusan Perimeter*, p. 45.

33. Center For Military History, *The Korean War: The Outbreak, 27 June-15 September 1950*, pp. 14-15.

34. Ibid., p. 17.

35. Ibid., p. 14.

36. Utz, *Assault From The Sea: The Amphibious Landing At Inchon*, p. 12.

37. RCT, a self-contained unit consisting of a rifle regiment brigaded with supporting artillery, tank, logistical support, transport, and sometimes air support elements.

38. Simmons, *Over The Seawall—U. S. Marines At Inchon*, p. 3

39. Montross and Nicholas, *U. S. Marine Operations in Korea, 1950-1953: Volume II, The Inchon—Seoul Campaign*, pp. 3-5; Simmons, p. 3.

40. Montross and Nicholas, *U. S. Marine Operations in Korea, 1950-1953: Volume II, The Inchon-Seoul Campaign*, pp. 9-11; Simmons, p. 3.

41. Simmons, *Over The Seawall—U. S. Marines At Inchon*, p. 6.

42. Montross and Nicholas, *U. S. Marine Operations in Korea, 1950-1953: Volume II, The Inchon-Seoul Campaign*, p. 25.

43. Ibid., p. 33.

44. Joe Sleger interview, Las Vegas, NV, September 24, 2000.

45. A senior NCO, pay grade E7; a company rated one senior NCO of this grade in a combat leadership billet of the same name.

46. Don Gagnon interview, September 24, 2000; Roger Chaput interview, Las Vegas, NV, September 24, 2000.

47. In combat, the five-tank platoon could be subdivided into a three-tank "heavy" section under the Platoon Leader, and a two-tank "light" section under the senior NCO.

48. Robert Miller telephone interview, December 5, 2000.

49. J. A. Merlino telephone interview, November 22, 2000.

50. Under the acting command of Major Haberle.

51. G. G. Sweet interview, Las Vegas, NV, September 24, 2000; Dial interview.

52. Sleger interview, Dial interview.

53. A steam generator used for heavy-duty cleaning with pressurized water, like a modern power-washer.

54. Operational Report, A Company, p. ii.

55. Even inside the closed turret, the noise of the 90mm. was stunning, and there was no ear protection. Some tank crews stuffed their ears full of toilet paper. Bart Clendenen telephone interview, March 20, 2001.

56. John Haynie interview, Las Vegas, NV, September 24, 2000; Sleger interview.

57. Montross and Canzona, *U. S. Marine Corps Operations in Korea, 1950-1953: Volume I, The Pusan Perimeter*, pp. 50-51.

58. The onboard gear such as tools, extra parts, and other items normally carried on the tank. This gear was stored separately to prevent damage or theft.

59. "Deck-loaded" means they drove the tanks off the LCUs and stored them in the well deck of the ship.

60. A circular device that carried a ring of electrical contacts. It allowed electrical circuits to function when the turret rotated.

61. The standard 2.5-ton military truck, with six wheels and six-wheel drive.

62. Prentiss Baughman telephone interview, October 21, 2000; Bill Robinson telephone interview, December 16, 2000; Operational Report "A" Company, p. ii.

63. The HVAP round was a sabot round with a tungsten penetrator and an aluminum ballistic sheath. Salt water would badly corrode the aluminum, causing improper seating; Robinson interview.

64. Montross and Canzona, *U. S. Marine Corps Operations in Korea, 1950-1953: Volume I, The Pusan Perimeter*, p. 63.

65. The official history says that the ships returned to California, but the interviewees and records dispute this.

66. An electronics repair specialist, usually seen only in the battalion repair shop.

67. Robinson interview; Gagnon interview.

68. Montross and Canzona, *U. S. Marine Corps Operations in Korea, 1950-1953: Volume I, The Pusan Perimeter*, p. 63.

69. Robinson interview; Gagnon interview.

70. Tank crewman Pete Flournoy of C Company recalls having available High Explosive, Armor Piercing, HVAP, smoke, and canister rounds. The HE was the most commonly used ammunition, with smoke used to mark targets. The other types were seldom used. Pete Flournoy telephone interview, October 16, 2000.

71. Spelled "Ozang-Won" in the Operational Report; Montross and Canzona, *U. S. Marine Corps Operations in Korea, 1950-1953: Volume I, The Pusan Perimeter*, pp. 91, 93-94.

72. Sleger interview.

Chapter 2: Defense of the Pusan Perimeter

1. Dial interview; Chavarria interview.

2. Montross and Canzona, *U. S. Marine Corps Operations in Korea, 1950 – 1953: Volume I, The Pusan Perimeter*, pp. 103-124.

3. Miller interview.

4. Operational Report "A" Company, p. vi.

5. Marines identify themselves by their regiment, or sub-unit within the regiment. For example, A/3/5 refers to Company A, 3rd Battalion, 5th Marine Regiment. The 5th Marines were the basis of the Marine Brigade in the Pusan perimeter.

6. Actually a Soviet-made 45mm Model 42 anti-tank gun. The World War II Japanese 47mm. Type 01 Anti-Tank Gun was patterned after Soviet ZIK-37s (an early version of the Model 42) captured in Manchuria in 1938-1939. The guns were very similar, and most of the older Marines were more familiar with the Japanese gun.

7. The rifleman was not dead or even seriously injured. By a strange coincidence Robinson later encountered the man in civilian life.

8. A group of four men, a leader, an automatic rifleman, and two riflemen. The fire team is the most basic fighting element of Marine infantry.

9. The Soviet-made GAZ-67 Range Car was a vehicle similar to the American jeep.

10. Rear slope defenses are a standard anti-tank doctrine. When a tank pulls over the crest of a ridge, a gun can fire into the thinly armored belly. This was Sweet's reason for having the blade tank blind the T-34 with a smoke round.

11. Cecil Fullerton telephone interview, October 21, 2000.

12. Operational Report "A" Company, p. x.

13. Ibid.

14. About ten inches or 25 cm.

15. Montross and Canzona, *U. S. Marine Corps Operations in Korea, 1950-1953: Volume I, The Pusan Perimeter*, p. 192.

16. Montross and Canzona, *U. S. Marine Corps Operations in Korea, 1950-1953: Volume I, The Pusan Perimeter*, p. 194; Operational Report "A" Company, p. x.

17. Marine divisions typically have a tank officer attached to the division commander's staff as an advisor. Craig utilized English in this capacity, and English told Ken Estes that Craig kept him "in his hip pocket."

18. Fullerton Interview.

19. Note that the recollection of this event is somewhat garbled. Some recall that Sweet ordered two tanks to make the roadblock, and the Operational Report places two tanks in the road cut. Others, notably Sweet, remember three. Sweet's account is likely the most accurate, although the precise relative positions of the tanks are understandably confused.

20. Fullerton Interview.

21. The official unit report (Operational Report "A" Company, p. x) states that Fullerton knocked out the leading T-34 with three rounds of APC (Armor Piercing Cap) shot, and there are similar discrepancies in the descriptions of the rounds used against the other T-34s. I have elected to use the recollections of the tank crewmen.

22. Lieutenant Colonel Arthur J. "Jeb" Stuart, at that time the Marine Corps' armored vehicle expert in the Plans and Policies Division, commented upon the obvious implication in the official report of this battle. Neither the 3.5-inch rocket launchers nor the 75mm recoilless rifles of the infantry actually stopped the T-34s; Estes, *Marines Under Armor*, p. 138.

23. Note that Fullerton recalls putting a second round into the lead T-34, another example of the massive confusion in this short and violent fight.

24. Gagnon Interview.

25. Moss Interview.

26. Montross and Canzona, *U. S. Marine Corps Operations in Korea, 1950-1953: Volume I, The Pusan Perimeter*, p. 196.

27. Operational Report, "A" Company, p. xii

28. Sweet Interview.

29. Nik Frye interview, Las Vegas, NV, September, 24, 2000.

30. Moss Interview.

31. A box with food for five men for a day. It contained canned bacon, candy bars, and other coveted items.

32. Montross and Canzona, *U. S. Marine Corps Operations in Korea, 1950-1953: Volume I, The Pusan Perimeter*, p. 211.

33. Craig was Winters's godfather; the elder Winters was a Warrant Officer who had served with Craig in China.

34. Di Noto was only seventeen years old. He was sent to the Philippines until his eighteenth birthday, and then returned to Korea—as an infantryman; Robinson interview; Merl Bennett telephone interview, December 19, 2000.

35. The Soviet-made 12.7mm. DShK 1938 was the standard heavy machine gun of the NKPA, and was similar to the American .50 caliber M2 Browning.

36. Gagnon Interview; Moss Interview.

37. In fact, part of the issue was probably Swinicke's height. Unusually tall, he could stand on the floor of the turret and expose his head above the hatch rim.

38. Gilbert, *Marine Tank Battles In The Pacific*, p. 129.

39. This may have been a Soviet-made Ba-64 armored scout car, a small four-wheeled vehicle used by the NKPA.

40. George Saunders telephone interview, June 17, 2001. The information is from Saunders's discussion with the late Joe Welsch, Pomeroy's Platoon Sergeant.

41. Sleger Interview.

42. Miller Interview.

43. Miller said that Staff Sergeant Christiansen stayed in the Marine Corps with a prosthetic foot; Miller Interview.

44. Saunders Interview.

45. A crewman from another tank. Sleger does not recall why he was in his tank that day.

46. The Soviets had supplied the NKPA with obsolete 14.5mm. Model 1941 PTRD Anti-Tank Rifles. This single-shot bolt-action monster fired a tungsten-cored shot.

47. Chappers and Jones, p. 21.

Chapter 3: The Inchon and Seoul Operations

1. Harry Milne telephone interview, November 11, 2000.

2. Able Company, 2nd Tank Battalion was re-designated as C Company, 1st Tank Battalion on August 7, and the battalion received its first new vehicles, eighteen M26 tanks, on that date. 1st Tank Battalion Diary, p. 1. The 1st Platoon of Dog Company was a 2nd Tank Battalion platoon deployed to the Mediterranean, and came by way of the Suez Canal to join the Division at Inchon. Stuart interview.

3. Vaughn Stuart telephone interview, November 12, 2000; Stuart unpublished ms., p. 13.

4. Darrell Snideman telephone interview, November 9, 2000.

5. Diagonal stripes worn on the lower sleeve of the dress uniform. Each indicated four years of honorable service.

6. Sanders interview.

7. Don Bennett telephone interview, October 15, 2000.

8. Few veterans have fond memories of this thick, greasy petroleum-based preservative grease.

9. Bruce later clarified this: he picked up his tank in Kobe, Japan.

10. Don Bennett, letter dated October 9, 2001.

11. The M1912 pump-action Winchester had a six-round magazine and a bayonet lug, and fired brass-cased rounds.

12. World War II-era cargo transports.

13. Don Bennett interview.

14. Snideman interview.

15. A non-firing procedure that aligns the gun sight with the axis of the gun tube.

16. Don Bennett interview.

17. Sanders interview.

18. Utz, *Assault From The Sea: The Amphibious Landing at Inchon*, p. 16.

19. Simmons, *Over The Seawall: U. S. Marines at Inchon*, p. 16.

20. Utz, *Assault From The Sea: The Amphibious Landing At Inchon*, p. 14.

21. Simmons, *Over The Seawall: U. S. Marines at Inchon*, p. 44; Utz, *Assault From The Sea: The Amphibious Landing at Inchon*, p. 19.

22. Simmons, *Over The Seawall: U. S. Marines at Inchon*, p. 23.

23. 1st Tank Battalion Diary, p. 4.

24. As each tank was unloaded, the boat rode higher in the water, and it would move farther up onto the beach.

25. Sleger interview.

26. Ibid.

27. Simmons, *Over The Seawall: U. S. Marines At Inchon*, p. 33.

28. The LVT(A)-5 was an improved version of the LVT(A)-4. Thinly armored and armed with a short-barreled 75mm. howitzer and machine guns, it was a tank in name only. Utz, *Assault From The Sea: The Amphibious Landing at Inchon*, p. 37.

29. Ibid., p. 38.

30. Simmons, *Over The Seawall: U. S. Marines at Inchon*, p. 41.

31. 1st Tank Battalion Diary, p. 41.

32. B Company was not supposed to be part of the initial landing. It may be simply that an unobservant boat commander approached too soon and stranded his boat.

33. Don Bennett interview.

34. Milne interview; Phil Morell telephone interview, October 18, 2000.

35. Milne interview.

36. Baughman interview.

37. Morell interview.

38. Ben Busch telephone interview, November 22, 2000.

39. Stuart, unpublished ms., p. 13

40. Simmons, *Over The Seawall: U. S. Marines at Inchon*, p. 44.

41. The unit diary credits Sweet's platoon with two tanks destroyed. 1st Tank Battalion Diary, p. 4.

42. A Soviet-made submachine gun, so called because of the distinctive sound.

43. Ibid., p. 48.

44. Miller interview.

45. Milne interview.

46. In the 1930s, the *Augusta* (CA31) was flagship of the Asiatic Fleet; Chester Nimitz was her captain.

47. 1st Tank Battalion Diary, p. 4.

48. Ibid., p. 5.

49. Alexander, *Battle Of The Barricades: U. S. Marines in the Recapture Of Seoul*, p. 7.

50. Miller interview.

51. Ibid.

52. Stuart, unpublished ms, pp. 13-14.

53. Ibid., pp. 14-15.

54. Michael O'Sullivan telephone interview, September 2, 2000.

55. The infantry expended a considerable number of rockets, lending further credence to Arthur Stuart's observation that the rocket launcher was a far from ideal weapon against the T-34.

56. 1st Tank Battalion Diary, p. 6.

57. Ibid., p. 6

58. Major General Frank Lowe was an Army Reservist who had served with Truman in World War I, and was Senator Truman's military assistant during World War II. After his visit to Korea, he became a vocal advocate of Marine Corps training.

59. The unit diary says the tank was hit on the engine deck , but this does not explain Viveiros's injuries. See 1st Tank Battalion Diary, p. 7.

60. Viveiros teased Sweet, a former NCO, so many times in this way that now he does it by habit.

61. Sweet interview; Sleger interview; Haynie interview; Merlino interview.

62. Merlino interview.

63. Probably a nearby masonry railway viaduct. Reentrants underneath sheltered the Forward Aid Station and CP of the 5th Marines.

64. Alexander, *Battle Of The Barricades: U. S. Marines in the Recapture Of Seoul*, p. 18.

65. Ridgway, *The Korean War*, p. 31.

66. 1st Tank Battalion Diary, p. 7.

67. Alexander, *Battle Of The Barricades: U. S. Marines in the Recapture Of Seoul*, p. 19

68. 1st Tank Battalion Diary, p. 7.

69. Alexander, *Battle Of The Barricades: U. S. Marines In The Recapture Of Seoul*, p. 30.

70. Ibid., p. 33.

71. Sanders interview.

72. The tanks could shrug off light mortar fire, but the NKPA was lavishly equipped with powerful Soviet-made 120mm. mortars. Sleger interview.

73. Robinson interview.
74. 1st Tank Battalion Diary, pp. 8-9.
75. Ibid., p. 2.
76. Ibid., p. 2.
77. Sleger interview.
78. The unit diary reports that this enemy attack commenced about 0330 hours. 1st Tank Battalion Diary, p. 2.
79. Morell interview.

Chapter 4: The Chosin Reservoir Campaign—Encirclement

The general outline of the northeastern Korean campaign presented in Chapters Four and Five, with certain exceptions, is drawn from the official history, *U. S. Marine Operations in Korea, 1950 - 1953: Volume III, The Chosin Reservoir Campaign* by Lynn Montross and Nicholas Canzona.

1. For example, McCullough, *Truman*, pp. 778-779, and Utz, *Assault From The Sea: The Amphibious Landing At Inchon*, p. 12.

2. Alexander, *Battle Of The Barricades: U. S. Marines in the Recapture of Seoul*, p. 53.

3. Ibid.

4. Miller Interview.

5. Like their Soviet military mentors, the NKPA organized new units from the remnants of old. Montross and Canzona, *U. S. Marine Operations in Korea, 1950 - 1953: Volume III, The Chosin Reservoir Campaign*, p. 105.

6. Ibid., p. 110.

7. Ibid., pp. 123-128.

8. Ibid., p. 131.

9. Moss Interview.

10. Montross and Canzona, *U. S. Marine Operations in Korea, 1950 - 1953: Volume III, The Chosin Reservoir Campaign*, pp. 133-134.

11. 1st Tank Battalion Diary, p. 10.

12. Stuart, unpublished mss., pp. 16, 17.

13. Jim Edwards telephone interview, November 11, 2000.

14. The confusion was such that Jim Edwards did not even know that he was assigned to the Provisional Tank Platoon. His experiences, Vaughn Stuart's recollection of his vehicle number, and photographic evidence place him in the Provisional Tank Platoon.

15. Stuart interview.

16. Some sources state that the Provisional Platoon moved forward on November 18; the November 19 date, however, is the one recorded in the unit diary. 1st Tank Battalion Diary, p. 10; Montross and Canzona, *U. S. Marine Operations in Korea, 1950 - 1953: Volume III, The Chosin Reservoir Campaign*, p. 137; Milne interview; Stuart interview.

17. 1st Tank Battalion Diary, p. 10.

18. Pack marks were calluses on the shoulders and back. Soldiers tended to have softer hands than the peasant farmers. Don Bennett interview.

19. Chaput interview; Merlino interview.

20. Division OPs Order 23-50, 0800 November 23, as cited in Montross and Canzona, *U. S. Marine Operations in Korea, 1950 - 1953: Volume III, The Chosin Reservoir Campaign*.

21. 1st Tank Battalion Diary, p. 12.

22. A dam across a stream that flowed northward into the Yalu River created the reservoir. Hydroelectric power was generated by diverting water off the steeper south edge of the plateau.

23. Stuart, interview, and unpublished mss., p. 18.

24. Ibid., p. 21.

25. Montross and Canzona, *U. S. Marine Operations in Korea, 1950-1953: Volume III, The Chosin Reservoir Campaign*, p. 149.

26. Ibid., pp. 86-87.

27. Ibid., p. 146.

28. Stuart, unpublished mss., p. 23.

29. Appleman, *Escaping The Trap: The U S Army X Corps in Northeastern Korea, 1950*, p. 55; O'Sullivan interview.

30. Appleman, *Escaping The Trap*, p. 55.

31. Montross and Canzona, *U. S. Marine Operations in Korea, 1950 - 1953: Volume III, The Chosin Reservoir Campaign*, p. 215.

32. Stuart, unpublished mss., p. 24.

33. Don Bennett interview.

34. Stuart interview.

35. Stuart unpublished mss., p. 32.

36. Baker Company, 31st Infantry, U. S. Army consisted in part of KATUSAs (Korean Army Troops, U S Army), semi-trained Korean conscripts used to fill out the depleted ranks. Most did not speak even rudimentary English.

37. 1st Tank Battalion Diary, p. 13.

38. Sanders interview.

39. Hammel, *Chosin–Heroic Ordeal Of The Korean War*, pp. 176-177.

40. Captain Bruce Clark's decision not to intersperse his tanks throughout the convoy remains controversial. Tankers naturally believe that their firepower could have helped salvage the situation. However, given the length of the convoy and the limited number of tanks, the vulnerability of the trucks, the difficult radio communication situation, and the overwhelming Chinese force, the presence of tanks dispersed throughout the convoy would in all probability not have materially altered the fate of Task Force Drysdale. In fact, had the tanks been trapped, and then wrecked or abandoned with the trucks, their wreckage might have blocked the later escape of the entire division.

41. Ibid., pp. 178-179.

42. 1st Tank Battalion Diary, p. 14; Harry Milne interview.

43. Several former tankers commented on this problem. Sudden changes in engine speed would slip the belts off the pulleys. Flournoy interview.

44. Montross and Canzona, *U. S. Marine Operations in Korea, 1950 - 1953: Volume III, The Chosin Reservoir Campaign*, p. 231.

45. Miller interview.

46. The despised M3A1 submachine gun was designed in 1942, and its principal virtue was its production cost of $22. It was prone to jams, and easily damaged.

47. A jeep-sized tracked amphibious vehicle, originally designed for arctic search and rescue work. They were commonly used as utility vehicles.

48. Don Bennett interview.

49. Ibid.

50. Don Bennett interview; Busch interview.

51. Official accounts state that Williams drew his tanks up in a defensive laager (or circle) off the road. However, all who were there say that the road space between the rail embankment and the drop into the river below was too narrow. The next morning the tanks were unable to move off the road even in daylight. This seems more consistent with Williams's decision not to simply move off the road past the wrecked trucks, and back to Koto-ri. Williams's position seems to have been an elongated perimeter rather than a classical circular laager.

52. Don Bennett interview.

53. Ibid.

54. Ibid.

55. Don Bennett interview; Hammel, *Chosin–Heroic Ordeal Of The Korean War*, pp. 204-205.

56. Ibid., pp. 204-205.

57. At this point the ditch was between the road and the elevated railway tracks was about fifteen feet wide. Miller interview.

58. American forces used red tracers, Chinese green.

59. Major John N. McLaughlin. The ranking officer, Lt. Colonel Arthur Chidester, the division's Assistant Logistics Officer, had been shot through both thighs and was unable to exercise command.

60. The Chinese were eager to infuse Americans with the Communist revolutionary ideal during the early days of the war. There were numerous incidents of such behavior, as well as the spontaneous release of American prisoners.

61. Hammel, *Chosin–Heroic Ordeal Of The Korean War*, pp. 204-205.

62. Don Bennett interview.

63. Ibid.

64. Ibid.

65. Busch interview.

66. Sanders interview.

Chapter 5: The Chosin Reservoir Campaign—Breakout

1. O'Sullivan interview.

2. Chappers and Jones, *Tank Teams*, pp. 22-23.

3. Hastings, *The Korean War*, p. 157.

4. In fact, 1/32 lost most of its heavy equipment east of the Reservoir. Surviving Army units that came out with the Marines brought their equipment. Both Army and Marine units scavenged abandoned equipment, as will be described later.

5. Sanders interview.

6. Captain Robert T. Drake's 31st Tank Company operated twenty-two M4A3 tanks, twenty armed with 76mm. guns, and two with 105mm. howitzers. Slowed by the heavy traffic along the road, they had not displaced far past Hagaru, and thus escaped the destruction of their parent unit east of the reservoir. These Army tanks are frequently misidentified in photographs as Marine Corps vehicles. The Marines did not operate the 76mm. gun tank. Appleman cited forty-six Army tanks, but misidentified them as M26s. Appleman, *Escaping The Trap–The U S Army X Corps In Northeastern Korea, 1950,* pp. 83-85, 306.

7. Stuart, unpublished ms., p. 26.

8. Ibid., p. 28.

9. Ibid., p. 29.

10. Technically, this type of device is called a pole charge.

11. Stuart, unpublished ms., p. 30.

12. Milne interview; see also 1st Tank Battalion Diary, p. 2.

13. A single engine observation plane with two seats. There were several types in service, but OY was the generic term.

14. 1st Tank Battalion Diary, p. 3.

15. Stuart, unpublished ms., p. 25.

16. Chappers and Jones, *Tank Teams,* p. 23.

17. Ibid., p. 23.

18. Probably Stuart's abandoned M4A3.

19. Chappers and Jones, *Tank Teams,* p. 23; O'Sullivan interview.

20. 1st Tank Battalion Diary, p. 2.

21. Battalion Memorandum Number 34-50, dated December 2, 1950, copy attached to 1st Tank Battalion Diary, December 1950.

22. Max English interview, Louisville, KY, October 1998.

23. Montross and Canzona, *U. S. Marine Operations in Korea, 1950-1953: Volume III, The Chosin Reservoir Campaign,* p. 277.

24. Ibid., p. 280.

25. 1st Tank Battalion Diary, p. 3.

26. Ibid., p. 3.

27. Ibid., p. 4.

28. Chappers and Jones, *Tank Teams,* p. 23.

29. Milne interview.

30. 1st Tank Battalion Diary, p. 4.

31. Hammel, *Chosin–Heroic Ordeal Of The Korean War,* p. 337.

32. 1st Tank Battalion Diary, p. 4; Stuart, unpublished ms., p. 34.

33. 1st Tank Battalion Diary, p. 4.

34. Stuart, unpublished ms., pp. 35-36.

35. The unit diary lists two tanks abandoned and destroyed, but Don Bennett recalls that B-15 was also included. 1st Tank Battalion Diary, p. 4; Don Bennett interview.

36. Duncan, *Korea, Sept 1950–Oct 1951, MCTA Magazine,* June 2001, p. 10.

37. Stuart, unpublished ms., p. 37.

38. Ibid., p. 37.

39. Duncan, *Korea, Sept 1950–Oct 1951, MCTA Magazine,* June 2001, p. 10.

40. Montross and Canzona, *U. S. Marine Operations in Korea, 1950-1953: Volume III, The Chosin Reservoir Campaign,* p. 314. The M16 was four fifty-caliber machine guns in an electrically powered turret, mounted on an armored half-tracked truck. The M19 was a pair of 40mm. automatic cannon in an open-topped turret, mounted on a light tank chassis. The Marines did not use either of these vehicles.

41. Stuart, unpublished ms., p. 38; Stuart interview; Miller interview.

42. Hammel, *Chosin–Heroic Ordeal Of The Korean War,* p. 409; Stuart interview; Sanders interview

43. Hammel, *Chosin–Heroic Ordeal Of The Korean War,* p. 409.

44. 1st Tank Battalion Diary, p. 5.

45. Stuart interview; Milne interview.

46. Stuart unpublished ms., p. 39.

47. Don Bennett, letter to author, dated October 9, 2001.

48. Hammel, *Chosin–Heroic Ordeal Of The Korean War,* pp. 409-410. Don Bennett believes that at that point in time there were probably fewer than twenty effectives in Hargett's platoon. Don Bennett interview.

49. Sanders interview.

50. Morell interview; see also Hammel, *Chosin–Heroic Ordeal Of The Korean War,* pp. 410-411. However, Don Bennett thinks that tank B-11 slid into the ditch because the steel tracks caused it to slide on the icy road. While this contradicts other accounts, it does possibly explain why the tank could later be moved. As the reader will soon discover, this was a very confusing night. Don Bennett, letter to author, dated October 9, 2001.

51. Some accounts say eight tanks, including the stalled vehicle, were trapped. The partial destruction of the rear guard is, understandably, one of the most confused episodes of the campaign. The confusion apparently revolves around the fact that some of the trapped tanks were eventually able to escape the blockage.

52. Don Bennett interview.

53. There is no indication in the chain of events as described in either command chronologies or interviews that the tanks were able to communicate, and the terrain seems the most likely explanation. Hammel, in *Chosin–Heroic Ordeal Of The Korean War,* p. 414, recounts how Lieutenant Hargett tried to get one tank to move "a dozen yards" to be able to fire around a turn, and states that the communications problems were the result of the terrain, although no specific evidence is cited.

54. Russ, *Breakout,* pp. 421-422.

55. Hammel, in *Chosin–Heroic Ordeal Of The Korean War*, p. 4 14, wrote that "the entire rearward tank platoon fell apart," and that the tanks crews "panicked." Given the precarious situation and the confusion, the author believes that the men are entitled to the benefit of the doubt.

56. Don Bennett interview.

57. Hammel, *Chosin–Heroic Ordeal Of The Korean War*, p. 415.

58. Ibid., p. 414, states that someone freed the frozen brake on the stalled tank, and Lett simply drove the tank down the pass. This is another example of the massive confusion that prevailed at that time. Bennett's account seems to agree most closely with the recorded number of vehicles lost.

59. Don Bennett interview.

60. Don Bennett, letter to author dated October 9, 2001.

61. Ibid.

62. 1st Tank Battalion Diary, p. 6.

63. Chavarias interview.

64. Duncan, *Korea, Sept 1950 Oct 1951, MCTA Magazine*, June 2001, p. 10.

65. Mullins and Sgt. Don Reisch had not shaved or changed clothing in over a month. Reisch was later killed in action.

Chapter 6: Offensives and Counteroffensives, 1951-1952

The general outline of the eastern Korea campaigns is drawn from the official history, *U. S. Marine Operations in Korea, 1950 - 1953: Volume IV, The East-Central Front,* by Lynn Montross *et al.* The spatial complexities of the seesaw battles of early 1951 were considerably greater than might be assumed from the brief outline presented here. For a better understanding, the reader is referred to Montross *et al.*

1. 1st Tank Battalion Diary, p. 6.

2. This unit was the 328th Ordnance Battalion. Estes, *Marines Under Armor*, p. 143.

3. Stuart, unpublished ms, p. 42.

4. Stuart, personal communication, November 22, 2000; Sanders interview.

5. Morell interview.

6. Busch interview.

7. Snideman interview.

8. Montross et al, *U. S. Marine Operations in Korea, 1950-1953: Volume IV, The East-Central Front,* pp. 12-13.

9. Ibid., p. 13.

10. 1st Tank Battalion Diary, pp. 7-8.

11. Ibid., p. 6

12. H. Smith interview, Las Vegas, September 14, 2000.

13. Despite its reputation as the most segregated of the services, the experiences of Wiggins and others suggest that the Corps seems to have been more effectively integrated than the Army by late 1950 and early 1951. The manpower shortage was more effective than policy in effecting desegregation.

14. Apparently a nickname for an ROK interpreter attached to the company.

15. Robert Mack telephone interview, June 26, 2001.

16. Ibid.

17. Ibid.

18. Ibid.

19. 1st Tank Battalion Diary, Summary, p. 3.

20. Saunders interview; Bruce interview.

21. Saunders interview.

22. Joe Welsch, who had been LT Pomeroy's platoon Sergeant in the Pusan fighting.

23. 1st Tank Battalion Diary, p. 13.

24. The friend was in Dog Company.

25. Robinson interview.

26. This was apparently 1st Lieutenant William Phifer. Although not hit by shrapnel, he suffered a spinal cord injury when he was blown off the tank. He had been with the platoon for barely a month. Robinson interview; USMC Casualty Records; Ken Estes, personal communication.

27. 1st Tank Battalion Diary, pp. 17-18. In World War II, the Marines were the primary American users of rocket artillery. These weapons provided a devastating barrage, dumping tons of high explosive on an area target in a short time. An improved model was used in Korea.

28. Robert Mack interview. Raisin jack was the generic name for an illicit moonshine made by allowing a mixture of fruit (raisins were the most commonly available material), water, sugar, and baker's yeast to ferment in an enamel-lined metal water can. Strained through a sock to remove solids, it tasted and smelled ghastly.

29. Bob Montgomery, a tank officer who served in the 1953-1954 period says that the practice of firing from ramps at high elevations would sometimes

lead to fractures of the traversing gear. "In fact, I broke a turret ring. Went back and they had to lift the whole turret off to replace it. If you were just firing at maximum elevation without getting up on that ramp you were all right. Once you tilted the tank up on that ramp, you put too much stress at that one point on the turret ring." Robert Montgomery telephone interview, June 17, 2001.

30. Clendenen interview.

31. Stuart, unpublished ms., p. 43.

32. Ibid., p. 44.

33. Ibid., p. 45.

34. 1st Tank Battalion Diary, p. 14.

35. Montross et al, *U. S. Marine Operations in Korea, 1950-1953: Volume IV, The East-Central Front*, p. 123.

36. Stuart, unpublished ms., p. 45.

37. Official sources, primarily the 1st Tank Battalion Diary, p. 14, cite only 112 counted enemy KIA in this action. The discrepancy between counted and estimated enemy KIAs is typical, and in the absence of any Chinese system for reliably reporting their casualties, the actual number will always remain a mystery.

38. Stuart, unpublished ms., pp. 22-23.

39. 1st Tank Battalion Diary, p. 14; see also Montross et al, *U. S. Marine Operations in Korea, 1950-1953: Volume IV, The East-Central Front*, p. 125.

40. Meid and Yingling, *U. S. Marine Operations in Korea, 1950-1953, Volume V, Operations In West Korea*, p. 435.

41. Firing ranging shots at a selected terrain feature. From this, the artillery computing staff can determine the relative positions of guns, observers, and targets in unfamiliar or poorly mapped ground.

42. Meid and Yingling, *U. S. Marine Operations in Korea, 1950-1953, Volume V, Operations In West Korea*, p. 435.

43. He weighed 155 pounds when captured. Maffioli interview.

44. In the days before tanks had intercoms, the tank commander signaled the driver to stop by pushing down on the back of his head with one foot.

45. Charles Sooter telephone interview, June 24, 2001.

46. 1st Tank Battalion Diary, p. 17.

47. Ibid., p. 17.

48. Stuart, unpublished ms., p. 46.

49. 1st Tank Battalion Diary, p. 2.

50. Ibid., p. 2.

51. A surveying device used by the artillery to determine the precise orientation of a line of guns, and to determine their alignment relative to true and magnetic north. Firing artillery is a complex exercise in applied trigonometry.

52. Artillery survey crews carefully map such locations to provide known reference points. The relative locations of artillery positions and targets can be determined by measuring distances and compass bearings from such known points.

53. Deflection is the side-to-side angle of deviation, the compass bearing from the gun to the target. A mil is a very precise angular measure used by the artillery. One mil in American military usage equals 0.0531 degree.

54. Walter Moore letter to author, dated 1 January 2002; this letter is an augmented transcript of an oral interview.

55. Ibid.

56. Ibid.

57. 1st Tank Battalion Diary, pp. 1, 10; see also Baker, *USMC Tanker's Korea*, p. 40.

58. Montross et al, *U. S. Marine Operations in Korea, 1950-1953: Volume IV, The East-Central Front*, p. 199.

59. Ibid., p. 245.

60. Baker, *USMC Tanker's Korea*, p. 62.

61. Baker, *October 16, Behind Enemy Lines*, in Chaput, *Korean War 50th Anniversary Operational Report, "A" Company Reunion*, 3 pages; also Baker, *USMC Tanker's Korea*, pp. 50-52.

62. Baker, *October 17, 1951 Base of Operations*, in Chaput, *Korean War 50th Anniversary Operational Report, "A" Company Reunion*, 2 pages.; also Baker, *USMC Tanker's Korea*, p. 55.

63. Ibid.

64. Walter Moore, letter to author.

65. 1st Tank Battalion Diary, October 31 entry, no pagination.

66. Donald Boyer telephone interview, March 19, 2001; see also Gilbert, *Marine Tank Battles In The Pacific*, pp. 35-40.

67. Estes, *Marines Under Armor*, p. 144.

68. Boyer interview.

69. Meid and Yingling, *U. S. Marine Operations in Korea, 1950-1953, Volume V, Operations In West Korea*, p. 45.

70. 1st Tank Battalion Diary, December 1951, p. 8.

71. Sooter interview.

72. The 'Little Joe' auxiliary engine previously described.

73. The concept of the 'spotter rifle' was later used on several vehicles, notably the M51 'Ontos' anti-tank vehicle used in the Vietnam War.

74. C. B. Ash, *Trench Warfare–1952*, p. 21.

75. Walter Moore letter to author.

76. Saunders interview.

77. Baker, *USMC Tanker's Korea*, p. 89.

78. C. B. Ash, *Trench Warfare–1952*, p. 21.

79. Ibid.

80. Walter Moore letter to author.

81. Meid and Yingling, *U. S. Marine Operations in Korea, 1950-1953, Volume V, Operations In West Korea*, p. 10.

82. Ibid., p. 10.

83. The troops, officers and men alike, would strip off their uniforms upon entering the showers. When they exited, they would be issued laundered clothing salvaged from a previous batch of shower occupants. Considerations such as proper fit and rank badges—often painted onto the cloth—were secondary.

84. Walter Moore letter to author.

Chapter 7: Battles for the Jamestown Line, 1952-1953

The chronology of defensive operations along the Jamestown Line is drawn from the official history, *U. S. Marine Operations in Korea, 1950-1953, Volume V, Operations In West Korea,* by Pat Meid and James M. Yingling.

1. Meid and Yingling, *U. S. Marine Operations in Korea, 1950-1953, Volume V, Operations In West Korea*, p. 12.

2. Ibid., pp. 13, 35.

3. Ibid., p. 18

4. Ibid., pp. 39-40.

5. Robert Post telephone interview, June 21, 2001.

6. 1st Tank Battalion Diary, August 1952, pp. 4-5.

7. Meid and Yingling, *U. S. Marine Operations in Korea, 1950-1953, Volume V, Operations In West Korea*, p. 45.

8. Walter Moore, letter to author.

9. Meid and Yingling, *U. S. Marine Operations in Korea, 1950-1953, Volume V, Operations In West Korea*, p. 45.

10. Flournoy interview.

11. Meid and Yingling, *U. S. Marine Operations in Korea, 1950-1953, Volume V, Operations In West Korea,* p. 73.

12. 1st Tank Battalion Diary, April 1952, pp. 1-2, 5-7.

13. Meid and Yingling, *U. S. Marine Operations in Korea, 1950-1953, Volume V, Operations In West Korea,* p. 73.

14. Walter Moore, letter to author.

15. Meid and Yingling, *U. S. Marine Operations in Korea, 1950-1953, Volume V, Operations In West Korea,* pp. 79-81.

16. Ibid., p. 98.

17. Williamson, *Dearest Buckie*, pp. 2, 13.

18. Specific types of enemy guns were usually not identified in period documents.

19. Zaloga and Grandsen, p.154

20. Meid and Yingling, *U. S. Marine Operations in Korea, 1950-1953, Volume V, Operations In West Korea,* p. 104.

21. Williamson, *Dearest Buckie,* p. 19.

22. Ibid.

23. Ibid., pp. 20-21.

24. Ibid., pp. 21-23.

25. Meid and Yingling, *U. S. Marine Operations in Korea, 1950-1953, Volume V, Operations In West Korea,* pp. 111-113.

26. 1st Tank Battalion Diary, August 1952, pp. 4-5.

27. Meid and Yingling, *U. S. Marine Operations in Korea, 1950-1953, Volume V, Operations In West Korea,* pp. 136-137.

28. Ibid., p. 138.

29. Estes, *Marines Under Armor,* p. 144; COL Elliot R. Laine, telephone interview April 20, 2002.

30. 1st Tank Battalion Diary, September 1952, p. 2; Williamson, *Dearest Buckie,* p. 51.

31. 1st Tank Battalion Diary, September 1952, p. 4.

32. Meid and Yingling, *U. S. Marine Operations in Korea, 1950-1953, Volume V, Operations In West Korea,* pp. 166-170.

33. Ibid., p. 186.

34. Boyer interview.

35. Meid and Yingling, *U. S. Marine Operations in Korea, 1950-1953, Volume V, Operations In West Korea,* p. 188. Despite the popular assumption to the contrary, at this stage of the war the CCF deployed many armored vehicles to

Korea. The heaviest was the forty-six ton ISU-152 self-propelled howitzer, built on the chassis of the IS-2 heavy tank.

36. 1st Tank Battalion Diary, October 1952, p. 3.

37. Meid and Yingling, *U. S. Marine Operations in Korea, 1950-1953, Volume V, Operations In West Korea*, pp. 192-*196*. Ranks of heavy machine guns were also set up, and the trajectories of the rounds carefully calculated. Fired *en mass*, the guns would rain unobserved fire on an area of enemy-held ground.

38. Ibid., p. 195.

39. 1st Tank Battalion Diary, November 1952, p. 2.

40. Ibid., p. 4.

41. Williamson, *Dearest Buckie*, p. 87.

42. Ibid., p. 121.

43. Dunstan, *Armour in Korea*, p. 38.

44. Saunders interview; Williamson, *Dearest Buckie*, p. 121.

45. Ballenger, *Final Crucible*, pp. 22-26.

46. Meid and Yingling, *U. S. Marine Operations in Korea, 1950-1953, Volume V, Operations In West Korea*, p. 232.

47. Flournoy interview.

48. Ibid.

49. Ballenger, *Final Crucible*, pp. 27-30; Williamson, pp. 152-153.

50. Williamson, *Dearest Buckie*, p. 143; Ballenger, *Final Crucible*, pp. 52-56.

51. Williamson, *Dearest Buckie*, p. 147.

52. Ballenger, *Final Crucible*, pp. 57-58.

53. Anonymous, p. 32.

54. Ballenger, *Final Crucible* , p. 59.

55. Williamson, *Dearest Buckie*, p. 147.

56. Williamson, *Dearest Buckie*, p. 169; Ballenger, *Final Crucible*, p. 59.

57. Anonymous, p. 32.

58. Corporal Marvin Dennis died of his wounds. Williamson, *Dearest Buckie*, pp. 148, 169; Ballenger, *Final Crucible*, pp. 60-61.

59. Ballenger, *Final Crucible*, p. 62.

60. Ibid., p. 62.

61. Ibid., p. 63.

62. Williamson, *Dearest Buckie*, p. 164. It was and is common military practice to search bodies for documents, maps, and other useful information.

63. 1st Tank Battalion Diary, March 1953, p. 2; Williamson, pp. 176-177. Force Troops were heavy units, including tanks and heavy artillery, held at corps

level to be used to reinforce divisions in the event of a major war, particularly one against the Soviet Union, with its powerful mechanized army.

64. A tank with heavy chains attached to a power-driven drum on the front. When the drum rotated, the chains beat against the ground, and—with luck—detonated mines.

65. 1st Tank Battalion Diary, March 1953, p. 2 and Appendix IV.

66. Meid and Yingling, *U. S. Marine Operations in Korea, 1950-1953, Volume V, Operations In West Korea*, p. 270.

67. Ibid.

68. This artillery tactic, a variation of the World War I box barrage, was designed to thwart the massive Chinese attacks. The artillery fired patterns that formed a box around the friendly outposts, making a nearly impenetrable curtain of fire.

69. Meid and Yingling, *U. S. Marine Operations in Korea, 1950-1953, Volume V, Operations In West Korea*, p. 270.

70. Ibid., p. 291.

71. Williamson, *Dearest Buckie*, p. 184.

72. Meid and Yingling, *U. S. Marine Operations in Korea, 1950-1953, Volume V, Operations In West Korea*, p. 304.

73. Ibid., pp. 307-308.

74. Ibid., pp. 316-317.

75. Meid and Yingling, *U. S. Marine Operations in Korea, 1950-1953, Volume V, Operations In West Korea*, p. 331; Lieutenant Colonel Robert J. Post, personal communication, October 2, 2001.

76. Assigned the US Army's 25th Division, the Turkish Brigade was an oversized unit with four infantry battalions and its own artillery and transport elements. Its size was the reason for assigning two tank companies; Laine interview.

77. Lieutenant Colonel Robert J. Post, personal communication, October 2, 2001.

78. Ibid.

79. Meid and Yingling, *U. S. Marine Operations in Korea, 1950-1953, Volume V, Operations In West Korea*, p. 339.

80. Lieutenant Colonel Robert J. Post, personal communication, October 2, 2001.

81. Meid and Yingling, *U. S. Marine Operations in Korea, 1950-1953, Volume V, Operations In West Korea*, p. 9

82. This is another example of beating ground with unobserved machine gun fire.

83. Truck-drawn wheeled rocket launchers of the divisional rocket artillery. When these weapons fired, the back blast produced an enormous cloud of smoke and dust, which revealed their firing positions to enemy observers. The usual procedure for the rocket artillery was to "shoot and scoot."

84. Lieutenant Colonel Robert J. Post letter to Director, Marine Corps Historical Center, HQMC, May 28, 1970, cited in Meid and Yingling, *U. S. Marine Operations in Korea, 1950-1953, Volume V, Operations In West Korea*, p. 341.

85. The Command Post was also subjected to artillery fire from 76.2mm and 122mm artillery, which Montgomery described as "a nuisance." Montgomery interview.

86. These were main telephone trunk lines, which various units could tap into at will.

87. Bryant had no way of knowing for certain, but this may have been Robert Post.

88. 1st Tank Battalion Diary, May 1953, p. 3.

89. Meid and Yingling, *U. S. Marine Operations in Korea, 1950-1953, Volume V, Operations In West Korea*, pp. 342-344.

90. Sooter interview

91. Karl Fontenot telephone interview, June 15, 2001.

92. Meid and Yingling, *U. S. Marine Operations in Korea, 1950-1953, Volume V, Operations In West Korea*, pp. 391, 394.

93. Ballenger, *Final Crucible*, p. 254.

94. Ibid., p. 388.

95. Lieutenant Colonel Robert J. Post, personal communication, October 2, 2001.

Chapter 8: Armistice and Withdrawal

1. This episode is detailed in Fehrenbach, *This Kind Of War*, pp. 396-412.

2. Driving the tank in reverse, dragging the lowered blade behind. This process smoothed the road surface and eliminated track marks that could throw a jeep or light truck out of control at higher speeds.

3. Navy Bureau of Personnel.

4. Dr. Vernon Osborn, telephone interview, April 8, 2001. Corpsmen are traditionally nicknamed "Doc" by Marines, but Osborn became a dentist after the war. "Doc" became an actual doctor of dentistry.

5. The extreme tidal range on the western coast of Korea causes these bores. When the tide comes in, it floods quickly into the mouth of the Imjin River, and seawater floods over the top of the water flowing out. This sends a churning wall of water racing up the river at high speed.

6. A. C. Bryant telephone interview October 17, 2001.

7. Dunnage is rough-cut lumber used to separate and pad heavy cargo aboard ship. This observation and comments on the incidence of disease are from Ed Bale interview, College Station TX, June 26, 1998.

8. "Slop chute" is Marine Corps jargon for a place where beer is sold, usually an enlisted men's or NCO club.

Select References

Readers will no doubt observe that the following list is rather short. As far as published materials dealing entirely or even in part with armored operations, Korea truly is the "Forgotten War." In addition to the oral histories that comprise much of this work, the primary source accounts for this book are the official history (five volumes) and the unpublished unit diaries.

Unpublished Source Materials

Chaput, Roger (compiler). *Korean War 50th Anniversary Reunion, 3rd Plt. "A" Company 1st Tank Battalion September 24-27.* Las Vegas, NV, unpaginated manuscript.

Stuart, Vaughn R. Unpublished manuscript, undated, relevant portions provided by the author.

United States Marine Corps. *Operational Report "A" Company 1st Tank Battalion 5th Marines (REINF) FMF*, 14 pages. National Archives and Records Administration, Suitland, MD.

United States Marine Corps. *1st Tank Battalion, Historical Diary Type B, August 1950 through December 1950.* This record is paginated by month and is available in electronic image form at the Marine Corps Historical Center, Washington, D. C.

United States Marine Corps, *1st Tank Battalion, Historical Diary, January 1951 through June 1953.* This record is paginated by month and is available in electronic image form at the Marine Corps Historical Center, Washington, D. C.

Published Source Materials

Alexander, Joseph H. *Battle Of The Barricades:U. S. Marines in the Recapture of Seoul.* Washington, D. C., Marine Corps History and Museums Division, Korean War Commemorative Series, 2000.

Anonymous. "It Was a Bloody and Dangerous February." *Leatherneck Magazine* (February, 1993), pp. 30-33.

Appleman, Roy E. *Escaping The Trap: The U S Army X Corps in Northeastern Korea, 1950.* College Station, Texas, Texas A&M University Press, 1990.

Ash, C. B. "Trench Warfare:1952." Marine Corps Tankers Association Newsletter, Vol. 8, No. 195 (January 1985), p. 21.

Baker, Roger G. *USMC Tanker's Korea:The War in Photos, Sketches, and Letters Home.* Oakland OR, Elderberry Press, 2001.

Ballenger, Lee. *The Outpost War: U. S. Marines in Korea, Volume I, 1952.* Washington, D. C., Brasseys, 2000.

———. *The Final Crucible: U. S. Marines in Korea, Volume II, 1953.* Washington, D. C., Brasseys, 2001.

Center For Military History. *The Korean War: The Outbreak, 27 June-15 September 1950.* Washington, D.C., U.S. Army Center for Military History, undated.

Chappers, George S. and James C. Jones Jr. "Tank Teams." *Leatherneck Magazine* (August 1951), pp. 21-23.

Duncan, George. *Korea, Sept 1950 - Oct 1951. Marine Corps Tankers Association Magazine*, Vol. 12, No. 2-01 (June 2001), p. 10.

Dunstan, Simon. *Armour of The Korean* War, 1950-1953. London, Osprey-Vanguard No. 27, Osprey Publishing, 1982.

Estes, Kenneth W. *Marines Under Armor:The Marine Corps and the Armored Fighting Vehicle, 1916-2000.* Annapolis, MD. Naval Inst. Press, 2000.

Fehrenbach, T. R. *This Kind of War.* Fiftieth Anniversary Edition. Washington, D. C., Brassey's, 1994.

Gilbert, Oscar E. *Marine Tank Battles in the Pacific.* Conshohocken, PA, Combined Publishing, 2001.

Hammel, Eric. *Chosin:Heroic Ordeal of The Korean War.* Novato, CA. Presidio Press, 1990.

Hastings, Max. *The Korean War.* New York, Touchstone, 1987.

McCullough, David. *Truman.* New York, Simon & Schuster, 1992.

Meid, Pat and James M. Yingling. *U. S. Marine Operations in Korea, 1950-1953, Volume V, Operations In West Korea.* Washington, D. C., Headquarters Marine Corps, Historical Division, 1972.

Mesko, Jim. *Armor In Korea: A Pictorial History.* Carrollton, TX, Squadron-Signal, 1984.

Millett, Alan R. *Semper Fidelis: The History of the United States Marine Corps.* New York, Macmillan Publishing, Free Press Edition, 1982.

Montross, Lynn and Nicholas Canzona. *U. S. Marine Operations in Korea, 1950-1953. Volume I, The Pusan Perimeter.* Washington D. C., Headquarters Marine Corps, Historical Branch, 1954.

——. *U. S. Marine Operations in Korea, 1950-1953. Volume II, The Inchon: Seoul Campaign.* Washington D. C., Headquarters Marine Corps, Historical Branch, 1955.

——. *U. S. Marine Operations in Korea, 1950-1953. Volume III, The Chosin Reservoir Campaign.* Washington D. C., Headquarters Marine Corps, Historical Branch, 1957.

Montross, Lynn, Hubard D. Kuoka, and Norman W. Hicks. *U. S. Marine Operations in Korea, 1950-1953. Volume IV, The East-Central Front.* Washington D. C., Headquarters Marine Corps, Historical Branch, 1962.

Ridgeway, Matthew B. *The Korean War.* New York, Doubleday, 1967.

Simmons, Edwin H. *Over The Seawall: U. S. Marines at Inchon.* Washington, D. C., Marine Corps History and Museums Division, Korean War Commemorative Series, 2000.

Utz, Curtis A. *Assault From The Sea: The Amphibious Landing at Inchon.* Washington, D. C., Naval Historical Center, 2000.

Williamson, John I. *Dearest Buckie: A Marine's Korean War Memoir.* Austin, TX, R. J. Speights, 1993.

Zaloga, Steven J., and James Grandsen. *Soviet Tanks and Combat Vehicles of World War Two.* London, Arms and Armour Press, 1984.

Index